Communicative Action and Rational Choice

Communicative Action and Rational Choice

Joseph Heath

The MIT Press
Cambridge, Massachusetts
London, England

Library of Congress Cataloging-in-Publication Data

Heath, Joseph, 1967–
    Communicative action and rational choice / Joseph Heath.
        p.   cm.—(Studies in contemporary German social thought)
    Includes bibliographical references and index.
    ISBN 0-262-08291-8 (hardcover : alk. paper)
    1. Habermas, Jürgen. 2. Ethics. 3. Act (Philosophy) 4. Communication—Philosophy. I. Title. II. Series.
B3258.H324 .H43   2001
170—dc21
                                                                            00-032918

For my mother and father

Contents

Contents

Preface

This book has been a very long time in the works. As the title suggests, the argument draws upon material from fields of study that are not usually in close communication. My ability to speak with any degree of understanding in many of these areas is due to the quality of the instruction that I have received over the years. As a result, I am very pleased to acknowledge first and foremost the contribution that has been made to this work by many of the fine teachers I have had—at McGill: James Tully, Charles Taylor, David Davies; and at Northwestern: Thomas McCarthy, James Johnson, Jeroen Swinkels, Michael Williams, and Jürgen Habermas. The idea of using rational choice theory to evaluate the claims that Habermas makes about the limits of the instrumental conception of rationality is one that I picked up from Jim Johnson. As well, the emphasis on accountability as the key characteristic of social action is something that Tom McCarthy impressed upon me, and that forms the core of his own systematic views.

Many people have read and commented on portions of this work over the years. They include Joel Anderson, Jim Bohman, David Davies, Gordon Finlayson, Jim Johnson, Tom McCarthy, Cheryl Misak, and Kevin Olson. I would like to thank them for their efforts. Also, I am indebted to the graduate students at the University of Toronto who have participated in my various seminars, especially Klaus Jahn, who lent further assistance in the preparation of the final manuscript.

This book incorporates, in revised form, material from previously published articles. I gratefully acknowledge the work of the editors and referees of the journals in which the articles appeared. Sections 2.3 and 2.4 are drawn from

"Is Language a Game?" *Canadian Journal of Philosophy* 26: 1 (Lethbridge: University of Calgary Press, 1996): 1–28; §3.1 takes a bit from "Threats, Promises, and Communicative Action," *European Journal of Philosophy* 3: 3 (Oxford: Blackwell, 1995): 225–241; §3.4 repeats material from "What Is a Validity Claim?" *Philosophy and Social Criticism* 24: 4 (London: Sage, 1998): 23–41; some of §4.1 and §4.4 was published in "The Structure of Normative Control," *Law and Philosophy* 17: 4 (Dordrecht: Kluwer Academic, 1998): 419–442; some of §6.2 in "The Problem of Foundationalism in Habermas's Discourse Ethics," *Philosophy and Social Criticism* 24: 4 (London: Sage, 1998): 23–41; and the argument in §§7.2–7.3 appears as "A Pragmatist Theory of Convergence" in *Pragmatism: Canadian Journal of Philosophy Supplementary Volume*, ed. C. J. Misak (Lethbridge: University of Calgary Press, 1999). My thanks to Blackwell Publishers, Sage Publishers, Kluwer Academic Publishers, and the University of Calgary Press for their kind permission to use this material.

Finally, I would like to thank the University of Toronto Connaught Fund, along with the Social Sciences and Humanities Research Council of Canada for financial assistance at various points in the development and execution of this project.

Introduction

For Kant the moral order "within" was an awesome mystery; for sociologists the moral order "without" is a technical mystery.
—*Harold Garfinkel*

This book is a critical study of Jürgen Habermas's theory of communicative action. Habermas's theory is important because it is the best attempt that has been made so far to produce a *general theory of social action*. It is a conspicuous feature of the social sciences that different disciplines are dominated by different theories about how people act—what psychological states govern their decisions, what incentives they respond to, and how the actions of multiple agents are coordinated. The most extreme disciplinary division has been between economists and sociologists. Economists have tended to emphasize the instrumental dimension of human action—the way that practical deliberation is concerned with discovering the most efficient means to the realization of given ends—whereas sociologists have argued that "social norms," or shared rules of conduct, play an important role in social action by directly motivating agents to conform to specific institutional patterns. Although these two views are not strictly incompatible, there is a significant tension between them. Insofar as agents are really following rules (i.e., respecting deontic constraints), there is no clear sense in which they can be selecting their actions as mere means to some further end. This tension has given rise to well over a century of debate, and although this has generated significant refinement of the positions on both sides, there has been very little narrowing of the gulf between them. In fact, the seeming intractability of this dispute has led many theorists to reject abstract social theory entirely in favor of local, interpretive studies.[1]

From Habermas's perspective, the reason that little progress has been made in this debate is that two pieces of the puzzle are missing. First, even though many social scientists have abandoned positivism as a methodological stance, the idea that "value judgments" or "moral questions" are rationally undecidable is still widely accepted. As a consequence, most social theorists simply assume that any agent who acts on the basis of a moral principle, or a social norm, is not rationally justified in doing so. This is what underlies the widespread tendency among social theorists to assume that instrumental action is the only form of rational action, and that norm-governed action must have some kind of nonrational source, such as conditioning, socialization, or habit. This leads to problems, however, because norm-governed action is often highly organized, reflexive, and adaptive.[2] If it is not rational, then the coherence of norm systems is extremely difficult to explain, since it could not be achieved through any specifically intentional process. This makes it tempting to abandon the action frame of reference and supply a purely functionalist explanations of these norms. This strategy has generated a lengthy and increasingly sterile debate about the merits of "micro" versus "macro" explanations, and the status of "methodological individualism."[3]

The most obvious problem with this debate, from a philosophical perspective, is that the assumptions about rationality that are accepted by all parties presuppose an extremely controversial form of moral skepticism. The traditional reason for thinking that normative commitments are irrational, or unjustifiable, depends upon a rather specific conception of rationality and justifiability known as *foundationalism*.[4] This conception of rationality, however, is one that has become increasingly discredited in philosophical circles, largely as a consequence of the so-called linguistic turn.[5] The impact of this change has been felt in debates over scientific methodology, but has still had little impact on the working theories of social scientists. Habermas is one of the first to bring a nonfoundationalist conception of rationality to the task of understanding the logic of social action. One of the consequences of this view of rationality is that he is not inclined to treat moral action as irrational. This means that he can explain conformity to social norms as a straightforward exercise of *rational choice*—except that "rational" is now to be understood in a noninstrumental sense. This allows him to explain the coherence and adaptability of norm-governed systems by appealing to cognitive resources that agents themselves can deploy in managing their interactions.

The second major piece of the puzzle that has been missing is an account of language. It may come as a surprise to some to discover that the instrumental model of social interaction most often used in the social sciences explicitly excludes any kind of linguistic communication among agents.[6] Given the absolute centrality of language for all forms of social life, it is hard to imagine that a theory of action that excludes communication could have more than limited applicability. A general theory of rational action must give some account of all rational activities—not just consumption and voting decisions, but also such paradigmatically rational activities as doing arithmetic, compiling data in a lab, debating economic policy, and even reading a book on rational choice theory.

This is a problem not just for instrumental theories of action. Theories that incorporate noninstrumental forms of action have generally not been any more successful at accommodating language and communication. Symbolic interactionism, for instance (despite the title), has remained focused on the way that specific actions acquire symbolic properties, and has never been able to explain how propositionally differentiated speech could emerge out of social action.[7] As a result, it provides no systematic account of our most powerful linguistic capacity, namely, the ability to use compositional semantic resources to *represent* possible states of affairs. Without such an account, it is impossible to explain how we use language to make requests, announce intentions, and so forth.

Habermas overcomes this deficit by incorporating *speech act theory* into his model of social action.[8] Thus his theory of action includes a full-scale theory of linguistic action. As a result, the cognitive resources that are simply presupposed by most action theories form an integral part of Habermas's own. For instance, most action theories presuppose that agents come equipped with all sorts of intentional states—beliefs, desires, preferences, values, and so on. Since all these intentional states are propositional attitudes, and since language is a social phenomenon, it would seem that the theory of social action should have the capacity to explain how these states come about (or at least how they acquire their *content*). But any action theory that starts out by *presupposing* these states will be structurally incapable of providing such an account. Habermas's theory of communicative action, because it incorporates a theory of meaning, is not vulnerable to this difficulty. It thus stands as an exemplar of how a philosophically sophisticated theory of action should be constructed.

The first half of this book is concerned with evaluating Habermas's action theory. At various points in its development, Habermas presents this theory as a part of a general critique of instrumental rationality (this is the central line of continuity between his work and the "Frankfurt school" tradition of critical social science). However, despite being pitched as a critique of instrumental rationality, Habermas's work is informed by only a somewhat vague grasp of the details of the instrumental view. My goal in the present work is to bring Habermas's theory into dialogue with the most sophisticated articulation of the instrumental conception of practical rationality: Bayesian decision and game theory. More specifically, I try to show that Habermas's central criticism of the instrumental view is broadly consistent with limitative results that have been obtained in game-theoretic analysis. The weaknesses that Habermas points to from "outside" the theory have also been pointed out from the "inside"—often more perspicuously. Thus critical theory and game theory, as James Johnson has observed, "converge in improbable but potentially productive ways."[9]

I begin in chapter 1 by presenting a basic outline of Habermas's theory of action. One of the major problems that arises from Habermas's lack of precision with respect to the instrumental model is that his theory has had little impact among those who are not already interested in finding an alternative to the instrumental view. By contrast, Donald Davidson's critique of decision theory, which is in many ways quite similar to Habermas's, has had a much greater effect.[10] This is despite the fact that Davidson's overall action theory is in some respects much less sophisticated than Habermas's (e.g., Davidson does not even try to generalize the action theory to social contexts). The difference is that Davidson gets the decision theory right, and so knows how to make his arguments stick. Since there are broad structural similarities between Davidson's view and Habermas's—particularly on the relationship between rationality and interpretation—I draw upon Davidson's work at various points in order to help situate Habermas's views.

In chapter 2, I present a general outline of decision and game theory, followed by an analysis of Habermas's major criticism of this model. The key idea in Habermas's theory of communicative action is that speech acts cannot be planned or executed with entirely strategic intent. To establish this claim, however, Habermas draws upon some rather controversial work in the philos-

ophy of language—in particular, J. L. Austin's distinction between illocutionary and perlocutionary components of speech acts.[11] My major task in this
chapter is to show that Habermas's claim can be established without appealing to any of these problematic claims, but through an entirely game-theoretic
analysis of the effects of communication systems on strategic interaction. I
develop this argument by showing that interactions among instrumentally
rational agents cannot confer semantic content upon any of their actions, and
so language could not arise out of strategic interaction. On the other hand, if
agents are simply assumed to have primitive linguistic competencies, then they
will be incapable of solving social interaction problems using strictly instrumental resources. The upshot of these two arguments is that recent game-theoretic research lends considerable support to Habermas's claim that speech
acts cannot be instrumentally rational.

This discussion takes care of the "critical" aspect of Habermas's action
theory. However, unlike many critics of the instrumental conception of rationality, Habermas does not forget the old saying that "you can't beat something
with nothing." Perhaps the more exciting feature of his work is that instead of
just criticizing the instrumental view, as so many others have done, Habermas
attempts to present a concrete alternative. This is what I examine in chapter
3. The key here again is Habermas's claim that speech acts are not instrumentally rational. Since there must be some sense in which language use is
rational, analyzing the "logic" of speech may help to reveal the "logic" of linguistic action. Here the connection between rationality and interpretation
becomes important. To interpret each others' utterances, we must assume that
we are at least minimally rational. This means that we can look at our practices of interpretation—how we confer semantic content upon expressions—
in order to discover what conception of practical rationality governs our
linguistic practices. In a sense, the best theory of meaning imposes a particular conception of practical rationality upon us. This argumentation strategy is
what Habermas employs to develop his alternative, "communicative" conception of practical rationality.

Although I endorse this general argumentation strategy, I have some disagreements with the specific theory of meaning that Habermas develops. At
the end of the third chapter, I criticize Habermas's attempt to analyze speech
acts using three different "validity claims" and outline an alternative to
this view. However, since the theory of meaning imposes a theory of practical
rationality, the changes that I suggest at the level of semantic theory have

ramifications for the entire theory of action. In chapter 4, I present the broad outlines of a multidimensional theory of rational action that includes "norm-governed" action as a specific type. This theory is similar to Habermas's, but adopts a different explanatory strategy when it comes to accounting for certain features of social order. The result is a model of rational action that contains roughly the same components as Habermas's, but arranges them in a different way.

The second half of this book is dedicated to a discussion of the more philosophical dimension of Habermas's conception of practical rationality. Because he does not approach the theory of action with a prior commitment to moral noncognitivism, Habermas is able to dispel much of the mystery that has surrounded the sociological conception of "norm-governed" action. However, this perspective will only be persuasive if he is able to give some account of moral reasoning that redeems his cognitivist intuitions. The attraction of Habermas's position, in this respect, is that instead of trying to provide an autonomous, "foundational" conception of moral reasoning that would ground the action theory, he imports elements of the action theory into his philosophical ethics, in order to explicate the *practice* of moral argumentation. Thus he draws upon the action-theoretic concept of a "social norm" in order to dispel certain classic problems in moral philosophy. So at the same time that suspending the noncognitivism postulate enables him to develop a more powerful theory of social action, this enhanced action theory is itself deployed in order to relieve some of the skeptical pressures that have traditionally favored moral noncognitivism.

The significance of Habermas's work in moral philosophy has more to do with the way that he situates the major problems than in the specific proposals that he has for resolving them. His major achievement in this respect is to have recognized that the skeptical problem that has motivated many popular forms of moral noncognitivism (often expressed by the question "why be moral?") is equivalent to the technical problem in theoretical sociology referred to as the "problem of order"—or more generally, that the solution to one of these problems would constitute a solution to the other.[12]

The "why be moral?" question is normally taken as a shorthand way of referring to a certain type of skeptical challenge to morality.[13] The question is usually not meant literally. When Hume asked why he should not prefer the destruction of the world to the scratching of his finger,[14] it would always have been possible to provide a straightforward response, for example, "The destruction of the world would bring about the deaths of billions of innocent people." This would be to miss the point. What Hume really meant was something more like "What reason could I have for placing the interests of others above my own?" Conflicts can arise between the demands of morality and those of self-interest, and it is unclear what would lead an individual to disregard her self-interest in the way that our moral intuitions often tell us we should. As Bernard Williams memorably put it, we are hard pressed to find ways of making moral obligations "stick" to a rational, self-interested agent.[15]

The "problem of order" refers to a set of questions in sociology concerning the nature of social organization. Humans interact with one another in complicated patterns, and they reproduce these patterns over generations. However, unlike other "social" animals, human behavior is characterized by significant genetic underdetermination. This means that we do not come equipped with many preset behavioral routines, but are capable of learning from our environment and adapting to circumstances on a case-by-case basis. As a result, we are also perfectly capable of opting out of the culturally prescribed patterns of conduct, as demonstrated by the occurrence of *crime* and *deviance*. The tricky question is why this does not occur more often, for example, why crime is the exception rather than the rule. Another way of posing this question is to ask how society is able to make its patterns "stick" to the individuals that compose it.

In both cases, the problem arises because demands and expectations are made of an agent that appear to be "external" to his or her own motivational system. The solution to this problem, one might reasonably suppose, will require some identification of the mechanism through which these external demands are translated into effective deliberative considerations. Habermas's key insight is that this mechanism is *the same* in the case of both morality and social order. Thus he develops what I call a "sociological" approach to moral philosophy. This is expressed in the following passage, which I think expresses the single most important idea in Habermas's philosophical ethics:

One has to take into account the fact that the normatively integrated fabric of social relations is moral *in and of itself*, as Durkheim has shown. The basic moral phenomenon is the binding force of norms, which can be violated by acting subjects. All basic concepts that are constitutive of normatively regulated action, then, already have a moral dimension, which is merely being actualized and fully employed when people judge conflicts and violations of norms. With the formation of the social world and the transition to norm-guided interaction, all social relations take on an implicitly ethical character. Golden rules and obedience to the law are ethical imperatives that merely sue, as it were, for what is already implicit in social roles and norms prior to any actual moral conflict: the complementarity of behavioral expectations and the symmetry of rights and duties.[16]

The basic idea, which Habermas correctly attributes to Durkheim, is that there is no *specific* socialization process through which agents acquire moral dispositions. *All* socialization is moral socialization, because all social interaction is governed by norms that function as deontic constraints. This means that acquiring the competences required to manage routine social interactions amounts to acquiring the dispositions and personality structures that we understand to be the essential elements of moral agency. Thus morality is not optional for us, simply because socialization is not optional for us. Socialization involves acquisition of a set of core human competencies that no one would ever choose to do without. Since many of these competencies are constitutive of our capacity for rational thought and critical self-examination, there is something incoherent about the very idea of choosing not to be moral. Thus the mechanism that translates "external" demands into "internal" motives will of necessity be reflectively stable. Becoming aware of this mechanism should give the agent no reason to want to change it. This "sociological" insight provides Habermas with the opportunity to develop what he calls a "transcendental-pragmatic" defense of morality.

In chapter 5, I offer a basic presentation of the conception of rationality that underlies Habermas's moral cognitivism, and I try to show how it draws upon the conception of communicative rationality elaborated in his action theory. Habermas's basic strategy in defending moral cognitivism is to reject the correspondence theory of truth and the foundationalist model of justification, both of which have served as major sources of moral skepticism. In the place of these older views, Habermas attempts to explain truth and justification in terms of the practice of argumentation. This is what generates his "discourse" theory of truth and "dialogical" model of justification, which underlie the broader philosophical program that he refers to as "discourse ethics."

The theories of truth and justification that Habermas develops are both, in a broad sense, antirealist. He does not attempt to provide any foundation for moral judgment that is outside the logical space of reasons. The danger with such a position is that it can easily open the door to relativism. It becomes difficult to explain why we should ever expect to secure agreement on moral questions, if there is nothing to which they are "ultimately" anchored. This is the problem of *convergence* (or the lack thereof). Although I endorse the general strategy that Habermas adopts in rejecting moral noncognitivism, I argue that his attempts to demonstrate that moral argumentation will exhibit convergence saddle him with an unnecessary burden of proof. I therefore reject, in chapter 6, his attempt to introduce a universalization principle governing moral discourse, and his criteria for distinguishing between moral and ethical problems. In chapter 7, I provide an alternative, more consistently pragmatist account of the level of convergence exhibited by moral argumentation. Both of these arguments draw upon game-theoretic models in order to specify more clearly the burden of proof that the theory of communicative action and discourse must assume.

Finally, in chapter 8 I turn to Habermas's "quasi-transcendental" defense of the discourse ethics project. This is the component of his view that has been perhaps most widely misunderstood in the literature. I therefore offer a brief clarification of the status of transcendental arguments, before going on to consider Habermas's more specific claims. Overall, I attempt to show that the claim to "universality" that Habermas makes for his theory follows fairly immediately from the pragmatic conception of language he endorses. Roughly speaking, if linguistic meaning arises from the use of particular expressions in a certain set of practices, then not all of these practices can be subject to discursive revision. Since our minds are language-dependent, and language is always embedded in particular social practices, these practices cannot be contingent, or "up for grabs" from our perspective. To assume otherwise is to treat cognition as the act of a disembodied intellect. In this respect, Habermas's transcendentalism is a direct and inevitable consequence of his rejection of the Cartesian conception of mind. I try to show that Habermas is correct in his claim that cultural relativism, in both morality and epistemology generally, rests upon broadly Cartesian assumptions that are inconsistent with the central insights achieved through the "linguistic turn."

Despite this final note of agreement, the overall tone of this book is critical. Over the course of the discussion, I reject two of Habermas's central theses, namely, that communicative action should be a fundamental category of action-theoretic analysis, and that his universalization principle can form the basis of a viable program in philosophical ethics. But having said this, I should note that my rejection of these two theses is subject to a significant qualification—I think that Habermas's basic insight is correct in both cases. The problems rest entirely in the details, in the particular way that he tries to cash out these insights at the level of more specific philosophical analysis. Thus at the same time that I criticize Habermas's specific views, I will also defend what I take to be the underlying intuitions, namely, that the instrumental conception of rationality does not provide an adequate theory of rational action in general, and speech acts in particular; and that a dialogical account of rational justification not only undermines the traditional bases of moral noncognitivism, but also supplies formal constraints on the content of acceptable moral norms.

In one sense, Habermas's work serves here as the scaffolding for the construction of my own view. In another sense, I am only rearranging the pieces of Habermas's theory, since I wind up disagreeing more with his way of carrying out the project than with the project itself. This means that at times the boundary between what Habermas says, what Habermas should say, and what I say, gets a bit blurred. Where our disagreements are significant enough, I have tried to draw attention to the differences. But in other cases, I have simply reconstructed Habermas's view in what I take to be its strongest form. This I take to be less an exercise of interpretive license than a way of doing philosophy in the spirit of Habermas's own work—not only is it a direct application of the maxim that the best interpretation is the one that is most restrained in its ascription of error, but it also reflects the fact that Habermas's project remains, now and I hope for a long time still, a work in progress.

I
Communicative Action

1

The Theory of Communicative Action

The first thing to notice about Habermas's theory of communicative action is that it is a *typological* theory. Habermas does not reject the instrumental conception of rationality and replace it with an alternative, "communicative" conception. Instead, he takes as his point of departure the assumption that agents always have available to them a set of different, often incommensurable standards of choice. Communicative action will turn out to be action governed by a particular standard, while instrumental action will be action governed by another. Thus Habermas is not committed to the claim that agents do not sometimes deliberate instrumentally; his claim is simply that instrumental models do not provide a sufficient basis for a *general* theory of rational action.

The locus classicus of this view is Immanuel Kant's moral action theory, where it is claimed that reasons for action can take the form of either hypothetical or categorical imperatives. Although Kant thought that the latter were in some sense superior to the former, he nevertheless granted that both could serve as the basis for rational action.[1] The difference lay in which "incentive" the agent allowed to determine his will. If one assigns priority to one's inclinations, then hypothetical imperatives determine what it is rational to do; if one assigns priority to one's duties, then the categorical imperative determines what it is rational to do.

The most significant inheritor of this view was Max Weber, who gave it a characteristically sociotheoretic twist. In Weber's analysis, Kant's two categories of rational action become transformed into *zweckrationalität* and *wertrationalität*.[2] The former is broadly instrumental, whereas the latter consists of action that is directly prescribed by some transcendent system of values. (The sociotheoretic twist comes in the further claim that the values in question are not directly prescribed through the exercise of pure practical reason, but come from a historically contingent set of ideals that is symbolically transmitted and reproduced.) Thus in his famous study of the "Protestant ethic," Weber argued that the capitalist economy, which functions as a system of predominantly instrumental interaction, owes its origins not to an instrumentalization of social relations, but rather to the peculiar value-commitments of early Protestant sects.[3] Thus even actions taken in a competitive market, which represent the most obvious instances of instrumental reasoning, can only be made sense of against a background of noninstrumental commitments and behavior.

This thesis was significantly generalized by Talcott Parsons, who argued that every organized system of instrumental action was sustained against a background of social institutions maintained through systematically noninstrumental (or non-utility-maximizing) behavior. For this reason, any persistent pattern of social interaction would have to be understood as a complex outcome of multiple agents acting on different types of practical considerations. In his early work, Parsons referred to action of the noninstrumental type as norm-conformative (or simply normative) action, in order emphasize the importance of rule-following in the organization of such interactions.[4] He later chose to speak of role-conformity instead of norm-conformity, shifting the emphasis away from shared rules and placing it on the system of shared *expectations*.[5] In Parsons's view, agents are socialized in such a way as to give them somewhat generalized dispositions toward satisfying shared behavioral expectations. The content of these expectations, insofar as it is symbolically coded and reproduced, constitutes the agent's *culture*.

These three conceptions of noninstrumental action, though on some levels quite dissimilar, nevertheless have certain important ideas in common. The most significant is that, in all three cases, the noninstrumental form of rational action is seen as incorporating *publicly shared* reasons for action directly into the agent's deliberative processes (categorical imperatives for Kant, values for Weber, and norms for Parsons). This incorporation of public reasons means that the agent can be held accountable for her conduct in a way that an agent acting from strictly instrumental motives cannot.

Under the instrumental conception of rationality, the agent's reasons for acting in a particular way are always, in at least one important sense, private. Actions, according to this view, are chosen as means for the attainment of the agent's preferred outcome. This implies that the reason for an action is always given through reference to some ranking that the agent has conferred upon the set of attainable outcomes. And under the standard interpretation of decision theory in terms of belief-desire psychology, this ranking is understood to spring from a set of subjective motivational states. The type of reason that such a ranking provides is necessarily agent-relative and nongeneralizable. It is a reason for some *specific* agent to perform a *particular* action. It is also private, in the sense that the agent is assumed to have privileged introspective access to information about her preference ordering. For those who lack this information about the agent, it will be impossible to identify any reason that she might have for doing anything.

This means that the only constraint imposed by practical rationality upon an agent's conduct is that her actions accurately reflect her preferences over outcomes. This places limits on the extent to which an agent can be held *accountable* for her conduct by other agents. The question "Why did you do that?" insofar as it seeks a rational explanation of the agent's conduct, can have no greater force than "Which of your goals was that action intended to achieve?" Similarly, imperatives that other agents might like to issue, or recommendations they might like to make, must be hooked in to this system of preferences in order to have any practical import. Insofar as another agent intends his counsel to have greater force, he is after something that reason alone cannot provide. As Bernard Williams put it, no matter how deeply we would like our recommendations to "stick" to the agent, "the only glue there is for this purpose is social and psychological."[6]

This analysis introduces a rather striking disanalogy between theoretical and practical rationality. In the case of beliefs, agents are usually held accountable to a system of publicly accepted facts. Asking an agent to justify a belief that she holds normally does not just mean, "How does this belief follow from your other (possibly crazy) beliefs?" but rather, "How does this belief follow from beliefs that *we* all accept?"[7] The demand for justification requires an account in terms of publicly shared doxastic commitments. Of course, according to the traditional view, we can make these sorts of demands upon agents in epistemic contexts because we have a foolproof way of making doxastic demands "stick," namely, we can confront them with the world (something we cannot do in the case of their desires).[8]

This idea—that we can set up a simple confrontation between beliefs and corresponding states in the world—presupposes a foundationalist theory of justification, which, as we will see further on, is deeply problematic. For the moment, it will suffice to note that this analysis is in tension with the logic of our usual practices of argumentation. At first glance, demands for the justification of conduct appear to take the same public form as demands for the justification of belief.[9] For instance, if one observes an opponent at chess surreptitiously rearranging pieces on the board when one appears not to be looking, the inclination will be to call her to account, saying something like "What do you think you are doing?" Clearly, the sort of answer that one is looking for here is not "trying to win," since an agent's *instrumental* reasons for cheating are fairly obvious. What one is looking for is perhaps (charitably) an obscure and unfamiliar rule of play, or else an admission that the action was illegitimate. Proponents of the instrumental conception of rationality, however, are committed to the claim that demands of this type are not, strictly speaking, invitations to participate in a process of reasoning or justification. At best, they represent nonrational psychological or social mechanisms for exerting pressure on others. (Naturally they have this effect; the issue is whether this is *all* that they have.) Thus, faced with the fact that agents tend to argue about action in terms of shared standards of conduct, just as they argue about beliefs in terms of shared doxastic commitments, proponents of the instrumental view of rationality are inclined to dismiss the phenomenon, suggesting that this type of argumentation is not, strictly speaking, rational.

The natural alternative to this view is to take seriously the "public" content of practical rationality and to question the generality of the instrumental mode of deliberation. This is one thing that the theories of Kant, Weber, and Parsons all have in common. For Kant, adopting the categorical imperative as the basis of one's actions means deliberating from the standpoint of a legislator in the kingdom of ends, a position that in principle every agent is able to assume. Since agents in the kingdom of ends deliberate qua noumena, from this standpoint every agent is interchangeable, and therefore every maxim adopted must be universalizable. This means that every agent who deliberates in this way will come up with the same answer. On the other hand, acting on the basis of hypothetical imperatives means deliberating in terms of one's empirically determined desires and inclinations. So even though Kant conceives of practical reasoning in completely individualistic terms, his framework is designed to ensure that the reasons underlying actions performed "from duty" will be *shared* by all agents. (In fact, the strict formalism of the categorical imperative follows directly from the monological conception of deliberation and the requirement of publicity.[10] To guarantee that reasons are shared, in the absence of genuine dialogue among agents, it is necessary to abstract away every feature that makes agents different from one another.)

If deliberative conditions are conceived less individualistically, we can see that both Weber and Parsons also conceive of noninstrumental reasoning in terms of essentially shared justificatory resources. For Weber, "values" differ from desires precisely through their public nature. For Parsons, norms and roles take the form of impersonal deontic prescriptions, such as "in situations of type x, agents of type y are to perform actions of type a." Giving an account of one's conduct then involves showing how it falls under a prescription of this type. This kind of theory makes it much easier to see what is going on in the chess-cheating example. Asking "What are you doing?" is an attempt to elicit a principle of action that is generalizable. What is characteristic about a rule of play, in this context, is that both players accept it. It therefore provides a publicly shared reason for action.

1.1 Outline of the Theory

Given its emphasis on public accountability, Habermas's conception of "communicative action" is closely related to this family of views; nevertheless, his motivation for introducing a noninstrumental action type differs significantly. The primary concern of the "classical" sociological theorists was to solve what Parsons referred as "the problem of order."[11] The instrumental conception of rationality, on this view, is incapable of explaining the empirical regularities exhibited in social interaction, because instrumental action does not provide the sort of "glue" needed to hold together stable human associations. The instrumental model fails to explain how a preponderance of "force and fraud" can be avoided in social interaction, just as it fails to explain how agents can generate the fund of trust needed to sustain shared cooperative activity.[12] Positing a set of publicly shared values that could be transmitted directly into action, on the other hand, seems to solve the problem. Not only does it provide precisely the sort of mechanism needed to patch up the theory of action, it also derives strong empirical support from the demonstrable role that religion and morality play in stabilizing and reproducing social structure.

The problem with the classical sociological theory of action is that its proponents have never been able to specify with any precision how values and norms interact with other intentional states—primarily beliefs and desires—in order to produce observed interaction patterns. When compared with, for example, contemporary rational choice theory, sociological models of action are woefully imprecise. Aaron Cicourel captured the basic problem quite sharply in a critique of Parsons (whose work in many ways provides the most sophisticated formulation of the classical sociological view):

> In focusing upon the interactional context for structural properties of social order, Parsons directs our attention to "common" value-orientations. But this apparent conceptual "answer" avoids the crucial questions of what passes as "common" and how our actors decide on their own or some collectivity's "common" value-orientations; how consistent are actions in honoring or excepting such orientations if we assume they exist; and how varying degrees of institutionalization would refer to value-orientations "more" or "less" common to a group? *Explicit cognitive procedures and a theory of meaning are absent from Parsons's formulation.*[13]

Habermas addresses this problem by adopting a different approach to the theory of action. Rather than introducing a type of publicly accountable action as a resource for solving the problem of order, he introduces it as a resource for explaining the *development of language*. He then uses this account of language to solve the problem of order. The lack of "explicit cognitive procedures and a theory of meaning" in Parsons's theory is, according to this view, merely symptomatic of his having collapsed these two distinct explanatory steps. Parsons uses public accountability to attack the problem of order directly. What he should have done is examine how public accountability gives rise to language, which then gives agents the *cognitive resources* needed to solve the problem of order.

The reason that public accountability is necessary for the development of language, in Habermas's view, is that the meaning of sentences is determined by the type of public commitments that speakers undertake through their utterances. This suggests that among strictly instrumental agents, whose interactions are not governed by such commitments, it would be impossible to develop a set of words or sentences whose meaning remained relatively independent from specific contexts of use. Since both words and sentences in our language clearly have such a property, it must then be the case that, as speakers, we are able to orient our conduct toward public forms of justification. Thus the conceptual need for a noninstrumental action type is established without appeal to the problem of order. But then how does this help *solve* the problem of order? According to Habermas, when language is used to coordinate social interaction, these linguistically incurred commitments reduce the range of action alternatives that are available to us, and so increase the "orderliness" of our interactions.

This discussion should make it clear that the set of considerations motivating Habermas's project differs significantly from those that exercised the classical sociological theorists. The type of theory that Habermas sets out to develop is what Donald Davidson refers to as a "unified theory of meaning and action."[14] The basic structure of such a theory is determined by the special constraints that an adequate theory of meaning and a theory of action must impose upon one another. It is widely accepted that a general theory of communication will have to parcel out the analysis of utterance meaning into semantic and pragmatic components. This is the origin of the mutual constraints between the theory of action and the theory of meaning. Since any semantic theory will leave certain aspects of communication to be "handled" by the pragmatics, a general theory of meaning requires a theory of action that explicates precisely those features. The semantic theory, by inducing a particular pragmatics, thereby places restrictions on what will serve as an acceptable theory of action. According to Habermas, it is considerations of this type that expose the inadequacy of the instrumental conception of rationality.

In Habermas's view, speech acts, by drawing upon a set of shared linguistic resources, necessarily involve the agent in a set of public commitments, and therefore cannot be modeled instrumentally. In Habermas's terms, each speaker raises a set of "validity claims" through her utterances, claims that can only be redeemed through appeal to public justificatory resources. To understand the utterance is, in this view, to know the conditions under which these validity claims could be redeemed. Thus public accountability is an intrinsic feature of linguistic communication. For Habermas, this serves as the basis for the division of action into two primitive analytic types: instrumental action and speech acts. He argues that these two forms of action correspond to two different "stances" that the agent can take toward others. Instrumental action involves a simple concern with the success of the action. Communication, on the other hand, requires that the agent adopt what Habermas calls the *performative stance*. The adoption of this stance commits the agent in a series of idealizing presuppositions. So while the success of an instrumental action rests in the attainment of its objectives, the success of a speech act rests in the achievement of mutual understanding (i.e., acceptance of the commitments undertaken).

The motivation for this view can best be grasped by contrasting it with Davidson's, which Habermas takes as his point of departure in later formulations of the theory.[15] Davidson argues that the instrumental conception of rationality, as expressed in preference-based decision theory, is flawed, insofar as it takes for granted agents' linguistic competence. Under the standard "psychological" interpretation of instrumental rationality, inherited from Hobbes and Hume, agents are thought to act on the basis of beliefs and desires. Beliefs and desires, however, are propositional attitudes, which means they take as their objects interpreted sentences of a natural language. How agents come to acquire these attitudes—where the grasp of language comes from—is usually either ignored or posited as primitive. The problem does not go away, in Davidson's view, if one opts for a "revealed preference" interpretation of instrumental rationality. Although revealed preference theory claims to rest on strictly behaviorist foundations, it assumes that agents' utility functions can be derived by observing their responses to complex wagers; the ability to understand these wagers, in turn, requires significant linguistic and computational ability, all of which must simply be presupposed by the model.

What this shows, in Davidson's view, is that the standard instrumental models of rationality start with a conception of agents in which the basic structures of theoretical rationality are already in place—knowledge of a language, a system of representational beliefs, mastery of the probability calculus, and so on. The attempt is then made to generalize this apparatus from the theoretical to the practical realm. This leads to philosophical commitments that are deeply antipragmatist, since the basic explanatory strategy precludes the use of practical (or social) considerations to elucidate the structure of theoretical reason. Thus the standard models all start out from what Davidson regards as a misguided reductionist strategy.

In Davidson's view, theoretical and practical rationality must be treated as equiprimordial.[16] He therefore sets out to reformulate the instrumental model, taking as a psychological basis three simple cognitive attitudes: belief, desire, and meaning.[17] All three of these attitudes are ascribed to agents in order to explain observed patterns in their behavior. The utility-maximizing conception of rationality, in this view, is a structure that we employ to resolve a set of observed preferences over actions into a set of ascribed beliefs and desires. Similarly, a *theory of truth* is a structure we can use to resolve a set of observations about which sentences an agent holds true into a set of ascribed beliefs and meanings.[18]

However, although the maximizing conception of practical rationality and the theory of truth in semantics impose formal constraints on the attitudes that we can coherently ascribe to agents, they do not come anywhere near specifying a unique solution. All our cognitive attitudes are interdependent, and a single attitude is never directly responsible for a particular behavioral display. When we observe an action, the desire we ascribe to an agent as an explanation of that action will depend upon what beliefs we also ascribe to her. For example, an agent who drinks a cup of coffee may be acting on a desire to stay awake during an upcoming meeting, or she may be acting on the basis of a mistaken belief that the cup is full of tea. Similarly, how we treat the agent's belief that "this is a cup of coffee" will depend upon what we take the agent to refer to by the word "coffee," just as what we take the agent to mean by a particular utterance will depend upon the set of background beliefs that we ascribe to her. This is what motivates Davidson's famous "principle of charity," which states roughly that our interpretations must be constrained by the requirement that we ascribe to the agent a set of beliefs and desires that are, in some sense, reasonable. In the case of beliefs, this means that we must attribute to the agent a system of beliefs that is predominantly true.

When Davidson initially outlined this project, he was of the opinion that behavior is divided into two natural kinds, speech and action. Understanding the former involved ascribing to the agent a set of beliefs and meanings, and understanding the latter involved ascribing beliefs and desires. Furthermore, he thought that in order to come up with an adequate interpretation of speech, it is not only necessary to focus on beliefs and meanings, but also at least temporarily to bracket the question of which desires the agent is acting upon. Thus he saw it as necessary, in order to ascribe meaning to the agent's words on the basis of which sentences she held true, that the agent's pattern of affirmative and negative responses be an accurate reflection of her underlying belief states. This amounted to positing something like a "desire to tell the truth" governing all speech. Similarly, Davidson thought that in order to determine an agent's desires and beliefs, by observing preferences over actions, it would be necessary to presuppose as given the meaning that the agent attributed to various sentences.

When his view is formulated from the standpoint of the interpreter, it can sound as if Davidson is suggesting that we must always ignore one contributing factor in understanding an agent's conduct. This is not the case. In Davidson's view, the method that must be followed for ascribing attitudes is *constitutive* of those attitudes. This is why the principle of charity is not a falsifiable assumption. Uncharitable interpretations do not count as interpretations, because they disavow the only standard that can be used to distinguish better from worse interpretations. As a result, beliefs are, in Davidson's words, "intrinsically veridical."

Because a desire to tell the truth must be ascribed to agents in order to interpret their speech, it follows immediately from Davidson's view that truth-telling must be constitutive of linguistic meaning. The action of speaking is "intrinsically veridical," in the sense that it must be, on the whole, motivated by a desire to tell the truth. And since language must be presupposed in order to ascribe desires to agents, the veridicality of speech is more basic than any particular desires that the agent may possess. This makes it incorrect to say that agents tell the truth when speaking *in order to satisfy their desires*. The fact that they tell the truth when speaking is a necessary condition for their having desires in the first place.[19] Thus it is a priori that speech cannot be a form of instrumental action, that is, action oriented toward the satisfaction of desire-based preferences over outcomes. (Naturally, agents are capable of lying, just as they are capable of having false beliefs. The point is that lying and error are intelligible only against a background of veracity and veridicality.)

Davidson, however, is unsatisfied with this typological construction, and he therefore suggests that it can be further unified. Instead of treating patterns of *preferring* and *holding true* as the basic data for the ascription of cognitive attitudes, he proposes instead that the same information can be garnered from identifying an agents' *preferences over which sentences are true*. An analysis of this pattern, he argues, will yield belief, meaning, and desire simultaneously. This suggestion is not developed in detail, and so it is not clear how it affects a variety of features of Davidson's project. For instance, he does not say whether the agent has to report these preferences, or whether they are supposed to be available to observation (the latter seems implausible).

Habermas's analysis of the two "elementary types" of action can be understood as motivated by the basic Davidsonian strategy, coupled with a rejection of the final "unification" attempt. Habermas, in other words, continues to view speech and instrumental action as fundamentally distinct types. They are distinguished, from the standpoint of the observer, by the different underlying cognitive attitudes that they reveal, and from the agent's perspective, by the different stance that must be adopted when performing actions of one or another type. When speaking, according to this view, the agent must set aside the particular set of mundane objectives that he might like to achieve and instead adopt a set of standardized intracommunicative goals, namely, to tell the truth (for Davidson) or to reach mutual understanding (for Habermas). This is what motivates Habermas's claim that mutual understanding is the "inherent telos" of communication. The point is not to deny that speech acts can be performed with the intention to mislead or confuse, but rather to affirm that an orientation toward mutual understanding is an enabling precondition of communication systems in general (in the same way that truth-telling is for Davidson).[20]

Thus instrumental action and speech form the two "elementary forms of action" in Habermas's analysis. "Elementary form" means a form that is identified in abstraction from all contexts of social interaction. Naturally, this is not to suggest that language is a presocial phenomenon. The point is simply to identify two orientations that the agent is able to assume toward her environment, before considering the implications of introducing other agents into that environment. The introduction of a second agent, in Habermas's terms, generates *social action*. Social action, in this view, is a complex phenomenon constructed out of the interaction of the two elementary forms of action. The most immediate consequence of introducing a second rational agent into the frame of reference is that it places agents in the position Parsons referred to as *double contingency*—what the first agent wants to do will depend upon what he expects the second to do, and vice versa.[21] Thus agents engaged in interaction are always in a position where they must "coordinate their action-plans," even if this means simply developing a stable set of expectations against which they can each proceed to pursue their private objectives. Thus every interaction involves a coordination problem.[22]

In Habermas's view, this problem of interdependent expectations can be resolved by drawing upon the resources of either elementary action type—instrumental action or speech. When the former is assigned priority, social action takes the form of *strategic action*, in the standard game-theoretic sense. However, when speech is used to resolve the coordination problem, it generates the form of action that Habermas refers to as *communicative action*. The difference is that communicative action explicitly draws upon the public commitments underlying linguistic interactions in order to secure coordination, and therefore creates commitments for all agents involved.

Habermas describes this difference as follows:

The two types of interaction can, to begin with, be distinguished from one another according to the respective mechanism of action coordination—in particular, according to whether natural language is employed solely as a medium for transmitting information or whether it is also made use of as a source of social integration. In the first case I refer to strategic action and in the second to communicative action. In the latter case, the consensus achieving force of linguistic processes of *reaching understanding* [*Verständigung*]—that is, the binding and bonding energies of *language itself*—becomes effective for the coordination of action. In the former case, by contrast, the coordinating effect remains dependent on the *influence*—functioning via non-linguistic activities—exerted by the actors on the action situation and on each other.[23]

It is important to note that communicative action is not the same as speech. It is a form of teleological action, that is, agents continue to pursue goals, to bring about states of affairs in the world. The distinguishing characteristic is that agents use language in order to solve the problem of "double contingency," and therefore use language to determine a set of shared goals. This use of language as an explicit coordination mechanism (rather than simply consistently aligning beliefs through strategic reasoning) imposes constraints on the types of goals that agents can pursue, and the means that they can employ.

Strategic action is also not a simple generalization of instrumental action. It relies upon linguistic resources as well. In this case, however, the intralinguistic objectives of speech acts are subordinated to each agent's individual projects. Language is still in the background, providing agents with the information against which they determine maximizing strategies, for example, common knowledge of preferences, action alternatives, a common prior on probability distributions over states of nature, and so on.[24] But it does not exercise any constraint on the range of action alternatives available to agents.

Thus Habermas's typology of social action is derived as shown in figure 1.1. In his view, the use of language to coordinate social interaction is what generates the structure of public accountability that Kant, Weber, and Parsons took to be a basic feature of norm-governed action. The idea, simply put, is that when agents use language to coordinate their expectations, they incur certain commitments. This is what renders their speech intelligible. However, these commitments are also, as Habermas puts it, *relevant to the subsequent interaction sequence*. They are not merely intralinguistic, but impose direct constraints on the agent's future conduct. These constraints are what generate social order. Thus Habermas claims that "with the concept of communicative action, the important function of social integration devolves on the illocutionary binding energies of a use of language oriented to reaching understanding."[25]

In practice, this means that agents, when performing actions that are linguistically coordinated, can be asked to justify their conduct. This is not an

Elementary action types combine to produce **social action types**

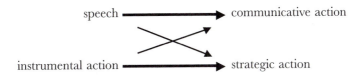

Figure 1.1

"external" demand that is imposed upon them by others. Rather, others simply call upon the agent to make good on commitments that she has already incurred through the use of the linguistic medium as a coordination mechanism. Naturally, since these commitments are generated by the use of an intersubjectively shared language, the agent's justification must also appeal to publicly shared argumentative resources. As Habermas puts it:

> To be sure, speech-act offers can develop an action-coordinating effect only because the binding and bonding force of a speech act that is both understandable and has been accepted by the hearer also extends to the consequences for the sequel of interaction that result from the semantic content of the utterance—whether asymmetrically for the hearer or the speaker, or symmetrically for both parties. Whoever accepts a command feels herself obliged to carry it out; whoever makes a promise feels himself obliged to carry it out; whoever accepts an assertion believes it and will direct her behavior accordingly.[26]

The sort of case that Habermas has in mind is when agents adopt a rule to govern their interactions—for example, when everyone agrees that a certain allocation problem will be handled on a "first-come, first-serve" basis. In the future, agents who were party to this agreement will be held accountable to the accepted norm. In Habermas's view, it is not an intrinsic feature of the norm that agents are held accountable to it. It is because the norm is established using the mechanism of communication oriented toward mutual understanding that all agents are held accountable to it. Thus the accountability of social action is not a primitive feature, but is inherited from the accountability of speech acts. Communicative action is precisely that segment of social action that inherits this characteristic.

1.2 Speech Act Theory

Naturally, what has been said so far is not sufficient to motivate Habermas's position. The goal has simply been to show in what way Habermas's basic framework for the analysis of social action differs from the classical sociological approach. Habermas expresses this difference in terms of a shift away from a *practical* toward a *communicative* conception of rationality.[27] Whereas sociologists have traditionally sought to introduce some shared motivational structure—a norm, value, role, etc.—into the analysis of interaction that would directly influence what agents decide to do, Habermas begins by abstracting from immediate problems of decision, in order to determine what interactive structures must be in place for agents to develop the cognitive and linguistic resources needed to deliberate rationally about action. His theory of practical rationality is then articulated as a consequence of the constraints imposed by this more general theory.

Habermas's stated motivation for making this break arises from his view that theorists in the sociological tradition have never succeeded in capturing the force of what he calls the *validity* of social norms. His intuition here is that when we act in accordance with a particular social norm, we do so because we recognize the norm as in some sense rationally compelling. In his view, norms make a claim upon us that is not contingent upon empirical features of our inclinations or character; the claim is one that is made upon us qua rational agents. This means that we are not permitted to reject norms arbitrarily, or simply be indifferent toward them. If an agent is going to reject a norm, she must do so for a reason. On the other hand, according to the traditional sociological story, normative authority arises when agents internalize the sanctions associated with the violation of socially generalized behavioral expectations. This type of internalization account, however, fails to capture the sense in which norms are considered valid by the agent. The fact that a person has been conditioned to behave in a certain way does not give him a good reason to continue behaving that way. He might just as easily decide to "decondition" himself so that he no longer wants to. Thus the problem with the sociological account, in Habermas's view, is that it is unable to account for the rational force associated with social norms.[28]

For Habermas, Frege's critique of the early Husserl, and Husserl's subsequent critique of "psychologism," represent the paradigmatic articulation of the tensions that arise when one attempts to reduce validity to facticity.[29] In the same way that logical rules cannot be reduced to inferences that agents are inclined to make, social norms cannot be reduced to patterns that agents have been socialized to uphold. By eliminating the dimension of validity, this kind of naturalizing account is unable to adequately reconstruct the normative authority that certain kinds of inferences have for us. In Habermas's view, the ultimate source of validity is language. Certain key practices associated with language use, such as argumentation, have a special sort of normative authority, because language is the *vehicle of thought*. Our ability to think is an ability to manipulate a set of linguistic symbols. These symbols only acquire meaning through the roles they play in certain social practices. Thus the authority that these practices retain upon reflective scrutiny derives from their role in constituting our reflective capacities.

The classical sociological analysis is unable to explain how social norms retain any authority upon reflective scrutiny. In Habermas's view, the authority of these norms derives ultimately from a set of linguistic commitments, and these linguistic commitments derive their authority from linguistic practices that are necessarily reflectively stable. Because it reconstructs the role of language in coordinating social interaction, the theory of communicative action is therefore able to explain how social relations come to be legitimately ordered, that is, ordered in a way that is valid. This is why Habermas thinks that his approach will be capable of explaining what the traditional sociological story was unable to accommodate.

Habermas believes that validity must be analyzed in terms of a type of commitment that agents undertake when they perform certain actions, namely, a commitment to provide a justification for their utterances. Consider the following example. An agent who believes that p is normally understood to have at least two types of commitments. Not only does she maintain that p is the case, she also maintains that she has some reason to believe that p. We would not hesitate to attribute a cognitive fault to someone who simply maintained the truth of p without any justification. Thus, in believing p, the agent maintains an epistemic commitment to the existence or potential existence of grounds for believing that p. In Habermas's terms, the agent, by making the judgment that p, raises a *validity claim* for p, thereby committing herself to the existence of justifying reasons for believing that p.[30]

What has been described here as the making of a validity claim is an *in foro interno* version of what Habermas takes to occur *in foro externo*. In the same way as through judgment we make a private commitment to the existence of

supporting grounds for our belief, through assertion we make a public commitment. In Habermas's view, speakers do not simply assert that particular states
of affairs obtain; they also claim that there is justification for believing that it is
so. Whether their assertions are valid depends upon the existence of supporting reasons that could motivate others to accept their assertion. However, this
feature of assertion is not an accidental feature of the speech act. It is the type
of discursive commitments that the agent undertakes in the performance of
such a speech act that *constitutes the meaning of the utterance*. This is what Habermas
refers to as the internal connection between meaning and validity.

The central implication of this view is that the capacity to understand
linguistic communication is internally connected to the ability to evaluate
the epistemic commitments that speakers undertake through their utterances.
To understand a speech act, in Habermas's view, is to know what makes it
acceptable. Thus Habermas endorses a form of *conceptual role* or *inferential*
semantics.[31] According to such theories, it is impossible to separate the understanding of an utterance from an evaluation of its content. As Habermas
argues:

> The interpreter cannot become clear about the semantic content of an expression inde-
> pendently of the action contexts in which participants react to the expression in ques-
> tion with a "yes" or a "no" or an abstention. And he does not understand these yes/no
> positions if he cannot make clear to himself the implicit reasons that move the partic-
> ipants to take the positions they do. For agreement and disagreement, insofar as they
> are judged in the light of reciprocally raised validity claims and not merely caused by
> external factors, are based on reasons that participants supposedly or actually have at
> their disposal. These (most often implicit) reasons form the axis around which processes
> of reaching understanding revolve. But if, in order to understand an expression, the
> interpreter *must bring to mind the reasons* with which a speaker would if necessary and
> under suitable conditions defend its validity, he is *himself* drawn into the process of
> assessing validity claims. For reasons are of such a nature that they cannot be described
> in the attitude of a third person, that is, without reactions of affirmation or negation
> or abstention. The interpreter would not have understood what a "reason" is if he did
> not reconstruct it with its claim to provide grounds; that is, if he did not give it *a ratio-*
> *nal interpretation. . . .*[32]

Naturally, Habermas is not here claiming that an interpreter cannot abstain
from judging the validity of an utterance. The view is that a speech act can
be understood only in terms of its relations to other speech acts, and that these
relations are epistemic, or more generally, justificatory. To get the meaning of
an utterance right, one has to get its relations with other utterances right, and

since these relations are epistemic, constructing a reasonable interpretation of the meaning of the utterance will involve situating it within a field of largely reasonable inferences. (This is a familiar consequence of the rejection of the analytic/synthetic distinction. It amounts to denying that "knowledge of language" and "knowledge of the world" are two separate things, so that one could be had without the other.[33] We cannot separate semantic from epistemic knowledge.)

A significant aspect of Habermas's approach lies in his emphasis on the fact that speech acts are tied up in a web of epistemic relations in the same way that beliefs have often been thought to be. This makes the practice of language use, like the holding of belief, by nature at least minimally holistic. The internal connection between belief and justification makes the idea of an agent having a single belief nonsensical. Since Quine and Davidson, this has become a common philosophical view. Beliefs are not punctual; they do not bear any direct relationship to suitably individuated chunks of the world. Instead, they are bound up in a complex set of epistemic relations with other beliefs, and it is out of these relations that beliefs are individuated and acquire content. The claim here is a strong one: it is not that an agent is somehow "forced" to think out potential justifications for her beliefs, but that the very idea of her having a belief *makes no sense* outside the context of there being a whole lot of epistemic connections with other beliefs. So if the agent could not think out some of these potential justifications, we would have no grounds for saying that she had a belief (she might have something else, but it could not properly be called a belief).

The parallel drawn here between belief and assertion illuminates the same dimension of Habermas's argument:

A speaker, with a validity claim, appeals to a reservoir of potential reasons that he could produce in support of the claim. The reasons interpret the validity conditions and to this extent are themselves part of the conditions that make an utterance acceptable. In this, the acceptability conditions point to the holistic character of natural languages; every single speech act is linked via logical-semantic threads to numerous other, potential speech acts, that could take on the pragmatic role of reasons.[34]

In this view, it makes no sense to say that someone made an assertion outside the potential for justifications that she could give for its content. It is the way an utterance fits into this web of assertions that gives it its meaning. The notion of a validity claim raised for an utterance highlights the fact that speech acts are tied up in a web of epistemic relations in the same way that beliefs are. In assertoric speech acts, action and validity are tied together in an especially intimate way, for understanding the action consists in knowing what makes it valid.

However, the fact that speakers raise validity claims when they make assertions does not have any obvious repercussions as far as the organization of social practice is concerned. The sociotheoretic implications of Habermas's position stem from his claim that not just assertions, but *all* the different types of speech act we employ should be analyzed in terms of the different validity claims they raise. Most importantly, he argues that in the same way that speakers raise a claim to truth for assertions, they raise a "rightness" claim for their imperatives. Since in the actual organization of institutional interactions all social norms are mediated through imperatives, this claim has obvious and significant implications for the general analysis of social practice. According to Habermas, when we tell someone to, for example, "do the dishes," his understanding of the utterance consists in a grasp of its validity conditions, which is to say, knowledge of the *reasons* that could be given for or against it. These will consist in reasons why he should do the dishes, and why the speaker is authorized to issue such an imperative. This means that insofar as people accept such imperatives and conform to them, they do so because they have accepted the validity of the speech-act offer.

To distinguish between speech acts such as assertions and speech acts that play a more direct role in the organization of social practice, Habermas draws a distinction between *weak* and *strong* communicative action. In weak communicative action, speakers simply state facts or announce intentions, and thus "do not as yet expect each other to be guided by common norms and values and to recognize reciprocal obligations."[35] In strong communicative action, on the other hand, agents use speech acts such as directives, commands, promises, and requests to generate specific normative obligations.

To motivate this analysis, Habermas argues that speech acts should be understood in terms of three basic types of validity claim. In the absence of any institutional context, speech acts divide up naturally into these three kinds. This division stems from the fact that language involves a tripartite relation between a speaker, a hearer, and the world.[36] Thus an agent can use the language to either *assert* that a particular state of affairs obtains in the world, *express* an intention that she has formed, or *request* that the other perform particular actions. These three basic modes, the assertoric, expressive, and regulative, are mutually irreducible and therefore form the three basic kinds of speech act.

All other speech acts, Habermas argues, can be resolved into some combination or variation of these more basic pragmatic modes.[37]

When an agent asserts that a given state of affairs obtains, she claims to do so truthfully. When she expresses the intention to perform a particular action, she claims to do so sincerely. And when she requests that the other perform an action, she claims to do so "rightly," that is, legitimately, or with authorization. Thus, corresponding to the three basic speech act types are three validity claims: truth, rightness, and sincerity. Understanding the speech act involves understanding the conditions under which the appropriate validity claim is satisfied: what state of affairs would have to obtain for the agent's assertion to be true, what actions the agent would have to perform in order to be considered sincere, and what norms would have to be in force in order for the agent's suggestion to be legitimate. Similarly, basic linguistic competence requires that the agent have the ability to redeem these validity claims when called upon to do so, for instance, to show that the state of affairs obtains, to perform the action that has been announced, and so on.

The principle difference between a speech act and an ordinary teleological action is that the speech act, by virtue of its content, renders explicit its own claim to validity. If one observes a person running down the street, one must *ascribe* to that person a set of propositional attitudes, then determine the rationality of his conduct by considering the redeemability of the validity claims associated with these attitudes. For example, if we think that a woman is running to catch a train, we evaluate her conduct in terms of the rationality of her belief that she is in danger of missing the train, and so on. A speech act, on the other hand, renders explicit its own propositional content. Thus the rational evaluation of a speech act must consider whether its content is redeemable. If an agent says "I'm going to be late," the rationality of the speech act must address the redeemability of precisely this belief. There is no need to *ascribe* the propositional attitude that is in need of evaluation; it is right there, a part of the action.[38] It is this characteristic of speech acts that is referred to as their *reflexivity*.[39]

Habermas analyzes the reflexive character of speech through the distinction, introduced by J. L. Austin, between the *illocutionary* and the *perlocutionary* component of speech acts. The illocutionary component specifies the type of action that the agent is performing with the associated propositional content; for example, "I declare that" indicates an assertion, "I order you to" indicates an imperative, and so on. Thus the illocutionary mode tells the hearer how to evaluate the propositional content, for example, as a state of affairs that currently obtains, or that the agent will cause to obtain, and so on. In this respect, the illocutionary mode renders explicit the type of validity claim that is being raised. By grasping the conditions under which this validity claim can be satisfied, the speaker comes to understand the semantic content of the utterance.

However, it is also possible to accomplish, by way of speech acts, certain things that are not rendered explicit in the illocutionary component. An agent may, for instance, make a promise to someone with a variety of "ulterior" motives, for example, to help put her mind at rest, to create a false sense of security, or to facilitate a business transaction. The latter are what Austin called the *perlocutionary* effects of the speech act. The key point is that these ulterior goals are not a "built-in" feature of the speech act in the way that the promising is. If an agent missed the illocutionary component of the promise, there is a clear sense in which she would not know "what was said." However, one can easily know what was said, but have no idea what perlocutionary goal it was intended to serve. The perlocutionary goal must therefore be read into the utterance through the ascription of additional propositional attitudes, much as in the case of ordinary teleological action. One need not understand the validity basis of the speech act in order to grasp its perlocutionary component, and understanding the perlocutionary component contributes nothing to the agent's understanding of the semantic content of the speech act. It therefore appears that although perlocutions can be "piggybacked" onto standard speech acts, they are not an essential component.[40]

This observation led Habermas to suggest that the difference between illocutionary acts and perlocutionary acts showed that in standard cases, the use of language is basically noninstrumental. Whereas speech acts can be used for instrumental purposes (as revealed by the fact that speech acts may contain a perlocutionary component), in their original, that is, *meaning-constitutive*, use, speech acts are not performed with the intention of achieving extralinguistic goals.

The teleological actor's orientation to success is not constitutive for the "success" of processes of reaching understanding, particularly not when these are incorporated into strategic actions. What we mean by reaching understanding has to be clarified solely in connection with illocutionary acts. From this it also follows that we cannot explain illocutionary success in terms of the conditions for the purposively achieved success of a teleological action.[41]

Habermas argues that speech acts must be understood as performed with the intention of achieving the standardized intralinguistic goal of mutual understanding/agreement.[42] The adoption of this goal is constitutive, insofar as agents must presuppose that such an orientation (i.e., the "performative stance") has been adopted by all parties in order to correctly situate the utterance within the field of associated validity claims, and thereby grasp its semantic content. This is what motivates Habermas's claim that mutual understanding is the "inherent telos" of communication.

This analysis of speech acts provides the basis for Habermas's reconstruction of the notion of norm-governed action. In his view, understanding an utterance is necessarily connected with evaluating it. An agent, in speaking to another, does not act upon the hearer instrumentally, but makes a *claim* upon her. The hearer, in order to understand the utterance, is drawn into an evaluation of the validity of the claims that the speaker associates with that utterance. But once drawn into the circle of evaluation, she cannot just dismiss the claim, but must respond with a yes or no. However, by responding in this way, she also raises validity claims, that is, she claims to accept or reject the speaker's offer for reasons. The hearer thus incurs commitments that are relevant to the further sequence of interaction. If the hearer responds to a speaker's assertion with acceptance, then she commits herself to act as if the state of affairs in question in fact obtained. If she fails to act in this way, she owes the speaker whose assertion she accepted an explanation of why she failed to act in an appropriate manner. Similarly, an agent who accepts an imperative must treat it as giving her a reason for action, and an agent who accepts a promise must proceed on the expectation that it will in fact be fulfilled. In each case, the hearer's commitment is entailed by the validity claim associated with her yes/no response to the initial speech-act offer.

Now, since social norms are conveyed through imperatives, and agents, in accepting these imperatives, express a sincere commitment to act upon them, all norm-governed action involves a moment of rational insight, in which the agent voluntarily, and for good reasons, accepts the obligations that are expressed in the norm. To understand the utterance, the agent must know the sort of reasons that the speaker could give for it. So in accepting the utterance, the hearer claims not only that the utterance itself is acceptable, but that it is acceptable in light of the reasons that could be given for it. This moment of acceptance, induced by the speech act, accounts for the *validity* associated with social norms that is missing in the sociological picture. And when the agent conforms to the norm, what she does is no more than fulfill the commitments that she undertook in her initial evaluation of the imperative through which the norm was communicated.

Habermas summarizes his argument in the following passage:

> If understanding a speech act depends upon knowing the conditions for its acceptability, then the speaker's illocutionary aim of being understood points to the further aim that the hearer should accept her speech-act offer. Acceptance or agreement on the part of the hearer is equivalent to recognition of a validity claim raised by the speaker. It is based on the good reasons that the speaker offers in order to redeem the validity claim in discourse (or else on a credible warranty issued by the speaker that she could provide such reasons, if necessary). And the hearer, with his "yes" to a validity claim he has accepted as worthy of recognition—that is, with his acceptance of the speech-act offer—also takes upon himself, as a rule, certain obligations relevant for the sequel of interaction, such as obligations to meet a request, to trust a confession, to believe a statement, to rely on a promise, or to obey an order.[43]

At the heart of this approach is an essentially contractualist intuition, namely, that the only rationally compelling forms of obligations are those that have been freely incurred by agents. In Habermas's framework, such obligations are those to which the agent has said "yes," where this "yes" represents the rationally motivated acceptance of a speech act offer, that is, acceptance with respect to the reasons that could be supplied to back it up. Habermas avoids the overly voluntaristic aspects of contractualism, however, through his claim that agents enter into rationally motivated agreements whenever they participate in linguistically organized social practices. The mere use of language as a medium of social integration imposes the constraint that social practices be grounded in such an agreement.

Habermas recognizes that, when stated baldly, this view has absurd consequences. It must therefore be qualified, in order to avoid the implication that all social practices are grounded in rational consensus: "Otherwise we would have to assume that the de facto validity of norms of action rests everywhere, and from the very beginning, on the rationally motivated agreement of everyone involved; this conflicts with the repressive character evinced in the fact that norms, demanding obedience, take effect in the form of social control."[44] He therefore argues that social institutions were *originally* stabilized through simple internalization of sanctions, but have slowly been transformed through the use of communicative action as a mechanism of social integration. This means that social institutions, over the course of their development, come to assume an increasingly voluntaristic character. This is the process that Habermas refers to as the "linguistification of the sacred," and it occupies a central role in his developmental account of our capacity to coordinate interaction through communicative action.

1.3 The Genesis of Communicative Action

Habermas believes that communicative action represents the tail end of a developmental process in which complex forms of social action have given rise to competencies that have in turn permitted the emergence of more sophisticated forms of action. This is an empirical hypothesis, which can be tested, in Habermas's view, by a historical reconstruction of cultural worldviews. It is also a developmental process that is recapitulated in ontogenesis, so that the emergence of each new form of sociocognitive competence can be observed in the growing child. These two arguments are developed in the fifth chapter of *The Theory of Communicative Action*, where Habermas provides a phylogenetic account of communicative action in the form of an interpretation of work by Emile Durkheim and George Herbert Mead, and in a paper entitled "Moral Consciousness and Communicative Action," where he tries to show that the stages in Lawrence Kohlberg's model of the development of sociocognitive and moral reasoning are isomorphic to the stages that occur in his own reconstruction of the development of communicative action.[45] Of these two accounts, the Mead-Durkheim analysis is the more significant, because it establishes the basic developmental framework.

In Habermas's view, the development of the capacity to engage in communicative action begins with the emergence of what he calls *symbolically mediated interaction*. At this stage, communication takes the form of holophrastic signaling. The development of such signaling capacities permits the transition to a stage of conventional norm-conformative action. Normative judgment, in turn, permits the differentiation of signaling languages into semantic, intentional, and conventional components. Communicative action then arises with the reintegration of these three components into propositionally differentiated speech acts of the type that we now routinely employ.

For Habermas, the first thing that needs to be explained in an analysis of the origin of symbolically mediated interaction is how certain actions come to have *conventionally fixed* meanings. To explain this, he argues, one must assume that agents acquire the ability to adopt a kind of noninstrumental action orientation. Whereas instrumental actions are performed in a stance that is oriented toward success (*erfolgsorientiert*), symbolization must be performed in a stance oriented toward mutual understanding. The burden of proof that Habermas assumes requires showing that conventional meaning is impossible without the ability to adopt a special stance of this type. This he develops by way of a critique of Mead.

In *Mind, Self, and Society*, Mead defines *simple acts* as goal-directed interventions an organism makes in the causal nexus of the physical world. This is the case when one dog bites another, or when someone pushes someone else in order to get him out of the way. But sentient organisms are generally able to anticipate the likely consequences of a series of physical movements they see unfolding before them, and so are liable to modify their behavior in order to avoid undesirable outcomes. This means that two interacting organisms tend to react to each others' acts before completion. If one agent moves to push another, the latter might quickly move out of the way. But seeing that the act cannot successfully be completed now that the other has reacted, the agent may cut it short and try something new. In this way, the initial phase of the act becomes a *gesture*, in which the agent calls out a response in the other, and hence brings about a certain result in the world merely by prompting a reaction in another organism.[46]

Mead observes that this can give rise to a *conversation of gestures*, in which two organisms reciprocally call out responses in each other. In the case of cognitively unsophisticated organisms, this conversation is unintelligent, because they are incapable of anticipating each other's responses. More sophisticated organisms—most obviously humans—are able to anticipate how others will respond to certain acts by inference from how they themselves would. Role-taking thus gives gestures the potential to become significant symbols. According to Mead, a pushing motion may no longer be aimed at pushing, but merely at evoking a response in another. Since the first agent begins by "calling out" this response in herself in the process of anticipating alter's behavior, the gesture takes on the meaning of alter's anticipated behavior, since both agents share it as a response. Gestures that arise frequently then become stylized into shared symbols, like shaking a fist at an enemy, and so on.

Although Habermas endorses Mead's conceptual strategy, he claims that this simple role-taking analysis is not fine-grained enough to account for the production of *identical* responses in both organisms. In his view, Mead does not take into consideration the fact that, as the level of role-taking competence increases, each agent must take over the attitudes of an increasingly sophisticated other. Thus role-taking has built into it a mechanism that propels actors on to more and more sophisticated cognitive operations. On an individual level, this can be illustrated by showing the recursive structure of role-taking operations, and thus singling out several distinctly different *rounds*, each adding a layer of complexity to the previous one. If an agent initially is not a role-taker at all, and puts himself for the first time in the shoes of the other, he will simply think of the other as responding to stimulus. But once this role-taking ability has been established, the agent will realize that the other is also able to role-take. Now, when the agent assumes the role of the other, he will have to take into account the fact that the other is also able to assume his position. This cycle obviously continues indefinitely, and the structure of anticipations becomes increasingly complex.

In Habermas's view, Mead's primary achievement was to recognize that symbolic action differs from instrumental action in that it rests upon a certain structure of convergent intentions and expectations. However, Mead failed to acknowledge the role that "higher-order" expectations play in social interaction, and so mischaracterized this structure. In the case of gesture-mediated interaction, if ego does a "single" role-take onto alter and performs the initial segment of a certain act *a* in order to provoke behavior *b*, then *a* acquires the meaning *b* for ego—but contrary to Mead's suggestion, the identical meaning is not shared between ego and alter. This is because alter has not done any role-taking at all, but is rather mistakenly responding to an act as if it were going to be carried through.

This asymmetry only arises, however, if ego does a single role-take, that is, assumes that alter does not do one. If ego invests alter with role-taking ability, that is, does a "double" role-take, once onto alter and then back to himself, he will realize that alter may interpret *a* as a gesture designed to bring out behavior *b*. Thus ego may produce the gesture not to bring out the behavior, but with the strictly communicative intent of having it interpreted as aimed at bringing out a response. However, if alter must understand a gesture not as directed upon, but rather as *addressed to* him, then he must realize that ego is giving him something to interpret, and that the success of the interaction depends upon a harmonization of their responses, not in the causal consequences of the act. This marks the point at which agents acquire the ability to distinguish between success-oriented and understanding-oriented action. Once this new orientation is established, according to Habermas, "the participants can differentiate between the social object in the role of speaker and hearer and the other as an object of external influence, between communicative acts addressed to one's counterpart and consequence-oriented actions that bring something about."[47]

This new structure of intentionality allows meaning to be detached from the specific behavior that the gesture was intended to elicit. But this raises the obvious question of how it is possible to *distinguish* between different meanings if no reference to the teleological intentions of the speaker is permitted. The answer is that meaning becomes conventionally determined. For meanings to become fixed, there must be rules for the proper use of symbols. And for an actor to follow a rule, she must do more than simply believe she has followed it. Her act must meet with approval, and so be considered an instance of following the rule, by at least one other partner in interaction. So to follow the rule, she must be able to anticipate how others will evaluate her performance. Habermas points out that this occurs simply through a third round of role-taking.

At the first level, ego anticipates only the behavior of alter. At the second level, ego begins to anticipate alter's interpretation of a gesture. At the third level, ego role-takes back onto alter and realizes that her act may or may not succeed depending on whether alter interprets it in the way intended. If ego fails to articulate a gesture correctly, or uses it in contexts where it is out of place, alter's lack of response functions as a signal to ego that a mistake has been made. When ego comes to "internalize this dismissive response," then she has learned to "anticipate critical responses" to her use of symbols. Habermas offers this "genetic explanation of Wittgenstein's concept of a rule" in order to show how meanings could come to be determined conventionally, and thus how sameness of meaning could be secured.[48]

The structure of intentionality underlying rule-following can be characterized in the following way: to say that ego is applying a rule, ego must perform an action with the intention of fulfilling alter's expectations, with the expectation that alter will acknowledge ego's act as a fulfillment of these expectations, and with the understanding that ego expects alter's response to be governed by these expectations.[49] This is a sort of complicated way of saying that the action must fit the expectations of both parties, and these expectations must also be expected. Since both parties, in this context, are doing nothing more that satisfying each other's expectations, the action in itself no longer has any instrumental significance—its only consequences are the effects it has upon the structure of expectations, that is, its meaning.

With this analysis, Habermas provides the foundation for his claim that there are two types of elementary action. Instrumental action is oriented fundamentally toward achieving outcomes in the world. But for actions to acquire conventionally fixed meanings, agents must suspend this orientation toward worldly outcomes and focus on satisfying each other's expectations. It must be recalled that when agents communicate, the actual sounds or gestures produced do very little of the work in conveying the speaker's meaning. It is the background structures of intentionality, shared to a greater or lesser extent by speaker and hearer, that allow these signs to communicate something *meaningful*. According to Habermas, it is only when action is oriented toward satisfying expectations, rather than outcomes, that the appropriate sort of intentional structures can arise.

The analysis so far explains only how actions can acquire symbolic properties. The next step in Habermas's story involves showing how, when the meaning of a set of symbols has become conventionally fixed, new possibilities for social coordination arise. At this point, "signals are embedded in interaction contexts in such a way that they always serve to coordinate the actions of different participants—the quasi-indicative meaning and the quasi-expressive meaning of the utterance form a unity with the quasi-imperative meaning."[50] Shouts like "Food!" are intrinsically action-guiding, in that they express a reaction to some feature of the natural world in a context where there is no question as to the desired course of action.

For Habermas, the transition to normatively regulated interaction is linked to the differentiation of these symbols into different modes. He argues that what is currently the propositional component of our speech acts originated in the differentiation of assertoric statements and statements of intention out of signal languages. "We can assume that in connection with the constitution of a 'perceptual world of physical objects' propositional elements are first of all differentiated out of the holistic utterances of context-bound signal languages."[51] These two different types of statement correspond to two possible types of relation to the physical world, that of an observer who describes events, and that of an actor who brings those events about.

As the idea of a "physical world" that can be described in assertoric speech acts develops, the "undifferentiated unity of world relations" that holds together forms of symbolically mediated interaction begins to fall apart. Assertoric statements equivalent to "That is a rabbit," or statements of intention like "I'm going to kill the rabbit," are then no longer automatically action-guiding. Thus the constitution of an objective world in experience provides an evolutionary challenge for forms of interaction based on signal languages:

To the extent that participants in interaction have linguistically at their disposal an objective world to which they relate with propositions or in which they can intervene in a goal-directed manner, their action can no longer be coordinated via signals. Only so long as the descriptive elements of meaning are fused with the expressive and imperative elements do signals have the power to steer behavior. It is true that the functional circuits of animal behavior break down at the stage of symbolically mediated interaction; on the other hand, signals remain tied to dispositions and schemes of behavior. It is because they are embedded in this way that signals have a binding power that is a functional equivalent for the triggering effect of gestures. At the stage of propositionally differentiated communication—of linguistic communication in the narrower sense—this kind of motivation gets lost.[52]

In something of a flight of fancy, Habermas then suggests that the branching off of propositional contents from symbol systems gives rise to the basic conceptual dichotomy between the sacred and profane (in the sense that Durkheim understood it). The now archaic "paleosymbols," which make up the repertoire of still intrinsically action-guiding holophrastic signals, that is, symbols capable of social integration, become "emblems" of the sacred. Meanwhile, the propositional elements, which have lost their integrating function and now merely serve to describe events and intentions, set off the realm of the profane.

To the extent that object perception and teleological action undergo development, propositional elements are differentiated out of signal language, elements that later take the explicit form of assertoric sentences and intentional sentences. As we have seen, speakers cannot replace the binding effects of signal languages with the communicative employment of these sentences. For this reason I would conjecture that there is a split in the medium of communication corresponding to the segregation of the sacred from the profane domains of life: religious signification, which makes possible a normative consensus and thereby provides the foundation for a ritual coordination of action, is the archaic part left over from the stage of symbolically mediated interaction after experience from domains in which perceptible and manipulable objects are dealt with in a more and more propositionally structured manner flow into communication.[53]

Thus group interaction comes to be regulated by the set of symbols that retain their integrative power. These sacred symbols, because of the function they serve, come to represent the group itself. Thus the correct execution of *ritual action* is secured by the group sanction as represented in sacred symbols. In this way, the authority of the collective is initially represented, and internalized by actors, as religious authority. Although this authority is used to secure the correct performance of religious rituals, it can lend support to other social institutions. In particular, those in leadership positions can draw upon this reservoir of sacred symbols in order to provide a normative foundation to their assumed role. "[A]t first moral and legal norms themselves had the character of ritual prescriptions. The more institutions are differentiated, however, the looser the ties to ritual practice become."[54]

Habermas refers to symbols employed this way as *appelative* sentences, which are used to express the "norm consciousness" of members in a society. Since the force of norms governs the correct performance of ritual acts, appelative expressions consist largely in critical responses to attempts at reproducing a certain type of conduct. Their use in conveying ideas like "this is how it is done," and "that is not how it is done," contains the basis for a right/wrong orientation toward the performance of nonlinguistic action. However, instead of representing the specific evaluation of a particular individual, this type of response now expresses the consensus of the community as to how certain actions should be performed. Internalization of this response, that is, of the "generalized other," then accounts for the development of norm-conformative motivations of the type posited by classical sociological theories of action.

To constitute communicative action, this normative regulation must be extended to include the use of speech acts. In pregrammatical profane speech, one can articulate a propositional content *p*, but one can only do so "baldly," so to speak. In saying *p*, an agent is not asserting the truth of it in such a way that the statement makes any claim upon others. Furthermore, the agent does not provide any implicit assurances that she has good reasons for asserting it. The agent is merely verbalizing a descriptive response. In sacred speech, on the other hand, agents are able to make a claim upon others as to the rightness or wrongness of an act with respect to a ritually secured action system. Thus statements made in sacred language demand the assent of all others and carry the authority of the collective.

In the transition to grammatical speech, this function of sacred language is extended in such a way that propositional elements get hooked up with the claim to rightness. Habermas illustrates this transition with the development of truth claims. In the case of assertoric statements, there must be an element of correspondence to the world if symbols are being used in accordance with fixed rules. Thus it is possible to name an object and to see the name as in some sense attached to it. At the same time, however, if meanings are fixed conventionally, it will be possible to get a fairly broad consensus as to whether the name has been used in such a way as to label the object correctly. Thus the act of naming takes on a significance analogous to that of ritual, in that it can be performed correctly or incorrectly (just as the connection between "naming" and "baptism" would suggest).

This is what gives rise to the development of a "validity claim" associated with assertoric speech. An assertion becomes criticizable as if it were a ritual action in a normative context. Assuming that a similar development occurs with truthfulness/sincerity claims, a system of language use then develops in which propositionally differentiated constructions can be used in making criticizable claims. Propositions representing states of affairs, executions of acts, or inner events can become the content of claims to truth, rightness, or sincerity respectively. This means that the elements that were first separated out of the signal language regain their coordinating power at a higher level. It is now possible to coordinate action through rationally motivated agreement about states of affairs in the external world, normative structures in the social world, and needs and desires experienced in the world of inner subjectivity.

It is because the intentional structure of linguistic understanding is built up on the basis of norm-conformative interaction that speech acts have a built-in normative dimension. At the same time, because speech acts allow agents to explicitly thematize and revise shared expectations, the development of propositionally differentiated speech transforms the action type upon whose base it initially emerges. Communicative action develops, in this way, as a generalization of primitive norm-conformative action. The primary difference is that with "full-blown" communicative action, only the weak binding force of communicatively achieved agreement underlies action coordination. Once it is developed, communicative action begins to replace norm-conformative action as the favored mechanism of social integration. Social norms—which Habermas thinks of as essentially "taboos"—begin to be replaced by communicatively achieved and hence discursively justifiable agreements.

Habermas refers to the process through which social integration is transferred from the "spellbinding" force of sacred symbols over to communicative action as the *linguistification of the sacred*. Habermas describes the process in the following way:

The validity basis of norms of action changes insofar as every communicatively mediated consensus depends on reasons. The authority of the sacred that stands behind institutions is no longer valid per se. Sacred authorization becomes dependent instead on the justificatory accomplishments of religious worldviews. . . . The *communicatively mediated* application of action norms depends on participants coming to shared situation definitions that refer simultaneously to the objective, the normative and the subjective facets of the situation in question. Participants in interaction must themselves relate the relevant norms to the given situation and tailor them to special tasks. To the degree that these interpretative accomplishments become independent from the normative context, the institutional system can deal with the growing complexity of action situations by branching out into a network of social roles and special regulations within a framework of highly abstract basic norms.[55]

It should be emphasized that the sacred is not simply replaced by linguistically steered interaction. Rather, the development of propositionally differentiated speech is an evolutionary step in a learning process that permits the emergence of more sophisticated forms of social organization.[56] With the development of communicative action, a new set of institutions springs up alongside the original set of religious ones. Because of the increase in societal complexity made possible by these developments, the sacred institutions are then replaced where they become dysfunctional, or else are bypassed in the development of more complex structures. Since both sets of institutions have roughly the same purpose, namely, social integration, the shift from one medium to another will not be terribly abrupt, nor will there be grounds for an upheaval in the basic content of normative structures.

Naturally, Habermas does not think that when social interaction is integrated through communicative action every agent is aware of the full battery of reasons that could be summoned in opposition to or in defense of every aspect of the practice. Communicative action is able to secure social integration because it is underwritten by a set of commitments, made by all participants, to justify the rules that they follow and expect to be followed. But these commitments can easily outrun any participant's actual ability to redeem them. In fact, given the structure of Habermas's speech act theory, the commitments that agents make when engaged in communicative action *necessarily* outrun their actual capacities to redeem them (since every speech act is said to raise three validity claims). As a result, agents explore these commitments, and the set of possible justifications, only when they are explicitly challenged to do so, or when one of the rules they are following somehow becomes problematic. The rest are simply consigned to the background. Participants may have some vague sense of how the argument would go, but they have no need to develop it explicitly until called upon to do so. Habermas refers to this taken-for-granted background as the *lifeworld*. The lifeworld functions to stabilize interactions that are integrated through the "improbable" mechanism of communicatively achieved consensus:

> The risk built into communicative action is *circumscribed* by those intuitive background certainties that are accepted without question because they are uncoupled from any communicatively accessible reasons that one could deliberately mobilize. Entrenched below the threshold of possible thematization, these behavior-stabilizing certainties that make up the lifeworld background are cut off from that dimension—opened up only in communicative action—in which we can distinguish between the justified accept-ability and the mere acceptance of beliefs and reasons.[57]

The developmental sequence that Habermas posits, from symbolically mediated to norm-governed and finally to communicative action, involves a series of cumulative gains. Norm-governed action arises when certain basic competences used in symbolic communication are put to use in the produc-tion of more complex behavioral structures. In the same way, the capacity to engage in norm-conformative action is taken up and transformed in the devel-opment of communicative action. Thus communicative action does not simply replace norm-conformity as the preferred form of action coordination, but rather sublates it. This means that norm-conformity is still an important devel-opmental prerequisite of communicative action. Habermas therefore suggests that these basic developmental stages are recapitulated in ontogenesis, as the child acquires increasing competence in analyzing and respecting patterns of social organization.

Habermas argues that this pattern can be discerned in the development of sociocognitive reasoning in children. Kohlberg analyzes this sequence using a framework that contains three levels of ability: preconventional, conventional, and postconventional reasoning.[58] At the preconventional level, the child is able to distinguish between the natural consequences of an action and those that follow from the disappointment of expectations, but adopts a uniformly instrumental orientation toward both. At this level rules are perceived as strictly external constraints, and they are obeyed only in order to avoid the punish-ment associated with failure to comply. At the conventional level, children have "internalized" these rules, either in the form of direct role expectations or com-mands. However, the attitude they exhibit toward these rules is one of pure conformity. There is no distinction drawn between the validity and the mere currency of a norm. At the postconventional level, norm-conformity is maintained, but the reasons for complying are now expressed in terms of abstract values or principles.

Habermas develops a lengthy argument—the details of which I will not discuss here—that attempts to show how the competences that the child develops at each level correspond to those attained at each primary stage of cultural evolution. The resources used in each transition are those drawn from the fundamental structure of action oriented toward mutual understanding. The use of these analytic tools for the reconstruction of the Kohlberg framework is thus intended to demonstrate the explanatory fruitfulness of the theory of communicative action, and to lend support to the broader developmental account offered in the analysis of Mead and Durkheim.

1.4   The Structure of the Argument

The problem with Habermas's linguistic analysis and his developmental reconstruction is that *as arguments for his position* both are extremely difficult to evaluate. The reconstructive argument, while making a commendable attempt to bring a broadly philosophical theory into dialogue with existing research in the social sciences, unfortunately makes use of this research in a highly speculative manner. The interpretations that Habermas uses to motivate his position often appear to be selected arbitrarily from among a range of equally plausible alternatives. So although I consider it extremely important that a philosophical account of social and moral reasoning be able to accommodate data such as that presented by Kohlberg, it is far from clear how a reconstruction of the type that Habermas develops lends any support to his view. Even Habermas's speech act theory, although considerably less speculative, involves taking sides on a number of extremely controversial issues in the philosophy of language. Habermas's position may in the end turn out to be correct, but the arguments he advances are in general insufficient to settle the difficult questions that must be answered in order to establish this.

Part of the problem is that Habermas never presents anything like a step-by-step defense of his position. As a result, it is difficult to discern exactly where the crucial burdens of proof lie. My strategy in the following two chapters will therefore be to reconfigure Habermas's basic theory as a step-by-step series of claims, then to evaluate each of these claims in sequence, making the strongest case for them that I can. In so doing, I will be attempting, wherever possible, to avoid controversial presuppositions, and where these are inevitable, to expand somewhat on the broader philosophical considerations that lead Habermas to favor the side that he does. Naturally, presenting the theory in this way will involve significant departures from Habermas's own work. However, my concern is not primarily to provide an exegesis, but rather to evaluate the correctness of Habermas's conclusions.

In my view, there are four major steps that need to be taken in order to defend a conception of communicative action of the type that Habermas presents:

1. Habermas must show that communication cannot be purely instrumental. The analysis of Mead is suggestive, but it does not really prove anything. A more powerful argument can be developed by showing that the standard instrumental model of rationality is unable to provide an adequate pragmatics for a theory of meaning. This shows that the existence of a shared language requires that agents engage in systematically noninstrumental behavior. And if speech acts are not rational in the instrumental sense, it suggests that they must be rational in some other, yet-to-be-specified sense.

2. Habermas must offer some explanation of *why* speech acts cannot be planned and executed with instrumental intent. This can be shown by establishing that the meaning of speech acts is given by the discursive commitments that are generated through their utterance. This would be the case if what Habermas calls acceptability conditions were capable of providing an adequate semantics for natural language. If propositional content were given by discursive commitment, it would explain why language cannot be instrumental, since commitments involve a failure of so-called sequential rationality, which is normally considered an important feature of the instrumental conception of rationality.

3. Habermas must then offer some characterization of the sense in which speech acts *are* rational. Here the notion of discursive commitment used to generate the semantic theory already suggests the answer. In the same way that beliefs are considered rational if and only if the agent is capable of justifying them, that is, redeeming the implied doxastic commitments, a speech act can be said to be communicatively rational just in case the agent is capable of justifying it, that is, redeeming the relevant discursive commitments. Thus the rationality of a speech act simply corresponds to the justifiability of its content.

4. Finally, Habermas must show that not only speech acts, but all actions coordinated through speech acts, are governed by standards of communicative rather than instrumental rationality. To establish this conclusion, Habermas argues that all norm-governed social practices are organized through the use of imperatives. To issue such imperatives successfully, agents must commit themselves to justifying their content, and thus the norms that govern their practices.

This argument, I will attempt to show, can be made to work all the way up to the last step. In chapter 2, I argue that Habermas's claim that speech acts are not, in their standard employment, strategic actions, can be established without appeal to the controversial distinction between illocutionary and perlocutionary acts. Rather than analyze meaning, in order to show that it cannot contain strategic elements, I analyze strategic reasoning, in order to show that it cannot include meaningful elements. I do so by showing, roughly, that when communication is introduced into instrumental models of social interaction, players are rendered incapable of determining maximizing strategies. This means that insofar as they do make use of linguistic resources in order to communicate, they cannot be planning or executing their actions with strategic intent. This analysis establishes Habermas's basic claim regarding the action-theoretic status of speech acts, but does so without requiring any controversial theoretical commitments, since the game-theoretic models that I employ are widely accepted as accurate implementations of the instrumental conception of rationality.

In chapter 3, I start out with an examination of the second major step in the argument, namely, the claim that a theory of meaning for speech acts can be given through some form of acceptability-conditional semantics. This is a more controversial idea, and so I provide a general characterization of the considerations that support this approach. The most significant, I argue, stem from the constraints introduced by Frege on theories of meaning, referred to as the "context principle," that words have meaning only in the context of a sentence, and the "compositionality principle," that the meaning of sentences is composed from the meaning of their parts. I endorse this approach to the theory of meaning, but argue that an acceptability-conditional semantics ultimately does not support the claim that the understanding of *imperatives* is given by reasons pertaining to the normative background of their utterance. This means that agents are able to issue imperatives without committing themselves to defending any particular set of social norms, and so the accountability of social action cannot be due to the use of language as a coordination device. So even if the third step of the above argument is plausible, the fourth is not. The transition from a *weak* to a *strong* conception of communicative action is unmotivated.

On the basis of this criticism, I will argue that classical sociological action theory is ultimately more coherent than Habermas's conception of communicative action. The two basic types of action, I will argue, are indeed instrumental and norm-conformative action, and accountability is a primitive feature of the latter. The reason speech acts cannot be modeled instrumentally, I will argue, is that they are a species of norm-governed action. The accountability of speech acts, which is essential to securing their intelligibility, is inherited from the fact that they are norm-governed actions. Thus Habermas's analysis gets the order of explanation exactly backwards. In chapter 4, I present an outline of a typological theory of action that includes norms of this type, but which retains a voluntaristic account of normative authority of the type that Habermas has sought to develop.

2

Language and Strategic Action

Habermas's view that rational action is divided into two primary types—strategic and communicative—is intended to be understood as a claim about the way agents deliberate. He is not claiming that action can be interpreted in two different ways, from a sociotheoretic perspective. He is claiming that agents go about their business in different ways, depending on the type of action orientation they adopt. As Habermas puts it:

I do not use the terms "strategic" and "communicative" only to designate two analytic aspects under which the same action could be described—on the one hand as a reciprocal influencing of one another by opponents acting in a purposive-rational manner and, on the other hand, as a process of reaching understanding among members of a lifeworld. Rather, social actions can be distinguished according to whether the participants adopt either a success-oriented attitude or one oriented toward reaching understanding. And, under suitable conditions, these attitudes should be identifiable on the basis of the intuitive knowledge of the participants themselves.[1]

For this difference to be as concrete as Habermas suggests, it must be the case that some actions can be rendered intelligible only relative to a particular orientation, that is, some actions must make sense only under the assumption that the agent is acting instrumentally, or acting communicatively. Naturally, some actions might plausibly be explained both instrumentally and communicatively, in which case only the agent in question would know the real reason for her action. But unless there is some extensional divergence—divergence that cannot simply be attributed to irrationality—there will be no difference between Habermas's view and the weaker "two aspect" thesis.

Habermas attempts to establish the stronger thesis by arguing that *standard speech acts* cannot be interpreted as instrumentally rational. His primary argument to this effect attempts to draw upon our "intuitive knowledge" of the distinction between illocutionary and perlocutionary goals, in order to suggest that we are not concerned with strictly extralinguistic objectives when performing speech acts. Nevertheless, this argument is quite weak, since it does not provide any reason for thinking that the intralinguistic goals that we pursue, for example, getting others to believe what we believe, cannot be characterized in instrumental terms. Furthermore, the illocution/perlocution distinction is itself extremely vague—in many cases it is very difficult to say where one component of the act stops and the other starts, making it hard to believe that these could constitute the goal states of two mutually exclusive action orientations.

Habermas adopts a much more promising argumentative strategy in later work, where he attempts to show that speech acts cannot be represented using standard decision theory models. There are a number of precise formal models that capture the key ideas underlying the instrumental conception of rationality. If some of the components that enter into the deliberation of agents in contexts of linguistic interaction could be shown to be absent in such models, or if certain essential patterns of speech behavior could be shown to be inconsistent with their predictions, then one would have a much firmer basis for maintaining that speech acts involve systematically noninstrumental reasoning. Furthermore, since speech acts play a central role in a variety of paradigmatically rational practices, such as scientific research, it would be deeply implausible to suggest that the noninstrumental character of linguistically mediated interaction could be written off as mere irrationality (as it is, for instance, by many economists in the case of moral conduct).

The argument that Habermas presents appeals to the claim that actions in the instrumental model are limited by the following three conditions: the goal of the action must be determined "(a) independently of the means of intervention (b) as a state brought about causally (c) in the objective world."[2] But a state of successful communication, he argues, cannot be described under these three constraints, since "*a.* illocutionary goals cannot be defined independently of the linguistic means of reaching mutual understanding"; "*b.* the speaker cannot intend the aim of reaching mutual understanding as something that is to be brought about causally"; and "*c.* finally, from the perspective of participants, the process of communication and the result to which this is supposed to lead do not constitute innerworldly states."[3]

This argumentation strategy is, I believe, one that can ultimately succeed. However, the specific claims that Habermas makes are inadequate. The limitations of the instrumental model that Habermas outlines are roughly accurate only as a characterization of decision-theoretic models. Decision theory, however, models only the deliberative processes of instrumentally rational agents acting in exclusively *nonsocial* contexts. The limitations that Habermas describes do not apply to game-theoretic models, or models of strategic action, which attempt to characterize the deliberative processes of agents acting in contexts of interdependent choice. Although it is correct that in such models an outcome must be a natural state of affairs, brought about by causal intervention, the action that brings about this outcome is observed by others, who in turn draw certain conclusions about the actor's state of mind. There is nothing in the instrumental conception of rationality that prevents an agent from performing an action with the goal of "setting up" others to draw some particular conclusions. Thus Habermas's argument shows only that speech acts cannot be modeled decision-theoretically; it says nothing about the possibility of a modeling communication as strategic action.

A number of theorists have presented models of language that use the more sophisticated, strategic conception of instrumental rationality for their pragmatics. David Lewis, for instance, models linguistic conventions using a signaling game in which player 1 alone observes an event, then performs one of a set of actions that will be viewed by player 2. Player 2 chooses an action that results in an outcome, with payoffs for each player having the structure of a coordination problem. Through fairly simple strategic reasoning it is possible for player 2 to infer which event has occurred by observing player 1's action. Thus player 1's action can be described as a signal that communicates the prevailing state of nature to player 2. Since player 1's reasoning mirrors player 2's, it can plausibly be said that player 1 sends the signal with the intention that player 2 form correct beliefs about which event has occurred. But player 2's belief is not brought about causally by player 1's action. Player 1, who knows the prevailing state, chooses an optimal action. Player 2, who does not observe the state, is able to form correct beliefs about it from the combination of observing player 1's action and knowing that player 1 is optimizing. Thus player 2 can *rationally infer* the information content, that is, the meaning, of player 1's signal.[4]

The important point is simply that strategically rational agents can perform actions not only with the intention of causing certain outcomes in the world, but also with the intention of *prompting* other players to change their beliefs. Because of this, Habermas's argument does not show what it purports to. But this is not to say that the conclusion is incorrect. Several limitations with models of the type that Lewis presents suggest that there are in fact very good reasons to believe that communication cannot be modeled game-theoretically. But establishing this requires a significantly more complicated argument than the one Habermas provides.

To seriously evaluate Lewis's proposal, and Habermas's claim, it is necessary to begin (§§2.1–2.2) with a precise specification of the decision theory and game theory models. I will then argue that Habermas is correct in his claim that communication cannot be modeled decision-theoretically. I proceed to assess the two available strategies for modeling communication game-theoretically. The first strategy, pursued by Lewis, attempts to show that the semantic content of linguistic utterances is given by their pragmatic role in strategic interactions. I argue (§2.3) that this program fails, because it is unable to account for the autonomy of linguistic meaning from particular contexts of use. The second strategy takes semantic content as primitive and attempts to introduce speech acts as a special category of instrumental action. In §2.4 I show that modifications of this type undermine the standard game-theoretic solution concepts, making it impossible for agents to determine a strategically rational course of action. This analysis yields a strong presumption in favor of Habermas's claim that speech acts cannot be planned or executed with strategic intent. I conclude (§2.5) by attempting to specify more precisely the characteristics of speech acts that make them resistant to strategic deployment.

2.1 The Instrumental Conception of Rationality

The instrumental conception of rational action has exercised a profound grip on the philosophical imagination over the last century. This phenomenon is, in a certain sense, quite understandable, since there is no denying that the instrumental model has a certain intuitive appeal. The natural place to begin when developing a conception of rational action is with the simple case of a single actor in a nonsocial environment. This framework is certainly the most basic, since action always occurs in the context of some natural environment, and only some of the time does this environment include other rational agents.

It therefore appears reasonable to begin by characterizing rationality for this simple case, with the intention of extending the framework to include social interaction at some later date. Following standard usage, we can refer to choice problems in such nonsocial contexts as *decisions*, and hence the theory that specifies how they should be resolved as *decision theory*.

Decision problems can be exhaustively represented using three primitive components: actions, states, and outcomes. All three of these are events. The difference between them is that an agent's action is an event under her control, whereas the state is an event that is outside of her control. The outcome is then a third event that is produced through the causal interaction of the first two. For example, suppose that Adam is about to walk to work and must decide whether or not to take an umbrella. He has two actions to choose from: A = {Adam brings an umbrella, Adam does not bring an umbrella}. For simplicity, let us say that there are two states that may obtain: S = {it rains, it does not rain}, and there are two possible outcomes O = {Adam gets wet, Adam stays dry}. Obviously, in a problem of this type, there will be a causal connection between the action that Adam chooses, the state that obtains, and the outcome he receives. This can be represented by a function that maps actions and states onto outcomes. Such a function associates an outcome with each pair of actions and states, for example, f(Adam does not bring an umbrella, it rains) = Adam gets wet. Insofar as the problem is well defined, this mapping will be exhaustive.

From the agent's perspective, two events are under her control: the action, which is *directly* under her control, and the outcome, which is *indirectly* under her control. Let us suppose for the moment that the agent has no knowledge about the world, that is, that she has no idea what state will obtain and no idea how actions and states map onto outcomes. In this context, we can see that her problem is not just one of deciding on an action. Each action sets off a chain of events, and to choose an action is, in a certain sense, also to choose its consequences.[5] Lacking knowledge of which outcome will *actually* follow a given action, the agent is confronted not just with a set of actions, but with a set consisting of each action and each possible outcome that could follow its performance. Since there is some possible world in which any action would cause any outcome, this set can be represented as $A \times O$.

So while *in fact* the agent only chooses an action (leaving the rest in the hands of fate, so to speak), from the agent's perspective, the problem is to choose an action-outcome pair. We can call each such pair an *option*, and represent it as $<a_x, o_y>$. So, for instance, if there are three possible actions, and three possible outcomes, then the agent's options can be organized into a table:

$$\begin{bmatrix} <a_1, o_1> & <a_1, o_2> & <a_1, o_3> \\ <a_2, o_1> & <a_2, o_2> & <a_2, o_3> \\ <a_3, o_1> & <a_3, o_2> & <a_3, o_3> \end{bmatrix}$$

Naturally, these are only possible options, not actual ones. In the actual world, each action will only bring about one outcome. It is because the agent does not yet know which options are the actual ones that this representation is appropriate. (Naturally, if the agent chooses an option that is not an actual one, she is in for a disappointment.)

Making a choice, in this context, involves selecting a row. To do this, the agent must find some way of narrowing down the field. The first and most obvious way of narrowing down this field would simply be to pick a row directly. If the agent happens to prefer one action over the others, she might simply decide "I want to do a_x." In this way, outcomes would not enter into the picture at all. Some people might be skeptical about the idea that an action could be intrinsically desirable in this way, but there is no a priori reason that it should not be so. Since both actions and outcomes are simply events, there is no reason to think that agents could not desire either.

The more standard case would involve selecting an action in order to bring about an outcome that the agent would like to see occur. This would require two choice criteria, one for picking a column, another for selecting a row. In the simplest case, we can think of a *desire* as an intentional state that selects a particular outcome as the agent's goal. Once an outcome is selected, the agent's options have been narrowed to the contents of a single column. However, of these remaining options, only one is actual. Thus the only way to get the outcome desired is to find out which is the actual option, and perform the associated action. A *belief* can be thought of as an intentional state that distinguishes actual from possible options. Action that is chosen through such a belief-desire combination is called "instrumental action," since the action is selected not as an end in itself, but as a means to the attainment of the desired outcome.

Beliefs of this type have traditionally been represented in the form of hypothetical imperatives, for example, "If you want o_2, do a_3." If desires are given the form, "I want o_2," then instrumental reasoning takes on a classic syllogistic form, with the conclusion "do a_3." However, I would like to suggest a slightly different representation. Where n_a is the number of available actions, each hypothetical imperative can be represented as an $n_a \times 1$ matrix, with a number 1 in the xth row of this matrix indicating that action a_x will bring about the desired outcome, and a 0 indicating that it will not. Thus the agent's system of beliefs can be represented, where n_o is the number of outcomes, as an $n_a \times n_o$ matrix:

$$B = \begin{bmatrix} 0 & 0 & 1 \\ 1 & 0 & 0 \\ 0 & 1 & 0 \end{bmatrix}.$$

The positioning of the zeros and ones here tells us that options $<a_1,o_3>$, $<a_2,o_1>$, and $<a_3,o_2>$ are actual (and so the matrix is equivalent to three hypothetical imperatives—"if you want o_3, do a_1," "if you want o_1, do a_2," and "if you want o_2, do a_3").

It is then a simple matter to represent the agent's desires as a $n_o \times 1$ matrix, in which a 1 in the xth row specifies that outcome o_x is desired, and a 0 that it is not. Thus "I want o_2" would be represented as:

$$D = \begin{bmatrix} 0 \\ 1 \\ 0 \end{bmatrix}.$$

Now, instead of hooking up the agent's beliefs and desires through a practical syllogism, we can just multiply matrices B and D:

$$U = BD = \begin{bmatrix} 0 & 0 & 1 \\ 1 & 0 & 0 \\ 0 & 1 & 0 \end{bmatrix} \cdot \begin{bmatrix} 0 \\ 1 \\ 0 \end{bmatrix} = \begin{bmatrix} 0 \\ 0 \\ 1 \end{bmatrix}.$$

This gives a $n_a \times 1$ matrix, in which a 1 in the xth row specifies that action a_x should be performed. In the example above, it shows that the agent should do a_3.

This sort of setup captures the basic idea underlying the instrumental conception of rationality, and corresponds roughly to the model that can be found in Hume, Kant, or Weber. However, it is limited by the fact that it treats both desires and beliefs as having binary values—an outcome is either desired or it is not, an option is either actual or it is not. Clearly, a desire can be more or less intense, just as a belief can be more or less certain. Thus a sophisticated conception of instrumental rationality would represent both desires and beliefs as having degrees of desirability or certainty, for example, as a set of weights distributed across outcomes or options. The model that results from these modifications is called *Bayesian decision theory*, or more commonly, the *utility-maximizing* conception of practical rationality. (The point of developing the matrix representation above was to show that Bayesian decision theory is a straightforward extension of the belief-desire model of action.)

To begin with, there may be some uncertainty as to exactly which outcome will result from a given action. Flipping a fair coin, for instance, has a 50 percent chance of turning up heads, and a 50 percent chance of turning up tails. We can accommodate this by representing the agent's beliefs about the consequences of an action as a subjective probability distribution over outcomes. In this way, the agent's system of beliefs can be represented as an $n_a \times n_o$ matrix as before, but with entries giving confidence levels between 0 and 1:

$$B = \begin{bmatrix} .2 & .2 & .6 \\ 1 & 0 & 0 \\ .1 & .9 & 0 \end{bmatrix}.$$

This can be read as representing that action a_3 has a 10 percent chance of bringing about o_1, and a 90 percent chance of bringing about o_2, and so on. Assuming that the set of outcomes is exhaustive, the entries in each row must sum to 1. (Here the matrix representation is useful, because hypothetical imperatives cannot be used to represent probabilistic beliefs.)

In a similar way, an agent may experience more or less intense desires for an outcome. Rather than either wanting or not wanting something, she may rank outcomes from better to worse. We can therefore represent the agent's desires as an $n_o \times 1$ matrix with entries giving intensity levels between 0 and 1:

$$D = \begin{bmatrix} .6 \\ 1 \\ .2 \end{bmatrix}.$$

This can be interpreted to mean that the agent would be indifferent between o_1 and a coin toss that gave her an even chance of getting o_2 or o_3.[6]

To decide which action the agent should perform, once again all we need do is multiply B and D. Now, however, instead of picking out a particular action, the result is a ranking of actions from best to worst:

$$U = BD = \begin{bmatrix} .2 & .2 & .6 \\ 1 & 0 & 0 \\ .1 & .9 & 0 \end{bmatrix} \cdot \begin{bmatrix} .6 \\ 1 \\ .2 \end{bmatrix} = \begin{bmatrix} .44 \\ .6 \\ .96 \end{bmatrix}.$$

The entries in U assign an *expected utility* to each action. For example, action a_1 gives the agent a .2 probability of getting outcome o_1, which is desired with an intensity of .6, making that chance worth .12. Action a_1 also gives a .2 probability of getting outcome o_2, which is desired with an intensity of 1 (so this chance is worth .2), and a .6 probability of getting outcome o_3, which is desired with an intensity of .2 (chance is worth .12). Adding these up gives the total expected value of the action as .44, which then appears in the first position in the U matrix.

Action a_3 is ranked highest, with an expected utility of .96. In selecting this action, the agent can then be said to be *maximizing* her expected utility. (This is why instrumental rationality is often referred to as the maximizing conception of practical rationality.)

All of this is fairly noncontroversial. In effect, it is just a precise development of the idea that agents decide what to do by ranking available outcomes and then choosing the action that they expect to provide the best result with respect to this ranking. Nowhere has it been suggested that agents act from self-interested motives, since the content of the outcomes they desire has been left unspecified. In fact, one of the strengths of the model is that it is not committed to any particular account of how agents' beliefs and desires are formed, but treats them as exogenously determined. There is nothing to stop the theorist from supplementing this model of action with a characterization of desire-rationality that places substantive constraints on the way agents rank outcomes. (The moral realist could claim, for instance, that just as true beliefs accurately reflect some objective probability distribution over states, good desires accurately reflect some objective order of values. The fully rational agent could then be characterized as one who seeks to believe what is true and desire what is good. In this case, all the model outlined would suggest is that knowing the truth, the rational agent then seeks to maximize the good.)

It will be fairly obvious from this discussion, however, that communication cannot be modeled using a simple decision-theoretic representation. (For this reason, Davidson's introduction of "meaning" into decision theory and Habermas's characterization of speech acts as an elementary action type are both extremely misleading.) To model communication decision-theoretically, it would be necessary to subscribe to something like a causal-associationist account of meaning of the Hobbes-Locke variety. In this view, words are tags attached to ideas. The meaning of the word is the idea that is associated with it in the mind, and speech acts are a case of perfectly ordinary teleological intervention in the world. By pricking someone with a pin, I cause her to start; by saying "horse" I cause the idea *horse* to appear before her mind. Translating this into decision-theoretic terms: the hearer's state of mind would be an *outcome* and the association that establishes the causal connection between word and idea a *state*.

The most serious problem with this type of causal-associationist account of linguistic understanding is that it cannot explain the role of what is sometimes called the "Gricean mechanism" in communication. In an influential paper, Paul Grice argued that recognition of an *intention* to communicate is required for linguistic communication to be successful.[7] Grice distinguishes between what he calls *natural* and *nonnatural* meaning. He illustrates the distinction using cases like the following: A person wants to suggest to a friend that her spouse has been unfaithful; he can (A) show her a photograph of the inappropriate conduct, or (B) draw a picture of the same. Herod wants to inform Salome of the death of John the Baptist; he can (A) show her the head on a charger, or (B) say to her, "John the Baptist is dead." In each of these examples, one individual intends to inform the other of something. But the difference between the A and B cases is that in the A cases recognition of this intention by the hearer is irrelevant to the success of the action, while in the B cases it is not. Thus the connection between the photograph or severed head and their "meanings" is in a certain sense natural. But in the B cases, communication would fail if the hearer interpreted the drawing as simply doodling, or the spoken words as just noises.

Grice went on to make the more dubious claim that the *specific* meaning of the utterance was also determined by the intention. But we do not have to accept this to see that the recognition of an intention to communicate is necessary for an action to be construed as meaningful. The hearer is not simply acted upon by the speaker, but participates actively in the exchange. Thus the mental state produced by communication cannot be an outcome, and hence the action cannot be modeled decision-theoretically. The nonnatural quality of linguistic meaning gives it no place in the state-outcome domain of the decision-theoretic ontology.

2.2 Game Theory

This is not the end of the story, however. A conspicuous feature of the decision-theoretic model is that it treats every element of the agent's environment as a state whose probability can be fixed prior to the agent's deliberations. This is not possible in a situation where the outcome is to be determined *jointly* by the actions of two separate agents—what rational choice theorists call "interdependent choice" (and Habermas, following Parsons, calls "double contingency"). It was mentioned earlier that both actions and states are events that combine to cause an outcome. Now what needs to be considered is the case in which the action of the first agent combines with the action of a second agent in order to produce an outcome. Recall that the only difference between an action and a state was that an action is an event under the agent's control, while a state is not. Thus the concept of a state is agent-relative. In a situation of interdependent choice, the first agent's action is a state for the second, just as the second agent's action is a state for the first.[8]

The question that arises is how agents are able to develop rational beliefs in such a context. In the decision-theoretic case, beliefs could be treated as exogenous to the choice problem. This meant that a Bayesian account of belief-formation (with subjective probabilities assigned to states on the basis of statistical induction) would suffice as a simplifying assumption. But when the first agent's state is actually the second agent's action, induction will no longer suffice (nor will any other mechanism that is exogenous to the choice problem). As John von Neumann and Oskar Morgenstern put it:

Every participant can determine the variables which describe his own actions, but not those of the others. Nevertheless, those "alien" variables cannot, from his point of view, be described by statistical assumptions. This is because the others are guided, just as he himself, by rational principles.[9]

In a simple decision problem, the agent could solve the problem of assigning probabilities to states first, and then move on to the problem of deciding what to do. But when agents are interacting with one another, each agent must solve both of these problems simultaneously. To decide what to do, the first agent must determine the probability of various states obtaining. But since these states are simply the second agent's actions, the first agent must determine what the second player intends to do. To figure this out, he must figure out what the second player's beliefs are. But since the second agent's beliefs about what state will obtain are equivalent to her beliefs about what the first agent will do, and since this is precisely what the first agent is still trying to decide, a regress of anticipations arises.

Since the state that will obtain for each agent is no longer given in advance of the decision problem, both agents must solve for two variables simultaneously. Not only must each decide which action is optimal, she must also determine which state will obtain. The problem is that which states will obtain depends upon which actions are optimal, and which actions are optimal depends upon which states will obtain. This presents a serious problem for the instrumental conception of practical rationality. Since states provide the link between outcomes and actions, the only way to reason back from a desired outcome to a favored action is via some knowledge of the state. Without some mechanism for pinning down these beliefs, *it will be impossible for agents to reason instrumentally in social contexts*.

There are two programmatic strategies that present themselves at this point. One is to suppose that social interaction presents a fundamentally new type of problem, one that agents require some additional cognitive resources in order to resolve. This is not at all implausible. Earlier, desires and beliefs were introduced as selection criteria that allowed the agent to eliminate choice options. It is always possible that the introduction of some new criterion might be called upon to resolve social interaction problems (one example of which would be Habermas's suggestion that communication is used to reduce the number of relevant contingencies). The alternative to introducing some specifically social form of decision criterion is to suppose that the regress of anticipations is not vicious, and that agents, given only the basic resources supplied under the decision-theoretic model, are able to find some way of pinning down states. The idea here would be to explore the regress to see if it stops somewhere.

This second option is what has developed into the program known as *game theory*. The object of game-theoretic analysis is to find a way of working through the regress of anticipations in such a way as to allow a stable set of beliefs to emerge for all players, without introducing any new sort of selection criteria. A game-theoretic "solution" is therefore an *equilibrium* of beliefs, and game theory is a general mechanism for determining beliefs about the relative probabilities of various states. For each player, *strategic reasoning* operates by working through the cycles of anticipation in such a way as to turn other players' actions (which have not yet been planned or performed) into events that will occur with specific probabilities. Once reduced in this way, each player's choice can then be handled as a simple decision problem.

Initially, the idea that interaction problems could be separated out into decision problems showed some promise. Consider the game illustrated in figure 2.1. Here, players 1's actions $A_1 = \{U,D\}$ are states for player 2, and $A_2 = \{L,R\}$ are states for player 1. (The expected utility of each outcome for both players is given in the associated square, player 1 first, player 2 second.) Obviously, when the players have not yet decided what to do, it will be impossible to assign any probability to the occurrence of any state.

But in this case, it takes only a small effort for both players to determine what the other will do. Both players might begin with a hypothesis of the form "suppose I decide to choose *x*," then consider how the other player would respond, and then how he would respond to that response, and so on, and see if this process levels off somewhere. With luck, they will be able to find a pair of responses that is consistent with *every* initial hypothesis, and this will solve their problem. In the game shown in figure 2.1, player 1 might think: "Suppose player 2 expects me to play U. In that case, she will respond with R. But if player 2 is going to play R, I would be better off playing D. So player 2 should expect me to play D. But if player 2 expects me to play D, she will continue to play R. So no matter what she expects me to do, she will play R. Therefore, I should play D." In this example, L is a *strongly dominated strategy*, that is, choosing it is always worse for player 2 than choosing R. Since no rational agent would ever play such a strategy, player 1 can predict R with certainty.

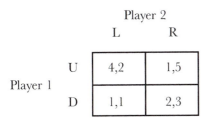

Player 2

		L	R
	U	4,2	1,5
Player 1	D	1,1	2,3

Figure 2.1

This effectively changes the game into a decision for player 1 between the (U,R) and (D,R) outcomes.

This example is particularly tidy, because the (D,R) outcome has the advantage of being both stable and convergent—stable because neither player has an incentive to switch strategies if (D,R) is the anticipated outcome, and convergent because every set of initial hypotheses about what either player will choose leads to the selection of this outcome. The regress of anticipations is therefore harmless, because it converges on the equilibrium outcome (D,R).

Unfortunately, not all games have outcomes that exhibit these two properties. In figure 2.2, the so-called Battle of the Sexes game, both (U,L) and (D,R) are stable, but no process of reasoning will lead players to converge upon one or the other. Under the hypothesis that player 1 will choose U, player 2 will choose L, but under the hypothesis that he will play D, she will play R. Because player 1's reasoning mirrors player 2's, there is no reason to favor either hypothesis.

Furthermore, there are some games in which no outcome is either stable or convergent. To see this, consider figure 2.3. Again, player 1 can start out: "Suppose player 2 expects me to play U. In that case, she will respond with R. But if player 2 is going to play R, I would be better off playing D. So player 2 should expect me to play D. But if player 2 expects me to player D, she will switch to L. But if player 2 is going to play L, I would be better off playing U ... (etc.)." No matter which hypothesis players take as their point of departure, this cycle of expectations develops.

The lack of convergent or stable outcomes form what are known respectively as the *equilibrium-selection* and the *existence* problems. Without some resolution, these problems suggest that instrumental rationality is radically deficient in social contexts.

Player 2

		L	R
	U	3,1	0,0
Player 1			
	D	0,0	1,3

Figure 2.2

Player 2

	L	R
U	3,0	1,3
D	0,3	3,1

Player 1

Figure 2.3

There have, however, been a number of creative solutions suggested for these two problems. The most successful has been in response to the existence problem. The first step is to allow players to randomize over their pure strategies, for example, to throw dice to determine which action to perform. So instead of just playing "pure" strategies like U and D, player 1 could also adopt a "mixed" strategy, like [.3U, .7D]. This is equivalent to expanding the set of outcomes to include not just the "pure" outcomes, but the entire set of randomizations over these outcomes. Subject to a few minor qualifications, this guarantees that every game has at least one stable outcome.[10] Such an outcome, in which neither player has any incentive to change strategies, given the other player's strategy, is called a Nash equilibrium. In the game illustrated in figure 2.3, the strategy profile ([.4U, .6D],[.4L, .6R]) is a Nash equilibrium. (Since these strategies give both players an expected utility of 1.8 for their actions, regardless of which one they choose, both are willing to play these randomizations over the two.)

With the introduction of the Nash solution concept, the game theorist can claim to have shown that some stable set of expectations exists for almost every strategic interaction problem. On the other hand, attempts to solve the equilibrium-selection problem have been notably less successful. In a game like the one shown in figure 2.2, there does not seem to be anything that could lead either player to prefer one action rationally over another. Instrumental rationality appears to leave them guessing. The general consensus among game theorists is that some additional element will have to be introduced into the theory to explain how players' initial expectations are formed. The best-known modification of this type is Thomas Schelling's "psychological" solution.[11] Schelling argued, roughly, that certain psychological associations that agents might have with particular actions or outcomes could make them "salient" or "focal" in a way that would serve to focus expectations. He presented a number of examples where such things as round numbers, equal shares, bright colors, and so on, by attracting agents' attention, seemed to favor outcomes exhibiting such properties. Similarly, he argued that an equilibrium might become focal by virtue of having been played before.

Picking up on Schelling's line of thinking, David Lewis argues that these types of focal-point effects could be used to explain the origin of social conventions. Lewis notes that agents are often faced with many possible ways of doings things, in situations that require that they both do it in the same way in order to succeed. Hume's example of two people rowing a boat is a case in point—they do not especially care how fast they row, as long as they match each other's stroke.[12] In a sense, there is a continuum of strategic equilibria here. Lewis suggests that while the rowers may vary their strokes for a while in order to get coordinated, once they hit upon an equilibrium, they will continue on that rhythm. An informal convention has now arisen between them. It consists in an equilibrium (the rhythm at which they are rowing) and a psychological association that makes that equilibrium salient (the habit they form once they "get into" the rhythm).

Lewis goes on to suggest that language can be understood as a set of conventions of precisely this type. With a name, for instance, the connection between the sound and the object that it refers to is arbitrary. What counts is only that the speaker and hearer take it to refer to the same thing. As a result, Lewis claims that linguistic communication is a gigantic multiple-equilibrium coordination problem. The meaning of linguistic expressions, in this view, is the set of psychological associations that make certain of these equilibria salient. In a sense, Lewis's model of meaning conventions modifies associationism in order to build in a Gricean mechanism. The recognition of an intention to communicate is modeled as part of the normal cycle of anticipations that hold together these equilibria. The Gricean mechanism is thereby shown to be nothing other than a special case of the standard strategic reasoning used in all contexts of social interaction.

This sort of proposal presents a challenge to Habermas's view. In game-theoretic models of action, agents must not only anticipate what states of the world will obtain, but also ascribe beliefs to one another, in order to anticipate each others' actions. An equilibrium exists at every point where these sets of ascribed beliefs can converge, or become mutually consistent. This makes it possible to model communication as a type of action that induces such a convergence of beliefs among players. Proposals of this type have been closely investigated by game theorists, who have long been interested in the kind of information that strategic action can communicate. The model of communication that Lewis develops is actually a particular instance of a more general class of games referred to as *signaling* (or *sender-receiver*) games. The evaluation of Habermas's position therefore requires an examination of these models.

2.3 Signaling Games

A purely strategic model of communication begins with the presumption that there is nothing intrinsically distinctive about speech as a form of social action. The "meaning" of any such action, if there is one, is given by the inferences that other players are able to draw from it using standard strategic reasoning. Thus the meaning of any speech act must be determined endogenously in every game, that is, one cannot assume that meanings are fixed prior to individual acts of communication.[13] The result is a somewhat peculiar refraction of the Wittgensteinian doctrine of meaning as use. To know the meaning of an utterance, one must examine its role in the language game. And the "game" in question is not constituted by any suspicious mental or semantic entities, but rather a set of practical, goal-directed actions.

In evaluating this proposal, the key question is whether or not such an account of the social interaction game is rich enough to capture the phenomenon of meaningful speech. Thus the most important task, for proponents of the instrumental conception of rationality, is to show that the components that go into building up various types of linguistically mediated interactions can be represented using game-theoretic tools. It must be possible to characterize any particular problem exhaustively in terms of beliefs, states, outcomes, and so on. To approach this task, two elements must be added to the method of representing games introduced in §2.2. First, a form of representation must be introduced that renders explicit the temporal order in which players select moves. This is necessary in order to model the way that players respond to actions performed with communicative intent. Second, for there to be interesting communication, it must be the case that one player knows something that at least one player does not. It will therefore be necessary to introduce asymmetric information.

Temporal order is introduced by representing the interaction in the form of an extensive form game. The extensive form of the "Battle of the Sexes" game from figure 2.2 is shown in figure 2.4.

The game tree diagram is a finite rooted tree, with an empty circle representing the origin. Each node represents a point where some player must select an action. The "move label" associated with each node indicates which player the choice belongs to. The branches represent the actions available to each player, and are labeled accordingly. In figure 2.4, player 1 moves first, selecting either U or D. This passes the initiative to player 2, who must select either L or R. The dashed line between player 2's nodes represents an information set, indicating that the player does not know which of the two connected nodes has been reached at the time she is called upon to move.[14] Finally, the terminal nodes of the game tree give the payoffs associated with the various outcomes of the game.

All of this information is taken to be common knowledge, that is, something that everyone knows that everyone knows that everyone knows, etc. The only form of "ignorance" present involves players not necessarily knowing what other players have done in the course of play, which is represented by information sets.

The Nash solution can be applied to games of this type, yielding (U,L) and (D,R) as pure strategy equilibria. However, the introduction of turn sequence brings to light one important detail that is obscured by the strategic form. In figure 2.4, player 2's willingness to do her part of the first equilibrium depends upon her believing that she is at the left-hand node of her information set with probability ≥.75, just as her willingness to play along with the second depends upon her believing that she is on the right with probability ≥.25. Because of

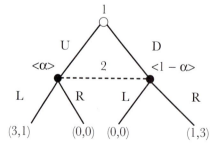

Figure 2.4

this, the equilibrium belief set must contain not only beliefs about what strategies will be played, but also some specification of the beliefs that players hold about where they are in the game at every point of decision. David Kreps and Robert Wilson refer to this kind of expanded belief set as an assessment.[15] The beliefs that players have at each information set about which node they are at is shown in the game tree diagram between angle brackets $\langle\langle\alpha\rangle\rangle$. In figure 2.4, the equilibria are therefore (U,L, $\alpha \geq .75$) and (D,R, $\alpha \leq .75$). Naturally, to be in equilibrium, the assessment must contain a belief system that is internally consistent. This means that the players' beliefs about where they are must not be inconsistent with their expectations about what moves the other players are likely to make.

These are just some of the complications that arise when temporal sequence is introduced into the game. However, the model elaborated so far is still not yet very useful, because both players have the same knowledge about the world. Games in which some players have private information—known as *games of incomplete information*—are normally represented in what is called "Bayesian" form. This formulation permits the translation of games of incomplete information, which are not mathematically tractable, into "Bayes-equivalent" games of complete but asymmetric information, by representing players with different amounts of information as different "types."[16] The idea, roughly, is to take the single game of incomplete information and represent it as a set of different subgames of complete information, where not all players know which subgame is being played. This means that differences in information about the world can be represented using information sets of the sort already introduced.

The game begins by having "nature," a pseudo-player who moves according to some fixed probability, determine which of the subgames is to be played.[17] One player observes nature's move (this player is said to be given a type). The other player does not. This can be represented by having the uninformed player's nodes appropriately grouped into information sets. This sort of game can then be used to model communication. The most general class of language game is called a *sender-receiver* or *signaling* game.[18] Player 1, the sender (S), has private information (i.e., a type), and player 2, the receiver (R), has none. S selects an action, called the "message," after which R chooses an action that determines the payoffs for both players.

Consider the following example. Two builders are busy at work. S is building a wall, while R is passing him the materials he needs. R cannot see the wall, and so only S knows what materials are needed at what time. Suppose there are two types of materials being used: blocks and slabs. This gives us two types of S: the "need-a-block" type and the "need-a-slab" type. S sends a message to R. After receiving the message, R passes S either a block or a slab. If R passes a block to the need-a-block type S, or a slab to the need-a-slab type S, then they have coordinated successfully. This game is illustrated in figure 2.5.[19]

In this game, the origin belongs to nature (player 0), which first determines the type of player 1. For simplicity, the two types are designated as equiprobable. Player 1, knowing his type, then chooses to send either the message "block" or the message "slab." Player 2 hears the message, but does not know player 1's type. This is indicated by the information sets connecting her left and right nodes. Player 2 decides to hand over a block or a slab. If a block is handed over to the need-a-block type, or a slab to the need-a-slab type, both players receive a payoff of 1, otherwise they each get 0.

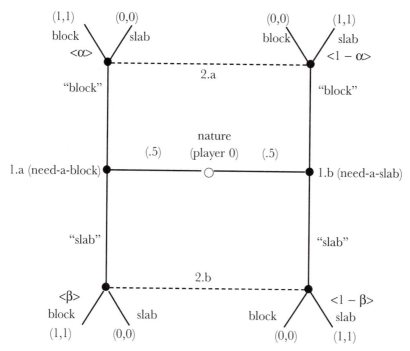

Figure 2.5

In this game, there are two pure strategy equilibria (informally): ([S says "block" at 1.a, S says "slab" at 1.b], [R passes block at 2.a, R passes slab at 2.b]), and ([S says "block" at 1.b, S says "slab" at 1.a], [R passes block at 2.b, R passes slab at 2.a]). Both these equilibria yield a payoff of 1 to each player. There is also a plethora of mixed-strategy equilibria, where both players randomize in various ways over their pure strategies. These all yield a payoff of $\frac{1}{2}$ to each.

Consider the first equilibrium. Given what the other player is doing, neither has an incentive to deviate. If R is passing a block whenever she receives the message "block," and a slab whenever she hears "slab," then obviously S has no incentive to shout "slab" when he in fact needs a block. And if S is shouting "block" only when he needs a block (etc.), then R also has no incentive to deviate. Knowing this, it is rational for R to assign $\alpha = 1$ when she hears the message "block," and $\beta = 0$ when she hears "slab," because these are the only beliefs consistent with actions S would perform. Thus the Nash equilibrium being played requires that R form correct beliefs about which node in her information set she has reached, and by implication, S's type. It is therefore no stretch of the imagination to say that the *meaning* of the messages "block" and "slab" are the types that they reveal in the equilibrium. By sending a message that allows the hearer to infer the true state of the world, the speaker has effectively communicated information to the hearer. The meaning of the expression is simply this information content.[20]

We now have a simple way of characterizing the second equilibrium. It is the same as the first, except that the meaning of the messages "block" and "slab" have been reversed. This illustrates nothing other than the conventionality of linguistic meaning. Both players are indifferent between the two equilibria, since their payoffs remain the same. They do not care which sounds have which meanings, as long as they are able to communicate effectively. Since there are no rational grounds for preferring one of these equilibria over the other, Lewis argues that the particular "meanings" messages have will be determined merely by force of habit. Once players have observed a certain number of plays of the game where the same equilibrium is selected, they will tend to stick to that equilibrium. In the same way, once we have met in a particular café a couple of times, we will tend to return to the same café if we want to meet again. Therefore, associationism retains a central role in communicative interaction, serving as a "psychological" equilibrium-selection mechanism.

There can be no doubt that this model of communication is extremely clever. Whenever the sender is divided into types, the receiver will have information sets in which different nodes correspond to different types. By determining which node she has reached, R is able to infer S's type, and thereby acquire its information content. But the problems with the model are somewhat obvious and have been noted by several authors.

The first problem relates to equilibrium selection. In the building game, there is a plethora of mixed-strategy equilibria in which both players randomize over their pure strategies (e.g., when R assigns a probability of $\frac{1}{2}$ to each action, S can select any randomization over messages, as long as it is the same for both types). These equilibria are counterintuitive, partly because they are suboptimal. Nevertheless, if R is flipping a coin to decide what materials to hand over, then S does not care what message he sends. And if S is flipping a coin to determine whether to say "block" or "slab," R will be completely indifferent between her two actions. This is an example of what game theorists call a "babbling equilibrium," in which the sender randomizes over the set of possible messages, and all other players ignore him. In this situation, all messages are meaningless.

These equilibria are extremely implausible, but there appears to be no way of eliminating them through refinements.[21] Lewis avoids the problem by legislating mixed strategies out of the model, an option that is not available in this context, since it undermines the generality of the Nash solution concept. In any case, it is an artificial solution, one that ignores the deeper problem. A babbling equilibrium seems to correspond to the case where there is no effective "Gricean mechanism." Words are treated like noises. And since the messages do not affect payoffs directly, that is, they do not accomplish anything in the world, they are ignored. But the babbling equilibrium is a Nash equilibrium like any other, with the same type of belief supports as the more "informative" ones. This suggests that game-theoretic reasoning alone does not capture the relevant dimensions of intentionality operative in communicative interaction, and that Lewis's "higher-order" belief diagrams may well overestimate the determinacy of the Nash solution concept.[22]

A more significant difficulty rests with the informative equilibria. The game-theoretic model makes the meaningfulness of the speech act dependent upon the payoff structure of the game. The unfortunate consequence is that "the informativeness of the most-informative equilibrium is limited by the degree to which the players' interests coincide."[23] The only way that R can get any insight into S's intentions is by considering the outcome S is pursuing, along with S's anticipation of the outcome R is pursuing, and so on. However, it is not always the case that a player will benefit from having another player anticipate his actions or know his type. In the case of a conflict of interest, S does not have any incentive to inform R of his type, and R, knowing this, has no reason to take any message as indicative of S's type. All messages in the model will therefore be meaningless. This is not a peculiarity of the specific game presented here. Vincent P. Crawford and Joel Sobel have established as a completely general limitative result that in the entire class of cheap-talk signaling games "perfect communication is not to be expected in general unless agents' interests completely coincide, and that once interests diverge by a given, 'finite' amount, only no communication is consistent with rational behavior."[24]

Suppose that S and R have been working on their wall for a number of days, and are comfortably playing one of the two informative equilibria. Suddenly S discovers that he is to be paid by the hour, not by the job. He no longer has any incentive to build the wall efficiently—in fact, he would like it to take as long as possible. Instead of the game having the payoff structure of a coordination problem, (0,0) and (1,1) for R's two actions, it now has (0,1) and (1,0), a conflict of interest. With these payoffs, S would benefit from a "tower of Babel" situation, in which he was no longer able to coordinate his actions with R through a common language. Miraculously, his wishes are self-fulfilling. *By simply acquiring this new incentive, all his speech suddenly becomes meaningless.* It is now impossible for R to understand anything S says, because the only equilibrium of this new game is a babbling one. Since S could never benefit from revealing his type, and since R knows this, R will ignore all of S's messages. Now when S calls out "block" it is just a sound, with no meaning whatsoever.

There is obviously something wrong here. But notice that associationism cannot save the day. One might criticize the example on the grounds that players, having responded to the message "block" with a certain action for so many days, would retain a residual association even after the game changed. But this is not the role that associationism played in the model. Past instances of communication were used to make certain *equilibria* focal, not give certain sounds meanings. The meaning of the sounds was always inferred from within the equilibrium. In this new game, the two informative equilibria have vanished entirely, and thus no *game-theoretic* account of language could possibly retrieve them. Linguistic conventions can exist only where there is a coordination problem, and there is no longer a coordination problem here. The new set of payoffs does not permit R to determine anything about S's intentions, and therefore no communication is possible.

This problem usually gets missed because of the tendency to use game-theoretic language in a rather vague and metaphorical sense. Lewis says language is a convention, and conventions exist where there is a common interest in achieving coordination. Since it is obviously in our common interest to be able to communicate, he reasons, meaning conventions must be the solution to a general social coordination problem. The problem is that it may be in our interest, in general and as a group, to have a common language, but game theory deals only with particular situations and individual players. And there are obviously many cases in which it is not in one person's interest to be able to understand another, for example, when being told to do something she does not want to do. It is therefore not adequate to show that social life, in general, has the structure of a coordination problem. It must be shown that on each and every occasion in which any meaningful communication takes place, the interaction has the structure of a coordination problem. This is not just a tall order, it is patently false.

Our normal response to the new building game would be to say that R still understands what S is saying, but is just no longer sure whether or not to believe him. What has clearly gone wrong is that meaning has become so closely tied to credibility that it has becomes impossible for anyone to tell an intelligible lie. This is because the players in this model determine each others' communicative intentions from what we would normally call their "ulterior" motives. This is not incidental. Recall that in the game-theoretic ontology, only outcomes can be the object of an action. Beliefs are developed incidentally. This means that communication can only be achieved indirectly. If alter's beliefs were the object of ego's action, then alter would have no way of developing beliefs, because she would have no way of grasping ego's intentions. Alter is able to infer ego's type only if ego is pursuing certain objectives in which alter's state of mind plays at most an instrumental role. Ego's primary objective in speaking to alter can never be to have her develop certain beliefs, because this is not an admissible outcome. Instrumentally rational agents cannot just talk to each other, or, as Lewis himself acknowledges, there can be no idle conversation.[25] Thus the attempt to model communication strategically turns out to reveal a dramatic limitation of the instrumental conception of rationality.

2.4 Cooperative Alternatives

In the games that have been discussed so far, players are able to form beliefs by drawing upon only two types of knowledge: knowledge of nature obtained through observation, which allows them to determine the relative likelihood of various states obtaining, and knowledge of rationality obtained through introspection, which allows them to anticipate the actions of others. The problems with signaling games suggest that knowledge of linguistic meaning cannot be derived from these other two types of knowledge. This eliminates the possibility of a strict game-theoretic reduction of language. However, suppose a new type of knowledge is ascribed to players—knowledge of language (e.g., English), which allows them to assign literal meanings to statements. Now when a player hears the word "block" she knows that it means (in some unanalyzed sense) *block*. Players can therefore make assertions about their type with the anticipation that they will be *understood*, even though they may not be *believed*. Such a model, even though it introduces unexplained semantic primitives, offers the prospect of providing a consistent instrumental account of the *pragmatics* of language use.

Clearly, if someone were to succeed in redeeming this somewhat narrower goal of providing simply an instrumental pragmatics for natural language, it would still undermine Habermas's claim that speech acts cannot be planned and executed with entirely strategic intent. Adding knowledge of semantic primitives to the instrumental model changes the game from a "noncooperative" into a "cooperative" game. Defending Habermas's position therefore requires showing that cooperative game theory is no more successful than noncooperative game theory at modeling linguistic interaction.

Standard game theory models, like the one I have developed so far, are concerned exclusively with interactions in which "each participant acts independently, without collaboration or communication with any of the others."[26] These are defined as *noncooperative* games. This imposes two restrictions: players are unable to *commit* themselves to a particular course of action, and players are unable to *communicate* to each other their intentions or observations. A *cooperative* game is one in which either of these restrictions is lifted. The two restrictions are related (as will be seen in the next chapter), but for the moment I will examine only cases in which the ban on communication is lifted.

Consider for the moment how a modification of this type would affect the building game. Clearly, a distinction must now be drawn in the model between messages and actions. For simplicity, a cooperative game of this type can be represented by dividing each player's nodes into those at which he can act, and those at which he can send messages. And since there are no restrictions placed on the content of these messages, instead of having a branch of the tree for each possible message, a strategy for this game can be defined as a set specifying an action for each node and a message for each message-node, for each possible history of messages received.

This reformulation looks as if it will clean up the building game quite nicely. In the coordination version, it eliminates the "babbling equilibria" as well as the informative one in which the "meaning" of the messages is reversed, leaving only the informative equilibrium in which "block" reveals "need-a-block" and "slab" reveals "need-a-slab." For the conflict version, the "babbling" mixed-strategy equilibrium remains the only solution, and so no effective communication can take place. But it is no longer the case that the sender's messages are meaningless; they are just not *credible*. There is nothing peculiar about this, since it appears to be an adequate characterization of the situation in which one party has a constant incentive to lie.

But what sort of solution concept will do this work? In keeping with the instrumental conception of rationality, players in cooperative games will presumably send messages for the same reason that they perform actions—to maximize their payoffs. The Nash solution concept therefore requires that no agent have an incentive to deviate unilaterally from the equilibrium strategy profile. For a cooperative game, the strategy profile would include both actions and messages; thus an appropriate solution for such a game would have to be one in which no player has an incentive to perform any action or send any message that is not part of the equilibrium strategy profile. Any message that is not a part of this equilibrium is referred to as a *neologism*. Thus the solution concept for cooperative games, due to Joseph Farrell, is called *neologism-proof* equilibrium.[27]

To see how this solution works, consider a version of the building game in which S has some other messages at his disposal. Suppose that he could also call out "pillar," even though the wall did not require any pillars and so the type need-a-pillar occurs with probability zero. In the informative equilibria, the word "pillar" would be a neologism. For these equilibria to be neologism-proof, it would have to be the case that S never has any incentive to deviate and send this message.

In the noncooperative game, the meaning of all statements is determined by the effective equilibrium. As a result, if R were to receive an unexpected message like "pillar," she could take it to mean anything that she wanted.[28] Since the meaning of all messages is determined by the equilibrium, and the neologism is not a part of that equilibrium, it effectively has no meaning. Thus there will always be consistent belief sets in which neologisms are simply ignored. In such cases, S will not have any incentive to deviate. This makes the informative equilibria in noncooperative sender-receiver games all neologism-proof.[29]

This does not hold, however, when statements are taken to have literal meanings. Since neologisms will always be understood, only statements that are not credible can be ignored by other players. Thus situations may arise in which players can benefit by deviating from equilibrium play and sending an unexpected message. To develop a strategy, S must determine how R would respond to all of the various messages that he could send. Farrell proposes the following analysis: Take T to represent the set of all possible types, and $m(X)$ to represent a neologism asserting that player S is of type $t \in X$, where $X \subseteq T$. It would be overly credulous of R, upon receiving this message, to infer that $t \in X$. Instead, she might infer that S is a member of some type that would *prefer that R believe* that $t \in X$. But then again, she might infer that S is of some type that would prefer that R believe that S is of some type that would prefer that R believe that $t \in X$, and so on. However, there is a special class of cases in which the set of types who would prefer that R believe $t \in X$ is just X, namely, those where S would like R to believe $m(X)$ just in case it is true. Farrell refers to these as *self-signaling* neologisms. They have the distinctive property of being *intrinsically credible*.

In the modified building game, "pillar" would not be a credible neologism. But there may be games in which S's utterance of a neologism would be credible, and so might cause R to change her beliefs, and thereby cause her to change strategies in a way that benefits S. It will therefore be a minimum adequacy criterion of any solution concept for games with exogenously determined meanings that under an equilibrium strategy profile no player have both an available self-signaling neologism and an incentive to use it. Unfortunately for cooperative game theory, it turns out that by this criterion, a wide range of games turn out to have *no solution*. An example of such a game is shown in figure 2.6.

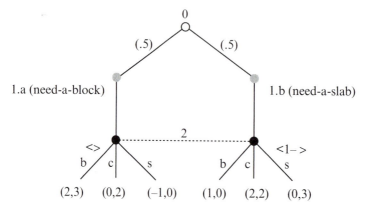

Figure 2.6

In this game, we can imagine player 1 (S) and player 2 (R) still working on their wall. Nature determines player 1's type as before, and player 1 then sends a message to player 2 (message nodes are indicated by gray circles). Since the messages are in English, they are not represented in the game tree diagram; instead the turn passes directly to player 2. Upon hearing the message, player 2 has three actions, {b,c,s}, which we will interpret as "pass a block," "take a coffee break," and "pass a slab" respectively. For the sake of discussion we can represent player 1's messages in the following way: anything asserting that he is at node 1.a will be referred to as $m(a)$, anything asserting 1.b as $m(b)$, and anything irrelevant, obscure, or equivalent to "I'm not telling" as $m(t)$.

Player 2's payoffs are fairly simple. She prefers to hand player 1 the correct materials, but when she is somewhat uncertain about what is needed ($\frac{2}{3} > \alpha > \frac{1}{3}$), that is, her belief about what materials are needed is close enough to the prior probability, she would rather call a coffee break. Player 1 wants to get the wall finished, but hates carrying slabs. When a block is needed he wants to receive the block, but failing that he would rather player 2 call a coffee break than hand him a slab. When a slab is required, he is happiest when player 2 calls a coffee break, and failing that, he would still rather be handed a block than a slab.

This game has no neologism-proof equilibria. Consider first the situation in which R takes all messages to be uninformative and calls a coffee break. Here, $m(a)$ is a self-signaling neologism. However, if R passed a block in response to

$m(a)$, she would also pass slabs in response to anything else. Then S would also want to send $m(a)$ when his type was 1.b., in which case it would be better for R just to call a coffee break. Thus for both players, reasoning about this game results in an irresolvable regress of anticipations.[30]

The fact that very simple games like this have no solution casts serious doubt on the claim that cooperative game theory can serve as the foundation for a general pragmatics of language use. The standard response among game theorists has been to add a mediator to the game, who controls the transmission of messages between players.[31] Although this move solves the technical problem, it is not available in this context because it makes the model too specific to serve as a general theory of action.

The problem of neologisms, however, is somewhat minor compared with some of the larger unanswered questions that arise within the cooperative framework. In the game considered above, all of the communication that takes place is completely public, that is, the content of the messages that are sent is common knowledge among players. But if private communication channels are available through which players can reveal their types to each other (without a mediator), then players in games of incomplete information will no longer be able to assign probabilities to each others' beliefs. This creates a situation in which players are no longer able to "mirror" each others' reasoning processes, making the regress of anticipations unsolvable. Introducing knowledge of language as a new *source* of beliefs therefore undermines the standard solution concept for games of incomplete information.

Furthermore, our attention so far has been confined to situations in which players use their available messages only to reveal their type. But as Roger Myerson has observed, the problem becomes more complex when we grant that players can also use messages to announce their intentions, or make requests.[32] In a multiple-equilibrium game, a player could use a message node as an opportunity to announce how he intends to play at a later point. This introduces extremely undesirable "forward induction" elements into the game. Since there is no game-theoretic account of equilibrium-selection (only the psychological focal point theory), it is unclear what effect this should have on the other players, and by implication, how the strategy underlying such an announcement should be characterized.

All of this makes cooperative game theory very unattractive as a fall-back position. Earlier I suggested that in order to establish the claim that game theory provides an adequate general theory of action, the rational choice theorist must show that linguistically mediated interaction can be modeled game-theo-retically, and that these models, once constructed, have solutions. When it comes to providing a game-theoretic account of communicative action, non-cooperative models fail on the former count, while cooperative ones fail on the latter. Noncooperative game theory cannot explain how a meaningful commu-nication could develop among instrumentally rational agents. The introduction of any significant divergence in players' interests gives them all an incentive to deceive one another, and so makes them incapable of drawing any conclusions about the prevailing state of nature from observing each other's actions. If, however, semantic resources are introduced by assumption, it has the effect of undermining the standard noncooperative solution concepts. The assumption "solves" the problem of accommodating meaningful speech, but only at the expense of rendering the strategic problem unsolvable.

2.5   The Nature of Communication

This analysis supports the contention that the instrumental conception of rationality cannot provide an adequate pragmatics for a theory of meaning. This suggests that insofar as agents do act communicatively, they have adopted some noninstrumental action orientation. This does not, however, bring us any closer to an adequate characterization of the orientation that they do adopt. Furthermore, it is not obvious exactly which features of language use make speech acts resistant to instrumental employment. I would therefore like to close this chapter with a few points of speculation on this subject.

One way of characterizing the difference between the types of noncooper-ative and cooperative game theory outlined above is in terms of how they treat beliefs. In a decision-theoretic framework, where there is only a solitary actor confronting a natural environment, beliefs can only play the role of selection criteria "in the head" of the deliberating actor. However, once a second ratio-nal agent is introduced into the frame of reference, beliefs are present not only in the deliberating agent's head, but also in the agent's environment (i.e., in the other agent's head). This makes it possible for beliefs to serve not only as selection criteria, but also as "objects" that can be acted upon. At the same time, it seems fairly obvious that beliefs cannot be acted upon in precisely the same way that natural states of affairs can be acted upon (and if they can, in most cases we do not know how to do it). Since communication is the primary mechanism through which agents influence each other's beliefs, it is therefore not surprising that modeling speech acts proves to be a challenge for game theory. The noncooperative strategy can be seen as one in which beliefs are not allowed to be treated as outcomes, and so can only be influenced indirectly through actions aimed at producing natural states of affairs. The cooperative strategy, on the other hand, assumes that beliefs form a special class of outcomes (and defines messages as the special class of actions that act upon them), but retains the view that agents act in order to maximize the satisfaction of their preferences over natural outcomes.

I have attempted to show that neither of these technical fixes will work. From a more general perspective, however, I think that this should be unsurprising. Game theory is a reductionist program. Its goal is to eliminate the regress of anticipations that arises in contexts of interdependent choice, allowing agents to parameterize both natural and social environments. Once this is accomplished, they will have effectively reduced the social interaction problem to a set of individual decision problems, which can be handled using the standard techniques of decision-making under risk. For this reduction to be carried out, it must be the case that nothing fundamentally new arises in the context of social interaction that might call for the introduction of more sophisticated decision criteria. However, it is obvious that something fundamentally new *does* occur in social interaction. When there is another person in the environment, it becomes possible to select actions that are aimed at influencing that person's beliefs. Adopting a somewhat reifying vocabulary, one might say that it becomes possible to act on a completely new type of object. It is not obvious that the same old instrumental model of action can be extended unproblematically in such a way that it can be applied to these beliefs.

Suppose, for instance, that one intended to expand the class of outcomes directly to include beliefs. It is, after all, widely thought that speech acts have as their goal the production of beliefs. When I say "It's seven o'clock" to my wife, I often do so with the intention of getting her to believe that it is seven o'clock. I choose this particular utterance because it is the most efficient means of getting her to form this belief, and hence of realizing my desired outcome. But in this case, the deliberating agent's preferences would have to include preferences over the beliefs of other agents. Since other agents must have beliefs about his preferences (this is the common knowledge of preferences presupposition essential to game theory), the deliberating agent must have preferences over their beliefs about his preferences, and so they must have beliefs about his preferences over their beliefs about his preferences, and so on. This

produces the same type of regress that motivated the original problem of interdependent expectations, except that instead of being a belief-belief regress, it
is now a desire-belief regress. The approach is therefore an obvious nonstarter,
since a regress of this type would have to be resolved before it would even be
possible to define players' payoff functions. This suggests that there can be no
well-defined utility function associated with beliefs as outcomes.

The alternative is to treat the "value" of a belief as a function of the payoffs
associated with the set of natural outcomes that an agent who holds that
belief might select. Thus player 1 might prefer that player 2 hold belief b_1 over
belief b_2, because then she is more likely to perform action a_1 instead of
a_2, and the outcome of a_1 is one that player 1 prefers over the outcome of a_2.
This is the proposal that was examined and rejected above. From a more
general point of view, I think it is clear that this type of proposal presents a
very unnatural view of communication. The idea that I can never speak to
someone with "merely" the intention of providing him with information, or
with changing his point of view, but that I must always have some further
objective pertaining to his nonverbal conduct, is simply implausible. While I
may, on occasion, say "It's seven o'clock" because I want my wife to wake up
and get out of bed, I am also capable of saying it just to let her know, or
because she asked me.

The fact that beliefs form a part of each actor's environment in every social
interaction problem provides an intuitive way of drawing Habermas's distinction between instrumental action and speech acts. All action is teleological,
and thus has a goal. An action that has a natural *outcome* as its goal is a *success-
oriented* action. An action that has another's *belief* as its goal (and does not
rely upon "natural" meaning) is an *understanding-oriented* action. Success-
oriented actions can be planned and judged instrumentally, whereas
understanding-oriented actions cannot. It is precisely the introduction of
beliefs into the actor's environment that introduces the distinction between
these two orientations, since beliefs cannot be handled using the tools associated with nonsocial decision problems. (One might also like to generalize this
by saying that any action that has another's *propositional attitude* as its goal is
understanding-oriented, so that the possibility of changing both people's
beliefs *and desires* is entertained.)

The objection that speech acts can *at times* be employed strategically can
then be dismissed in the manner that Habermas suggests.[33] Strategic uses of
language are parasitic upon communicative uses in the same way that break-

ing promises is parasitic upon the practice of keeping promises. Parasitic here has a precise meaning: an action type is parasitic if it can only succeed in the event that one's interaction partner *makes an error* in the determination of one's attitude or intent. If everyone always broke their promises, then the entire practice would collapse. It is precisely because people, for the most part, keep their word, that it is possible for some people to defect profitably. Similarly, if everyone always communicated strategically, then the institution would collapse, as the above analysis shows. However, strategic uses of communication are possible if one player adopts an instrumental orientation while the second maintains an understanding-orientation. In this case, a regress of anticipations does not occur, because only one player is acting instrumentally. However, if the second player detects the first's orientation and also switches to an instrumental orientation, then their interaction may become an unsolvable strategic problem (although, as the above analysis shows, this will be less of a problem when their interaction happens to have the structure of a coordination problem). Thus a strategic use of language may only be successful if one-sided, and may only remain one-sided if undetected.

This way of construing Habermas's project would leave decision theory in place, granting that it provides an adequate characterization of rational decision in nonsocial contexts. Communicative action would arise in specifically social contexts, because the introduction of beliefs into the agent's environment presents a new set of variables that cannot be handled instrumentally, primarily because they cannot be directly manipulated through causal intervention. Habermas's basic rationale for introducing communicative action as a second type of rational action is therefore quite sound, even though the argument that he presents to motivate this position falls short of establishing its necessity. As far as the instrumental model of rationality is concerned, the fact that agents are able to communicate successfully is completely mysterious. This means that any attempt to expand the notion of rational action to account for communication *starts out* with a certain prima facie plausibility.

3

Communication and Justification

Stepping back momentarily from the details of the position, it is worth noting that Habermas's claim that communication cannot be sustained through instrumental action is consonant with a number of at least prime facie intuitions that we share as speakers and hearers. In fact, when looked at from the standpoint of everyday practice, the instrumentalist view can appear incredible. Our willingness to form beliefs on the basis of information communicated to us by others, and our capacity to communicate information to others with the expectation that it will be believed, presupposes a *generalized system of trust*. For the most part, we simply trust people to tell us the truth, or what they consider true given the evidence available to them. Furthermore, we expect that others will extend the same expectation to us when responding to our speech behavior (and we are usually offended if they do not). In the vast majority of cases, neither expectation is based on any calculation of the material advantage that either party expects to derive from the interaction.

The importance of trust for communication is expressed in different ways by different theorists. For the later Wittgenstein, it takes the form of the assumption that agents are playing a language game. In this view, agents are following rules because they have been trained or conditioned to do so, not because of the outcomes that they expect to achieve. Because they are reasoning nonteleologically, they can be *trusted* not to defect from the game when it is in their interest to do so. For Quine and Davidson, it enters the picture with the assumption that agents are being sincere when they present their reports on which sentences they hold true. This way, agents can be *trusted* to tell the truth, even when it may be in their interest to lie. For Brandom, making an assertion involves adopting a set of deontic commitments, which one must be *trusted* to uphold.

It is important that, in all of these views, the system of trust is not introduced as an afterthought. We could not have invented language first, then decided to employ it in a social practice governed by a generalized system of trust. Language could only have arisen *in* such a practice. This is because, in all of these views, the meaning of words is derived from some aspect of their use, and without some regimented pattern of use, there would not be enough stability to fix linguistic meaning. Instrumental action, because it is ultimately based on subjective preference, is too capricious to provide the needed stability. Instrumentally rational agents can be trusted only to do what they want to do, which is equivalent to saying that they cannot be trusted at all.

Habermas's version of this claim takes the following form. When we perform a speech act, we do so with the goal of bringing about mutual understanding/agreement. We can accomplish this only indirectly, by striving to make claims that are warranted, that is, susceptible to some form of publicly acceptable justification. This is why speaking involves attempting to bring about agreement. Habermas goes on to claim that the hearer's understanding of the utterance consists of nothing more than a grasp of the conditions that make it acceptable.[1] Thus striving to reach agreement is the same as striving to reach understanding. We may succeed in bringing about understanding, yet fall short of reaching agreement, because the hearer may know what conditions would make our utterance acceptable, but deny that they obtain.

The element of trust in communication stems from the fact that the agent, in making an utterance, claims that the utterance is, in some general sense, warranted. This idea is captured by Habermas's view, already mentioned, that speakers raise "validity claims" when making speech acts. To claim that an utterance is warranted is equivalent to expressing a willingness to provide such warrant, thereby making it legitimate for *others* to demand that one provide such warrant. Thus in practice the speaker's claim takes the form of a commitment to provide, upon demand, the reasons that warrant the claim. According to this account, we influence one another's beliefs, not by saying things that we want others to believe, but by sayings things that we think are warranted. Since we also try to believe what we think warranted, others believe what we have said when they trust, or recognize, that our warrant is good.[2]

This has the potential to be an extremely compelling view, if the following argument could be made: If the meaning of an utterance is given by its acceptability-conditions, and if the agent, in making the utterance, commits herself to the claim that these conditions are satisfied, then the meaning of the utterance is given by the commitments that the agent makes in performing it. It is widely believed, however, that there is a deep tension between the notion of commitment and the instrumental conception of rationality. If instrumentally rational agents are incapable of making commitments, and communication requires a practice in which speakers incur justificatory commitments in order to establish linguistic meaning, then in principle communication cannot be based on a system of instrumental interaction. This would explain why the results presented in the previous chapter obtain, but also provide a concrete indication of the type of social action that is required to sustain language use. This argument therefore takes us one step closer to the goal of specifying the structure of communicative action.

In the first three sections of this chapter, I will show that this portion of Habermas's position can be successfully defended. Here Habermas has already provided the outline of a workable argument, so I will confine my remarks to filling in some of the blanks, and expanding on some of the literature that he draws upon. In particular, Habermas takes from Parsons the claim that instrumental rationality is incompatible with commitment. I will begin in §3.1 by updating this argument slightly and presenting it at a greater level of generality. Habermas also presents his "acceptability-conditional semantics" in somewhat rough form and relies heavily on Michael Dummett's critique of truth-conditional semantics to establish the centrality of discursive commitment.[3] In §3.2 I review the motivation for Dummett's views, in order to provide a more accessible account of Habermas's reasons for claiming that the meaning of speech acts is given by their associated validity claims. I then present (§3.3) a slightly cleaned-up version of Habermas's "three validity claims" doctrine.

Having provided this reconstruction of Habermas's speech act theory, I go on to conclude (§3.4) that it ultimately does not support his contention that communication is able to generate obligations that are "relevant to the sequel of interaction."[4] In particular, I argue that Habermas's analysis of imperatives in terms of "rightness claims" does not support his claim that agents, in issuing such imperatives, commit themselves to justifying the norms that underlie their practices. The only validity claim that is internally connected to the meaning of the utterance is the truth claim. Because of this, the accountability of social action cannot be explained as a result of the fact that we use language to coordinate our interactions.

3.1 Commitment and Instrumental Rationality

A long time ago, Hobbes argued that the state of nature would be unstable because rational agents, left to their own devices, would be untrustworthy. He argued that our everyday notion of commitment is incoherent, since "he that can bind, can release; and therefore he that is bound to himself only, is not bound."[5] It is not that people are bad, or that they want to be unjust, it is simply that when presented with a set of options, they will select the action that leads to the best outcome. Anything that they have said or done in the past is irrelevant; it is only the present and future that count. The fact that an agent at one point thought that it would be a good idea to perform a particular action, or announced that she would perform that action, in itself provides her with no reason to perform that action when the time comes.[6] There is nothing to stop her from changing her mind, and rationality seems to require that she do so whenever there is any evidence that circumstances have changed.

The technical term for the phenomenon that Hobbes identified is *reoptimization*. The idea is simply that agents, given the chance, will update their plans using whatever new evidence or opportunities have become available. Rationality requires that one adapt in this way, and not stay "locked in" to a particular plan of action. The intuition here is familiar from the case of belief. To have rational beliefs, one must not ignore new information when it comes along, but rather update one's beliefs in order to incorporate it. The opposite of rationality here is "dogmatism," which indicates a commitment to a particular belief that renders the agent insensitive to changes in his epistemic circumstances. In the case of action, the same intuition applies. Consider the following popular adages: "let bygones be bygones," "ignore sunk costs," "don't cry over spilt milk," "don't throw good money after bad," "that was then, this is now," and so on. The general idea is that a rational agent should stay flexible, and should select the action that is best given current information and current options. The idea of a commitment to an action is in tension with this view, because it appears to eliminate this flexibility, and therefore to guarantee the agent an inferior outcome.

The idea that agents will reoptimize forms the central component of many of the refinements of the Nash equilibrium solution concept that have been introduced over the years. The Nash solution states that each player's strategy must be a best response to the strategies of the others, where a strategy is a set of actions that each player intends to perform. However, when the game has a temporal structure, players may know the results of their first action when it comes time to perform the second (or someone else's first action, or their second, etc.). And it makes no sense to say that a given strategy is part of an equilibrium profile if it contains actions that look good at the start, but that later in the game would no longer be desirable to perform. The Nash solution contains no mechanism to ensure that this type of defection from one's own strategy will not occur. To correct this problem, game theorists introduced the notion of *sequential rationality*, which specifies, roughly, that a strategy should contain only actions that maximize each player's expected payoffs *at the point in the game at which they are to be played*. Reinhart Selten's *subgame-perfection* refinement provides a simple illustration of this concept, shown in figure 3.1.[7]

Figure 3.1 provides an extensive-form representation of a game with two Nash equilibria: (U,R) and (D,L). Suppose (U,R) is the projected outcome. If player 2 is playing R, then player 1 is best playing U, and if player 1 is playing U, player 2 has no reason to switch to L. Similarly with (D,L). Thus these outcomes are self-enforcing, since no player has an incentive to deviate from them.

However, it is easy to see that there is something unreasonable about the (U,R) equilibrium. The only reason that player 2's "choice" of R over L does not affect her payoffs is that she does not get a chance to move when player 1 selects U. However, if she *were* actually called upon to move, she would choose L. So although it is true that player 1 cannot benefit by deviating from the equilibrium so long as player 2 is playing R, if he *were* to deviate, player 2 would certainly not play R, but would in fact switch to L. Thus, under the (U,R) equilibrium, player 1's belief set contains a false counterfactual. If he corrects this belief, it will lead him to play D in order to get the higher payoff of 3. This effectively unravels the equilibrium.

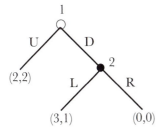

Figure 3.1

It appears, then, that the only reasonable equilibrium in this game is (D,L). On these grounds, Selten argues that a reasonable equilibrium strategy profile would have to be not only a Nash equilibrium in the large game, but that the relevant subset of it would also have to be Nash in any proper subgame, even if this subgame is never reached in the course of play. The idea is that players' strategies must be optimizing both on and off the equilibrium path, otherwise some player might stand to benefit from a deviation that would cause other players to switch strategies. In figure 3.1, player 2's decision node forms the origin of a subgame that is not reached in the (U,R) Nash equilibrium. Since R is not a Nash equilibrium of this subgame (since it is not a utility-maximizing choice for player 2 at that point), (U,R) is not a subgame-perfect equilibrium of the larger game. Thus subgame perfection eliminates the "unreasonable" Nash equilibrium.[8]

The example in figure 3.1 is interesting for our purposes because the (U,R) equilibrium can be interpreted as an interaction based upon a threat. Under the (U,R) equilibrium, player 2 receives a payoff of 2, whereas under (D,L) she receives only 1. Clearly, it would be to her advantage if she could in some way publicly *commit* herself to playing R in the event that she was called upon to move. If player 1 believed that player 2 would choose R, then he would select U, which would be to player 2's advantage. Player 2 could perhaps threaten player 1 with the (0,0) payoff in order to force his hand. Unfortunately, this will not work. Player 2 could make such a threat, but as a rational agent she would never carry it out if called upon to do so. To threaten, players have to be willing to engage in non-utility-maximizing actions. But since this is precisely what instrumentally rational agents are unwilling to do, there can be nothing but empty threats in strategic contexts. The same analysis can be applied to promises, except that the action in this case is unilaterally damaging to the promiser.[9] To see this, suppose player 2 choosing L gave a payoff of (3,3) and R gave (0,4). This would lead player 1 to choose U, since he would expect player 2 to choose R given the opportunity. If player 2 could promise to choose L, then both would get 3. Instead they both get 2, a suboptimal result.

The irony is that Selten's refinement of Nash equilibrium, which was motivated by strictly technical considerations, rediscovered in the heart of game theory the feature of instrumental rationality that had troubled theorists as far back as Hobbes, namely, that instrumentally rational agents cannot credibly commit themselves to future actions, even when the adoption of such commitments would benefit all. There are clearly many cases in which it would be advantageous for agents *not* to reoptimize at every point. Under such circumstances, the requirements of rationality appear to conflict with the dictates of self-interest. This presents something of a puzzle.

In *nonsocial* contexts, reoptimization is always advantageous. It is impossible to construct a decision problem in which an agent could benefit from making a commitment.[10] In *social* contexts, however, commitment can allow agents to achieve nonequilibrium outcomes. This is extremely useful, because the strategic equilibria available within any game are often either disadvantageous or suboptimal. (In the former case, an announced commitment would be a threat, in the latter, a promise.) The commitment can be advantageous in social contexts because, when effective, it allows one agent to generate beliefs in others that are different from those that would normally be ascribed to her as the product of strategic reasoning. The strategies that these other agents adopt in response to these beliefs may then turn out to be better for one or more of the agents.

The problem, however, is that agents are not obviously capable of "turning off" their capacity to optimize when it suits them. For example, being crazy makes one immune to most types of blackmail and extortion, so it would be very much in our advantage to be able to go mad when we like. Unfortunately, most of us are unable to do so, and therefore remain potential targets. Furthermore, it will always be in our advantage to convey the appearance of being crazy, inflexible, or committed (as the case may be), but then reoptimize when it comes time to act. Since everybody can see this just by examining the structure of the interaction, it seems unlikely that instrumentally rational agents would take any commitments seriously. For this reason, Hobbes thought that even though everyone could see that they would all be better off with the ability to make commitments, it would remain wishful thinking so long as everyone would be better off still with the ability to make *and break* commitments.

However, if Hobbes is correct and instrumentally rational agents are incapable of making commitments, then a serious explanatory difficulty arises. What is one to make of the fact that agents *do* routinely make and honor promises, and that these commitments provide the foundation for the development of all large-scale cooperative activities, including agriculture, industry, construction, and navigation? Hobbes's idea—that this cooperation is secured entirely through the imposition of external sanctions—is both empirically and conceptually implausible.[11] For this reason, many theorists committed to defending the instrumental conception of rationality have attempted to modify the basic framework in order to incorporate commitment. (The alternative, of course, is to suppose that commitments represent the expression of some other, noninstrumental form of rationality.) However, if one takes seriously the teleological structure of instrumental rationality, this is exceedingly difficult to do.

First of all, any attempt to build the capacity for commitment into the decision-theoretic foundations of game theory is an obvious nonstarter. Decision theory is a mechanism for using empirical beliefs to project a set of preferences over outcomes onto a set of actions. Tacit in this view is the idea that only outcomes count.[12] Actions are assumed to have no intrinsic properties that make them more or less desirable; only outcomes have these properties. Actions acquire them indirectly through the outcomes they promote. Commitment, on the other hand, introduces a property of *actions* that makes them desirable independent of the outcome they produce. An action may become desirable because it is "part of the plan," "something I promised," or "something I intended to do." These sorts of considerations are, in principle, not instrumental. They can be incorporated into the agent's ranking of actions, but only at the expense of changing the weight that the relevant outcomes exert on the ranking of the action. It would then be necessary to keep track of these effects, because subsequent changes in the agent's information about the prevailing state would generate only a reduced impact on the agent's payoff expectations. It is impossible to treat an agent's commitments as just one more sort of preference, because the two are structurally disanalogous, and so one would always need to keep two sets of books on the agent (at which point the theory of action would no longer be, strictly speaking, instrumental).

This explains why proponents of commitment models seldom attempt to build it in on the "ground floor" of rational choice theory. The more usual approach is to take the agent's utility function as given by the standard decision-theoretic apparatus, and build in commitments by rejecting sequential rationality as a constraint on equilibrium solution concepts. (This has the considerable advantage of treating commitment as a strictly social phenomenon, which it obviously is, but at the risk of compromising the reductionism of the game theory project.) Some theorists, like Nicholas Rowe, have suggested that agents should be able to "lock in" to particular strategies at the beginning of the game, in such a way as to prevent themselves from later reoptimizing.[13] David Gauthier has presented an slightly more complex scheme, which would allow agents to *selectively* forego reoptimization.[14] In both cases, agents would no longer be maximizing utility in their selection of particular actions, but rather would be selecting actions in conformity with a larger "plan" that is utility-maximizing overall.

Despite the mode of presentation, however, these sorts of theories still have the effect of introducing a class of noninstrumental reasons for action. If an agent chooses some action a with an expected utility of 2 over action b with an expected utility of 3, because a is the tail end of a larger plan, then the agent's reason for choosing a is not governed by its anticipated outcome and is therefore not instrumental in form. Although the agent's reasons for adopting the plan may have been instrumental, the reasons for performing any of the component actions cannot be. For this reason, many game theorists have criticized Gauthier, among others, for helping himself to standard utility functions. Ken Binmore, for instance, has argued that if adopting a plan makes an agent more likely to choose a than b, then this should be accommodated by changing the agent's utility function around, so that a is now worth 3, and b worth 2.[15] If this suggestion is accepted, then commitment has been filtered out again, and so all the old problems return.

If, however, one grants to theorists like Gauthier the use of standard utility functions, and grants that agents can engage in non-utility-maximizing actions when these are prescribed by a certain class of noninstrumental reasons, a number of questions still remain unanswered. First of all, the rejection of sequential rationality significantly increases the indeterminacy of strategic reasoning. Not only does it eliminate all of the existing refinements of Nash equilibrium, starting with subgame-perfection, but it expands the set of admissible equilibria to include a wide range of what were previously considered irrational strategies. The ability of agents to resolve strategic interaction problems depends essentially upon their ability to "mirror" each other's reasoning processes. Allowing agents to make private commitments, and therefore introduce a different class of reasons into their future deliberations, makes it all but impossible for agents to accomplish this task, and therefore all but impossible for them to reason their way to a maximizing course of action.[16]

There is also in Gauthier's proposal the unargued assumption that plans must be adopted for instrumental reasons. But why could plans not be selected on the basis of larger plans? I might return my friend's book because it is part of a plan that involves promising, but I may adopt that plan because it is part of a larger plan to make my mother proud of me. To suppose that there are noninstrumental reasons for action, but then claim that these are all "ultimately" backed by instrumental reasons, requires some sort of philo-sophical justification.[17] But once we start admitting that there can be nonin-strumental reasons for action, it raises all sorts of fundamental questions about the nature of practical rationality. This opens a rather large can of worms. Gauthier, in effect, tries to pluck one out and clamp the lid back on. There is something ad hoc about this. If we are going to start entertaining candidates for noninstrumental reasons for action, we should put all the options on the table and evaluate each one on its substantive merits—and not simply shop around for one that will help rescue rational choice theory.

The moral of the story is that even though the claim that the instrumental conception of rationality excludes commitment is not universally accepted, there are serious and substantial grounds for thinking that the two are ulti-mately incompatible. (Furthermore, few theorists who endorse instrumentalist views of commitment have considered any of the counterintuitive conse-quences of their claims. If, for instance, instrumentally rational agents were capable of making commitments as easily as Gauthier says, then markets would not function, since price competition is an interfirm Prisoner's Dilemma. Needless to say, Gauthier does not see himself as undermining the microfoundations of neoclassical economics.)

It should be noted that this problem with commitment is what generates the "Hobbesian problem of order" that motivated the classical sociological theo-rists to introduce social norms, or rule-following, as a primitive action-theoretic component of social interaction. This argument was given its most influential formulation by Parsons, and it is to this argument that Habermas appeals at various points.[18] Thus Habermas's claim that speech acts cannot be instrumentally rational exploits a certain local version of the problem of order. In this sense, Habermas is not presenting an alternative to the traditional soci-ological critique of instrumental rationality, but is developing a special case.

3.2 Discursive Commitment

This discussion of the incompatibility between commitment and instrumental rationality sets up the background for Habermas's most important claim, namely, that the meaning of speech acts is determined by the commitments that speakers undertake through their performance. Habermas's views on the noninstrumental character of communication are a direct and obvious conse-quence of this claim. More important, however, is the fact that this analysis of communication in terms of commitment also allows Habermas to effect a clever inversion of the explanatory order presupposed by proponents of the instrumental conception of rationality. That commitment cannot be justified instrumentally does not mean that instrumental rationality cannot be characterized as a certain structure of commitment. The instrumental model of rationality, as is generally acknowledged, presupposes that the agents' reasons for action—beliefs and desires—are propositional attitudes. If the meaning of speech acts, and hence propositions, is given by a set of commitments that agents undertake through their performance, then Habermas is in a position to claim that the rationality of instrumental actions is actually derived from the rationality of some underlying structure of commitment.

The attractive feature of this claim is that it provides Habermas with an extremely simple way of giving a uniform characterization of the rationality of both instrumental and communicative action:

Consider two paradigmatic cases: an assertion with which A in a communicative attitude expresses a belief and a goal-directed intervention in the world with which B pursues a specific end. Both embody fallible knowledge; both are attempts that can go wrong. Both expressions, the speech act and the teleological action, can be criticized. A hearer can contest the truth of the assertion made by A; an observer can dispute the anticipated success of the action taken by B. In both cases the critic refers to claims that the subjects necessarily attach to their expressions insofar as the latter are intended as assertions or as goal-directed actions. This necessity is of a conceptual nature. For A does not make an assertion unless he makes a truth claim for the asserted proposition p and therewith indicates his conviction that his statement can, if necessary, be defended. And B does not perform a goal-directed action, that is, he does not want to accomplish an end by it unless he regards the action planned as promising and therewith indicates his conviction that, in the given circumstances, his choice of means can if necessary be explained.[19]

One of the characteristics of instrumental action mentioned in the first chapter is that in order to understand it, one must ascribe a set of propositional attitudes to the agent. In Habermas's view, this amounts to ascribing a set of commitments to that agent.[20] The rationality of the action will then be determined by the agent's capacity to redeem these commitments. On the other hand, when the action is a speech act, there is no need to ascribe commitments to the agent; rather, the agent explicitly undertakes commitments through performance of the action. But the rationality of an action of this type is determined in exactly the same way—by whether the agent is capable of redeeming these commitments. Thus Habermas claims that the rationality of all social action is determined by its "susceptibility to criticism and grounding."[21] The only major difference between speech acts and instrumental actions is that, in the former case, the commitments undertaken *constitute* the action, while in the latter case they only underlie it.

However, Habermas's ability to turn the tables in this way depends entirely upon his ability to make the claim that linguistic meaning—and hence the content of propositional attitudes—is given by speakers' discursive commitments. Unfortunately, this claim is likely to strike many readers as simply unmotivated. Among philosophers of language it is not a particularly unusual view, but to explain the reasons for it requires an understanding of a number of relatively abstruse developments in analytic philosophy of language. Habermas moves through these so quickly that any reader not already familiar with the relevant literature can easily fail to notice than an argument has even been presented.[22] To lend some assistance to Habermas's cause, I will therefore go through the major steps that are needed to motivate the "acceptibility-conditional" semantics that he develops: §3.2.1 discusses the need for a compositional semantics for natural language; §3.2.2 explains his acceptance of Dummett's "critique of truth-conditional semantics"[23]; §3.2.3 defends his substitution of an "inferential semantics" for truth-conditional[24]; and §3.2.4 interprets inference pragmatically, in terms of commitment to particular moves in the language-game of "discourse."[25] Once these steps are completed, it will be possible to move on to consider Habermas's distinctive "three validity claims" thesis.

3.2.1 Compositionality

One of the reasons that developing an adequate theory of meaning for a language is so hard is that competent speakers are able to grasp the meaning of a potentially *infinite* number of expressions (or equivalently, are able to understand expressions that they have never heard before). This implies that the meaning of expressions in a language cannot be fixed directly by stipulation, as they could be in a system of signals, but must in some way be generated from a simpler set of semantic resources.[26] An adequate theory of language will therefore have to explain the semantic machinery that allows us to "put together" meanings in this way. This feature of language is referred to as its *compositionality*. The meaning of a sentence, according to this view, is constructed from the meaning of its parts. A compositional theory of meaning attributes to competent speakers knowledge of the meaning of a finite number of semantic primitives, along with a finite number of rules for combining these primitives. By recursive application of these rules to the primitives, the agent has the capacity to produce and understand an infinite number of sentences.[27]

Unfortunately, this presentation makes the problem appear deceptively simple. Since the meaning of the whole has to be explained in the terms of the meaning of its parts, the obvious place to start would appear to be with an analysis of the smallest parts. Once these are adequately characterized, it will then be possible to build up the more complex meaning. Since the best candidates for semantic primitives are words, the most direct procedure would be to explain how words get their meaning, and then show how various rules of grammar and syntax allow us to put them together into sentences. This procedure seems so natural that it has exercised a near-total grip on the human imagination throughout the entire history of thought. The revolution in philosophy carried out by Kant and Frege lay in the simple recognition that this procedure is wrong.[28]

What Frege claimed, simply put, is that words do not have meaning all on their own. Their meaning is derived from the contribution they make to the meaning of larger semantic units. This idea is expressed in Frege's context principle, which states that one must "never ask for the meaning of a word in isolation, but only in the context of a proposition."[29] Speakers learn a finite number of these larger expressions, and from this, determine the meaning of component words from the systematic contribution they make to the meaning of these larger units. Having grasped the meaning of the words in this way, speakers are then able to go on to construct new expressions. This gives the theory a complicated pattern: starting with a higher structure, speakers work their way down to the lower level of words, and then work their way back up to the structure they began with and beyond. We can refer, following Dummett, to a construction of this type as a *molecular* (as opposed to an *atomistic*) theory of meaning.[30] There are many consequences that follow from adopting a molecular theory. Possibly the most significant is that the notion of reference cannot be taken as primitive. In an atomistic theory, the meaning of a word like "dog" is characterized in terms of the relationship between the symbol and the set of entities to which it refers, namely, dogs. In a molecular theory, the reference relation will "fall out" of the derivation of word meaning; it will not be fixed in advance.[31] What "dog" refers to will ultimately be determined by the contribution that the word "dog" makes to the semantic significance of larger linguistic expressions in which it occurs.

The most significant programmatic decision in the development of a molecular theory involves selecting the larger semantic unit that is to be taken as basic. It goes without saying that since the smallest unit of communication is the utterance, or speech act, a finished theory of meaning will have as its central objective the characterization of utterance meaning. This does not mean, however, that the utterance must be taken as the basic semantic unit for the account of compositionality. It is possible that only one component of utterance meaning is fully compositional. This component would then be integrated with a finite set of other meaning resources in order to produce the finished utterance.

This issue is an important one. Because the compositional theory will be very complex, it is important to keep the compositional component of the theory of meaning as simple as possible. This requires picking out the smallest unit with which to begin analysis. Consider the following illustration: Suppose someone has a job working in a bakery, attempting to copy all of the cakes that I produce in mine. I have only twelve different types of icing recipes, but am in possession of a recipe algorithm that allows me to generate an infinite number of cakes. My rival has to reproduce each cake that I make. Naturally, in order to do this, he will have to know both the icing and the cake type. How will he proceed? As far as the frosting goes, he can just taste it, then look it up in a list and identify it. The cake is a bit different. Since he cannot just look it up, his best hope is to figure out from the taste what ingredients I used, along with the manner in which they were combined. Obviously, his cake theory is going to be the hard part of the "reverse engineering" job.[32] So even though cake-plus-icing will be the basic unit of reproduction, success in reproduction will involve primarily identification of cake-type. In fact, the problem is roughly equivalent to one in which I have only one type of icing. (Note also that by not distinguishing between frosting and cake, a number of irrelevant permutations will be introduced into the cake theory, making the compositional account needlessly, and perhaps hopelessly, complex.)

A central line of disagreement in early analytic philosophy of language involved the question of whether an utterance is more like a cake, or like a cake-plus-icing. Broadly speaking, proponents of the *speech act project* take utterances to be the basic semantic unit (and thus like a cake).[33] Proponents of the *formal semantic* approach, on the other hand, divide utterance meaning into pragmatic and semantic components. Characterization of the contribution of these components is performed by a theory of *force* and *sense* respectively. In this view, the sense of a *sentence* is given compositionally (and so is like a cake); this sentence is then employed with particular force to make an utterance (icing on the cake).

There is a broadly emerging consensus that the formal semantic approach is the correct one. The considerations that weigh in its favor arise from what Davidson calls the "autonomy" of linguistic meaning, that is, that "once a feature of language has been given conventional expression, it can be used to serve many extra-linguistic ends; symbolic representation necessarily breaks any close tie with extra-linguistic purpose."[34] In other words, once the meaning of a particular set of symbols has become more or less settled, they can then be applied in a variety of novel practical contexts. When it comes to analyzing these utterances, it will then be the case that a core component of their meaning is invariant to the specific use to which the utterance is put.

Apart from this general consideration, there is also the fact that no one has any clear idea how compositional principles could be derived directly from utterances (without positing something like a sentence with literal meaning, or a "generic" utterance type that fixes literal meaning). Consider two speech acts:

(1)   Put four plates on the table.

(2)   There are four plates on the table.

No matter how one cuts things up, these are going to belong to two totally different utterance types, since (1) is an imperative and (2) is an assertion. Now what is going to give us the meaning of the word "four" as it appears in these two utterances? (If we reject atomism, we cannot say that "four" has meaning all on its own.) The speech act theorist, following Austin and the later Wittgenstein, claims that utterances are the smallest unit with which we can use language to *do* something, to make a move in a language game. This implies that we intend to explain the meaning of words in terms of the systematic consequences they have for the pragmatic outcomes of any speech act in which they are used. The problem with this analysis is that it does not supply an impressive level of uniformity, since the two speech acts above have completely different pragmatic roles. What is going to connect the meaning of "four" in imperatives with the meaning of "four" in assertions? What is to stop "four" from meaning *four* when used in assertions and *five* when used in imperatives?

Furthermore, the speech act analysis leaves open the following, unusual possibility. According to this view, we can imagine someone who understands (2), and recognizes that (1) is an imperative, but does not understand it (i.e., knows what it would mean to assert that the state of affairs that he is ordered to bring about obtains, knows how to recognize when he is being ordered to do something, but does not understand an imperative ordering him to bring this state of affairs about). This is a straightforward consequence of the claim that the meaning of words is determined by their contribution to the *utterances* in which they are used.

The proponent of formal semantics suggests, on the other hand, that both the assertion and the imperative above have something in common. They both employ a reference to a state of affairs—there being four plates on the table. Thus the same proposition (understood as the meaning of a sentence) is uttered in both (1) and (2), but with different force. In the first case, the speaker orders another to bring the state of affairs about, in the second, she asserts that it obtains. Knowing the proposition and recognizing the force with which it is employed allows the hearer to infer the meaning of the utterance as a whole. It is only this propositional component that is given compositionally. To illustrate, when someone says "Can you type this?" and the hearer does not know whether it is a question or a request, what he understands is the *sense* of the expression, what he does not yet know is the force. The counterintuitive consequence of understanding (2) but not (1) is thereby excluded: if we know what the assertion in (2) means, and we know what it means to issue an imperative, we can simply transfer our semantic knowledge of the propositional content over to generate an understanding of (1).

This suggests that we can make the theory of meaning more manageable by analyzing utterances in terms of two components, consisting of a proposition, taken from an infinite set of possible propositions, and an illocutionary component, taken from a finite set of possible forces. (Hence the now-standard Ip representation of speech acts, where I gives the force [illocutionary mode] and p the sense [propositional content].) This means that since the meaning of the words is distilled from the contribution they make to larger semantic units, and the compositional portion of the theory involves propositional contents, then the sentence will be the basic unit. This account, once constructed, provides a characterization of sentence meaning that is uniform across speech acts. The theory of force would then account for how sentences are transformed into utterances. This may still involve a transformation of the meaning of the sentence; the only crucial thing is that the set of such transformations be finite (e.g., that there be no recursively applicable rules for the formation of arbitrarily complex illocutionary modes).

But so far this is a strictly negative account. What is it about sentences that makes them a plausible basic unit? One suggestion has been that sentences are the smallest piece of language that can be true or false. Words can then be said to get their meaning from the contribution they make to the truth-conditions of sentences in which they appear. Note, however, that truth-conditions are not truth-values, and sentences are not assertions. To know the truth-conditions of a sentence is to know what *would* make it true. When this sentence is used to make an assertion, this means knowing what state of affairs is said to obtain. When this sentence is used in an imperative, it means knowing what action constitutes compliance, and so on. So adopting a truth-conditional *semantics* does not automatically commit one to the view that fact-stating discourse constitutes the primary mode of language use.

3.2.2   Critique of truth-conditional semantics

What is the intuition underlying the identification of knowledge of sense with knowledge of truth-conditions? Habermas has an unfortunate tendency to dismiss truth-conditional approaches to semantics offhand. In his view, formal semantics in the tradition of Frege has labored under an arbitrary limitation of its analysis to the single dimension of validity—truth—when it might have proceeded more fruitfully by analyzing the full panoply of claims. This is a result, he suspects, of a cognitivist bias permeating the cultural ethos of Anglo-American philosophy. Thus he does not present much of an argument against truth-conditional approaches—the closest that he comes is to endorse, at various points, Dummett's critique.

This dismissive attitude prevents him from delving too deeply into the types of considerations that have led so many philosophers to think that linguistic meaning must be analyzed in terms of truth-conditions. This is unfortunate, because precisely these same considerations, under a slightly different interpretation, motivate inferential approaches to semantics and ultimately serve as the basis for the connection that Habermas wants to draw between meaning and validity. Because Dummett takes truth-conditional views more seriously, these considerations are all rendered explicit in his work.

The first step in understanding Dummett's critique is to consider why anyone might ever have thought that knowledge of meaning is given by knowledge of truth-conditions (a question Habermas never directly considers). This discussion will seem somewhat obvious to those familiar with post-Fregean philosophy of language. But it is precisely this obviousness that I believe is at the root of a major problem in the reception of Habermas's work. The reasons for focusing on truth-conditions are so often taken for granted by analytic philosophers that they are seldom explicitly discussed, and as a result, often perceived by those outside the tradition as merely a prejudice.

Naturally, if one takes utterances as the primitive unit of semantic significance, then the truth-conditional approach will appear to arbitrarily privilege assertoric forms of discourse. A wide variety of utterances cannot be characterized as true or false, including imperatives, questions, and promises. It is only if one accepts the division of labor between the semantic and the pragmatic components of the theory of meaning that the truth-conditional approach even begins to appear reasonable. In this view, truth-conditions do not give the meaning of the utterance as a whole, but only its compositional component. This propositional content is then given a certain force by being used in one or another illocutionary mode. Each different illocutionary mode can be characterized in terms of how it deploys these truth-conditions, for example, assertions can be characterized along the lines of "It is the case that p is true," imperatives as "Make it the case that p is true," questions as "Is it the case that p is true?" and so on.

Accepting the semantic/pragmatic distinction is therefore essential for getting the truth-conditional approach off the ground. The remaining question is why grasp of truth-conditions appears to be equivalent to an understanding of sentence meaning. One way of looking at this is as follows. To know the *truth-value* of a sentence, one has to know what the sentence means, and how the world is. This can be rewritten in order to get rid of the appeal to meaning by saying that to know the truth-value of a sentence, one has to know how the world must be in order for the sentence to be true, and how the world in fact is. Here knowledge of truth-conditions has effectively been substituted for knowledge of meaning. But what has been gained? How are we to understand what it is to know "how the world must be in order for the sentence to be true"?

The most direct way of cashing this out would be in terms of the "picture-theory" of language developed by Wittgenstein in the *Tractatus Logico-Philosophicus*.[35] Here knowing the truth-conditions amounts to having a mental representation of a state of affairs that may or may not map onto an equivalent state of the world. The problem with this view is that only whole sentences have truth-conditions, and whole sentences have internal semantic structure. For these sentences to map directly onto the world, the world would also have to have an essentially linguistic structure. This is a difficult idea to accept. Our inclination is to think of the world as consisting of objects, *about which* we are capable of making true or false statements.

The implication of this view is that the truth-conditions of a statement cannot be grasped directly, like a picture, but must themselves be built up out of more basic relations, which is to say, they must be given compositionally. As a result, most proponents of truth-conditional semantics are not naive representationalists or empiricists. They rest their case on the claim that the compositional principles that govern the determination of truth-conditions are the same as those that determine the meaning of sentences. The theory of truth is privileged because it appears to have a formal structure that makes it suitable to serve as a theory of meaning.

The most intuitively accessible example of this structural homology involves the rules that govern the familiar logical constants, like "and," "or," etc. The rule for "and" is recursive in the following way: I can take two sentences and conjoin them using the word "and" to form a new sentence. I can then take this sentence and conjoin it to another using the word "and" to form another new sentence, and so on. The meaning of each new sentence formed in this way will depend upon the meaning of the original sentences, and the manner in which they are connected, for example, by an "and" and not an "or." Thus knowing the meaning of the sentences p, q, and r, along with the meaning of "and," I can figure out the meaning of new sentences, like:

(3) p and q.

(4) q and r and p.

This example is something of a simplification. Since the sentential connectives can be used to combine already complete sentences, the above account treats entire sentences as semantic primitives. The more basic compositional features of language are exhibited in the way words are combined in order to produce new, but logically simple, sentences. This requires that objects and predicates (which themselves do not express complete thoughts) be taken as semantic primitives. Consider the following sentence:

(5) Dogs eat mushrooms.

If we are able to figure out the meaning of this sentence, it is because we know what dogs are, what mushrooms are, what it is for something to eat something else, and how these fit together to form a coherent thought.

So why would anyone think that knowledge of meaning consists of knowledge of truth-conditions? The compositionality requirement suggests that knowing the meaning of a complex sentence involves breaking it down into parts. But similarly, knowing the truth conditions of a sentence will involve breaking it down into parts as well, and, as it turns out, these parts are the same. In other words, the basic units of *semantic significance* are the same as the units required to characterize the *truth-conditions* of the sentences. This suggests that the semantic significance of each part might just be the contribution it makes to the truth-conditions of the whole.

To put this in more concrete terms: to understand (3), as mentioned above, the agent must understand the semantic primitives $\{p, q\}$ and the meaning of the sentential connective "and." But what must she know in order to know the truth-conditions of (3)? Obviously, she must know that "p and q" is true if and only if p is true and q is true. In other words, she must know the truth-conditions of the semantic primitives $\{p, q\}$, along with the truth table governing the "and" operator. The key point is that the sentence breaks down in the same way in both cases. To know the truth conditions of the logically complex sentence, one must break it down in precisely the way that one must break it down to get at its meaning.

Truth-conditions function in a similar way at a subsentential level, although the logical machinery involved is more complicated and too lengthy to get into here. The intuitive idea is as follows: to assess the truth of (5) one has to determine whether the specified relation "eat" obtains between the class of objects specified by "dogs" and that specified by "mushrooms." Names can be defined extensionally, as the set of objects that they designate. The predicates can be defined as the set of ordered *n*-tuples of objects that satisfy them. The sentences will then be true if the objects picked out by the names also satisfy the predicates. Once again, the point here is sufficiently obvious that it can easily be overlooked. To determine the truth-conditions of the sentence, one must break it down in exactly the same way that its meaning appears to be constructed. Furthermore, if someone knows everything that is needed to assess the truth of this sentence, there does not appear to be anything further needed to grasp the meaning of the sentence.

When this account is incorporated into a nonatomistic theory of meaning it can be somewhat counterintuitive, since theories of this type do not attempt to characterize the meaning of individual words directly. The truth-conditional perspective itself leaves open a number of ways of specifying these. In a molecular theory, the exact designation of "dog" will be whatever satisfies some canonical class of sentences that we hold true about dogs. What the truth-conditional conception of meaning attempts to do is merely to capture certain structural features of the way that the meaning of a complex sentence is constructed. The reason that truth-conditions have played such a central role in formal semantics is therefore not necessarily owing to a cognitivist bias, as Habermas assumes. It is because there are few other conceptions that appear able to offer a comparable reconstruction of semantic structure.

3.2.3   Inferential semantics

The most serious traditional rival to the truth-conditional theory involves variations on the claim that to know the meaning of a sentence is to know its method of verification. A word of caution is in order here. Modern verificationism, as exemplified by the work of Michael Dummett and Crispin Wright, has little in common with the earlier "verificationist criterion of meaning" used by the logical positivists to disparage nonscientific forms of reasoning. This type of verificationism was just crude empiricism transplanted into the philosophy of language. Modern verificationism, on the other hand, has developed from specifically language-theoretic considerations. The basic claim is that ascribing knowledge of truth-conditions to an agent is gratuitously strong, since knowledge of justification-conditions will in all cases suffice to explain linguistic competence. In this view, the claim that agents grasp the truth-conditions of a sentence, despite its initial appearance of intelligibility, turns out on closer examination to harbor considerable ambiguity.

The basic suggestion can be articulated most clearly using sentence (3) as an example. It was pointed out that knowing the truth-conditions of "p and q" would involve knowing the truth-conditions of p, the truth-conditions of q, and the truth table governing the "and" connective. This suggested that a recursive specification of truth-conditions for the sentences of a language would yield an adequate characterization of their meaning. But truth is not the only possibility here. Consider, for instance, that in order to know how to *prove* "p and q" one would have to know how to prove p, how to prove q, along with the *introduction rule* for "and" in a natural deduction system. In logic or mathematics, a recursive definition of provability can be provided that yields the same compositional analysis of complex sentences as the truth-conditional analysis does. Thus proof, or justification, would appear to do the same work as truth.

The meaning of subsentential components can be characterized in a similarly epistemic fashion. Instead of characterizing the agent's understanding of a term such as "dog" as a cognitive grasp of some set of objects, it can characterized as a practical ability to identify dogs. Similarly, the agent's understanding of properties and relations can be characterized as the ability to carry out the procedures necessary to determine whether certain objects possess these properties, or stand in the appropriate relations.

Given these two competing accounts, what considerations can be used to decide one way or the other? Those impressed by Wittgenstein's private language argument claim that in order to intelligibly ascribe knowledge to someone, there must be some way in which the agent is able to exhibit this knowledge. This provides what Crispin Wright calls the "manifestation argument" against truth-conditional semantics:

Understanding is essentially knowledge which can be distinctively displayed in behaviour; it is a network of discriminatory and responsive skills. So there is no place, in an acceptable philosophical account of understanding, for imputation of conceptions of (potentially) "transcendent" states of affairs; whatever ability corresponds to such a conception, it cannot *show* itself as different from the abilities constituting knowledge of the *use* of the statement of whose truth-conditions it supposedly constitutes grasp. Only as a complex of recognitional skills can understanding be distinctively manifest in behaviour; understanding a statement is manifest in the ability to recognize when circumstances warrant the assertion, or denial, of it and of compound statements containing it, and to recognize its logical consequences and ancestry; this is all anyone can overtly do with the statement, and for the description of these abilities it is otiose "theoretical slack" to invoke the notion that the speaker possesses a conception of a (potentially) transcendent state of affairs. His abilities can be fully described in terms of states of affairs which he can recognize: conditions justifying assertions and denials involving that statement, and decidable logical relations between it and other statements.[36]

For a number of different classes of statements it will be impossible to directly manifest a grasp of the truth-conditions, for example, statements involving unrestricted quantification over infinite domains, referring to inaccessible regions of space-time, or reporting inner experiences. According to Wright, the most that a speaker could ever manifest would be an ability to recognize evidence for the truth of these statements. A theory of meaning is therefore unwarranted in attributing to the speaker anything more than a knowledge of justification conditions.

The intuition here is straightforward. The only way one can ever tell that a person understands the meaning of the word "dog" is if that person is capable of identifying dogs in the environment and making correct inferences using that concept, for example, "dogs are mammals," and so on. There might be something further that underlies these public displays, such as a complex reference relation between the word "dog" in the agent's mind and the actual dogs in the word, but we have no evidence for the existence of such relations. And furthermore, since language is learned from observing the public behavior of others, it is unclear how anyone would ever acquire a grasp of these purely private relations. In any case, since nothing beyond the grasp of inference rules and verification procedures is ever publicly manifested, these are the only components of meaning that must be shared in order for language to function effectively, that is, to provide a system of shared meanings. This means that even if one wants to posit a grasp of truth-conditions, these will play no explanatory role in the theory of meaning. Thus the central appeal of the verificationist alternative to truth-conditional semantics is that it exhibits greater parsimony in its postulation of unobservables, but has exactly the same explanatory power.

It should be noted that a verificationist (or *justification-conditional*) semantics of this type can be developed in ways that make it easy to confuse with truth-conditional approaches. The most direct way of doing verificationism is simply to eliminate any appeal to truth-conditions in the compositional component of the theory of meaning. However, it is possible to retain truth as the "central notion" in the theory of meaning by reinterpreting the predicate so that it no longer refers to recognition-transcendent "realist" truth, but rather to some kind of epistemically constrained "antirealist" truth. If truth is defined as, for instance, warranted assertibility, then one can proceed to construct a truth-conditional semantics knowing that "knowledge of truth-conditions" can always be cashed out in terms of some concrete epistemic capabilities of the knower.[37] This ambiguity will become significant later on, as Habermas is not always clear about which of these two strategies he subscribes to.

3.2.4   Pragmatic interpretation

Dummett's verificationism is limited by the fact that it remains closely tied to the model of formal languages. To put it to work on Habermas's behalf, it needs to be pragmaticized. This can be accomplished in a few relatively well-rehearsed steps. (I will refer, following Brandom, to this type of pragmatic theory as an "inferential semantics.")[38]

First of all, in verificationist semantics the basic intersentential compositional rules are given by the logical connectives, which are interpreted as providing rules for the construction of proofs. In natural language, these rules should instead be understood to govern arguments, which can be characterized as linked sets of warranted assertions. In this way, the introduction rule for "and" states that if one is warranted in asserting p and warranted in asserting q, then one is warranted in asserting "p and q." Thus the semantic rule represents a certain type of practical *entitlement*. Similarly, the elimination rules can be understood as principles that specify the "downstream" consequences of accepting some particular set of assertions. This makes them equivalent to a set of practical *commitments*.

The second major difference is that in natural languages, most of the inferential relations that people work with will not incorporate explicitly logical vocabulary, but will be so-called material inferences. This is an idea that Habermas picks up from Stephen Toulmin's argumentation theory.[39] It implies that an inference, like "it rained, so the streets will be wet," is directly constitutive of the meaning of words like "rain," "wet," and so on. Additional logical vocabulary can be introduced in order to formalize this inference using an assertion, a conditional, and detachment, but this is merely a form of representation; it is not constitutive of the meaning of any terms in the utterance.

Finally, the question of what counts as "verifying" particular ascriptions of properties or relations to objects can be loosened without altering the basic semantic structure of the theory. The important claim is simply that there be noninferentially acquired entitlements that can serve as "entry-moves" into the language game.[40] In some cases these will be simple recognitional capacities, such as the ability to correctly identify primary colors, household animals, and so on. In other cases, recognitional capacities may depend upon theoretically sophisticated analysis and interpretation of the environment, and thus need not be representational in any straightforward sense. What counts is simply that the speaker's responses covary with aspects of the environment in such a way as to give content to some set of logically simple utterances.

In a view of this type, the meaning of any utterance is given by its inferential role—the entitlements from which it flows, the commitments that it entails. These will provide a compositional analysis of the meaning of the sentence. To figure out whether the speaker is entitled to a logically complex claim, one must break it down into simpler claims and determine whether the speaker is entitled to those. One then needs to break down the logically simple claims into their various semantic components, and determine what one would have to do to show that the objects possess the properties ascribed to them, or that the relations obtain, and so on. All of these steps must be understood not as abstract mental operations, but as specific demands that one is entitled to make of the speaker. Since these entitlements correspond to the speaker's commitments, understanding the utterance can therefore be said to consist in a grasp of the commitments that the speaker has undertaken through its performance.

To summarize briefly: Habermas's claim that the meaning of an utterance is given by the procedure that the agent would have to follow to justify the content of that utterance is motivated by the following considerations drawn from the philosophy of language. A theory of meaning must be compositional, which means that it much include a set of general rules for the construction of meaningful sentences out of meaningful subsentential expressions. Inference rules and verification procedures provide precisely the sort of rules that are needed, and do so without any of the metaphysical baggage associated with the use of truth tables and satisfaction relations. When inference and verification are interpreted pragmatically, that is, in terms of natural language, they correspond to the norms that establish the conditions for warranted assertibility, which cover both legitimate "language-entry" moves and permissible "material inferences." Thus the epistemic relations between sentences are not something that are added later, after the meanings of those sentences are fixed. Instead, it is the epistemic (or more broadly justificatory) relations that the sentence is embedded in that determine its meaning. As Brandom puts it, "communication is the social production and consumption of reasons."[41] This is why there is an internal relationship between meaning and validity.

3.3 The Three Validity Claims

This reconstruction sketches out the general motivation for Habermas's claim that "we understand a speech act when we know the kinds of reasons that a speaker could provide in order to convince a hearer that he is entitled in the given circumstances to claim validity for his utterance—in short, when we know *what makes it acceptable.*"[42] Speakers raise validity claims through their utterances. Raising a validity claim amounts to incurring a commitment to provide, upon demand, a justification for the utterance. Understanding an utterance therefore consists of knowing how its corresponding validity claim could be redeemed, which is equivalent to knowing the commitments that the speaker has incurred through its performance. It is precisely because it is the agent's commitments that pin down the content of her utterance that speech acts resist purely instrumental employment.

However, this is not yet sufficient to motivate Habermas's more general ambitions for a theory of communicative action. The above account shows that speakers cannot make meaningful utterances without incurring commitments. But so far all of the commitments they incur remain specifically *discursive* commitments. Making a speech act appears to commit the agent to nothing more than *other speech acts*. To get from discourse to communicative action, Habermas must show that the use of linguistic exchange to coordinate social action necessarily generates commitments that extend *into* the anticipated interaction. Communication must generate extradiscursive obligations that are "relevant to the future interaction sequence [*interaktionsfolgenrelevante*]."[43]

To establish this, Habermas argues that there are three types of validity claims that speakers can raise through their utterances, and therefore three types of commitments that they can make. Each of these different types of commitment can be redeemed only in a corresponding type of discourse, and understanding the utterance consists in a knowledge of the conditions under which all three of these claims could be redeemed. These three types of validity, as mentioned above, are truth, rightness, and sincerity. In making a validity claim, a speaker makes a certain commitment about how things stand in three different domains (Habermas uses the term "world"). Truth claims concern the way things are in the physical world, rightness claims concern the way things are in the social world, understood as the totality of legitimately ordered interpersonal relations, and sincerity claims concern the way things are in the subject's private domain of inner experience.[44] These three relations capture the representational, conventional, and expressive dimensions of speech, respectively.

The reason speech acts carry obligations that are relevant to the future sequence of interaction is that the speaker, in making a rightness claim, commits himself to a certain view about how the social world should be organized. If the listener accepts this speech act, then she also accepts this view of how things should be done. In both cases, the speakers commit themselves to defending their claims with reasons. When they are able to successfully coordinate their action-orientations in this way, it means that they have reached a rationally motivated consensus. Action that is coordinated through agreements of this type, and motivated by the underlying illocutionary commitments, is referred to as *communicative action*. As Habermas puts it:

> In explicating the meaning of linguistic expressions and the validity of statements, we encountered idealizations that are bound up with the medium of language. . . . These idealizations inhabiting language itself acquire, in addition, an *action-theoretic* meaning if the illocutionary binding forces of speech acts are enlisted for the coordination of the action plans of different actors. With the concept of communicative action, which brings in mutual understanding as a mechanism of action coordination, the counterfactual presuppositions of actors who orient their action to validity claims also acquire immediate relevance for the construction and preservation of social orders; for these orders *exist* through the recognition of normative validity claims.[45]

The crucial idea, from Habermas's point of view, is that not only is the content of these action-coordinating plans fixed by speech acts, but also the relevant obligations. The capacity of communicative action to secure social integration is derived entirely from the "weak binding force of illocutionary commitments." In other words, if an agent were later to ask why he should do his part in a communicatively achieved agreement, the appropriate answer would be that he had committed himself to doing so through the speech acts in which the plan was initially selected. This is what I referred to earlier as the "contractualist intuition" that informs Habermas's project. It is because we have already tacitly agreed to play our part in these plans that we are later obliged to do so. This obligation is a rational obligation, because our agreement was necessarily motivated by an appreciation of the reasons that could be given for the plan, since our understanding of the proposed plan *consisted in* a grasp of the reasons that the speaker could have given in support of it. If we accepted the plan, this amounts to having accepted these reasons as good (at least from our own point of view). This explains the rational motivating force of communicatively achieved agreements. The primary difference between this view and standard contractualism is that the agent does not have to agree or promise explicitly in order to incur an obligation. The point of Habermas's speech act theory is to show that these obligations are automatically and necessarily generated by the process of reaching agreement through language. As Habermas summarizes it:

> If understanding a speech act depends on knowing the conditions for its acceptability then the speaker's illocutionary aim of being understood points to the further aim that

the hearer should accept her speech-act offer. Acceptance or agreement on the part of the hearer is equivalent to recognition of a validity claim raised by the speaker. It is based on the good reasons that the speaker offers in order to redeem the validity claim in discourse (or else on a credible warrant issued by the speaker that she could provide such reasons, if necessary). And the hearer, with his "yes" to a validity claim he has accepted as worthy of recognition—that is, with his acceptance of the speech-act offer—also takes upon himself, as a rule, certain obligations relevant for the sequel of interaction, such as obligations to meet a request, to trust a confession, to believe a statement, to rely on a promise, or to obey an order.[46]

All of this hinges, however, on Habermas's ability to make the claim that language involves not just assertoric, but also *normative* commitments. It is essential that the speaker not only incur commitments about how the world is, or may become, but also about how it *should be*. Thus the introduction of rightness claims, on analogy with truth, represents a crucial step in the argument. To see why, consider the following scenario. Imagine a language in which speakers are only capable of making claims about the truth or falsity of states of affairs. When the speaker says that the door is open, and the hearer accepts this speech act with a "yes," both have committed themselves to the existence of a certain state of affairs. Thus the hearer has incurred a commitment to act as though the door is open, even if she has no evidence other than the speaker's report. At an action-theoretic level, however, this commitment does not in any way interfere with her ability to pursue her objectives in an entirely instrumental fashion. It simply means that, in attempting to satisfy her preferences over outcomes, she should treat "the door is open" as the prevailing state when it comes to selecting actions. Thus speech acts of this type generate only what Habermas calls *weak communicative action*.[47]

If, however, the agent is able to perform a speech act that, rather than committing himself to the fact that the door is open, commits him to the claim that the door should be open, then the situation changes dramatically. The hearer, in accepting such a speech act offer, thereby commits herself to a normative proposition specifying that the state of affairs should obtain. At an action-theoretic level, this commitment is capable of interfering with her antecedently given preferences. The agent, by accepting the claim that the door should be open, commits herself to doing what is in her power to ensure that the state of affairs is brought about. This is not necessarily something that can be smoothly incorporated into her existing preferences; it may require the preemption of some of her projects. Furthermore, if the speaker makes the claim that a certain type of action should be performed, and the agent accepts this claim, then the agent's commitment now precludes the possibility of pursuing her objectives in an instrumental fashion at all, since the commitment prescribes an action to the agent directly, without reference to any outcomes or preferences that she may have. The commitments incurred through normative claims of this type provide the agents not just with information, but with *reasons for action*. This is what Habermas calls *strong communicative action*.

Certainly there is no question that agents are capable of making commitments of this type. Making a promise is an obvious instance. If I say, "I'll walk to work today," the content of my commitment precludes my subsequent adoption of an instrumental orientation toward my commute. (The commitment may not ultimately succeed in *motivating* me to refrain from adopting an instrumental orientation, but that is a separate question.[48] It does provide me with a reason to refrain.) The burden of proof on Habermas is to show that these types of normative commitments are bound up not just with special speech acts like promises, where the normative dimension is explicit, but also with the more generic speech act types used to discuss action plans. This general claim must be established in order to show that normative commitments are inevitably incurred whenever language is used to coordinate social interaction. Failure to establish this claim would amount to a concession that suspension of the instrumental orientation is merely an *optional* outcome of agents' decision to employ language as a mechanism for coordinating their interactions.

The other thing Habermas must show is that in order to understand the rightness claim made in a speech act, agents must know what reasons the agent could give for the rightness of the claim. That is, the agent must have some sense of why things *should be* the way the speaker says they should, not just what it would mean for things *to be* the way the speaker says they should. This is necessary in order for the commitment that the agent incurs to be a rational commitment, since the agent must have some appreciation of the reasons that could be given for the action that she is to perform. Just as the agent must be able to situate a truth claim within the language game of assertion, in which reasons for belief are tested, so the agent must able to situate a rightness claim within a practical language game, in which reasons for action are tested. Habermas refers to a language game of the latter sort as *practical discourse*.[49]

Habermas has made at least two discernible attempts to defend this position. Throughout his discussion of validity claims, it is clear that he takes truth as the paradigmatic instance of a validity claim. The other claims, he argues, are introduced on *analogy with truth*.[50] However, he does not specify what the basis of this analogy is, that is, which characteristics rightness and sincerity share with truth that other predicates do not. Habermas's first attempt to develop a general theory of speech acts relied upon a very weak analogy between truth and rightness or sincerity, and as a result, did not support the more general claims about communicative action that he wants to make.[51] The problems with this attempt were fairly obvious, but it is worth reviewing them here, because the difficulties that he experienced help to show exactly what is required in order to discharge the burden of proof that the account must assume. This attempt, which dominated Habermas's early writings, in particular "What is Universal Pragmatics?" unfortunately serves as the basis for the most common interpretation of his views.[52] It is suggested by formulations such as the following:

[A participant in communication] claims truth for a propositional content or for the existential presuppositions of a mentioned propositional content. He claims rightness (or appropriateness) for norms (or values), which, in a given context, justify an interpersonal relation that is to be performatively established. Finally, he claims truthfulness for the intentions expressed.[53]

Here Habermas is attracted by the following architectonic analogy. The meaning of a speech act is usually broken down into three components: literal meaning, conventional force, and speaker's intention. Habermas argues that theories of meaning can be classified according to which component of utterance meaning they take as primary: formal semantics in the tradition of Frege is concerned primarily with literal meaning; "use" theories of meaning inspired by the later Wittgenstein take conventional force as the primary linguistic phenomenon; and intentionalist semantics of the Gricean variety look primarily to speaker's intention for the key to analyzing utterance meaning.[54] Habermas then suggests that his speech act theory is able to integrate all three approaches, by supposing that each of these three components of utterance meaning (semantic/pragmatic/intentional) maps on to one of his validity claims (truth/rightness/sincerity). In this view, knowledge of literal meaning consists in knowledge of the truth conditions, knowledge of conventional force consists in knowledge of the rightness conditions, and knowledge of speaker's intention consists in knowledge of the sincerity conditions.

Thus the speaker, in making an utterance, raises precisely three validity claims, one for each of the components of the utterance's meaning. Understanding the meaning of the utterance consists in knowledge of the conditions under which each of these claims could be redeemed. The difference between the three major classes of speech acts—assertoric, regulative, and expressive—is that they thematize, or assign priority to, one of the three claims. Thus in making an assertion, the speaker claims, first and foremost, that the utterance is true; in issuing an imperative or promise, the speaker claims that the utterance is right; and in making an declaration or avowal, the speaker claims that the utterance is sincere.

This analysis has a certain architectonic elegance but is rather dubious as a theory of meaning. The problems can be seen clearly in the example that Habermas offers in support of his view. He claims to show that every speech act raises three claims on the grounds that the hearer is always capable of rejecting a speech act for three different types of reasons. He gives the following example.[55]

A professor directs the following imperative toward a seminar participant:

(6)   Please being me a glass of water.

The participant can then "reject this request under three validity aspects." He can contest the normative rightness:

(6′)   No. You can't treat me like one of your employees.

He can contest the sincerity of the request:

(6″)   No. You really only want to put me in a bad light in front of the other seminar participants.

Or he can deny that "certain existential presuppositions obtain":

(6‴)   No. The next water tap is so far away that I couldn't get back before the end of the session.

On the basis of this example, Habermas concludes that:

Speech acts can always be rejected under each of the three aspects: the aspect of the rightness that the speaker claims for his action in relation to a normative context (or, indirectly, for these norms themselves); the truthfulness that the speaker claims for the expression of a subjective experiences to which he has privileged access; finally, the truth that the speaker, with his utterance, claims for a statement (or for the existential presuppositions of a nominalized proposition).[56]

The general problem with this view is that it severs the relationship between the rightness/sincerity claims and the propositional content of the utterance.

In this view, what the rightness claim is "about" is the agent's own speech act, not the action or state of affairs that the agent is talking about. (This is what Habermas suggests when he refers above to "the aspect of rightness that the speaker claims for *his action* in relation to a normative context.")[57] One awkward consequence of this view is that since each agent can raise a rightness claim only for his own speech act, it will be impossible for agents to thematize and discuss any particular rightness claim. Rightness claims would be essentially indexical and so could not form the "topic" of practical discourses in the way that truth claims can in theoretical discourses.

However, the more significant problem is that in the case of truth claims, the relationship between meaning and validity, that is, between understanding the utterance and knowing how to justify it, is established by the need to provide a compositional account of the meaning of the propositional content. But the illocutionary component of the speech act has little or no semantic structure, and so there is no obvious need for a compositional theory to explain how it can be understood. This means that if the rightness claim pertains only to the illocutionary component of the speech act, then Habermas's claim that we must know the *reasons* that could be given for or against the rightness and sincerity claims associated with an utterance is completely unmotivated. The need for a compositional theory provided the essential connection between truth claims and justification. Insofar as the illocutionary and expressive dimensions of the speech act are not compositional, there is simply no reason for justification to enter into the story.

This problem is embarrassingly evident in Habermas's treatment of the validity claims associated with (6). In this example, *none* of the three commitments that Habermas ascribes to the speaker pertains directly to the propositional content of the utterance. The rightness claim is for the propriety of the imperative itself and is not specific to its content (e.g., it would make no difference to the rightness claim whether the professor asked for water, coffee, or tea). The sincerity claim concerns the professor's motives and again has nothing to do with the specific content of the request. And the truth claim pertains, not to the propositional content, but to the existential presuppositions that the professor must make in association with the claim. At best, understanding any of these validity claims *presupposes* an understanding of the propositional content of the utterance. But precisely for this reason, the hearer's understanding of the latter could not possibly *consist in* a grasp of the conditions that would make the former acceptable. Without some direct relationship between the propositional content of the utterance and the validity claims, there are simply no grounds for the claim that grasping the reasons that could be given in support of an utterance is essential to understanding it. [58]

This point is sufficiently important that it is worth belaboring with a further example. If Bill says to me "do the dishes," according to this version of Habermas's analysis, I understand this utterance only if I understand the reasons for the associated rightness claim, namely, why Bill considers it appropriate for him to assign household chores. However, there is no reason that my knowledge that Bill is the one assigning household chores today cannot consist in just that, the knowledge that Bill is the one assigning household chores today. No further knowledge is required (and certainly not knowledge of the conditions under which this arrangement could be discursively redeemed). On the other hand, my knowledge of what it means to "do the dishes" cannot consist in simply knowledge of the meaning of "do the dishes," since a theory that ascribed knowledge of meaning to me in this way would wind up assigning an infinite number of primitive knowings, if it were to adequately reconstruct my linguistic competence. By instead ascribing to me knowledge of the procedures needed to determine whether the corresponding state of affairs obtains, the theory is able to characterize my knowledge of the meaning while positing only a finite set of cognitive resources.

Thus there is no reason to think that understanding the rightness claim, on this account, must involve knowing how to justify that claim. It may be that understanding the illocutionary meaning of an imperative always *coincides* with knowledge of how the associated rightness-claim could be discursively redeemed (although even this is unlikely), but there is no reason to say that the latter *consists in* the former. Thus there is no "internal" connection between meaning and validity in the case of rightness claims. With respect to the propositional content, on the other hand, there is such a connection, because an analysis of meaning in terms of inferential role promises to provide an explanation of our ability to understand the meaning of the sentence in terms of a finite set of subsentential components. If the propositional content is given by the truth claim, then it is only the agent's understanding of the truth claim that will require (indeed, *consist in*) knowledge of how the utterance could be justified.

Furthermore, if the meaning of the propositional component of the utterance is always given by its truth-conditions, as this version of Habermas's position suggests, then the theory of meaning would not require anything more than a standard truth-conditional semantics. Rightness and sincerity claims would not really belong in the theory, because grasping these claims would contribute nothing to the agent's understanding of the "speech" component of the speech act (it would be like icing on the cake). In making any speech act, the speaker in a certain sense "claims" to have performed the action correctly, in accordance with the relevant norms. But this is not a feature that is specific to speech acts. If this is all that it means to raise a rightness claim, then *every* norm-governed action makes a rightness claim. Every time I follow a rule, I am in a certain sense "claiming" to follow it correctly. But we would not want to say that by sliding into second base, opening the door for a colleague, or lifting my glass for a toast, I am raising a rightness claim. The fact that a speech act can be rejected by a hearer when it is "not right" demonstrates nothing at all about the validity basis of language, since any of the above nonlinguistic actions can be rejected on the same grounds. Thus the fact that a speaker can reject an imperative with arguments like (6′) has no tendency to show that there is a meaning-constitutive rightness claim raised in (6). If the capacity to reject an action on these sorts of grounds were all it took to demonstrate that a rightness claim has been raised (e.g., "No, you didn't touch first base"), then it could easily be shown that every rule-governed social action raises its very own rightness claim. And if understanding this rightness claim meant knowing how it could be discursively redeemed, then this view would wind up presupposing from the start that all social action is accountable, not just speech acts. Not only would this beg the question against the instrumentalist, but it would also undermine Habermas's own thesis that the accountability of social action is inherited from the accountability of speech acts.[59]

The obvious alternative to this view, which Habermas advances in later work, is to suppose that truth, rightness, and sincerity claims do not govern different *components* of every utterance, but that they consist in alternative ways of *presenting the propositional content*.[60] In this view, speakers use different illocutionary modes to raise different types of validity claims for the associated propositional content. Habermas articulates this idea in the following passage:

Let *Ip* represent any explicit speech act, where *I* stands for the illocutionary component and *p* for the propositional component; and let I_c designate the cognitive use of language, I_e the expressive, and I_r the regulative. We can, in terms of basic attitudes, distinguish intuitively the senses in which speakers want the propositional components (of their speech acts) to be interpreted. In a valid utterance of the type $I_c p$, *p* signifies a state of affairs that exists in the objective world; in a valid utterance of the type $I_e p$, *p* signifies a subjective experience that is manifested and ascribed to the internal world of the speaker; and in a valid utterance of the type $I_r p$, p signifies an action that is recognized as legitimate in the social world.[61]

The key idea here is that with regulative uses of language, the agent does not claim that her own speech act is "recognized as legitimate," but that the action she is instructing the other to perform, p, is recognized as legitimate. Thus understanding the rightness claim that an agent raises with a given imperative requires understanding not why the agent feels justified in issuing it, but rather why the hearer should perform the action specified. In this way, understanding the rightness claim is clearly related to the meaning of the utterance, because the hearer must understand what it is that she is being asked to do, in order to determine whether it is right or wrong.[62]

According to this view, when making an assertion the agent claims that the state of affairs described by a certain propositional content is true, that is, obtains in the world. When issuing an imperative, the agent claims that the state of affairs described by a certain propositional content is right, that is, should be brought about. (This is the key difference: rather than claiming that the utterance itself is right, the speaker claims that the action *referred to* by the utterance is right.) The following sentences render explicit the illocutionary force of an assertion and an imperative, respectively:

(7)   It is true that p.

(8)   It is right that p.[63]

Because the rightness claim is being raised directly for the propositional component, and not just self-referentially for the speech act proper, it can plausibly be maintained that knowledge of the justification conditions for the rightness claim would constitute an understanding of the propositional content. Because of this relationship, it would then be the case that the rightness claim associated with an imperative would be specific to speech acts, and would not be raised by social actions in general. Rightness would therefore figure as the "central notion" in a theory of meaning for imperatives, and participants in practical discourse would be able to thematize and discuss particular rightness claims, in the form of the propositional content of the utterance that the agent committed herself to defending in her regulative utterance.

According to this interpretation, each validity claim would connect up with its respective discourse by serving as a *designated value* in a corresponding system of logic or inference (broadly conceived). Knowing the reasons that could be given in support of an utterance in the appropriate types of discourse would then constitute a grasp of the meaning of that utterance. In Habermas's view, each of the validity claims is supposed to present a different *type* of condition for the acceptability of the utterance. He cashes out this categorial distinction with the idea that each validity claim is tested and redeemed or dismissed in its own matching form of discourse, each of which is conceived of as its own language game, with its own special rules. Truth claims, in this view, are subject to testing in theoretical discourse, just as rightness claims are tested in practical discourse. These discourses are distinguished not by differences in topic, but by differences in structure. There is no generic form of discourse, applied as the case may be to questions of how the world is, or what should be done. Instead, there are (at least) three different types of discourse, governed by different rules of inference corresponding to the type of claim being redeemed.[64]

It is therefore an important characteristic of validity claims that they be related to these different discourse types in the proper way. The nature of this relationship can be tricky to identify. For instance, when an agent says, "the cow is brown," the agent has not raised a "brownness claim" that needs to be redeemed in a special "brownness discourse." Rather, a truth claim has been raised, initiating a theoretical discourse whose *topic* will be cows and brownness. However, when an agent says "murder is wrong," in Habermas's view, she does not initiate a theoretical discourse on the topic or murder and wrongness. Rather, she has raised a "rightness claim" that needs to be redeemed in a special practical discourse. So what exactly makes "is wrong" different from "is brown"?

The characteristic of the truth predicate that appears salient in this context is that it ascribes a property to sentences that is *preserved through valid inference*. Whatever property of sentences it is that truth identifies, it is a property that any inferential consequence of these sentences must also possess. This is not the case with most other predicates. Thus truth appears to have a special, internal relationship to logic, inference, and argumentation. Outside of classical two-valued logic, the property of sentences that is preserved through valid inference is sometimes referred to as *designatedness*, and truth is regarded simply as one type of designated value.[65] If rightness and sincerity are thought of as other types of designated values, each governing nonclassical systems of logic, this provides a natural way of interpreting Habermas's contention that each validity claim is "redeemed" in a corresponding *form* of discourse.

In this view, the structure of the sentence "murder is wrong" is similar to sentences such as "the Duhem thesis is false." Rather than ascribing a property to an object, both sentences render explicit validity claims associated with the sentences that are referred to by their subject. Properly expanded, using the schemas given in (7) and (8), these read something like:

(9)   It is wrong that agents perform acts of murder.

(10)   It is false that verification is holistic.

Redeeming the validity claim then involves showing that the associated propositional content can be warranted in the appropriate form of discourse.

This interpretation makes the best sense out of Habermas's overall view, but it is inconsistent with some of the things that he says. For instance, it should be noted that in adopting this interpretation, one must reject Habermas's claim that speakers raise all three validity claims in every speech act. In fact, I consider this portion of Habermas's view to be a hold-over from the earlier "universal pragmatics" position.[66] If the validity claims must be associated with the propositional content of the utterance in order to motivate the claim that understanding the utterance consists of knowing its justification-conditions, then it makes no sense to suppose that the agent could raise any more than a single validity claim with any given utterance. The agent may incur other commitments through the performance of the speech act, but these cannot be usefully characterized as the result of having raised validity claims, since a grasp of these commitments is not essential for an understanding of the speech component of the speech act.[67] The advantage of the interpretation I am urging is that, by preserving the intrinsic connection between meaning and validity, the strong analogy between rightness/sincerity and truth is able to provide a foundation for the more general theoretical results that Habermas needs to extract from speech act theory.

3.4   The Analogy between Rightness and Truth

In Habermas's view, agents engaged in communicative action are bound by three constraints:

• They pursue their illocutionary aims with the help of speech acts in a performative attitude, which demands an orientation toward reciprocally raised, criticizable validity claims.

• In doing this, they make use of the binding (or bonding) effects of speech-act offers, which come about when the speaker, with his validity claim, gives a credible guarantee for the validity of what is said.

• Whereby the binding (or bonding) effect of a comprehensible and accepted speech act carries over to the commitments relevant to the sequel of interaction that emerge from the semantic content of the speech act—whether asymmetrically for the hearer or for the speaker, or symmetrically for both sides.[68]

The first two points are relatively unproblematic. The point that still needs to be established is the third, which states that commitments relevant to subsequent interaction emerge from the *semantic content* of the speech act. We have seen that for the commitments that fix semantic content to also govern subsequent interaction, it is necessary that the rightness claim pertain directly to the propositional component of the utterance. Thus rightness must be able to serve as what Dummett calls the "central notion" in at least one part of the theory of meaning.[69] Furthermore, for the relevant commitments to be justificatory, rightness must also ascribe a property to sentences that is *preserved through valid inference*, which is to say that it must be able to function as a designated value in a system of logic. These two qualities establish the required relationship between meaning and validity, since it is precisely the relationship between inference and validity claims that makes the latter capable of providing a compositional semantics for natural language.

Unfortunately, even with this clarification of the nature of validity claims, there remains some ambiguity in the way Habermas develops the semantic component of his speech act theory. There are two programmatic strategies available for handling utterances such as imperatives, which are not obviously capable of truth or falsity. These options are summarized by Dummett as follows:

In most languages, there are many sentences whose utterance would not normally be described as saying anything that could be true or false, although they bear a systematic syntactic relation to sentences the utterance of which would be so described. The theory of meaning may be formulated so as not to attribute truth or falsity to such sentences, but to associate with them conditions of a parallel kind, e.g. obedience-conditions in the case of imperatives; in that case, it must make explicit what may be done by uttering a sentence which has a truth-condition, and what other things may be done by uttering a sentence which has a condition of some other kind.[70]

If one adopted this strategy, a natural way of setting up Habermas's formal pragmatics would be as follows: When speakers make assertions, they make a truth claim for a certain propositional content. To understand the utterance is to know its truth-conditions, that is, the conditions under which the validity claim would be satisfied. In a similar way, when speakers make regulative utterances, for example, imperatives, they raise a rightness claim for the associated propositional content. To understand this utterance is to know its rightness-conditions, that is, the conditions under which "an imperative with the content p [is] legitimate or enforceable."[71] Knowing the rightness-conditions would consist in knowing how the speaker could defend the legitimacy or enforceability of an utterance with this content.

On the other hand, to pick up on Dummett again:

> Instead of using the distinct pairs of notions truth/falsity, obedience/disobedience, we could use a neutral pair of terms, say "correct" and "incorrect," for both. . . . The conditions for the correctness or incorrectness of a sentence could then be considered as endowing it with a certain descriptive content, which is in general independent of whether it is being used to make an assertion or give a command; this descriptive content corresponds precisely to what Frege calls the sense of a sentence, or the thought it expresses. In order to understand the sentence, to know its use, it will be necessary that it should contain another symbolic element, conveying the force with which it is used. . . .[72]

If Habermas were to adopt this strategy, the logical connectives could be taken as primitive rules of inference, defined in such a way as to preserve some generic designated value (say a "1"). The content of a proposition would be given by its inferential role, with again some appropriately formulated recursive function specifying the contribution of subsentential components to the inferential role of the sentence as a whole. In this view, the illocutionary mode of the utterance would provide something like a semantic interpretation of the designated value associated with the propositional content: in the case of assertions it would specify that "1" means "true," in the case of imperatives it would specify that "1" means "right," and so on.

Thus the compositional mechanism would provide speakers with generic content, while the illocutionary mode would specify how this content is being used, by embedding it in a speech act that gives it a certain conventional significance, for example, saying something about how the world is, saying something about what actions are normatively prescribed, and so on. The meaning of the validity claims would be given not by any property of sentences that

they refer to, but rather by their performative role in rendering explicit the illocutionary force associated with moves in these language games. To understand
the meaning of the utterance as a whole, it would therefore be necessary to
understand not only the propositional content, but also how this propositional
content is being used.

Both of these strategies, however, have serious problems. The first view,
according to which the propositional content of imperatives is given by
the rightness-conditions of the utterance, is the natural way of interpreting
Habermas's claim that his theory of meaning represents a *generalization* of the
traditional truth-conditional approach.[73] But despite its appealing simplicity,
this strategy generates a number of difficulties. First of all, it makes it difficult
to explain how uniformity of meaning is secured across speech-act types. Thus
it suffers all of the difficulties that beset the original "speech act" project. If
the meaning of terms is given by their contribution to the validity-conditions
of utterances, and different utterances raise different types of validity claims,
there is no reason that any word has to mean even roughly the same thing
when used in different types of speech acts. There is no reason, on this view,
why "plates" could not mean "cows" when used in imperatives, and still mean
"plates" when used in assertions.

Furthermore, although an understanding of the meaning of "plates" is
clearly central to the determination of whether an assertion like (2) is true, it
is not necessarily important for the normative authorization of (1). It is easy
to imagine cases in which there is nothing specific about plates that makes the
content of an imperative like (1) normatively authorized, or "right." The
person could just as well be asking to have cups or bowls placed on the table.
Thus it is implausible to think that, in the case of imperatives, the meaning of
the utterance components is determined by the contribution they make to the
satisfaction of the validity claim associated with the utterance as a whole. So
even though the rightness claim is raised for the propositional content of the
utterance, the rightness claim cannot seriously be thought to provide the *content*
of the utterance.

As well, the idea that different validity claims are associated with different
discourses, and hence different justificatory procedures, means that utterances
of different speech act types will be governed by different compositional principles. For instance, the introduction rule for "and" in theoretical discourse will
be very different from the rule in practical discourse, since the truth of two
sentences, taken separately, entails their truth taken together, whereas the right-

ness to two actions performed separately, does not entail their rightness performed together. If knowing the meaning of an utterance really is knowing
how it could be redeemed in discourse, the consequence appears to be that
"and" means something different when used in assertions than it does when
used in imperatives.

Finally, there are a variety of circumstances in which we use logical connectives to conjoin factual claims and normative authorizations. Thus the
meaning of $a \rightarrow b$ cannot be given as a function of the truth-conditions of a
and the truth-conditions of b in cases where a is true, but b is right. For instance,
the norms that specify sanctions for rule-violations normally combine a
description of an offense with a prescription indicating how it should be punished. A statement like, "He crossed the line, so he should be disqualified," is
difficult enough to classify according to illocutionary mode; it is even more difficult to say what validity claim the inference preserves.

In summary, the use of parallel truth-conditions and rightness-conditions to
provide the meaning of assertions and imperatives makes it difficult to explain
the uniformity of semantic and logical features of language. And the introduction of multiple validity claims makes it difficult to account for the validity of inferences that, in some contexts, preserve a particular type of validity
claim, while in others, appear to convert one type of validity claim into
another.

The second major strategy does not fare much better. It is possible to
imagine that the propositional content is given by some generic notion of
"validity." And certainly the idea that propositional content is given by something that is neutral between the different validity claims fits better with what
Habermas says on the topic, particularly when he distinguishes between the
"success" conditions of an imperative, associated with its propositional
content, and its "illocutionary meaning."[74] And it appears to be the only interpretation that will account for several obvious features of language use.
However, it is still beset by a number of problems.

First of all, the problem of mixed inferences and sentences does not go away.
There is no longer a problem explaining how a *valid* conditional could take a
factual premise to a normative conclusion, since validity will be defined simply
in terms of generic values, 0s and 1s. However, there is now a problem explaining how a single speech act could confer different interpretations onto the designated value, that is, how the "1" in the antecedent could come out as "is
true" and the "1" in the conclusion could come out as "is right," since by

hypothesis there is nothing in the propositional content to distinguish the validity-conditions of the antecedent and the conclusion. Furthermore, given a performative analysis of truth and rightness, it is difficult to see how mixed sentences could be possible at all.

The biggest problem, however, is that an account of propositional content that is uniform across different speech act types requires compositional principles that are similarly uniform. This makes it difficult to believe that there could be structurally dissimilar forms of discourse corresponding to the different validity claims. If the meaning of "and" is fixed with respect to preservation of some generic designated value, then the truth-conditions of an assertion with "and" as its primary connective cannot differ from the rightness-conditions of a sentence with the same content used in an imperative. But this means that the introduction rule for "and," or any other logical connective, cannot differ in theoretical and practical discourses.

These considerations cast doubt upon the idea that there could be any sharp distinction drawn between practical and theoretical discourse.[75] Without special rules of inference, it is not clear that there is anything distinctive about practical reasoning, other than its topic. But a difference in topic can easily be accommodated without introducing a special theory of practical discourse; a pragmatically sophisticated deontic logic will suffice. Since the standard deontic operators are defined truth-functionally, deontic logic is governed by the same validity claim as propositional or modal logic. The difference is strictly one of content, not form, that is, deontic logics have a special set of *axioms*, but the same set of inference rules.

The problems with the idea of a practical form of discourse become even more severe when it is recognized that most arguments about practical questions are conducted with the use of assertions. A speaker may begin with an imperative speech act that raises a rightness claim, but when this claim is challenged by others, the speaker will defend his speech act not with further imperatives, but with assertions. As a result, both theoretical and practical discourses consist in speech acts that raise "truth" claims. This seriously diminishes the plausibility of Habermas's claim that practical discourse is governed by a special set of inference rules. But if there is only one form of discourse, and the validity claim governing speech acts in this discourse is truth, then the only speech act type that connects up the propositional content of an utterance with its inferential role is assertion. This means that the claims to rightness and sincerity, although perhaps important to understanding the speech act as a whole, are not essential to understanding its compositional component. Thus only the truth claim establishes the internal connection between meaning and validity that is at the heart of Habermas's analysis.

Habermas himself has an example that indirectly illustrates this point. Ernst Tugendhat suggested as a counterexample to Habermas's analysis of imperatives in terms of rightness claims that "When a child beggar in Lima says to me 'give me a *sol*' he is neither commanding me nor is he appealing to any validity claim."[76] Habermas responds as follows:

Knowledge of success conditions, which can be derived from the propositional component "*p*" of the imperative "*Ip*," is not sufficient for understanding the illocutionary meaning of this speech act, namely, its specific character as an imperative. Knowledge of (1) the success conditions must be augmented by knowledge of (2) those conditions under which the speaker has reason to regard an imperative with contents (1) as valid, i.e. normatively justified—e.g. that children in the streets of Lima may beg from arriving foreigners.[77]

Notice that Habermas is careful to specify that the rightness claim refers to "an imperative with contents (1)," thereby distancing himself from his earlier "universal pragmatics" position. However, the same type of problem that undermined the earlier view shows up here: it is entirely possible to understand the rightness-conditions associated with this imperative, that is, to be familiar with the institution of beggary, without understanding precisely *what* was said, for example, the precise number of *sols* the child was asking for. On the other hand, if this same propositional content were used to form an assertion, it would be impossible to grasp the truth-conditions of the utterance without also grasping its specific content. This means the internal relationship between meaning and validity, which obtains because the success-conditions are given compositionally, does not hold for all validity claims, only truth. Knowing how the assertion can be justified constitutes knowledge of the success-conditions, knowing how the imperative can be justified does not.

Thus the use of some neutral concept, such as inference, or "success-conditions," to provide the propositional content of utterances provides a more promising basis for the development of an adequate theory of meaning, but seriously weakens the motivation for introducing "rightness" and "sincerity" as separate types of validity claims. If neither type of validity claim is going to play a significant role in the compositional component of the theory of meaning, and if neither is preserved through special patterns of inference, then introducing them generates nothing more than unnecessary confusion.

These considerations lead to the conclusion that with respect to the two interesting characteristics of the truth predicate, that is, those characteristics that establish the internal connection between meaning and validity, there is not a strong analogy between rightness or sincerity and truth. The reason that knowledge of the meaning of an assertoric utterance might be thought to *consist in* knowledge of its truth-conditions is that the latter can be given through a finite set of recursive functions, which would satisfy the compositionality requirement on theories of meaning for natural language. If new validity claims are introduced, claims that are also supposed to capture the compositional aspect of linguistic meaning, then it is difficult to see how uniformity of meaning is secured across speech act types. On the other hand, if the compositional element in the meaning of an utterance is severed from the validity claim, and truth, rightness, etc. are introduced through the illocutionary component, then there cannot be a separate "logic" of practical discourse. Furthermore, it appears that a rightness claim of this type bears a very different relationship to the propositional content of the utterance than the truth claim does.

This means, however, that since it is only knowledge of the propositional content that must be analyzed in terms of the agent's capacity to redeem validity claims discursively, and since it is only in assertions that a validity claim is raised that is internally related to this content, then the built-in structure of accountability of speech acts could only concern what Dummett calls their "descriptive content," that is, their truth-conditions. This means that the second half of Habermas's central argument—the claim that social action inherits its accountability from the use of language as a coordination mechanism—does not go through, because the intelligibility of imperatives does not rest upon any commitment to justification of the background social norms.

When agents issue imperatives under standard circumstances, they may in fact commit themselves to justifying these imperatives with good reasons. However, the preceding analysis shows that this commitment is only *conventionally* bound up with the speech act. It is conventional because the utterance would still be intelligible in the absence of such a commitment. With assertions, on the other hand, the commitments that the agent incurs through their performance are not conventional, because the utterance would be unintelligible in their absence. Thus assertions are rightly privileged in most theories of meaning, on the grounds that the pragmatics of assertion, that is, the structure of theoretical discourse, provides the compositional rules governing the construction of sentences. (This much seems intuitively correct, precisely because the propositional content of every utterance is descriptive in nature. The propositional content of an imperative is a description of a state of affairs in the *physical world*, not in the *social world* of "legitimately ordered interpersonal relations.")

As a result, any commitments that are incurred through a conversational exchange in which one agent issues an imperative to another cannot merely be a product of the illocutionary force of the speech acts employed. The only commitments that need to be generated to produce meaningful communication are commitments to further speech acts, or to actions that reflect a belief that the relevant states of affairs obtain. In no case does understanding a speech act require taking up a commitment to a pattern of nondiscursive action that would restrict the agent's capacity to pursue her objectives in an instrumental fashion. Thus the fact that agents do suspend the instrumental orientation in order to fashion and reproduce social order cannot be explained as the result of the binding/bonding effects of their speech acts. There must be something else at work.

This is an indirect way of saying that the accountability of social action cannot be a product of the accountability of speech acts. However, the results of chapter 2 show that denying the accountability of social action is also a nonstarter, since without some conception of accountability it is impossible to model linguistic communication. My solution, therefore, is to take accountability as a primitive feature of a certain type of social action. Rather than defining instrumental action and speech as the elementary action types, I take instrumental action and norm-governed action as the two elementary types. Speech acts, in this view, are accountable because they are a type of norm-governed action. This is, of course, a reversion to the "classical" sociological position. In the next chapter, I will defend this reversion by showing how a simple concept of norm-governed action makes better sense of precisely those features of linguistic communication that motivated Habermas's account.

4

The Origins of Accountability

Habermas's theory of communicative action takes as its point of departure the observation that the medium of language is peculiarly resistant to instrumental employment. This is what motivates his attempt to ground an alternative, noninstrumental conception of practical rationality in speech act theory. The discussion in the previous two chapters has shown, I believe, that there is a lot to be said for this as an analysis of the limits of instrumental reason, but that it does not provide adequate foundations for an alternative conception of rational action.

However, it is not necessary to look so far to find the limits of instrumental rationality as a model of social action. Both the "classical" sociological analysis of the problem of order and Habermas's claims regarding the "inherent telos" of communication focus on rather spectacular failures of the instrumental model. But there is a less glaring and even more persistent problem with the instrumental model that has received comparatively little attention. This is the problem of indeterminacy.[1] The problem of order and the problem of language both reveal cases where strategic models of social interaction systematically predict something close to the opposite of what actually occurs. The problem of indeterminacy, however, does not involve the same sort of predictive or explanatory failure. What it involves is the failure of instrumental rationality to significantly narrow the range of action alternatives available to agents in many deliberative contexts. The problem is not that the model delivers the wrong answer, but that it often does not deliver an answer at all.

In this chapter, I will attempt to show that the problem of indeterminacy—not the problem of order or language—provides the most powerful motivation for the introduction of a conception of norm-governed social action. I begin (§4.1) by defining the problem in precise terms. I show how the instrumental model, when generalized to social contexts in the manner of "orthodox" game theory, yields hopelessly indeterminate practical recommendations. I provide a brief overview of the results that have led most game theorists to believe that some exogenous choice criteria will have to be introduced in order to stabilize the model. In §4.2, I examine two such proposals, the "psychological" and the "cultural" solutions to the problem of equilibrium-selection, both of which lead to "heterodox" solution concepts. These proposals work by introducing affective and normative standards, respectively, as a basis for the development of shared expectations. I provide a formal analysis of these proposals, in order to show how the relevant beliefs are derived. In section §4.3, I endorse both solutions, but argue that they only work under the assumption that these additional criteria supply different *types* of reasons for action. These different types of reasons, I then argue, not only complement, but also compete with, standard instrumental reasons for action. They therefore constitute, in limiting cases, three different classes of rational social action.

In §4.4, I outline a multidimensional theory of rational action that incorporates these three standards of choice, corresponding to instrumental, normative, and affective reasons for action. This construction provides deliberative microfoundations for the basic typology of social action that has occupied a prominent place in sociology and cultural anthropology since Parsons.[2] I then attempt to show that the accountability structure of speech acts can be explained by the fact that they are a class of norm-governed actions. I conclude (§4.5) by providing an overview of the difference between this theory and Habermas's own. In particular, I argue that while eliminating the contractualist idea that participants in social interaction have always already committed themselves to justifying their actions, the theory is nevertheless able to defend the idea that social order ultimately depends upon a normative consensus among all participants.

4.1 Equilibrium Selection

In chapter 2, the concept of a strategic equilibrium was introduced as a solution to the regress of anticipations that arises when two instrumentally rational agents interact. However, it was also shown that agents are in most cases incapable of "powering" their way through to a solution by systematically entertaining strategic hypotheses. Only in cases where the iterated elimination of dominated strategies removes all but one of every player's feasible actions is there a *procedure* that anyone can follow to determine his or her utility-maximizing course of action.

Nash's solution concept gets around this limitation by effectively ignoring the question of how agents arrive at any particular set of equilibrium beliefs. What Nash saw was that a set of beliefs could *not* be in equilibrium if it contained a certain sort of defect, namely, if it was self-defeating. A self-defeating set of beliefs is one that, if players actually adopted it, would lead them to act in a way that was contrary to the expectations contained in that very belief set. What Nash proposed, plausibly, is that it be a minimal constraint on the acceptability of an equilibrium belief set that it not contain an intrinsic flaw of this type. The definition of Nash equilibrium—that each player's strategy be a best response to the strategies of the others—is just one way of formulating this constraint.

What Nash left entirely open was the question of how agents are supposed to *get* to a belief set that satisfied this or any other constraint. This question is especially pressing when a game has more than one Nash equilibrium. Furthermore, Nash's proposal for solving the existence problem—the introduction of mixed strategies—has the effect of increasing the number of belief sets that satisfy his constraint in most games. Nash thought that this portion of the theory would be fleshed out by future research, but there has been very little progress on this front (if one excludes the resort to heterodox solutions like Schelling's, which will be dealt with in the next section). In fact, it has been "one step forward, two steps back" throughout the history of attempts to solve the equilibrium-selection problem.[3]

Nash's promissory note has been outstanding for so long that many theorists have simply forgotten that it needs to be redeemed. It is often forgotten that Nash's solution does not really *solve* the interaction problem in a way that would be useful to the agents involved; all it does is eliminate a bunch of possible "solutions" that are obviously defective. (It is as if a someone tried to sum up the rationality of scientific inquiry by saying "we try not to believe anything manifestly false." This is certainly a good start, but one senses that there must be more to the story.) If game theory is to provide a workable theory of action it must focus on more than belief sets in the abstract; it must specify a procedure through which these belief sets can be developed by actual agents. Cristina Bicchieri states this requirement in the following way:

This admittedly limited definition of mutually rational beliefs would be completely satisfactory were game theory just bound to define what an equilibrium is and the conditions which make it possible. . . . Yet normative game theory's aim is to prescribe actions that will bring about an equilibrium, which means providing a *unique* rational recommendation on how to play. Indeed, if the task of the theorist were limited to pointing to a set of rational actions, the players might never succeed in coordinating their actions, since different agents might follow different recommendations. Thus a unique rational action for every player must be recommended, together with a unique belief about the behaviour of other players justifying it.[4]

There have been a variety of proposals aimed at resolving this difficulty consistent with the overall reductionist ambitions of the game theory project. Initially it was hoped that the introduction of *refinements* on the Nash solution concept would eventually result in the selection of a unique equilibrium outcome. The idea was simply to keep eliminating belief sets by imposing additional constraints, until only one belief set remained. However, the most widely accepted refinements have resulted in only a slight reduction in the size of the solution sets. Some of these refinements, like *subgame-perfection* and *trembling-hand perfection*, simply correct for the fact that the Nash solution concept places no constraints on players' responses to zero-probability events.[5] While these refinements are clearly simple extensions of the formal conception of strategic rationality, a number of other refinements go much further, introducing substantive constraints on the range of admissible outcomes. These include, for instance, restrictions that serve to eliminate Pareto-inferior equilibria.[6] Although these are in some sense quite plausible, they clearly introduce exogenous choice criteria. Since this represents an obvious departure from the instrumentalist program, solution concepts of this type are not relevant to the immediate discussion.

In any case, it quickly became apparent that there was only so much that could be accomplished by way of refinements. In a game like Battle of the Sexes (figure 4.1), which has two perfectly symmetric pure strategy equilibria, there is, from a purely rational standpoint, simply no relevant difference between the equilibria that could serve as a basis for eliminating one or the other. Refinements serve to exclude Nash equilibria that are, in some often subtle sense, defective. Here there is simply nothing defective about either of the equilibria. It therefore seems quite unlikely that the general equilibrium-selection problem can be adequately addressed through refinements alone.

The second major hope was that equilibrium selection problems might be due to the fact that simple "one-shot" games, like the one in figure 4.1, rep-

Player 2

	L	R
U	3,1	0,0
D	0,0	1,3

Player 1

Figure 4.1

resent too short a time-frame for agents to effectively coordinate expectations. It was hoped that over repeated plays of the same game a dominant equilibrium might emerge. Thus the concern expressed by Bicchieri—that players might never succeed in coordinating because each could follow a different recommendation—would be resolved over the course of repeated interactions.

This hope was dashed by the discovery that over repeated plays of the same game, where players are able to choose actions for each stage game that are conditional upon the actions taken by other players in the previous game, the set of equilibria is dramatically enlarged. Most importantly, proof of the so-called folk-theorem established that for infinitely repeated games, or finitely repeated games where there is some uncertainty as to when the interaction will end, the set of sustainable equilibria is infinitely large.[7] Although this wild proliferation of equilibria does not occur in all finitely repeated games, under no circumstances is the number of equilibria reduced. The basic reason is that iteration of the game allows players to adopt strategies that prescribe a complicated pattern of different actions for different stages. Furthermore, it allows players to perform actions that would be out of equilibrium in any single instance of the game. This not only increases the size of their strategy sets, but makes it so that their past actions become an unreliable indicator of their intentions in future play.

The final and perhaps most widely shared hope was that the introduction of some kind of communication system would help players select an equilibrium. The idea was that a communicative interaction could be modeled as a special type of multistage game, in which one player's choice of action allowed others to make accurate inferences about his beliefs or intentions (as in the game presented in §2.3). A communication system of this type could then be pegged onto a variety of standard games as a "preplay" segment, allowing one or more players to effectively announce their intentions before beginning the game.

This idea was abandoned when it was discovered that models of this type also increase rather than decrease the number of equilibria.[8] The "problem of neologisms" mentioned in §2.4 is the primary source of this difficulty. In non-cooperative games, since the meaning of messages is determined by the effective equilibrium, the occurrence of any message that is not anticipated under the equilibrium is a zero-probability event. This means that Bayesian reasoning places no constraints on the meaning that players can ascribe to such a message. This gives rise to a new batch of equilibria in which players assign to any message that is not expected the same meaning as one of the messages that is expected, rendering the sender indifferent between the two. Because messages in these games are not directly associated with payoffs, none of the standard equilibrium refinements is able to screen out such deviant interpretations. Thus, assuming that players have available a compositional language, this means that the equilibrium set of every such game will be infinitely large.

It should also be noted, as an aside, that all of the attempts that have been made to solve the problem of order through the introduction of commitment mechanisms have the effect of increasing the set of admissible equilibria. This is because any proposal that eliminates sequential rationality amounts to a coarsening of Nash equilibrium, since it allows players to select actions that are not best responses to the actions of the others. Furthermore, since these types of proposals give players the ability to "lock in" to particular strategies, they have the capacity to generate considerable indeterminacy, insofar as players cannot immediately determine whether their opponents are locked in or not. Gauthier tries to counter this difficulty by claiming that players are "translucent" with regard to their intentions, but this amounts to little more than assuming that people have a magical ability to determine each other's mental states.[9] Barring ad hoc postulates of this type, there is no way that introducing commitment can resolve the equilibrium-selection problem, since the point of such a mechanism is precisely to increase the number of strategies available to agents.

The intractability of the equilibrium selection problem effectively undermines the game theory project in its strict reductionist form. This has significant consequences for the instrumental conception of rationality, since it demonstrates that, in a wide variety of social interactions, agents are simply not able to make the inference from a desired outcome back to a favored action. The seemingly plausible idea that agents make decisions by ranking outcomes, then choosing the action that gives them the best outcome, turns out to be false, simply because agents involved in social interactions *are not capable of doing so*. In nonsocial contexts, we might expect them to reason this way, but in social contexts, we must consider the possibility that some new choice criterion must be introduced into the problem.

4.2 Two Solutions

Failure to solve the equilibrium-selection problem has led most game theorists to abandon the strict reductionist program. Even Roger Myerson—one of the strongest proponents of rationality-based game theory—has conceded that the indeterminacy problem reveals "an essential limit on the ability of mathematical game theory to predict people's behavior in real conflict situations and an important agenda for research in social psychology and cultural anthropology."[10] This reflects the general opinion that some additional theory is required to produce an initial specification of which outcome should be expected. What this means, roughly, is that beliefs and desires (as defined in §2.2, i.e., beliefs about states and desires for outcomes) are not always sufficient to provide an agent with good reasons for action in contexts of social interaction. Agents certainly have beliefs and desires, it is just that these often cannot be hooked up in such a way as to yield a determinate practical recommendation. This means that if we want a theory of action in which agents are generally thought to act on the basis of good reasons, some other kind of reason for action must be postulated.

Schelling's "psychological" solution to the problem of equilibrium selection is an example of this strategy.[11] Unfortunately, while Schelling provided a number of persuasive examples of how psychological factors can focus expectations, he did not attempt a formal analysis. In particular, he did not suggest any account of how the psychological states induced by the "salient" or "focal" properties of certain actions were supposed to interact with the belief-desire states posited by standard decision theory. As a result, there has always been a cloud of mystery surrounding Schelling's solution, because no one has been able to state clearly the intentional mechanism through which the results are achieved.[12] At various points, Schelling suggested that the specification of "salience" should be provided by some causal theory, the development of which could simply be farmed out to psychologists. But this is a rather unhelpful suggestion, since its serves only to defer, rather than address the problem. To correct this deficiency, I would like to provide a reconstruction of Schelling's "focal point" theory that incorporates an explicit analysis of the belief-supports that favor the focal equilibrium.

First, I would like to suggest a general principle governing the development of rational expectations. I take it as uncontroversial that rational expectations cannot simply be pulled out of the blue—the rational agent must have some reason to believe that an event will occur in order for her to develop even a prima facie expectation that it will occur. In contexts of social interaction, it therefore seems plausible to suggest that (where A_x is the set of actions available to player x, and $S_x \subseteq A_x$):

(RE) It is prima facie rational for player y to expect player x to do S_x if and only if player y has grounds to believe that player x has a reason to do S_x.

This is subject to a few qualifications. First, having a good reason to do S_x should be interpreted in the weakest sense possible, and should include having positive grounds for performing actions in S_x, and/or positive grounds for not performing actions in the set consisting of every member of A_x that is not in S_x. Thus where $A_x = \{L,M,R\}$, and M is a strongly dominated strategy, the agent could be said to have a good reason to do $\{L,R\}$. This allows the (RE) principle to capture the process by which agents not only pick out particular actions, but also the process by which they eliminate others.[13]

When S_x contains more than one element, player y's expectation may take the form of a probability distribution over this set. When these probabilities are unknown, the expectation simply takes a disjunctive form, for example, player y expects player x to do L or R. An expectation of this type is indeterminate in a very strong sense, in that the agent is unable to assign any probability to the occurrence of either event. In strategic contexts with multiple equilibria, the agent cannot even fall back on Laplace's principle of insufficient reason—assign equal probability to events unless given some reason not to—because such an assignment would constitute the ascription of an out-of-equilibrium mixed strategy to the other player, making any belief set that contained it obviously self-defeating. (For similar reasons, the agent cannot decide what to do by just picking an equilibrium at random, because the resulting randomization over her actions will be a mixed strategy, which will either be out of equilibrium—and so not rational to perform—or else simply one of the elements in S_x.)

The second major qualification is that (RE) specifies what it is rational to expect prima facie, not all things considered. The idea is to capture how an initial rational expectation can be formed. This expectation may then serve as the basis for further inferences that may in turn undermine that expectation (as in the case where player x's anticipation that player y will expect him to do S_x gives him a reason *not* to do S_x). Similarly, there is no specification that the grounds for belief have to be good grounds, all things considered.

The problem of equilibrium selection in multiple-equilibrium games is an obvious consequence of (RE). Although A_x can be narrowed down so that S_x includes only the actions that are included in the various equilibrium strategy profiles, there are no grounds for assigning probabilities to any of the elements of S_x. Without any further expectations regarding S_x, player y has no good reason to choose any particular action in S_y. This means that player x cannot develop further expectations regarding S_y, and so has no good reason to choose any particular action in S_x. In this situation, neither player will have any idea what to do. The only way that this problem can be solved is if some additional reasons for action are introduced that are, in some sense, not caught up in this cycle of interdependent expectations.

At this point, it is helpful to recall the distinction that was drawn earlier between actions and outcomes. In §2.1, I argued that the easiest way for the agent to select an action from among the available options would be simply to choose an action on its own merits. In standard decision theory, however, this is precluded by the instrumentalist assumption that agents only invest outcomes with motivational significance. But since outcomes and actions are both simply events, there seems to be no reason the agent could not invest an action with a similar significance, and therefore select a row "for its own sake." We might imagine that agents start out with two preference orderings, one over the set of outcomes, the other over the set of actions. The goal of practical deliberation, in this case, would be not only to "project" the agent's preferences over outcomes back onto the set of actions, but also to integrate these preferences with the antecedently given attitudes toward the actions themselves.

In the instrumentalist model outlined in chapter 2, "desire" was introduced as a term of art used to refer to an intentional state that expresses a preference over outcomes. Using the Kantian schema, we can say that desires are intentional states with the form "I want o_x." To motivate a specific action, these desires must be hooked up with beliefs, which can be represented in the hypothetical form "If you want o_x, do a_y." Now, if we assume that agents also have

direct preferences for actions, then these will take a categorical form "do a_z."
Thus practical reasoning will generate two sets of "do a", one *derived* from the
agent's beliefs and desires, the other springing directly from her categorical
preferences. The key question then becomes how the interaction between these
two sets of recommendations should be handled.

At the risk of some confusion, I will use the term "principle" to refer to the
intentional state that generates a direct preference for an action.[14] We can
assume that the agent starts with a set of principles and a set of desires, each
having a certain intensity level. These can be represented by matrices, as in §2.1.
Suppose there are three available actions, and three possible outcomes. The
principles can be represented as a set of direct preferences over the actions:

$$P = \begin{bmatrix} 1 \\ .5 \\ 0 \end{bmatrix}.$$

The desires are given as a set of preferences over outcomes:

$$D = \begin{bmatrix} 1 \\ .5 \\ 0 \end{bmatrix}.$$

The first thing that needs to be done is to transform this desire-based ranking
of outcomes into a ranking of actions. This is what instrumental reasoning
accomplishes. A system of beliefs is introduced, for example:

$$B = \begin{bmatrix} 0 & 0 & 1 \\ 1 & 0 & 0 \\ 0 & 1 & 0 \end{bmatrix}.$$

The desire can then be translated into a ranking of actions by multiplying these
matrices, as before:

$$U = BD = \begin{bmatrix} 0 \\ 1 \\ .5 \end{bmatrix}.$$

We now have two preference orderings over actions: one based on princi-
ples: $a_1 \succ a_2 \succ a_3$, and one based on desires: $a_2 \succ a_3 \succ a_1$. For the agent to decide
what to do, these orderings must be integrated. Since the two orderings are

inconsistent, it will be necessary to trade off desires against principles in some way. The easiest way to do this is simply add the P and U matrices together, and see which action has the most support. But to do this, we must provide some basis for comparison between the intensity level of desires and principles. One way to do this is to assign some kind of weight k to principles, which says how much they are worth relative to desires. We can then define the agent's *composite utility function* as:

$$V = kP + U$$

The number that is given to k will vary depending upon the agent's disposition, but also according to the scale that is used to represent the intensity level of her desires and principles. In this example, if we suppose that the agent is indifferent between her strongest desire (for o_1) and her most cherished principle (for a_1), then we can assign k a value of 1. This gives us a composite ranking of her actions as: $a_2 \succ a_1 \succ a_3$. This ranking, it should be noted, is not the same as the ranking represented in either P or U.

Note that this composite utility function is not equivalent to a utility function constructed using the standard von Neumann–Morgenstern procedure.[15] This is because such utility functions represent only preferences over outcomes. One of the virtues of the belief-desire formulation of decision theory presented in chapter 2 is that it renders this assumption explicit. The von Neumann–Morgenstern-style derivations, on the other hand, have a tendency to slip the assumption in through the back door. Rather than directly claiming that agents cannot be motivated by intrinsic features of an action, this possibility is indirectly excluded by one of the choice axioms (usually referred to as "reduction of compound lotteries").[16]

One of the major reasons that so little attention has been paid to the possibility that agents may have preferences over actions is that, in decision theory, the fact that these preferences are associated with actions, and not outcomes, can safely be ignored. This is because there are no circumstances in which the two components of the function could come apart. In game theory, however, the situation is quite different. When strategic reasoning fails to generate a single equilibrium, it means that agents are unable to develop a set of beliefs about which state will obtain. This makes it impossible to say which actions will lead to which outcomes, and as a result, makes it impossible to project the agent's preferences over outcomes back onto the set of actions. For an agent with a standard utility function, this then leaves her without any reason to choose any action. But for an agent with a composite utility function, it just makes the desire component of the function drop out, leaving the original ranking in terms of principles intact.

As an example, consider a case in which I am hoping to meet my friend at a café, and there are two places that we might go. If we both choose to go to the same one, we will be happy, but there is no way for either of us to tell in advance what the other will choose. This means that I know which outcome I prefer, but I do not know which action will bring it about. Absent the needed belief, instrumental reasoning gives me no guidance. So what should I do? One obvious suggestion is that I could simply give up on trying to coordinate and go to the café that I like best. In the original problem, my principle was subordinate to my overriding desire to meet. But having no idea how to satisfy this desire, it simply drops out of the picture, leaving me with just the principle.

The important thing about these principles is that they provide a mechanism that can generate Schelling's psychological solution to the equilibrium-selection problem. Suppose my underlying preference to go to café x is common knowledge. My friend can then guess that, when I give up on trying to coordinate, I will go there. According to (RE), she can then form a rational belief about where I will be. However, once this belief is formed, it then allows her to act on her desire to meet me there. But anticipating this gives me a belief about where she will go, and so the ability to act on my desire. In short, the principle gets converted into a stable pair of instrumental reasons, thereby selecting one of the two strategic equilibria. It is able to do this because it supplies a reason for action that is not caught up in the cycle of interdependent expectations that renders the strategic problem indeterminate.

There is one point that should be noted about this solution. It is crucial that a sharp distinction be maintained between the two *types* of reasons for action. The solution only works if principles are not treated as simply extensions of the set of desires. If this distinction is not maintained, then one might be inclined to simply rewrite the *payoffs* of a game in such a way as to include the effects of principles. Suppose, for example, that we want to modify the game shown in figure 4.1 in order to give player 1 a principle that favors playing D. Many rational choice theorists would be tempted to incorporate this principle simply by increasing the *payoff* associated with the (D,R) outcome to (2,3).

The problem is that the principle is associated not with the outcome, but with the action. So rewriting the payoff function to factor in principles results in a significant loss of information. And the loss of this information eliminates, a priori, the possibility of developing a Schelling-style solution to the problem of equilibrium selection of the type that has been presented here. Writing principles into the payoffs just increases the value of some outcomes, without providing any basis for the development of rational expectations. In figure 4.1, for instance, giving player 1 a principled reason to play D would make (D,R) the focal equilibrium. However, if this principle is introduced into the model simply by increasing the payoff of (D,R) to (2,3), it does not give the players any reason to favor (D,R) over (U,L). It is precisely because principles are *not* associated with outcomes, but with actions, that they are able to escape the regress of anticipations that generates the equilibrium-selection problem. Writing principles into the payoffs gratuitously obscures the fact that some component of the agent's motive for performing the action is noninstrumental, and therefore eliminates an important difference between the two types of criteria that that agent can use to select an action. It is therefore important to always keep two sets of books on the agent's motivations, keeping separate track of principles and desires. Furthermore, the strategic component of social interactions should be modeled using only the U utility function, not V.

Naturally, acting on the basis of a principle can always be redescribed as some kind of instrumental reasoning. So one could say, for instance, that in going to my favorite café, I am not really selecting an action on its own merits, but rather selecting it for some further outcome, such as my enjoyment of the coffee, or the ambiance. But this is to miss the point entirely. The distinction between a principle and a desire flows from the distinction between an action and an outcome, which is in turn determined by the way that events in the decision problem are divided up into those that are under the agent's control and those that are not. In the café example, my going to café x is an action, whereas my meeting my friend at café x is an outcome, since the latter depends upon factors outside my control, namely, her decision, in a way that the former does not. This distinction can be fairly ad hoc in decision problems (since nothing is ever entirely under my control, anything can be called an outcome). But in games the distinction is strict, determined through triangulation of the causal chain of events initiated by either player.

It is important to note, however, that whatever merits this version of the "psychological" solution to the equilibrium-selection problem may have, it remains in many ways quite low-powered. Since it places no substantive constraints on what can count as a reasonable principle, in cases where it does generate a focal equilibrium it still does not place any constraints on the type of equilibrium chosen. This means that, given this mechanism, there is no guarantee that, for example, a Pareto-inferior or risk-dominated equilibrium will not be selected. This might make some people inclined to supplement the model presented here with some account of principle-rationality, paralleling the account of desire-rationality earlier suggested as one the moral realist would like to introduce (or the account of belief-rationality that everyone assumes should be provided). Naturally, the theory of practical rationality—strictly construed—can leave the cognitive status of the agent's principles an entirely open question (just as standard decision theory leaves open the question of where the agent's desire-based preferences come from). But if principles are construed as entirely subjective, then the incorporation of this additional motive into the agent's deliberations will do very little to solve the problem of order. It is only when principles are widely shared—like beliefs—that they can reasonably be thought to increase the orderliness of social interaction.

To see this, consider the café coordination game again. Without knowing where my friend intends to go, I have no instrumental reason for choosing one café over the other. However, if my friend's favorite café is café x, then she would have a reason to select that café. If her preference for café x is common knowledge, this gives us both instrumental reasons to go there. However, since this preference is purely subjective, there is no reason that I must share it. In fact, if it is also common knowledge that my favorite café is café y, then a problem develops. She might get smart, and instead of choosing her own favorite café, choose mine, and vice versa. The problem is then that she starts out with a reason to choose café x, and I start with a reason to choose café y, from which she immediately acquires an instrumental reason to choose café y, and I acquire an instrumental reason to choose café x. These new reasons would then prompt each of us to switch reasons again, and so on ad infinitum. This means that principles are of only limited value in solving equilibrium-selection problems.

If, however, both of us like the same café, then the problem disappears. (Note that the problem does not disappear because the outcome of meeting there is Pareto-superior to the outcome of meeting elsewhere; rather, it disappears because our principled reasons for going to that café are complementary, and so generate a complementary set of instrumental reasons.) This means that the focal-point solution only works on the condition either that the players' principles are complementary, or only one player has principles, or only one player's principles are common knowledge. Since the latter two cases are somewhat marginal, one can see why Schelling's examples of focal-point coordination all draw upon qualities of actions that are associated with widely shared psychological propensities, under the assumption that they would provide complementary rankings of the available actions. In his coordination problems, people try to meet at 12 noon in the central square, armies cease to advance at the shores of the river, and so on. (There is also evidence that people in coordination problems often do not act on their own principles, but on expectations derived from the ascription of "typical" principles to others.)[17] Many theorists, however, have found this to be too narrow a base to provide an adequate account of coordination. They have argued instead that the need for a stock of complementary prescriptions to focus expectations provides an opportunity to explain the role of *culture* in social interaction.[18]

The "cultural" solution to the problem of equilibrium selection differs from the "psychological" solution only in that it takes the relevant intentional states to be derived from a body of shared rules rather than originating in a set of psychological propensities (such as the fact that 12 noon "sticks out" in one's mind). In the café example, a simple rule prescribing a meeting location would eliminate our dependence upon the fortuitous coincidence of principles. This is because a shared rule, unlike a set of subjective principles, has the advantage of providing a set of *complementary* practical prescriptions. This is by virtue of the fact that a rule can specify either obligations for all parties, or else some combination of obligations and entitlements, that result in every agent having a favored action. It is therefore no accident that agents' expectations converge—norms eliminate most of the guesswork involved in coordination through psychological propensities.

Consider the following example: In the so-called Battle of the Sexes game shown in figure 4.1, a husband and wife want to go out together, but the husband's preferred form of entertainment is the wife's least preferred, and vice versa. Now suppose the couple lives in a society in which there is a certain expectation of "gentlemanly" conduct, such as a widely shared norm that "husbands should defer to wives in their choice of evening entertainment." Or they might live in a society with less sex-role differentiation, where alternation on a weekly basis is prescribed. The point is simply that any such norm can provide a focal point that serves to favor one equilibrium over another.

However, if norms are to provide a mechanism to generate equilibria, they must in some way provide agents with reasons for action. We can represent a norm as a profile, $(a_{1x}, a_{2y}, \ldots a_{nz})$, that prescribes an action for some or all players involved in an interaction.[19] To be guaranteed effective, the norm must be common knowledge among all players. An agent who decides to employ a particular norm in making a decision takes the portion of the norm that pertains to her and adopts it as a selection criterion. We can refer to a principle that is adopted in this way as a *normative reason*, and action motivated by such reasons *normative action*. By contrast, we can call any action motivated by purely subjective categorical preferences as *affective action*.

In the Battle of the Sexes game, the "gentlemanly" norm would take the form (L). This rule provides player 2 with a normative reason to select L, player 1 an expectation that player 2 will select L, player 1 an instrumental reason to play U, player 2 an expectation that player 1 will play U, and therefore, player 2 an instrumental reason to play L. The same result would emerge if the rule assigned player 1 an entitlement to play U. (In this way, both obligations and entitlements are equivalent "normative" expectations; it is just that the player under obligation fares worse under the prescribed equilibrium than he would under some other.)

In this way, principles provide an intentional mechanism through which patterns can be transmitted from the level of cultural knowledge to that of concrete social interactions. The reason standard instrumental theories encounter a "problem of order" is that, according to the instrumental view, culture can determine behavior only indirectly, by patterning agents' desires. When agents then seek to satisfy these desires in an instrumental fashion, it generates both the suboptimality and indeterminacy that is characteristic of strategic interaction. This is why instrumental action can be expected to "scramble" any cultural pattern that it encounters. The alternative is to give culture a more direct role. Social norms, at the level of society, and principles, at the level of the individual, provide an alternative mechanism for culture to pattern social interaction. When agents act on the basis of a rule that prescribes particular actions—when they adopt this rule as a *reason for action*—the regress of anticipations that generates strategic indeterminacy never has a chance to get started. The analysis presented here is intended to provide a simple account of how the deliberative considerations that spring from such rules can be integrated with the belief-desire states posited by standard decision and game theory.

4.3 A Problem

With this heterodox account of equilibrium selection developed, it is now time to face a very important question. So far, I have focused exclusively on situations in which affective or normative reasons for action can be *converted* into instrumental reasons. In such cases, the agent whose principle provided the initial set of rational expectations was endowed with a set of redundant reasons for action. In the Battle of the Sexes game with the "gentlemanly" rule, for instance, player 2 wound up with both a normative and an instrumental reason to choose L. In this sense, his motive for choosing L was overdetermined.

What has not yet been considered are cases in which these reasons conflict. Consider a game with payoffs as in figure 4.2, but where a fairness rule prescribes ([.5U,.5D], R). Although this gives each player an attractive outcome of (2,2)—the highest symmetric payoff available—it is not a Nash equilibrium (since player 1 would defect to D). The only Nash equilibrium is the mixed strategy profile that gives the Pareto-inferior (1.8,1.8) outcome. Presenting the psychological and cultural action theories as "equilibrium-selection mechanisms" and narrowing the relevant action sets in advance to those included in equilibrium strategy profiles, tacitly suggests that instrumental reasons should automatically trump other types of reasons. The question now is why, or whether, this should be so.

It certainly cannot be denied that principles should be capable of motivating people to act. In a social context in which the agent is totally ignorant of the other players' preferences, he cannot have any instrumental reasons for

		Player 2	
		L	R
Player 1	U	3,0	1,3
	D	0,3	3,1

Figure 4.2

doing one thing or another. This makes him, from an instrumental standpoint, completely indifferent among his actions. But unlike Buridan's ass, he will not stand transfixed; he will look to see which action he most prefers. This case is somewhat different from the standard equilibrium selection problem in that the use of a principle in the agent's practical deliberation does not generate any further instrumental reasons for action. Even after the principle has been adopted as a reason for action, the agent will still have no way of knowing which state will obtain, and so will not be able determine which outcomes are associated with which actions. In such cases, it is natural to assume that the agent will not only adopt the principle as a reason for action, but will proceed to perform the action that this principle prescribes.

It is this presumption—that when unable to reason instrumentally, agents will perform the actions that they most prefer—that allows principles to provide the mechanism that solves the equilibrium selection problem. But if this is acceptable, then on pain of denying (RE), we are committed to the view that agents can be effectively motivated by different types of reasons for action. And if each of these types of reasons is able, independently, to motivate the agent, then these reasons can, in principle, conflict. Conflicts can arise precisely because different *types* of reasons for action are at stake: for example, instrumental reasons, which pick out actions for the sake of the outcomes they can produce, and normative reasons, which pick out actions for their intrinsic merits.[20] What this analysis reveals is a kind of structural conflict within the will that cannot arise in ordinary instrumental reasoning.

From a purely technical standpoint this is not really a problem. The potential for conflict between desires and principles was simply assumed in §4.2 when k was introduced to represent the relative weight that should be assigned to each consideration. The philosophical problem arises when one asks how *much* value should be assigned to each consideration. An agent faced with incompatible instrumental and normative reasons for action (as in the figure 4.2 plus "fairness rule" example) is, in effect, confronted with a *higher-order choice problem*. She must not only decide what to do, she must decide *how* to decide what to do. She must determine which set of reasons to assign the greatest weight in determining her actual conduct.

This higher-order choice problem was first clearly identified by Kant, in his later work on practical philosophy.[21] His typological action theory incorporated two types of incentive—inclination and duty—that would often lead to contradictory practical prescriptions. In Kant's view, there is nothing intrinsically wrong with adopting either inclination or duty as the basis for the determination of the will.[22] Thus the agent is faced with the higher-order problem of determining what type of reasons to assign *priority* in his practical deliberations. To argue that morality is rational, Kant considers it his task to show that the rational individual would rank reasons stemming from duty above those stemming from inclination. His strategy is argue that the agent's particular choices reflect an underlying disposition (*Gesinnung*), which is the "ultimate subjective ground" for the adoption of maxims. He then suggests that something like *authenticity* requires us to adopt a fundamental choice disposition that gives priority to the moral law. By taking up inclination as the incentive of his maxim, the agent uses his free will to act in the same way that he would act if had no such freedom. He thereby fails to live up to his potential as a rational, free being.[23] As a result, the only choice disposition that would remain stable under critical reflection is one that assigns the moral law deliberative priority.

The details of this argument are not terribly persuasive, but the way that Kant sets up the problem is essentially correct. Of course, Kant assumes that the agent's fundamental choice disposition must provide a lexical ordering of reasons for action (this is, in part, what generates his famous moral rigorism). This is consistent with his characterization of hypothetical imperatives, whereby states are treated as though they were always known with certainty ("if you want o, do a"). When states are treated probabilistically, it becomes more natural to treat both desires and principles as having intensity levels (perhaps "appropriateness" levels in the latter case), and to regard the fundamental choice disposition as assigning a certain weight to each factor. So if we assume that an agent's full set of reasons for action can be represented using a *composite utility function*, as defined earlier ($V = kP + U$), then k represents precisely the fundamental choice disposition that Kant identified.

The other major insight in the way that Kant sets up the problem lies in the way that he tried to solve it. He develops the appeal to authenticity because he sees quite clearly that he cannot appeal directly to either moral or prudential considerations as reasons for a particular choice of fundamental disposition. If we are trying to decide what type of reasons for action to consider, we clearly cannot appeal to considerations that have force only relative to one of these sets of reasons. Instrumental reasons for reasoning instrumentally and normative reasons for reasoning normatively are question-begging, but from this perspective, so are instrumental reasons for reasoning normatively, and normative reasons for reasoning instrumentally.[24] (Translating this into the idiom used here: one might argue that k should be assigned a high value, because this maximizes U in the long run. But why maximize U? Why not maximize P? To develop an argument that is not question-begging, it will be necessary to advance some considerations that do not already presuppose that either U or P is more important.)

This is a point that needs to be emphasized, because large segments of the history of moral philosophy have consisted in attempts to develop instrumental reasons for assigning normative reasons for action priority (e.g., Socrates: "injustice, wherever it occurs, be it in a city, a family, an army, or anything else, results in making it incapable of achieving anything as a unit because of the dissensions and differences it creates.")[25] One might argue, for instance, that since in figure 4.2 conformity to the fairness rule gives each agent a higher payoff than the strategic equilibrium, each of them has an instrumental reason to assign a high value to k. (This is, more or less, David Gauthier's central claim in *Morals by Agreement*, although he also assumes that the fundamental choice disposition must provide a lexical ordering of reasons for action.) Unfortunately, this is faulty instrumental reasoning, since each agent would get an even higher payoff by appearing to assign a high value to k, but then actually defecting when the time comes. This produces a "higher-order" Prisoner's Dilemma in the choice of fundamental disposition. This is a very general feature of instrumental arguments for reasoning morally. Such arguments often sound plausible when formulated at a high level of generality, but have invariably proven to be invalid when the attempt is made to specify them in any detail.[26]

One thing, however, that Kant's argument shares with the more standard instrumentalist ones is the assumption that something internal to the structure of rational agency requires that some particular type of reason for action be given priority. On the other hand, the way that the problem has been set up here—in terms of alternative selection criteria—suggests that the question may just be indeterminate. There may simply be nothing intrinsic to the structure of decision that makes it uniquely rational to rank actions directly, rather than via outcomes, or vice versa.[27] Thus the question "Is it rational to do such-and-such?" may only be answerable once it has been specified what type of reasons one is looking for.

To clarify this, it is helpful to draw a comparison between the agent's fundamental choice disposition and the agent's attitudes toward *future* satisfaction. The choice between acting for the sake of an action and acting for the sake of an outcome is structurally analogous to the choice between acting for the sake of an outcome *now* or acting for the sake of an outcome *later*. In many situations, agents are faced with not just a single outcome, but a stream of future outcomes. To select a utility-maximizing course of action, the agent must have some way of comparing the present value that satisfying some desire at time t_1 has against the present value of satisfying it at time t_2. The standard way of doing this is to introduce a discount rate that reduces the present value of future payoffs at some uniform rate. This discount rate is normally assumed to reflect the risk that future outcomes will not be achieved, but also an element of pure time-preference. This is owing to the psychological fact that, all uncertainty aside, future satisfaction appears to be worth less to us, at present, the further removed it is in time.

Informally, the way we discount the future reflects the way we balance our "short-term" against our "long-term" interests. Putting it this way might lead us to ask, naively, "What is the optimal rate of time-discounting?" or "What rate of time-discounting would a rational agent select?" But it is easy to see that this question is senseless if "optimal" and "rational" are understood instrumentally. There is no such thing as a utility-maximizing rate of time-discounting, because utility-maximization is defined as maximization of *time-discounted* expected utility. Thus every rate will be reflectively endorsed by the person who has that rate. This is trivially so, because it is in one's short-term interest to favor one's short-term interests, and in one's long-term interest to favor one's long-term interests.

So from the standpoint of an individual engaged in deliberation, it is senseless to ask what rate of time-discounting should be adopted. At best, agents will simply favor whatever rate it is that they have. Similarly, I would like to suggest that it is senseless for an individual to ask which type of fundamental choice disposition she should have. The question only makes sense after such a choice has been made. It is no surprise to then find that each choice standard will be reflectively endorsed by any agent who has adopted that standard. One will be better at achieving one's instrumental goals if one assigns instrumental reasons for action deliberative priority, just as one will be better at fulfilling one's normative obligations if one assigns normative reasons for action deliberative priority. If this is correct, then the agent's fundamental choice disposition, like her rate of pure time-preference, should be taken to be exogenously determined from the standpoint of practical rationality.

Of course, to say that the agent's fundamental choice disposition is not determined by practical rationality is not to say that it is arbitrary. It just means that the agent does not choose it. This does not mean that it cannot be determined by environmental factors, such as evolutionary selection or socialization. It is worth noting that, from the strict first-person perspective, there is no reason for an agent to select one discount rate over another. However, if agents are in a position to promote particular discount rates *for each other*, they may have significant reasons for favoring a longer planning horizon. This is because agents who discount the future less heavily are able to sustain a greater range of cooperative behavior, which provides potential benefits for all those who interact with them. Perhaps this is why socialization plays an important role in shaping our rate of time-preference. From a very early age, we are pressed to acquire discipline, to be less impatient, to defer gratification, and so on. Similarly, there are obvious evolutionary reasons why natural selection would favor organisms with a planning horizon suitable to their natural lifespan. I do not intend to argue in favor of either explanation here; I simply want to point out that the introduction of a social and environmental perspective provides a number of resources for explaining the source of the discount rates that we employ.

The same kind of analysis can be applied to the fundamental choice disposition. Not only are agents who possess fundamental choice dispositions that assign significant weight to normative reasons for action less likely to experience coordination failure, they are also able to engage in patterns of cooperative activity that would otherwise be unavailable. When the strategic outcome of an interaction is suboptimal, such agents are able to adopt a social norm that makes the set of actions that generates a Pareto-superior outcome obligatory (thereby "solving" the Prisoner's Dilemma). Thus it is not surprising to find that many of our socialization practices are aimed at promoting cooperative behavior. Through socialization, we teach children to control their impulses, to subordinate their self-interest when need be, and above all, to acquire the self-mastery needed to conform to the set of shared social norms.[28] The overall consequence of successful socialization, I would argue, is that it produces individuals who weigh normative reasons much more heavily than instrumental ones (which, in the limiting case, takes the form of a lexical ordering of choice standards).

4.4 Social Norms

For an agent who is endowed with a fundamental disposition that provides either a weighting or a lexical ordering of the various choice standards, and who is acting in the context of a system of social norms that provides the basis for a set of shared expectations, each social interaction problem can be given a determinate solution. The sort of considerations that might combine to recommend a particular action can be very complex. For instance, the agent could decide that a_1 is obligatory on normative grounds, and then proceed to perform it. On the other hand, she might eliminate a_3 on normative grounds, but decide that both a_1 and a_2 are permissible. She could then decide that o_1 is the most desirable outcome, discover that a_1 will be the most efficacious in bringing about o_1, and so decide on instrumental grounds to opt for a_1. Both deliberative processes produce the same action, except that the former relies upon strictly normative reasons, while the latter combines normative and instrumental reasoning (and is thus "multidimensional").[29] Most social interaction involves a complex combination of considerations, but insofar as one type of reasoning predominates, we can distinguish between various pure types of rational action.

This model provides microfoundations for the classical sociological theory of action, expressed paradigmatically by Parsons in his middle works.[30] Parsons thought that reasons for action could be divided into three types: instrumental/cognitive, normative/moral, and affective/expressive. He referred to the set of reasons that were assigned priority by the deliberating agent as his or her "orientation."[31] The particular orientation that is to be expected from agents in any particular interaction is then given by a set of "pattern variables," which are generalized social expectations that specify when it is appropriate to let one or another orientation prevail.

The account developed so far provides a plausible reconstruction of what it means to adopt a "normative orientation," but it does not yet explain why social norms have the structure of accountability that featured prominently in Parsons's analysis, and that motivated Habermas's detour into speech act theory. Habermas, it will be recalled, claimed that agents are held accountable to a set of social norms because of commitments that they have tacitly incurred, through speech acts, prior to the interaction sequence. In my view, the accountability structure of social norms is to be explained not by such antecedent commitments, but by the mechanism that must be in place in order to ensure that agents acquire the correct fundamental choice disposition through socialization. This is a line of argument that was initiated, but inadequately developed, by Parsons.

Accountability is an excellent term because it captures two related aspects of the structure of norm-governed action, namely, that agents can be called upon to verbally justify their actions vis-à-vis the relevant norms (to "give an account)," and that they can be sanctioned for failure to comply with the prevailing normative expectations (they can be "held accountable"). The model developed so far does not make norm-governed action accountable. For example, if player 1 in figure 4.2 simply ignored the fairness rule and played his maximizing strategy, this would disappoint player 2's expectations, but the theory does not specify a change in either player's normative status, such as an obligation to offer an explanation, or an entitlement to take punitive action.

To understand the accountability of social action, it is necessary to examine more closely the nature of the sanctions that accompany norm-violation. There is something about these sanctions that has often struck theorists as mysterious. To clarify this, it is necessary to draw a set of distinctions between the various ways that agents can disappoint the expectations of others in an interaction. According to standard game-theoretic usage, agents are said to *defect* when they adopt a utility-maximizing strategy that does not belong to the strategy profile that other players expect to be played. Thus defection refers to unexpected actions that occur in contexts of instrumental interaction. *Dissent* can be characterized as a situation in which an agent adopts a normative reason for action other than the one expected by other agents. The agent is still respecting a principle, just not the one that others think should be followed. Dissent therefore arises entirely within a norm-conformative orientation. *Deviance*, on the other hand, is a technical term used by Parsons to characterize the state of affairs in which an agent disappoints the expectations of others by adopting an inappropriate action orientation, for example, by assigning instrumental reasons priority over normative ones. Naturally, this can only be detected—when it can be detected—indirectly, via the action performed.

The indeterminacy of the higher-order choice problem means that every norm-governed social interaction harbors the potential for deviance.[32] Parsons argued that the key to understanding the sanctions that accompany social norms is to recognize that they are in place to deter this *deviance*, not defection or dissent. Thus these sanctions do not punish the agent for failing to perform a certain set of expected actions; rather, they punish the failure to employ a particular type of standard in deciding which action to perform. For this reason, actions are sanctionable only insofar as they reveal a failure to adopt the correct standards of choice (which is why we hesitate to punish those who have engaged in acts of civil disobedience). This insight provides the key to understanding the accountability structure of norm-governed social action.

The sanctions that accompany social norms have often appeared mysterious because theorists have tried to understand them as an attempt to discourage defection or dissent. The most common view is that sanctions exist to control defection, providing agents with an instrumental reason for conforming to a favored strategy profile. This idea underlies the Hobbesian "solution" to the problem of order. The claim, roughly, is that agents adopt a strategy profile that calls for sanctioning those who fail to conform to that profile. They are willing to adopt such strategies because the associated equilibrium is Pareto-superior to one that involves no sanctioning system. Thus the fact that agents conform to the rules, and the fact that agents punish those who fail to conform to the rules, can be explained from an entirely instrumental point of view.

As is well known, this idea encounters significant difficulties, both empirical and theoretical. Since punishing people is usually costly or inconvenient for the person doing the punishing, a free-rider problem emerges that undermines the integrity of the punishment mechanism.[33] Furthermore, reoptimization undermines the credibility of the threatened sanction—once the crime has been committed, the deterrent force of the sanctions has failed, and so what is the point of incurring the costs associated with carrying out the punishment? In both cases, the problem can be solved only by having an escalating hierarchy of threats—someone must threaten to punish anyone who fails to punish those who break the rules. This is the basic flaw in Hobbes's proposal—it requires a so-called perfect tyranny, which is impossible to construct in the "pyramid" shape that the state assumes.[34] One can construct a decentralized enforcement system that functions in this manner, but such systems work properly only under rather specialized conditions.[35]

Apart from these conceptual difficulties, there are a number of empirical problems with attempts to understand social sanctions in purely instrumental terms. First of all, there is the obvious evidence that agents often conform to rules and sanction violations even when it is clearly against their interest to do so. Normally, it does not require a "policeman at the elbow" to stop people from littering in parks or stealing from each other's vegetable gardens. Furthermore, people often carry out punishments even when they have no real incentive to do so. Certainly there are times when people are being honest when they say "this is going to hurt me more than it hurts you." In both cases there is a sort of commitment involved that, as we have seen, cannot be captured in instrumental terms.

The more significant empirical observation, however, is that most social sanctions do not have any intrinsic punitive quality. Often all they do is signal a shift in attitude. For example, when an agent violates certain rules of the road and incurs the "natural" punishment of a collision, the disuasive power of the sanction is clear. But similar sorts of violations may lead to the "social" sanction of being honked, yelled, or gestured at. It is not as obvious how these constitute punishments, since the sound of a horn does not in itself "harm" anyone. Similarly, when an agent says "I'm very disappointed in you" to a friend, this constitutes an extremely powerful social sanction. But it is entirely symbolic in nature. Sanctions of this type take effect by promoting feeings of guilt, shame, regret, and so on in the agent, but this can only work on people who are already in some way moved by the collective sentiments that back conformity to the rule. This is what inspired Emile Durkheim's claim that sanctions do not so much enforce the rules as articulate and reaffirm them in the face of violation. Thus sanctions are only the *external sign* of an underlying shared normative obligation, not a constitutive element.[36]

Durkheim attempted to explain social order by supposing that agents come to be motivated to conform to social norms by internalizing the sanctions associated with their violation. According to this view, after having been sanctioned a few times, agents will conform to a norm of their own volition, because failure to do so triggers feelings of guilt, shame, or remorse. For similar reasons, when fully socialized agents fail to respect the normative order, the sanctions applied against them can be largely symbolic in nature, because they are used only to activate these underlying feelings. According to this view, sanctions exist initially to punish, but punishment has a socializing effect by virtue of our capacity for internalization. This permits the punishment sequence to become abbreviated, and finally, rendered entirely symbolic, as internal control mechanisms slowly come to take over from external ones.

Durkheim's view lends itself quite easily to a somewhat oversimplified behaviorist interpretation. According to this view, the function of sanctions is to condition agents to conform to particular behavioral expectations. The sanction serves as a psychological mechanism that instills the appropriate principle in the agent. Thus it is not the anticipation of a punitive sanction that causes the agent to alter her course of action, but rather the imposition of the sanction that builds up a negative cathexis of the action that triggered it, thereby making it less likely to be repeated. The agent's relation to the sanction therefore has a "backward-looking" rather than a "forward-looking" character. But if the agent's only reason for not performing an action is this accumulated negative cathexis, then the inhibition appears somewhat irrational whenever there is evidence that the sanction has been removed. More importantly, this model cannot account for the flexibility of the dispositions that agents acquire through socialization. The behaviorist model claims that agents internalize the sanctions associated with particular patterns of action, but agents seem to have the capacity to modify most acquired routines significantly and even to substitute alternatives. Often, what agents appear to acquire through socialization is a set of extremely diffuse goals, for example, a desire to be a "good person," to "get along with others," and so on. The diffuseness of these commitments is reflected in the fact that their social competences are quite flexible; agents are able to substitute other cultural practices for their own. Furthermore, the mechanism through which they make such substitutions involves a variety of explicitly cognitive resources (hence the difference between primary and secondary socialization).[37]

Observations such as these led Parsons to suggest a conception of socialization according to which agents do not acquire a set of specific dispositions to perform particular actions, but rather an entirely formal disposition to assign a certain class of practical considerations deliberative priority. According to this view, agents are not punished for failing to conform to a particular normative pattern per se, but only insofar as their actions reflect a failure to assign normative reasons for action deliberative priority. Socialization designates the process through which *these* sanctions are internalized. So according to this Parsonian conception, sanctions secure social order not by punishing simple violation of the rules, but by punishing *motivated* violation of the rules, that is, deviance. This means that sanctions provide agents with an instrumental reason to follow the rules, but also, when internalized, they provide a disposition to assign normative reasons deliberative priority over instrumental.

According to this view, normative integration requires at least some agents who are disposed to assign normative reasons priority, and for those agents who are not so disposed, an effective system of sanctions giving them instrumental reasons for conforming to the normative pattern. There are two important components to this view. First, the norm-conformative orientation is understood to consist in both a disposition to assign normative reasons priority in one's practical deliberations, and *the disposition to punish those who do not.* Thus punishment of deviance is not a specific normative obligation, but a structural feature of the norm-conformative orientation. The second component of the view is that social sanctions, when implemented through a norm-conformative orientation, function simultaneously as a mechanism of *socialization* and *social control*. Social control refers to their instrumental significance—sanctions make deviance unprofitable, from an instrumental point of view. Socialization refers to their symbolic quality—through their expression of disapproval and the internalization mechanism, sanctions generate the disposition to assign normative reasons for action deliberative priority.

Parsons's argument in support of this view begins by considering the limiting case of what he calls "full institutionalization." In interactions of this type, there is a perfect complementarity of expectations and obligations, that is, both the content and the mode of application of all relevant norms are accepted and common knowledge among both ego and alter, and both agents assign priority to normative reasons for action. This arrangement "will lead to perfectly articulated, conflictless action on the part of the several actors."[38] Furthermore, fully institutionalized interaction cannot be destabilized through simple deviance, since the disposition to assign normative reasons priority includes a disposition to punish those who fail to do so. Thus entry into a fully institutionalized interaction context gives any agent who does not share the norm-conformative orientation an instrumental reason to conform to prevailing normative expectations.

Thus social order can remain stable even with some variation among agents in the strength of their fundamental choice dispositions. Under conditions of full institutionalization, each agent's motive is essentially overdetermined, because his normative obligations *coincide* with his self-interest. (It is this overdetermination of the motive that, according to Parsons, is the "hallmark of institutionalization.")[39] As long as a sufficient number of other agents can be expected to retain a normative orientation, it does not really matter what orientation a particular agent adopts. Thus "motivational orientations within the personality system might vary among different individuals who conform equally with the same set of expectations."[40]

Naturally, even though the sanctions are addressed to the instrumental rationality of potential deviants, they are not motivated by instrumental considerations on the part of those applying them. This means that agents will punish deviance only under the condition that they themselves retain a normative orientation when confronted with it. Situations may arise, however, in which an agent can, through his deviant conduct, motivate others to deviate as well.

Having switched to an instrumental orientation, these agents will then reoptimize and decide not to apply sanctions. This gives rise to the problem of collective deviance: "Alter's and ego's alienative need-dispositions, that is, may match each other's, so that instead of imposing negative sanctions for ego's deviant tendencies, and driving ego to alienation from him, alter tends to act in such a way as to reward them."[41] For this reason, there is always some potential for instability in any social order.

The first barrier to this sort of collective deviance is the fact that any agent's fundamental choice disposition may be highly resistant to deviance. It may simply not be possible to induce some agents to suspend sanctions in a given situation. The second barrier to collective deviance arises from the structure of instrumental action itself. Since agents cannot be motivated to deviate through normative considerations, they must be given instrumental incentives. But this will often not be possible. Because the initial deviant is not acting out of a normative orientation in the first place, he cannot credibly *commit* himself to providing any of the benefits that he may be in a position to offer those who join him. Furthermore, the potential for suboptimal strategic equilibria makes collective deviance problematic. The fact that "there is no honor among thieves" makes it difficult to sustain collective deviance, and therefore seldom tempting for others.[42] In the end, it is the *instability of social orders based on instrumental forms of action* that makes large-scale deviance highly problematic.[43]

It is important to keep in mind what this argument does *not* claim. It is nowhere supposed that under conditions of full institutionalization agents are actually motivated by the negative sanctions. This is the primary point of disagreement between Parsons and the Hobbesian. It is only if an agent happens not to assign priority to the normative point of view that the sanctions become relevant. For example, I do not kill people who get in my way because, from a normative point of view, I consider murder wrong. This motive has, to date, always been sufficient (in the sense that murder has never entered into my practical deliberations as an option to be considered). But if for some reason I chose to take a more instrumental perspective, the fact that others consider murder wrong and express this attitude in part through an organized penal system, ensures that I also have instrumental reasons for not murdering others.

Of course, this argument shows only that institutionalized interaction patterns can remain stable. The second part of the Parsonian account is the claim that noninstitutionalized interaction patterns tend to become institutionalized over time, that is, agents will come to regard their de facto interaction patterns as obligatory. All interaction contexts can be located somewhere on a continuum between two pure types: institutionalization and *anomie*. Anomie is roughly equivalent to an instrumental "state of nature," characterized by the "absence of structured complementarity of the interaction process."[44] This lack of complementarity means that each agent's sanctions bear no systematic relationship to the set of social norms, and so there is room for all sorts of conflict between an agent's normative obligations and her self-interest. According to Parsons, anomic conditions are inherently unstable. There is a mechanism built into the structure of social action that (ceteris paribus) pushes interaction systems toward the institutional end of the continuum.

Parsons argues that sanctions are effective because they "are treated as 'expressions' of the appropriate attitudes, not simply as discrete rewards and punishments."[45] He suggests that this is because the agent develops a sensitivity not only to the actions of others insofar as they affect his gratification-deprivation balance, but also to their *attitudes* toward him, insofar as they reflect a positive or negative evaluation of his performances:

> Thus, sanctions have two kinds of significance for ego. First, alter's intentional and overt action, which can change ego's objective situation, may have direct significance to ego by increasing his opportunities for gratification or limiting them, insofar as alter controls important aspects of ego's situation of action. But ego through generalization also becomes sensitive to alter's attitudes toward him and his action, so that even where alter has no specific intentions in the situation, it will still matter to ego whether alter approves or disapproves of his action—whether he shows love, hostility, or some other attitude toward him.[46]

Parsons argues that it is through the *mechanism of attachment* that the agent develops this "social-relational" need. When the agent perceives a pattern of sanctioning response to his actions, he generalizes this to apprehend the rule that governs alter's expectations. He may do so at first merely as a way of determining how best to avoid such sanctions in the future. But insofar as his relation with the other is a supportive one, he may also displace his cathexis from the actual sanctions to the attitudinal state that determines them; for example, he may acquire a desire to please the other agent, or earn her respect, and so on. (This is why strong emotional attachments play such an important role in early childhood development.) The agent can then be said to "internalize" the other's expectations, in the form of the rule that governs them.[47]

But so far, this does not provide the agent with a genuine normative orientation, because his motivation is still quasi-instrumental. And the interaction is "one-sided" in a way that a normed interaction is not, since one agent is simply trying to satisfy the other's expectations. This one-sidedness leaves open the possibility that the other's response pattern may not be norm-based. For example, a parent may not be imposing a set of normatively licensed expectations, but simply a set of personal preferences. According to Parsons, these two conditions are related. It is only when one agent's attitudinal cathexis of the other becomes a "reciprocal attachment" that a genuine normative orientation can emerge in either agent.[48]

Alter's initial pattern of sanctioning allows ego to construct a conception of the attitude of the other. If ego responds in kind, that is, by sanctioning the pattern of action initially exhibited by alter, then alter becomes in turn concerned to elicit the correct attitude in ego. However, at this point, the agents' attitudes have come to form something of a closed circle. Ego wants to satisfy alter's expectations, but alter only wants to satisfy ego's expectations. The only thing left that can pin down the content of these expectations is the norm that prescribes them. Thus under conditions of reciprocity, being motivated to satisfy the attitude of the other becomes equivalent to being motivated by whatever norm applies to the interaction. In this way, the normative orientation comes to lose its association with the particular attitudes of the significant others who guided the agent through primary socialization, and comes to assume the form of a generalized disposition toward conformity to shared norms. This is the primary difference between Parsons's model and the simple behaviorist view—it is not a particular pattern of action that the agent internalizes; according to Parsons, the agent constructs, through internalization, an increasingly generic disposition toward norm-conformity.[49]

The details of this account are, of course, ultimately empirical questions to be settled by research in developmental psychology. Here I would just like to make a few comments on the logical structure of the proposal. The first thing to notice is that the mechanism of reciprocally imputed expectations and sanctions that Parsons considers central to the development of the norm-conformative orientation is essentially the same as the mechanism that Habermas takes to be the source of the "orientation toward mutual understanding" in his reconstruction of Mead's symbolic interactionism. Specifically, Habermas argues that a particular gesture comes to have the same meaning for two organisms when alter sanctions ego's performance based upon a set of expectations that, in turn, ego uses to judge the correctness of alter's response. However, Habermas appeals to this mechanism to explain only the genesis of symbolic meaning.[50] He does not consider the possibility that it could supply the groundwork for a general account of norm-governed action. The view outlined here takes the existence of reciprocally imputed, sanctionable expectations to provide the foundations for a general disposition for rule-governed action, of which linguistic symbolization will be an important special case.

However, the crucial component of the view developed here is the idea that sanctions are used to reinforce the disposition to assign priority to normative considerations, not to enforce some specific pattern of action. If this basic analysis of institutionalization is accepted, then the precise details of how socialization works are of secondary importance. The fact that the normative *orientation* is enforced—not the norm—can be used to provide a simple explanation for the special accountability structure of social action. Agents are "held accountable" to the system of norms by being sanctioned for failure to assign normative reasons for action deliberative priority. However, whether or not an action is the expression of deviance cannot be read off its surface. Failure to conform to specific normative expectations may also be the expression of dissent (disagreement about which norms are, or should be, in force) as well as error (failure to grasp salient features of the situation), and these types of actions are not sanctionable. Thus when an agent initially disappoints expectations, she may be given the "benefit of the doubt" in the form of an opportunity to "give an account" of her reasons for action. If she can justify the action with respect to some set of norms or situational features, this generates the presumption that the action was in fact motivated by an underlying normative orientation. This may constitute an excusing condition, exempting her from blame, or it may prove to others that their expectations were incorrect.

This can be illustrated through the example given earlier of catching one's opponent surreptitiously cheating at chess. Upon seeing a move that violates the game rules, one might immediately conclude that one's opponent is subordinating norm-conformity to her desire to win. The usual response in such a situation would be to sanction the other, for example, by refusing to play further. However, one might give one's opponent the benefit of the doubt (perhaps a rule that I don't know? perhaps she forgot that it is my turn?), and ask for an explanation. In this case, if the agent wants to avoid the sanction, she must show that the action is licensed by some prevailing norm. In cases where there is a norm that licenses the move, then it will stand. In cases where the agent thought there was a norm that licensed the move, but was mistaken, the status quo ante will be restored, but the agent will not be punished. When no plausible case can be made for the move, it is assumed that the agent has adopted an instrumental orientation, and will therefore be sanctioned.[51]

4.5 Differences from Habermas

The analysis presented here explains the accountability structure of social norms without appealing to specifically linguistic commitments, but also without characterizing norm-conformity as merely the product of conditioning. When agents follow social rules, in this view, they do so for reasons that are, in principle, open to thematization and revision. Only the priority of the norm-conformative orientation is instilled through socialization, not the disposition to conform to any particular pattern. The fact that agents are held accountable to these norms is explained without reference to any antecedent commitments they may have made, but simply through the structure of expectations and sanctions that sustain the norm-conformative orientation. A conception of norm-governed action of this type differs from Habermas's on two key points, pertaining to (§4.5.1) the theory of meaning and (§4.5.2) the voluntaristic character of social order.

4.5.1 The theory of meaning

According to this view, linguistic communication develops as a special form of norm-governed action. A basic explanation of how language could develop from pragmatic resources of this type has been developed by Robert Brandom and need only be summarized here. Norm-governed practices can be characterized in terms of what Brandom calls "deontic scorekeeping."[52] Each agent, when entering into a given practice, assumes a particular set of commitments and entitlements, that is, recognizes a set of ascribed obligations and permissions. Each action performed by the agent changes her "deontic status." She assumes a new commitment, discharges an old one, acquires a new entitlement, and so on.

According to Brandom, all of this can be explained without presupposing that agents possess full-blown intentional states, that is, mental states with *propositional content*. The basic set of pragmatic abilities can be explained on the narrower assumption that agents have the capacity to respond differentially to features of their environment, and to sanction each other's performances. (In the above discussion, I have helped myself to the use of intentional states—

beliefs, desires, principles—to explain the structure of norm-governed action. This was done simply to keep the presentation manageable. A more perspicuous development of the action theory would start by explaining proto-norm-governed action, without any appeal to intentional states. It would then use this to provide the pragmatic foundations for an account of the development of language, after which, following the Sellarsian narrative, one could explain the development of norm-governed action as a fully rational action type.)[53]

The notion of deontic status can be used to define the concept of justification. In baseball, when a runner moves from first to second base, she discharges a commitment to touch second, and acquires an entitlement to run to third. In a norm-governed practice of this type, the *significance* of any action is the way in which it changes the deontic status of the agent (e.g., the significance of being on second is that one can then move on to third).[54] An action is *justified* if the agent was entitled to it at the point of its initiation. Thus the justification for running to second base is the action of having arrived safely at first (where "action" in understood in terms of the alteration in deontic status achieved through a particular behavioral event).

In this view, all social practices involve sets of actions linked together through deontic relations of this type. Every action is either susceptible to justification through reference to a deontic status that licenses it, or else can serve as justification for other actions by bringing about a deontic status that licenses them. What makes linguistic practices different from social practices is that they involve a special form of commitment that Brandom calls *assertional commitment*. An assertion, in his view, is simply an action that, in principle, "can stand in need of (and so be liable to the demand for) a reason; and it is something that can be offered as a reason."[55] This is how it differs from an ordinary practical action, which can be justified but is often not capable of justifying anything further, or which may justify what one person does, but cannot be used as a justification by some other:

The idea exploited here, then, is that assertions are fundamentally fodder for *inferences*. Uttering a sentence with assertional force or significance is putting it forth *as* a potential reason. Asserting is giving reasons—not necessarily reasons addressed to some particular question or issue, or to a particular individual, but making claims whose availability as reasons for others is essential to their assertional force. Assertions are essentially *fit* to be reasons.[56]

The meaning of assertions is, as before, simply the set of commitments that they presuppose and entail. Because assertions can serve as reasons and stand in need of reasons, these commitments and entitlements can be characterized as the *inferential role* of the associated assertion. Assertions acquire conceptual content by virtue of the inferential entitlements from which they flow and the commitments they entail. Naturally, linguistic practice remains bound up with the sensuous world, because an agent's particular entitlement to any given assertion does not *need* to be inferential. Observing a red object under standard perceptual conditions may entitle an agent to assert "this is red." The point is simply that, in principle, this assertion is also capable of being justified, for example, by reasons that refer to the agent's reliability as a detector of red objects. It is this inferential articulation that supplies the assertion with its conceptual content.

The significance of Brandom's way of drawing this tight connection between assertion and inference is that it allows him to develop a compositional theory of meaning for natural language. Sentences as a whole acquire their conceptual content from their inferential role. Subsentential components acquire content through the contribution they make to the inferential properties of sentences in which they appear. In both cases, the mechanism of substitution isolates the contribution that any particular component makes to an inferential relation. The contribution of different sentences or subsentential components can be identified through the particular configuration of commitments and entitlements generated by different patterns of substitution. The general outline of this style of semantics has already been given in §3.2.

The most significant contrast between this sort of approach and Habermas's is that it privileges assertion as the basic content-conferring category of linguistic action. Assertoric speech is the language-game that generates conceptual content. Once this content is developed and available, it can be used in a variety of ways; for example, it can be plugged into different social practices, such as telling people what to do, explaining what one intends to do, and so on. But the latter types of action are not "essentially fit" to serve as reasons, or to be supported by reasons, in the way that assertions are. Insofar as one must be entitled to issue an imperative, this will be a feature of the social practice of issuing imperatives, and not a general condition on the possibility of intelligible speech. (The lack of inferential articulation of imperatives is reflected in the fact that they must be *transformed into assertions* in order to be embedded in conditionals without semantic anomaly.) Furthermore, there is no reason that imperatives could not be employed instrumentally, so long as the associated interaction problem is solvable.

Conceiving of assertion in terms of commitment helps to render more intelligible the finding that language cannot arise out of systems of purely instrumental interaction, and thus the set of limitative results outlined in chapter 2. There it was suggested that social action forms two natural types, depending upon whether agents select either an outcome or else a propositional attitude of some other person as their goal. Action of the former type was said to be "success-oriented," action of the latter "understanding-oriented." However, in the analysis of Habermas's speech act theory undertaken in chapter 3, the concept of action oriented toward mutual understanding was seen to have somewhat misleading implications. In theoretical discourse, agents do not literally take the beliefs of others as their goal. Instead, they attempt to make warranted assertions, that is, speech acts to which they are normatively entitled, given the prevailing discursive norms and the state of the language game. They influence the beliefs of others only indirectly. Insofar as others are attempting to form only justified beliefs, they will believe what the agent says when they judge that it is in fact warranted.

For this reason, Habermas's claim that there is "a telos of mutual understanding" inherent in communication has overtones that all but invite instrumentalist misunderstandings. Linguistic action is oriented toward mutual understanding only insofar as it is norm-conformative, since it is precisely by grasping the deontic commitments associated with the speech act that speakers understand its linguistic meaning. Speech acts, being norm-conformative, have no goal in the instrumental sense. In speaking of an inherent telos, Habermas is adopting a somewhat misleading Kantian idiom, in which both actions prescribed by hypothetical and those prescribed by categorical imperatives are described as having a teleological structure. In the latter case, this goal is said to be merely "formal" because, whereas with hypothetical imperatives the goal prescribes the action, with categorical imperatives the action prescribes the goal. And since the action is choice-worthy a priori, the associated goal is also intrinsically worthy, that is, it is an end-in-itself. (This is how one gets the second formulation of the categorical imperative from the first—a step that is also notably subject to instrumentalist misunderstandings.)

Brandom's account of linguistic action allows us to take this analysis one step further. Beliefs, in his view, are nothing other than a shorthand way of referring to features of an agent's assertional commitments. Not only are beliefs not objects that we can attempt to affect directly through our actions, they are not objects at all. To keep score in the assertional language-game, it is necessary to keep track of one's own deontic status as well as the status of others. An agent's beliefs, in this view, are just the set of discursive commitments that one ascribes to oneself as part of this process, which is to say, the commitments that one would be willing to acknowledge.[57] When we make an assertion, our goal is to undertake a commitment that others can use. Insofar as we succeed, we have, in effect, given them a belief. Thus beliefs are the "formal end" of linguistic action—they are objects that we posit in order to describe communication in teleological terms.

In this way, the classification of action developed in chapter 2 can be retained, except that the direction of explanation is reversed. It is not because speech acts take beliefs as their goal that they cannot be employed instrumentally; rather, it is because assertoric speech acts are not employed instrumentally that it makes sense to posit the intentional states that can then be described as their goal.

4.5.2 Voluntarism

The second major difference between this view and Habermas's is that rejecting the "primacy of communication" thesis for the "primacy of norms" thesis in the explanation of the accountability of social action appears to undermine the voluntaristic basis of social order. Habermas places considerable emphasis on the way in which, with the development of communicative action, "the validity basis of norms changes insofar as every communicatively mediated consensus depends upon reasons."[58] In this view, primitive systems of norm-conformative action are held together through the spellbinding power of paleosymbols that have retained their action-guiding force from the stage of simple holophrastic signaling language. This sacred authority, which ultimately rests upon purely motivational dispositions, is gradually replaced when the propositional elements differentiated out of these primitive symbol systems are reintegrated with the normative elements to create the "three validity claim" speech act. Thus the emergence of communicative action is transposed onto a new base, in which interactions are linked only through the weak binding force of illocutionary acts.

The significance of this "linguistification of the sacred," in Habermas's view, is that social orders based on sacred authority are not, in the end, rational, whereas social orders based on communicative action are. This is because sacred authority compels agents to conform simply by triggering dispositions that are instilled through socialization. Their claim to validity is inextricably linked to a moment of purely factual motivational power. Social orders based on communication, however, rest in the end upon the acceptance of reasons for or against the particular form of organization. When social integration is secured through the issuance of imperatives, each speaker will have associated with her imperative a "rightness" claim that involves a commitment to justify the content of the assigned obligation in practical discourse. Anyone who accepts such an imperative does so because she accepts the corresponding validity claim, and therefore grants that good reasons could be given in support of the utterance. For this reason, social orders based on communication are underwritten by a set of promissory notes that, at any point in time, any agent can call upon any other to redeem.

I argued earlier that at the heart of this conception of social order is a fundamentally contractualist intuition—that the rules must always already be accepted in order to be binding. However, one of the peculiar consequences of this view is that it leaves Habermas without any good explanation of why social norms are *sanctioned*. This problem actually generates one of the most serious confusions in Habermas's view. According to his position, social norms (of the sacred variety) are sanctioned only because of a failure to distinguish normative and instrumental reasons (a fusion of facticity and validity). As a result, with the rationalization of the lifeworld, social norms get split up into moral norms and positive laws. The former constitute merely a type of "cultural knowledge" that tells us how we ought to behave, while the latter form a concrete action system with enforced compliance. However, it is a consequence of this view that all concrete action norms that regulate interpersonal interactions on an informal and day-to-day level, and which can only be justified from the moral point of view, are not enforced.[59] Insofar as these rules form part of agents' lifeworld, and so govern actions from within the performative stance, there is no reason that agents would ever need to be sanctioned, since there is no reason that they would not always follow up on their illocutionary commitments. If agents are inclined not to comply, it must be because they have adopted an instrumental orientation. However, Habermas believes that the regulation of agents who have adopted an instrumental stance can only be achieved through the mechanism of positive law (this is precisely what makes the law "positive"—agents are free to comply either because they respect the law, or to avoid the associated sanctions).

As a result, Habermas takes the characteristic of social action that Parsons regarded as the key to *institutionalization* (viz., that agents are free to comply either because they subscribe to the underlying normative reasons, or because they seek to avoid the sanctions associated with deviance), and displaces it entirely into the sphere of law. He is driven to take this position because he thinks that, if the accountability of social action is derived from the account-ability of speech acts, then ultimately there is no place for sanctions within the framework of communicative action proper. As a result, any sanctions that do regulate lifeworld exchanges must be the result of some confusion (as with archaic norms), or an external mechanism (such as positive law). This is, however, strikingly unrealistic as an account of how morality and social norms function within the lifeworld. It is a general feature of social norms that, even within the framework of a fully differentiated and rationalized lifeworld, they continue to be enforced. As Harold Garfinkel has shown perhaps most clearly with his "breaching experiments," social action is regulated down to its smallest detail, and there are serious sanctions associated with any motivated departure from the prevailing expectations.[60]

The problem shows up clearly in passages from Habermas such as the following:

The move from knowledge to action remains uncertain, on account of the vulnerabil-ity of the moral actor's precarious, highly abstract system of self-control, and in general on account of the vicissitudes of socialization processes that promote such demanding competencies. A morality that depends upon the accommodating substrate of propi-tious personality structures would have a limited effectiveness if it could not engage the actor's motives in another way besides internalization, that is, precisely by way of an institutionalized legal system that *supplements* postconventional morality in a manner effective for action.[61]

Something is clearly wrong here. Certainly a stable social order could not be generated through internalization alone. But if all punishment has to be legal (and if what distinguishes law from morality is strictly that the former is enforced), then the category of the legal to going to be stretched beyond recog-nition. But these difficulties are merely symptomatic of a more general problem. Sanctions drop out of the account of morality and the lifeworld because Habermas has no explanation for their presence. This is because his account of social order is a bit *too* voluntaristic. This stems from his derivation of the accountability of social action from illocutionary commitment. If instead one takes the accountability of social action as primitive, grounded in a structure of mutually imputed, sanctioned expectations, then the mystery disappears. The difference between law and morality, in this view, is not the difference between sanctioned and unsanctioned, but between formally sanctioned and informally sanctioned rules of conduct. The view that I have been developing retains the Durkheimian insight that morality is institutionalized in the form of sanctioned social norms. However, because these sanctions do not enforce particular normative obligations, but the norm-conformative disposition in general, they do not introduce an element of facticity into the agent's motive for conforming to any *particular* set of norms.

Unlike Habermas, I do not claim that merely by engaging in and reproducing a particular norm-governed practice, agents must be committed to defending this practice with reasons. However, to generate orderly interactions, in my view, social norms must not only provide agents with reasons to perform particular actions, they must also serve as a shared resource for fixing the expectations of others. To function successfully, norms must be accepted by all those whose conduct is directly governed by them, and be common knowledge among all parties to the interaction. Thus norms do not work by providing a brute disposition to act in a certain way; instead, they function at a cognitive level by coordinating a certain structure of expectations. And they function correctly only if everyone shares this same structure. This means that any participant will be in a position to destabilize an interaction simply by refusing to adopt the relevant norm as a reason for action. Assuming that such a refusal is not sanctioned as deviance, the result is that normative orders rest upon the ongoing willingness of all parties to "play by the rules."

When a particular normative consensus has been disrupted, language provides a variety of resources that can be used to reconstruct it. These vary from routine "management" techniques, like "I'm sorry, I meant to . . . ," "What do you mean by . . . ?" and "Why don't we both . . . ?" to full-blown "practical discourses" in which a suitable interpretation or justification of the norms governing the interaction is achieved through explicit argumentative procedures. The reason that communication forms the obvious recourse is that language has the *expressive resources* needed to thematize the problematic interaction pattern. It allows us to talk *about* our practices, and this allows us to decide in a straightforward manner how we are going to conduct them. The only non-linguistic alternatives capable of restoring a disturbed normative consensus involve processes of *tâtonnement*, in which intentions and expectations are slowly adjusted in response to repeated coordination failure.

Thus the development of language does lead to a change in the way norm-governed action is conducted, insofar as it provides us with a powerful resource for constructing and modifying normative orders. Instead of being a sedimentary product of tradition, norms can be explicitly developed and reflexively implemented. This does not, however, fundamentally restructure the basis of social order, shifting it over to a new mode of integration, nor does it change the underlying mode of practical deliberation. Social integration continues to be brought about through the binding force of social norms that function as deontic constraints in practical deliberation.

According to this view, when interactions become problematic, agents do not shift into discourse because there was already some tacit commitment on all sides to discursively redeem the norms. If they shift into discourse, it is because discourse provides an obvious resource for working out a new agreement, one that enjoys significant pragmatic advantages over the alternatives. Naturally, what I have been calling Habermas's "contractualist intuition," that the legitimacy of norms rests upon a "yes/no" response to validity claims, has been significantly diluted. It is still a consequence of my view that social integration requires acceptance on all sides of a set of social norms; it is just that this acceptance is not thought to be backed by any antecedent commitment to provide a justification for them. It is not even clear why such a commitment would be thought necessary. When a norm becomes problematic, how else is one going to sustain it other than by trying to provide some form of justification?

Of course, one alternative to restoring the disturbed normative consensus is simply to switch to instrumental action. But Habermas is never in a position to claim that when social integration breaks down, participants are *forced* to enter into a practical discourse. He has always granted that when social integration is disrupted, agents have the option of adopting an instrumental orientation. The commitments generated by the validity claims raised in the communicative interaction have no force against individuals who choose to ignore them. It is only from the moral point of view (or the normative orientation) that any agent is obliged to engage in the discursive redemption of his validity claims. But for agents to be subject to such an obligation, it is not necessary for there to be any antecedent commitment. From my position, it is still reasonable to claim that agents have a normative obligation to restore disturbed interaction patterns through discourse. They should do so, however, not because they have already committed themselves to it, but because it is simply the most efficient and effective way of restoring the normative consensus. Thus as far as the relationship between social action and discourse is concerned, all of the normative intuitions that motivated Habermas's position can be sustained without supposing that language provides the validity basis of all social interaction.

At this point, the discussion is beginning to stray from Habermas' action-theoretic claims into a discussion of his metaethical views. I have attempted to show, in the analysis developed in these last sections, that the basic set of claims Habermas makes about instrumental rationality and communication can be redeemed when reconstructed within the framework of a modified "sociological" theory of action. One of the characteristics of my analysis is that it rejects the idea, central to Habermas's view, that social norms acquire their binding force from an associated rightness claim. By treating social norms as a sui generis form of social action, with a built-in structure of accountability, the analysis can be rendered consistent with a theory of meaning that reconstructs propositional content in terms of a single dimension of validity, namely, truth or warranted assertibility. The relationship between the theory of action and the theory of meaning is reversed, but the two remain closely connected, insofar as the conception of norm-governed action provides precisely the conceptual resources needed to develop an inferential semantics along the lines suggested by Brandom.

However, the idea of a "rightness claim" plays a much more significant role in Habermas's overall system than simply that of a connecting link between speech and social action. It also plays a crucial role in his strategy for defending moral cognitivism, in the program he refers to as *discourse ethics*. In this view, the fact that social norms come with an associated rightness claim that must be redeemed in a special form of practical discourse allows him to reject metaethical views that deny the cognitive content of moral judgments on the grounds that they do not admit of truth or falsity. Habermas's speech act theory, which reconstructs propositional content in terms of rightness conditions, provides an obvious resource for denying the intelligibility of any such views. Denying that communication involves any validity claim beyond assertoric truth obviously undercuts this argument, and therefore threatens to undermine the entire discourse ethics project.

In the second half of this book, I will attempt to avoid this consequence by showing that Habermas makes a programmatic error in granting the noncognitivist's claim that moral judgments do not admit of truth or falsity. His own discourse theory contains sufficient resources to reject both moral noncognitivism and relativism, without having to posit special validity claims or structurally dissimilar forms of discourse. Furthermore, I will argue that the concessions he makes about truth leave him with an unnecessarily heavy burden of proof, which leads him to posit an implausibly strict universalization rule for practical discourse. I will attempt to show that these problems with discourse ethics can be ironed out if one adopts the view that practical discourse is governed by a deflationary truth predicate. The point of this is to show that the theory of meaning and action outlined in the first half of this book provides a more secure foundation for a program in philosophical ethics of the type that Habermas sets out to develop.

II

Discourse Ethics

5

Foundations of Discourse Ethics

In his work on communicative action, Habermas goes to great pains to show that social order is the product of commitments that are generated endogenously through the use of language to coordinate interaction. In particular, he argues that whenever agents issue imperatives, they make a commitment to defend the normative force of their utterance in a specifically practical form of discourse. However, there is a well-known line of argument in philosophical metaethics that simply denies that it is possible to justify normative claims. According to this view, although agents can reach a "rationally motivated consensus" about what the world is like (descriptive judgments), it is impossible to reach such a consensus about what it should be like (prescriptive judgments). Thus Habermas's theory of communicative action may show that it is rational to act on the basis of normative commitments, but it still does not show that it is possible to *have* rational normative commitments in the first place.

In response to such a challenge, Habermas develops, alongside his analysis of communicative action, a defense of the rationality of moral argumentation. This is the program that he refers to, following Karl-Otto Apel, as "discourse" or "communicative" ethics.[1]

The argument of the first half of this book is intended to show that Habermas's particular way of construing the relationship between language, commitment, and social interaction is ultimately not successful. However, none of this diminishes the need for something like the discourse ethics program to supplement the theory of action. The "multidimensional" theory presented in the previous chapter appeals to three different intentional states: beliefs, desires, and principles, in order to model practical deliberation (with an eye toward explaining the orderliness of social interaction). However, according to conventional wisdom, there is a significant asymmetry between beliefs and desires. Beliefs are generally regarded as "cognitive" states, and it is often assumed that the belief states of different individuals will exhibit some tendency toward *convergence*. Desires, on the other hand, are generally regarded as "noncognitive" states. Often they are thought to reflect purely subjective tastes. According to this view, desires will exhibit little or no tendency toward convergence.

For the introduction of principles into the deliberative framework to have any explanatory value with respect to the problem of order, it must be the case that principles resemble beliefs more closely than desires, as conventionally understood. If each agent's principles are completely "subjective," or immune to rational revision, then it will not be possible to assume that these principles ever coalesce around a set of shared social norms. When two people disagree about the color of a ball, or the height of a tree, we assume that something has gone wrong—that one of them has made a mistake. However, when two people disagree about what restaurant they want to go to, or what color they should paint their house, we do not automatically assume that one of them is mistaken. They simply want different things. What happens, then, when two individuals disagree about what norm they should follow? Is this a reasonable difference of opinion, or must one of them be mistaken? Or does the case fall somewhere in between?

Habermas refers to the view that norms are less susceptible to rational justification than beliefs as *moral noncognitivism*.[2] Thus his exposition of the discourse ethics program is governed by the stated desire to defend a *cognitivist* conception of moral judgment.[3] Unfortunately, Habermas thereby uses the term "noncognitivism" in a somewhat broader sense than has become standard in analytic metaethics. Thus I will begin by clarifying the terminology, along with the various strands in the debate (§5.1), before going on to discuss the primary arguments that Habermas presents against noncognitivism.

5.1 Moral Noncognitivism

The task of developing a theory of moral reasoning is simplified by the fact that Habermas's theory of rational action already explains the structure of practical deliberation at the point of decision. In day-to-day contexts, agents engage in "moral reasoning" simply by applying social norms to their interaction problems and respecting the commitments that are part of the settled background pattern constituting their lifeworld. The difficulties arise only when these background certainties are problematized.[4] (In the same way, the full resources of theoretical rationality are deployed only when our everyday empirical beliefs become problematic.) Agents are then faced with the task of using the general resources of speech in order to reconstruct the disrupted normative order. Thus discourse ethics, in Habermas's view, is a mechanism used only to address the general question of what the content of the norms that regulate the interactions of a community should be. Its role, as Habermas puts it, is "to clarify the moral point of view."[5] Thus it is structurally equivalent to what I have been calling a theory of "norm-rationality."

According to Habermas's view, norms, like beliefs, are linguistically formulated. Thus any associated intentional state ascribed to individual actors has semantic content. Given Habermas's commitment to an inferential semantics, this means that the content of these states is determined by the inferential articulation of the associated propositions. But to say that they can be inferentially articulated is to say that, in principle, any one of these states can be thematized and rationally debated. Since principles and desires, just like beliefs, have semantic content, they should be equally open to discursive contestation. Thus there is, from Habermas's perspective, something of a presumption *against* moral noncognitivism. If beliefs about the empirical world are to be assigned some privileged status, their definition alone will not do it. Some further argument must be introduced that will justify the privilege.

It is important to emphasize here, once again, that the instrumental conception of rationality does not itself presuppose or depend upon any sort of moral noncognitivism. In chapter 2, "beliefs" and "desires" were defined entirely formally—as selection criteria used to narrow down the range of options in a choice problem. Beliefs were taken to be subjective probabilities, desires to be subjective preferences. Their content was taken to be determined by some mechanism exogenous to the theory of practical rationality. Principles were added later in the same way—using an entirely formal definition. At no point was there any reason given to think that one of these criteria is more "rational" than some other, or more susceptible to justification.

Nevertheless, we have a strong set of intuitions, stemming from our everyday experience dealing with other people, that although it is possible to argue someone out of having a belief, it is sometimes quite impossible to argue someone out of having a desire. We often say that beliefs are something that we *form*, whereas desires are something that we *experience*. This active/passive distinction reflects a tendency to think that our desires are outside of our control in a way that our beliefs are not. Of course, there are many counterexamples to this claim—just try believing that 2 + 2 = 5, or that the sky is red. Furthermore, our everyday vocabulary still reflects the influence of a dubious sort of mind-body dualism, according to which beliefs are traditionally associated with the mind, and desires or emotions with the body. Thus the standard contrasts that are drawn between belief and desire are typically invalid. The question of what sort of parallels may or may not exist between the two types of intentional states is a fair bit more complex.

The question that is relevant to Habermas's project is, luckily, somewhat narrower. Habermas is concerned primarily with the issue of whether agents are able to conduct a rational debate on the subject of normative questions. He grants that in the case of needs and desires it is possible to have irreducible differences of opinion. Thus agents have the option of replying to demands for further justification of their desires with the claim: "that's just what I want."[6] With beliefs, on the other hand, the demand for justification can never be avoided. It is never permissible (strictly speaking) to say: "that's just what I believe." Habermas's goal is to show that, in the case of social norms, such a move is also inadmissible. Norms must always be justified.

Habermas's motivation for taking this stance stems from the fairly straightforward intuition that when we encounter someone violating a social norm, we are not likely to dismiss this as a mere difference of opinion about what is right and wrong. We are inclined to demand some type of justification. We do not behave this way, however, when someone performs an action that merely reveals an idiosyncratic preference. This feature of everyday interaction, according to Habermas, generates a presumption in favor of treating beliefs and norms as "on par" with one another.[7] Anyone who endorses moral noncognitivism must therefore, as the saying goes, be "in the grip of a theory."[8] So instead of developing a cognitivist theory per se, Habermas assigns himself the somewhat lighter task of rejecting what he takes to be bad arguments that have led people to adopt moral noncognitivism, despite their everyday moral intuitions.

Habermas focuses on two arguments that he takes to be responsible for the popularity of moral noncognitivism. In the first argument, the noncognitivist points to the fact that disputes over basic moral principles "ordinarily do not issue in agreement," and infers that the justification of moral judgments must rely in the end upon premises that are agent-relative or arbitrary.[9] This challenges the view that there could be any straightforward procedure through which the rightness or wrongness of any particular moral claim could be established to the satisfaction of all parties. In the second argument, the noncognitivist points to the fact that every attempt to explain what it might mean for normative propositions to be true has failed, and suggests that this is because moral judgments do not admit of truth or falsity.[10] This argument has been taken by many people to suggest that moral questions have some kind of intrinsic cognitive fault that makes them incapable of being rationally debated.

The terminological confusion over the use of the word "noncognitivism" arises from the fact that, in the Anglo-American philosophical tradition, "moral noncognitivism" is used to designate only arguments of the latter type. Thus a moral noncognitivist is someone who claims that moral statements lack truth-values.[11] This can be extremely confusing, since according to this definition, Habermas himself would be classified as a noncognitivist. (After all, he does think that the validity claim governing moral claims is rightness, not truth.) To avoid hopeless confusion, I will therefore use the term "moral noncognitivism" only in Habermas's sense, as a term for the view that norms are less susceptible to rational justification than beliefs. Thus the view that moral statements lack truth-values is not, according to this definition, itself a form of noncognitivism. It may, however, *imply* noncognitivism if this lack of truth-value somehow impairs our ability to justify these statements.

The confusion is exacerbated by the fact that whether or not individuals are able to reach an agreement on the subject of moral claims is usually thought to be the problem of *relativism*, or *subjectivism*, not noncognitivism.[12] Habermas, however, assumes that in order to defend his own version of moral cognitivism he must provide some reason to believe that moral disputes will issue in agreement. Why he thinks he must do so is not entirely clear. The mere fact that agents are unable to reach agreement does not mean that their claims are not rationally justified. They may simply have started out from different premises. Thus there appears to be no obvious tension between relativism and cognitivism. The reason that Habermas feels such a pressing need to preclude relativism therefore needs to be explored more deeply.

This discussion, however, will be deferred until the next chapter. Here I would like to focus simply on the two arguments that Habermas develops in response to the noncognitivist, because these provide the two basic components of the discourse-theoretic view. He claims, first, that the noncognitivist's concerns about the truth-aptness of moral judgments has significant consequences only if one assumes that truth represents some kind of correspondence relationship between sentences and states of affairs in the world. If one denies that this sort of "objectivity" plays any role in vindicating the truth-claim associated with beliefs, then our ability to justify beliefs will have nothing to do with their reference to the physical world. Thus one can grant that moral claims lack truth-values, but deny that this constitutes a cognitive fault, or that it precludes the possibility of rational justification. Similarly, when the relativist questions the ultimate justifiability of moral judgments, the argument is persuasive, in Habermas's view, only if one presupposes a *monological* conception of rational justification. If one assumes instead that justification is always *dialogical*, that is, involving an attempt by one person to justify a claim to some other person, then there is no longer any a priori reason to think that moral questions are any less decidable than empirical or scientific ones.

Thus one can defeat noncognitivism, according to Habermas, by rejecting both the received view of truth and the received view of justification.

In the following section (§5.2), I will examine Habermas's theory of truth, in order to specify more precisely his strategy for responding to the concern about moral statements lacking truth-values. However, the particular way that Habermas chooses to disarm this concern will no longer work, given the problems with his "three validity claim" thesis identified in chapter 3. I will therefore argue that his "illocutionary-act" analysis of the truth predicate, when developed consistently, allows him to claim that moral judgments admit of straightforward truth and falsity. This renders entirely superfluous the complicated ruse of introducing "rightness" claims (§5.3). I then turn to Habermas's second argument and provide a more detailed articulation of the dialogical conception of rational justification (§5.4), in order to show how it is able to provide a response to the relativist. I then conclude (§5.5) by examining briefly the way that Habermas tries to put these ideas together, in order to develop a "formalist" ethic in the Kantian style, grounded in the set of formal constraints that stem from his theory of argumentation.

5.2 The Discourse Theory of Truth

What does it mean to say that a certain class of statements "lacks cognitive content"? Often, this is interpreted to mean that statements of the designated type do not express propositional attitudes. For instance, a noncognitivist about pain-reports would argue that the utterance "I am in pain" should not be analyzed as an assertion that expresses the subject's belief that he is in pain, but rather as a sophisticated way of saying "arghh!" Similarly, a moral noncognitivist might argue that the statement "murder is wrong" does not express a belief about the propriety of murder, but rather expresses the subject's disposition to feel abhorrence when confronted with a certain type of action.

One way of formulating the sense in which moral judgements lack cognitive content is to say that they are incapable of truth or falsity. In this view, there is some property of sentences—call it truth-aptness—that makes them able to be true or false. In the same way that chairs and tables lack this property, many philosophers have also felt that a variety of linguistic phenomena—such as poems, imperatives, or moral judgments—also lack this property. Of course, it is not immediately obvious in what sense this lack of truth-aptness is a defect. Poems may lack truth-value, but there are still better and worse poems. The same could be said for moral judgments. Thus the mere claim that moral claims lack truth-values does not mean that they cannot be rationally debated, or that they could not be the subject of a rationally motivated agreement. Similarly, the mere fact that a particular assertion is capable of truth or falsity does not itself help us to decide whether or not to endorse it, since the evidence needed to ascertain its truth-value may be absent.

So for the claim that moral statements lack truth-values to form an impediment to the realization of Habermas's project, it must be strengthened somewhat. In general, there are two ways in which this can be done. The first involves the familiar idea that the meaning of a sentence is given by its truth-conditions. According to this view, any type of sentence that lacks truth-aptness cannot have truth-conditions, and therefore cannot have any meaning. If propositions are understood as the meanings of sentences, then moral judgments cannot have propositional content, and so must be just expressions of emotional states or the like.[13] The second claim is that what distinguishes a valid from an invalid inference is that the former is truth-preserving whereas the latter is not. This means that sentences lacking truth-values cannot appear as premises or conclusions in valid inferences. Otherwise put, since the logical connectives are defined truth-functionally, that is, using truth tables, sentences lacking truth-values cannot be subject to the standard logical transformations (and so cannot be embedded in conditionals).

This second criticism is the one that is the more fundamental (since the claim that inference must be understood truth-functionally undermines any attempt to develop an inferential semantics as an alternative to the truth-conditional). The point of this criticism can be seen most clearly by considering again the case of noncognitivism about pain-reports. Here the noncognitivist would claim that when someone says "I am in pain," it is useless to argue with her. If one were to counter with "No, you are not," this would be to treat her utterance as an assertion that p, and to counter with not-p. But when the utterance is correctly analyzed as "argh!" it can be seen that countering with "not-argh!" is to say something different, but not contradictory. The logical operator "not" flips the truth value of a sentence, but "argh!" has no truth-value. The same problem shows up if one tries to argue, for example, "If you are in pain, you should be writhing." Here the antecedent is neither true nor false, and so the truth-value of the conditional is undefined.

The moral noncognitivist might therefore maintain that arguments over moral judgments face the same difficulty. The usual view is that moral judgments are like pain-reports in that they are both essentially indexical locutions. The indexicality of "argh!" is given by the fact that the speaker can only use this speech act to express her own pain. For this reason, responding with "not-argh!" would be equivalent to saying "Really, I am not," rather than "No, you are not." Similarly, when people say "Murder is wrong" they are expressing nothing but their own attitude toward murder. If someone counters with "No, murder is okay," this person not contradicting what was said, but is just expressing her own attitude toward murder. There is no real disagreement here, any more than there is between two individuals, one of whom is in pain and the other of whom is not.

It is important to notice that central to this view is the unstated assumption that truth is a substantive, nonepistemic property that sentences may or may not possess. This is what allows the theorist to *define* inferential validity in terms of the sentential operations that preserve this property. So, for instance, according to the correspondence theory of truth, all true sentences share the common property of standing in a certain metaphysical or causal relation of correspondence to the world. There will then be some simple fact of the matter as to whether any given sentence satisfies this relation. This fact must obtain in a way that is independent of our ability to ascertain it, because if the truth of a sentence in any way depended upon our ability to know it, and our epistemic access involved any form of inference, then one could not provide a truth-functional definition of valid inference without obvious circularity.

But not every philosophical account of truth treats it as a substantive property of sentences. Any theory that defines truth in terms of warranted assertibility, verification, or even "Schema T," must on pain of circularity take the notion of valid inference to be more basic than truth. Adherents of any such view would think it backward to say, as the noncognitivist does, that certain sentences cannot appear in valid inferences because they are incapable of truth or falsity. Thus one clear strategy for responding to the noncognitivist is to adopt a theory of truth in which the truth-aptness of moral statements is no longer seen as relevant to their cognitive status or role in argumentation. This is the approach that Habermas takes, putting him in a position to grant that moral statements lack truth values, but to deny that this constitutes a defect.

The most basic assumption underlying the claim that truth is a substantive property of sentences is the idea that when we affix the predicate "is true" to a sentence, what we are doing is ascribing some property to that sentence. Naturally, the grammatical form of these sentences lends itself to such an interpretation. In Habermas's view, however, the truth predicate does not refer first and foremost to a kind of property that a sentence can have, but rather to a type of validity claim that we can raise *using* that sentence. The kind of validity claim raised determines the illocutionary force associated with the sentence, but it does not in any way determine the semantic content. Thus to say that a given sentence "is true" is not to ascribe a substantive property to that sentence; it is merely to employ a linguistic device that has the function of rendering explicit the illocutionary force of the assertion.[14]

Thus Habermas claims that predicates like "true" and "right" should not be confused with predicates that express *properties* like "yellow" or "white." They are "higher-level predicates" that are introduced to provide a "metalinguistic reformulation" of speech acts whose illocutionary force is only tacit.[15] This "illocutionary-act" analysis of truth (which is inspired by the work of P. F. Strawson)[16] suggests that the truth predicate has its origin in formulas like "It is true that . . . ," which should be analyzed through analogy with more obviously performative formulas like "I promise that. . . ." If this analysis of truth is correct, it would clearly take the wind out of the moral noncognitivist's sails. If ascribing truth to a sentence amounts to no more than rendering explicit the illocutionary force of asserting it, then any sentence that is capable of being asserted is *eo ipso* capable of truth or falsity. Thus truth-aptness becomes a matter of mere grammatical form. Moral judgments would then qualify as truth-apt by virtue of the mere fact that they can be formulated assertorically.

The important question, then, concerns the kind of considerations that lend support to the claim that there is a disanalogy between *validity claim* predicates like "truth" and *property* predicates like "yellow." In general, the view that "truth" does not represent a "real" or "substantive" property of sentences is referred to as *deflationism*.[17] Since Habermas's analysis of truth as a kind of validity claim constitutes a form of deflationism, I will address this question by looking at some features of the truth predicate that support the deflationary interpretation.

All deflationary theories of truth take as their point of departure the observation that the necessary and sufficient conditions for the application of the truth predicate to a sentence are supplied by the sentence itself, without reference to any other predicates that might apply to that sentence, or relations that might obtain between that sentence and some other object or state. This idea is captured by so-called Schema T, which states that:

(T)   "*p*" is true iff *p*

Alfred Tarski, who first drew attention to this fact, suggested that any adequate theory of truth for a language would have to satisfy the "material adequacy condition" that it *entail*, for every sentence *p* of the language, an instance of Schema T.[18] In Tarski's view, each instantiation of Schema T is a platitude (the stated intuition being that a sentence like "snow is white" is true if snow is white, and false if snow is not white). Since a theory that failed to entail at least this would be manifestly inadequate as a theory of truth, Schema T was to serve for Tarski as a check on the acceptability of the various candidate theories.

Deflationary views of truth, on the other hand, suggest that the various instantiations of Schema T are not *constraints* on the adequacy of an analysis of truth; they *are* the analysis.[19] What Schema T shows is that affixing the truth predicate to a sentence adds nothing to the simple assertion of that sentence. The intuition underlying deflationism is often expressed as the suggestion that there is no "one thing" that constitutes a sentence's being true, or no "substantive property" of sentences that the predicate labels. To determine whether "snow is white" is true, we simply have to determine whether snow is white; to determine whether "grass is green" is true, we only have to determine whether grass is green. This shows that knowing all the instantiations of Schema T is everything we need to know in order to decide, for any statement, whether or not it is true, but nothing about truth tells us how to decide whether snow is white, or whether grass is green.

But if the truth predicate is "redundant" when affixed to sentences in the way that this analysis suggests, what reason could there be for introducing it into the language? In Habermas's view, it is because it renders explicit the illocutionary force associated with assertions, a role that is obscured in semantic analysis of the standard form. One of the peculiarities of formalized languages is that all of their sentences are tacitly understood to be assertions. In other words, the use of a formalized language for discussion is a language game in which we assume assertoric force. Although the truth predicate may appear perfectly redundant in a language-game of this type, in a language that contains a variety of speech act types, it would obviously be quite useful.

To see this, it is helpful to reexamine the analogy between making an assertion and making a promise. Consider a language-game in which to utter a sentence describing some state of affairs is understood as the undertaking of a commitment to bring about this state of affairs. For instance, to say:

(1)   I will be at the station at 4 P.M.

is to commit oneself to being at the station at 4 P.M. These sorts of language-game moves will constitute, in the context of general linguistic interaction, a *type* of illocutionary act. Logicians sometimes use symbols to identify these illocutionary forces, for example, a turnstile for assertions, an exclamation point for imperatives, etc. Naturally, if it is helpful to have symbols to keep track of illocutionary modes in written formulas, it will also prove convenient to have some verbal formula that render them explicit in linguistic interactions. For instance, after producing a commitment-generating utterance, one might like to remove any ambiguity as to its force. This can be accomplished by adding a tag phrase that renders it explicit, for instance:

(2)   I will be at the station at 4 P.M. That's a promise.

The paratactic construction can be avoided by rewriting this as follows:

(3)   It is promised that I will be at the station at 4 P.M.

The same analysis can be applied to truth. Suppose that instead of promising to be at the station at 4 P.M., I merely want to state that, as a matter of fact, I am going to be there. To make this clear, I can add a different tag phrase:

(4)   I will be at the station at 4 P.M. It's true.

which can also be rewritten as:

(5)   It is true that I will be at the station at 4 P.M.

Since any assertion can be rephrased in this way, our use of the truth predicate is captured by the so-called Equivalence Schema (which, ignoring certain technicalities, we can take to be equivalent to Schema T):

(E)   It is true that p iff p.

According to this analysis, although the truth predicate plays no significant semantic role, it is far from useless. Because the truth predicate renders explicit the illocutionary force associated with assertion, understanding the truth predicate requires understanding the norms governing the practice of assertoric utterance, and this is a substantive form of pragmatic knowledge. This explains the fact that, as Dummett has observed, to grasp the concept of truth is to grasp the "point" of the language game of assertion.[20] And it is precisely the Equivalence Schema that ensures that this grasp of the truth predicate consists in an understanding of the relevant practice. The important point is that the kind of knowledge involved in understanding truth is not semantic, and in particular, it is not a grasp of a kind of property that sentences can have. What the person must grasp is a way of acting, a way of using sentences. Thus, as Habermas says, "The redundancy theory can be said to be based on a correct observation: that 'p' is true adds nothing to the assertion that 'p.' Precisely by asserting 'p' I make a truth-claim for 'p': therein lies the pragmatic meaning of assertion."[21]

Unfortunately, nothing is ever quite so simple. The analysis of the truth predicate provided by Tarski's Schema T is not capable of handling all occurrences of the truth predicate in natural language. In particular, Schema T treats only "freestanding" uses of the predicate—cases when it is applied to complete sentences. But sentences like the following suggest an obvious problem:

(6)   Everything that Bill believes is true.

Neither Schema T nor the illocutionary-act analysis can account for this usage of the predicate, because analyzing this sentence using Schema T would generate a sentence fragment—"everything that Bill believes"—on the right-hand side of the biconditional. In this case, the truth predicate is clearly not redundant.

This is not an issue that Habermas considers, but it does stand as an obvious objection to his line of analysis. There are a number of responses available, all of which have the effect of rewriting sentences like (6) in such a way that the appearance of the truth predicate can be analyzed as an instance of Schema T. I would like to examine one such line of response, partly to disarm this line of objection to Habermas's analysis, but also to lay the groundwork for my later evaluation of the way that he introduces the "is right" predicate for moral judgments.

It has already been argued that the truth predicate plays an expressive role in its "freestanding" uses—it renders explicit an aspect of the utterance that remains tacit in its standard employment. I would like to show that it plays a similar role in "embedded" contexts like (6). The general reason that the truth predicate shows up at all in such contexts is due to a grammatical oddity of natural language. In formal languages it is common to use variables to stand for all kinds of things, including objects, predicates, and sentences. However, it is a conspicuous features of natural languages that they do not contain expressions that can play this role with the same generality. The closest thing we have to variables in English are pronouns "he, she, it" and demonstratives "this, that." However, pronouns and demonstratives are normally consigned to the subject or object positions in sentence, which means that they can generate grammatical problems when they are not used to designate objects. For example, consider the way that the following sentence is rendered in English:

(7) $(\forall x)(x$ is a raven $\rightarrow x$ is black)

(8)   For each object, if it is a raven then it is black.

Here the generic term "object" and the pronoun "it" replace the variable x. This aspect of their use makes pronouns and demonstratives very important pieces of expressive vocabulary, because there are some things that can only be said using variables. In particular, to use quantifiers, one must have variables that can be bound by them. However, it is possible to compress sentence (8) in such a way as to conceal its underlying quantificational structure. One can start by nominalizing the first predicate, and ascribing the universal quantifier to it as an adjective. This has the effect of constructing a noun phrase that refers to all objects satisfying the first predicate. One can then use the second predicate to modify this noun phrase, resulting in the succinct:

(9) All ravens are black.

No mischief occurs so long as the pronouns eliminated refer to objects. However, pronouns are less flexible than variables. In a formal language, I can easily use variables to stand for sentences and quantify over them:

(10) $(\forall p)$(Bill believes $p \rightarrow p$)

But translating this into English is a problem, precisely because I cannot uniformly substitute pronouns for p. The problem is on the right-hand side. The procedure used to arrive at (8) from (7) in this case yields:

(11) For each proposition, if Bill believes it then it.

Formal English requires a subject-predicate structure in any unit which is to play the role of a sentence. The "it" pronoun, even though it *stands for* a whole sentence, only fills a subject position in any sentence in which it occurs. There is no problem on the left-hand side of the conditional, because we are ascribing a predicate to the sentence referred to by "it," namely, that Bill believes it. However, on the right-hand side we are not asserting anything *about* that sentence, we are simply asserting it. So we wind up with just "it," which by itself is not a sentence. What can we do? What we need is a dummy predicate, something that can be ascribed to "it" that will fulfill the grammatical requirement without changing the meaning of the expression, that is, we need a predicate that will be "redundant." But this is exactly what the truth predicate provides. With Schema T at our disposal, we can rewrite the original sentence (10) as follows:

(12) $(\forall p)$(Bill believes $p \rightarrow p$ is true)

The English translation of this sentence then reads:

(13) For each proposition, if Bill believes it then it is true.

This is perfectly grammatical. However, if we then compress this sentence in the same way that we did with (8), we get:

(14) Everything that Bill believes is true.

This sentence is highly misleading. The "is true" was stuck into sentence (13) as a redundant predicate, just to fulfill a grammatical requirement.[22] However, when the sentence gets compressed the second predicate migrates, concealing its original grammatical role. This transforms "is true," which is obviously redundant in (13), into what looks like a substantive predicate in (14). But it is a grammatical illusion, one that is dissipated as soon as the logical structure of the sentence is revealed.

Thus the truth predicate is important, because it is only through the availability of such a predicate that pronouns can be used to stand for sentences within the confines of English grammar. This allows us to say things that we would not be able to say otherwise, in particular, it allows us to quantify over sentences. And all embedded uses of the truth predicate, it has been argued, can be analyzed in terms of some role in the use of pronouns and demonstratives as propositional variables.[23] The ability to use language in this way is important, because it allows us to say extremely general things about sentences. In fact, there are some types of claims that can only be made with the use of such a device. In particular, certain kinds of anaphora (e.g., when one doesn't know exactly what someone else said, but wants to assert it as well), and claims at a certain level of generality (e.g., saying something about all of someone's beliefs), can only be achieved with propositional variables. This means that the truth predicate plays an important expressive role, both within sentences and without, but it does not pick out any particular property that sentences may or may not possess.

It would be easy to infer from this that the truth-aptness of moral judgments is a trivial property of their grammatical form. For instance, Schema T can obviously be instantiated in such a way as to produce sentences like:

(15) "Lying is wrong" is true iff lying is wrong.[24]

In this view, the fact that moral statements possess truth-conditions is a surface feature of their linguistic structure. As long as the statements are assertions, and so can be embedded without semantic anomaly in negations, conditionals, and other logical connectives, then they are truth-apt.

5.3 The Discourse Theory of Rightness

While many would be content to leave it at that, Habermas adds a peculiar twist to the argument. He adopts from the noncognitivist tradition the idea that moral judgments are best analyzed not as assertions, as in (15), but rather as imperatives.[25] As we know, Habermas maintains that social interaction is governed by a set of discursively incurred commitments that agents conform to for noninstrumental reasons. However, these commitments are formulated at a certain level of generality and are not always common knowledge among agents. This means that social interaction must be managed in its details through the issuance of imperatives, prescribing particular duties to specific individuals. In such cases, the imperatives do not represent the arbitrary will of the individual issuing them, but are merely particular instantiations of more general normative obligations. This practice of issuing normatively authorized imperatives constitutes a distinct language game, comparable to the promising game outlined above. As a result, moral imperatives are governed by their own validity claim, which, as we have seen, is supposed to be analogous to the truth predicate that governs assertoric discourse.

Thus Habermas argues that moral statements should be analyzed as moves in the game of issuing normatively authorized imperatives. (Unauthorized imperatives, in Habermas's view, should be analyzed as concealed assertions: "either you do a_1, or I will do a_2.")[26] Here he is expanding the traditional Kantian view, which regards morality as the actions of an agent conforming to self-directed imperatives, to incorporate social context, in which the agent conforms to imperatives issued by others. Just as Kant did not regard the categorical imperative as "true," or the object of determinative judgment, Habermas argues that social norms are neither true nor false. Thus he accepts the view, shared by many noncognitivists, that the associated imperatives lack truth-conditions. He suggests instead that imperatives have "rightness-conditions." Rightness as a property of imperatives is then analyzed using a type of equivalence schema. Thus the general imperative formulation of a norm, such as:

(16)   Help the poor

is, in Habermas's view, equivalent to:

(17)   It is right that one help the poor.[27]

The "is right" in this sentence, again, just renders explicit the illocutionary force of the imperative. Thus:

(18)   It is right that one help the poor iff one ought to help the poor.

Or more generally:

(19)   It is right that p iff one ought to p.

However, it should be noted that "is right" is not redundant in this sentence. This is because adding the "is right" predicate to the imperative in (16) has the effect of transforming it into an assertion. This is reflected in (19) by the fact that the right-hand side of the conditional contains an "ought." However, arguments are truth-preserving only because truth is perfectly redundant in its freestanding uses in the language game of assertion. So long as rightness is not redundant in the same way, it will be impossible to sustain the analogy that is required between rightness and truth (see §3.4 above). The mere fact that a conclusion follows from premises that are right will not entail that the conclusion is also right.

The problem stems from the fact that rightness has been taken out of the language game of imperatives and is being defined in the language game of assertion (19). To create a redundant rightness predicate, it must be defined within its home language game. But doing this requires that a certain amount of logical vocabulary be introduced into that game as well. Consider the case of "is promised," and the language game of commitment introduced earlier. An interpretation of "iff" for this language-game can be given by specifying that to utter "p iff q" is to commit oneself to the action that consists of performing either both or neither of actions described by p and q. For example, when an agent commits himself to p, and to p iff q, one can infer that he has committed himself to q. The conditions governing appropriate use of the prefacing phrase in (3) can then be given by the following schema:

(P)   It is promised that p iff p,

where this sentence is to be understood as a commitment-generating speech act like the others (i.e., where the occurrence of p on the right-hand side of the biconditional is understood as a promise, not an assertion).

The "is promised" predicate will then be redundant within the commitment-generating language game, in the sense that it will add nothing to the speech acts to which it is conjoined. But although it may not change the meaning of sentences, or alter their pragmatic force, it will have the same useful properties that the truth predicate has for assertions. Suppose that my friend Bill has just committed himself to some set of actions, and I would like to commit myself to the same actions. I can do so by saying:

(20)   Everything that Bill said is promised.

This is of course short for:

(21) $(\forall p)(\text{Bill said } p \rightarrow p)$,

stated in the language game of commitment. Using Schema P, this can be converted into:

(22) $(\forall p)(\text{Bill said } p \rightarrow p \text{ is promised})$,

which can be directly translated into English without grammatical problems.

  Rightness can be analyzed in the same way. First, "iff" would have to be defined by specifying that to utter "p iff q" is to instruct someone to perform either both or neither of the actions described by p and q. The rightness predicate can then be defined using an equivalence schema:

(R)   It is right that p iff p.[28]

Once defined in this way, the predicate "is right" will operate for normatively authorized imperatives in the same way that "is promised" does for commitments, and "is true" does for assertions. With this definition, valid moral arguments will be "rightness-preserving," just as valid assertoric arguments are "truth-preserving." Naturally, this will not be a substantive fact about the arguments, but rather a logical consequence of the rules that specify what is to count as an acceptable inference, combined with the definition of rightness and truth in terms of their respective equivalence schemas. Thus the adoption of a theory of truth and rightness of this type clearly disarms the claim that moral statements lack cognitive content because they are not truth-apt. Rightness, according to this view, is just as good as truth.

  But notice how strange (R) is. For this definition of rightness to work, (R) must be understood as itself a normatively authorized imperative. However, it is a conspicuous feature of our existing practices of issuing such imperatives that we have no vocabulary allowing us to generate logically complex commands. When logical vocabulary is used in imperatives, it is embedded in the propositional content, and is understood truth-functionally. For instance, when someone says "you break it, you fix it," he is not saying that "if it is right that you broke it, then it is right that you fix it." He is saying that "it is right that the one who broke it be the one who fixes it." The conditional is used to describe a logically complex state of affairs, not to issue a logically complex imperative. (The fact that I needed to *define* a biconditional for the promising game and the imperative game reflects the fact that everyday usage does not supply us with this kind of logical vocabulary for anything other than assertions.)

Another way to see the point is to observe that although imperatives can occur as conclusions of conditionals (e.g., "he crossed the line, so disqualify him!"), they can never occur as antecedents. To embed a normatively authorized imperative in a conditional, in must be converted into an assertion. We cannot say, "if help the poor, then get to it!" but must say, "if you should be helping the poor, then get to it!" The significance of this point is that only assertions function as arguments. And if the truth predicate articulates the illocutionary force of assertions, then the only kind of "validity claim" that we can argue about is the truth-claim. (And if one is committed to an inferential semantics, this means that the propositional content of any utterance, even an imperative, corresponds to its truth-conditions.)[29]

This means that although the "is right" predicate may appear analogous to the truth predicate when tacked on to an imperative sentence, it does not play a role comparable to truth, because the language game of issuing imperatives does not play a role in language that is comparable to the language game of assertion. The big difference is that we are only able to *argue* in the language game of assertion. This suggests that Habermas's strategy for defusing moral noncognitivism—introducing validity claims other than truth—is not a good one.

However, even if Habermas could make the formal analogy between truth and rightness work, he would still have to claim that moral judgments are capable of truth and falsity, simply because they can be formulated as assertions. If, in Habermas's view, to make an assertion is to raise a truth claim for one's utterance, then to say "murder is wrong" is to associate the validity claim of truth with this statement. This is an unavoidable consequence of Habermas's illocutionary-act analysis of the validity claims. So whether "murder is wrong" can be reformulated as an imperative that raises a rightness claim is irrelevant, especially since it can only be deployed in practical discourse when given this assertoric form. Thus Habermas's own analysis of truth renders his strategy for rejecting noncognitivism unnecessary. The obvious recourse is simply to grant that moral judgments can be straightforwardly true or false: "murder is wrong" is true just in case murder is wrong, and false if it isn't.

But what about the analysis of rightness suggested by (19)? Doesn't this suggest that there is some disanalogy between the predicate "is right" and everyday empirical properties like "is yellow"? In my view, what the connection between the rightness predicate and "ought" sentences shows is that rightness should not always be treated as a simple property of actions, but that it sometimes expresses a *modality*, in this case a deontic one. The better comparison is not between "is right" and "is true," but between "is right" and predicates like "is possible." As is well known, one can define a set of deontic operators: O for "is obligatory," P for "is permitted," F for "is forbidden," in a way that parallels the standard "alethic" modalities: necessity (N), possibility (M), and impossibility (I). The deontic modalities are interdefinable in the same way: Pp iff $\neg O\neg p$ iff $\neg Fp$. Right and wrong can then be defined using these deontic operators:

(23)   It is wrong that p iff Fp.

(Rightness is a bit tricky, because the predicate is ambiguous between Op and Pp.) In any case, (23) can be compared with:

(24)   It is possible that p iff Mp.

Modalities are often expressed in English through verb modification. So if we want to render "Mp" into English we can say either "it might be true," or "it is possible." Similarly, to say "Fp," we can say "it should not be done," or "it is wrong." (This is why the right-hand side of the biconditional in (19) needed to have an "ought" in it.) Interpreting the basic set of moral terms as deontic modalities, on analogy with the alethic, also gives sense to the intuition that moral statements are not straightforwardly descriptive in the way that factual claims are. In the same way that "it is possible that p" does not describe a state of affairs in the actual world, but rather claims that p is true at some possible world, "it is obligatory that p" can be interpreted to mean that p is true at some suitable possible world, namely, a *deontically perfect world*.[30] Norms can then be interpreted as selection functions that determine which set of possible worlds qualify as deontically perfect.

The idea that there is some connection between a sentence being "true" and its being "descriptive" rests upon a simple failure to recognize the way modalities function in natural language. There is a sense in which normative statements do not purport to tell us what is true. But in the same sense, statements about the past do not purport to tell us what is true, they tell us what *used* to be true. And statements about possibilities do not tell us what is true, they tell us what *might* be true. Normative statements simply tell us what *should* be true. But these are just different ways of articulating the force of the various modalities; they do not in any way suggest that the associated propositions lack descriptive content, or that the entire statement cannot be straightforwardly true or false when the modality is expressed in other ways.

I mention this because it is a source of enormous confusion in the literature, confusion that Habermas does not entirely escape.[31] In general, Habermas retains a residual adherence to the idea that "truth" has some connection with description, and so "rightness" needs to be introduced to capture the imperative dimension of morality. He fails to recognize that the real connection is the one between truth and assertion, and that it is the practice of assertion that gives descriptive character to the propositional content of all utterances, including imperatives. Adopting a deflationary view of truth eliminates the suggestion that truth involves some kind of correspondence relation between mind and world. This allows the theorist to say that moral statements are straightforwardly true, without suggesting that there are moral facts out there to which they correspond.[32] (Similarly, it allows the theorist to say that modal statements are straightforwardly true, without suggesting that there are possible worlds out there to which *they* correspond.)

It should be noted, however, that the metaphysical neutrality of the deflationary theory does no more than disarm a traditional source of moral noncognitivism. It does nothing whatsoever to specify what sorts of circumstances or arguments might license moral claims. It has the effect of unloading all of these problems onto the theory of justification. This is not to say that developing a deflationary analysis of truth is a waste of time. The notion of truth has given rise to an enormous amount of muddled thinking—the deflationary theory has the laudable effect of eliminating one source of the bad metaphysics that gave rise to moral noncognitivism.[33] However, it remains to be shown that there are epistemic standards governing moral argumentation that can guarantee less than arbitrary or parochial outcomes of this practice. This is what Habermas hopes to achieve in his theory of practical discourse.

5.4   The Dialogical Theory of Justification

The most common source of moral noncognitivism is, of course, not some abstract philosophical conception of truth, but rather the frustration that many people experience when they try to argue about moral claims, or even to justify their own moral commitments. It is often difficult to avoid the feeling that, at some point, "the spade turns." This kind of experience is what generates the common view that moral claims are somehow "irrational" because they rely upon premises that are, in the end, culturally relative, or even purely subjective. Informally, the case for this position seems fairly easy to make. The relativist simply points to the existence of intractable moral disputes—over abortion, euthanasia, etc.—or to the differences in moral obligations among cultures, and denies that there are any reasonable grounds to expect that these differences can be eliminated through argument.[34]

However, there is a significant difference between this informal argument and the more general relativist position. Showing that a particular argument has not issued in agreement provides no reason to think that it will not, someday, issue in agreement. (We have many examples of arguments that have taken thousands of years to resolve.) The relativist is in any case not in the business of making mere predictions; she wants to claim that, in principle, moral arguments cannot be resolved through explicit discursive procedures. Normally, the way we determine whether an argument is resolvable is to pursue the argument, to see whether it resolves itself. To claim, in advance, that an argument is not resolvable is to make a rather special kind of philosophical claim, one that presupposes a certain kind of external knowledge about the epistemic status of the argument. Thus the informal defense of relativism, while it may provide the intuitive motivation for the position, comes nowhere near establishing its truth. To defend the position, the relativist must actually produce an epistemological theory, one that specifies in general how we come to have well-justified beliefs, and why moral judgments in particular fail to be well justified by these criteria.

Generally speaking, relativists do have such a theory. The structure of this underlying theory can be discerned quite clearly in J. L. Mackie's influential argument against the possibility of "objectively valid" moral arguments:

Let us suppose that we could make explicit the reasoning that supports some evaluative conclusion, where this conclusion has some action-guiding force that is not contingent upon desires or purposes or chosen ends. Then what I am saying is that somewhere in the input to this argument—perhaps in one or more of the premises, perhaps in some part of the form of the argument—there will be something which cannot be objectively validated—some premise which is not capable of being simply true, or some form of argument which is not valid as a matter of general logic, whose authority or cogency is not objective, but is constituted by our choosing or deciding to think in a certain way.[35]

At first glance, this may appear to be nothing more than a *statement* of the relativist position. But looking at it more carefully, it is possible to pick out a particular theoretical conception of how justificatory relations are to be properly analyzed. Mackie suggests that to determine the soundness of a particular conclusion, we must lay out the entire chain of reasons that supports it. However, it is well known that any attempt to justify a given statement inferentially gives rise to a trilemma. Each new argument that we introduce in support of our conclusion will contain premises that themselves stand in need of justification. If we introduce some new argument in order to discharge these premises, then we have simply introduced a new batch of premises that will themselves need to be discharged. The only way to break out of this regress is to use one of the conclusions as a premise (i.e., reason in a circle), or simply break off the chain of reasons (i.e., make an undefended assumption).

In its most general form, this regress argument suggests that all of our judgments are, at some level, "constituted by our choosing or deciding to think a certain way." Assuming that an infinite chain of supporting reasons is unacceptable, all of our beliefs must be either self-confirming or arbitrary. Naturally, if this were the case, then there would be nothing especially dubious about moral judgments. To get moral relativism without general relativism, the theorist must claim that certain types of knowledge-claims are not undermined by the regress argument. The most popular strategy for grounding this claim has been to suggest that a class of "basic" beliefs are noninferentially justified. For instance, it has been claimed that some beliefs are intrinsically justified by virtue of their content, or that the agent is justified in believing certain things about the world by virtue of standing in the appropriate sort of causal relation to the objects or events in question. This strategy for responding to the regress problem is referred to as foundationalism.

When Mackie speaks of our moral arguments being based upon a certain kind of "input," he is supposing that the right way to handle the regress argument is to cut it off with a set of undefended assumptions, that is, he is suggesting that the formal structure of epistemic relations is foundationalist. To this he then adds a substantive thesis about the kinds of beliefs that can function as undefended assumptions without introducing an element of arbitrariness. Moral beliefs are not on this list. Thus:

When we ask the awkward question, how we can be aware of . . . the truth of these distinctively ethical premises or of the cogency of this distinctively ethical pattern of reasoning, none of our ordinary accounts of sensory perception or introspection or the framing and confirming of explanatory hypotheses or inferences or logical construction or conceptual analysis, or any combination of these, will provide a satisfactory answer; "a special sort of intuition" is a lame answer, but it is the one to which the clear-headed objectivist is compelled to resort.[36]

The idea here is that our ordinary empirical beliefs escape from the regress of justification by virtue of the fact that they are ultimately grounded in perception, a form of experience that is inherently veridical. Because our perceptions are taken to represent a physical world that is shared by all agents, empirical beliefs can be expected to be the same for all agents. This means that empirical inquiry can be expected to exhibit convergence, as mistakes are corrected and more information becomes available (it will thus be "objective"). Moral arguments, on the other hand, because of their prescriptive character, cannot ultimately be grounded in any direct experience of the physical world. The relativist then suggests that they are grounded in something else, something that may be shared to a greater or lesser degree. This varies from pure self-interest to widely shared cultural values. In each case, however, the level of convergence exhibited by the discourse will depend entirely upon the extent to which the resources that serve as "input" into these moral arguments are shared. Argumentation itself will be incapable of producing any greater level of agreement than that which agents already bring with them.

A common response to this line of argument has been to accept the formal component of the foundationalist analysis, but to reject the substantive list of belief-types that are claimed to be capable of "objective validation." Naturalist, realist, and intuitionist theories of morality all attempt to show that moral judgments can be "grounded" in some class of noninferentially justified beliefs that will be uniform across individuals and cultures. All of these theories suffer from well-known difficulties, so the relativist position appears quite strong in this context. However, what all of these theories have in common is that they accept the basic foundationalist strategy for responding to the regress argument, seeking only to deny the narrow empiricist interpretation that it is usually given. A different strategy would be to reject the argument at its first step, denying the force of the regress argument entirely.

One reason that some theorists have been inclined to take this more radical step is that foundationalism does not offer a very persuasive justification for any kind of belief, including empirical ones.[37] If the theory cannot handle this best-case scenario, it is no surprise that it cannot handle more sophisticated types of claims, like moral judgments. What should be clear from the argument presented above is that Mackie does not have a specific argument against the claim that moral statements can be well justified. The argument that he deploys against morality is actually just a form of general skepticism, that is, skepticism about *all* knowledge. Having used this skeptical argument to undermine his opponent's beliefs, he then claims that his own favored set of beliefs are exempt from the same set of skeptical doubts (a position whose defense he alludes to, but does not articulate).[38] But the problem with using skepticism to undermine your opponent is that it tends to undermine your own position as well. (This is an error to which philosophers are exceptionally prone—attempting to use general skepticism to defeat a *particular* theoretical position.)

But apart from the difficulties that Mackie's own argument embroils him in, there is a well-known Kantian argument against the kind of regress problem that foundationalists like Mackie employ against moral cognitivists. Kant interprets the foundationalist response to the regress argument as a naive application of the following principle of reason: "if *the conditioned is given, the entire sum of conditions, and consequently the absolutely unconditioned* (through which alone the conditioned has been possible) *is also given.*"[39] Basic beliefs, in the standard empiricist version of foundationalism, correspond to the unconditioned in this sense. The assumption is that for an agent to be justified in holding any particular belief, the entire support structure for this belief, both inferential and factual, must already be given. Thus the agent must have all of the other supporting beliefs in her head, and must have already made all the correct inferential moves linking these beliefs to the conclusion that is under investigation. In Kant's view, this picture involves a certain illegitimate hypostatization of these inferential relations. This is why, for example, he rejects the type of causal regress argument that motivated philosophers to posit a "first cause" of the universe:

The principle of reason is thus properly only a *rule*, prescribing a regress in the series of the conditions of given appearances, and forbidding it to bring the regress to a close by treating anything at which it may arrive as absolutely unconditioned. It is not a principle of the possibility of experience and of empirical knowledge of objects of the senses, and therefore not a principle of the understanding; for every experience, in conformity with the given [forms of] intuition, is enclosed within limits. Nor is it a constitutive principle of reason, enabling us to extend our concept of the sensible world beyond all possible experience. It is rather a principle of the greatest possible continuation and extension of experience, allowing no empirical limit to hold as absolute. Thus it is a principle of reason which serves as a *rule*, postulating what we ought to do in the regress, but *not anticipating* what is present *in the object as it is in itself, prior to all regress.* Accordingly, I entitle it a *regulative* principle of reason.[40]

The way Kant avoids the force of the regress argument here is to endorse a certain form of antirealism about the objects of inquiry. The causal relations between events are not there in advance; causality is a kind of interpretation that we place on events in the course of inquiry. Thus Kant says that, for example, questions about the beginning of time have no sense, because the chronological ordering of events is, in principle, constituted by the activity of inquiry. In contemporary philosophical jargon, we would say there is no "fact of the matter" as to when the universe began. Naturally, we do not have to accept Kant's antirealism about the external world to see that a comparable antirealist stance could be adopted toward mental states, the traditional objects of epistemic inquiry.[41] Kantians respond to the epistemic regress argument by simply denying that there is any "fact of the matter" as to whether an agent is justified in holding a particular belief. Epistemic relations are not intrinsic or built-in features of our beliefs; they are constituted by the activity of justification. Asking whether an agent is justified in believing *p* is just an oblique way of asking about the agent's capacity to justify that belief. This relieves the Kantian of the desire to specify, in advance, a set of "unconditioned," or basic beliefs to terminate the regress. Although the Kantian does not deny that justification involves a regress in the chain of supporting reasons, he does deny that all of the arguments in the supporting chain must already be given for the conclusion to be justified. Giving these reasons is a task, not a prerequisite.

This basic Kantian line is the one that Habermas adopts in defending the integrity of moral argumentation. For this reason, in his epistemological work, he does not attempt to specify necessary and sufficient conditions for moral statements to *be justified*. Instead, he attempts to articulate a set of regulative principles that must be followed in order *to justify* such statements. Thus Habermas rejects the traditional project of analytic epistemology, which has been to find, for example, "a set of substantive conditions that specify when a belief is justified,"[42] or to specify "what conditions must be satisfied in order for a cognitive state to constitute a genuine instance of propositional knowledge."[43] This way of posing the question, in Habermas's view, already prejudices the answer. Habermas's way of articulating this is to say that by conceiving of justifiability as a property of beliefs, one tacitly treats justification as an essentially "monological" process, that is, one involving only the agent's cognitive states and the objects of representation. Since the agent's capacity to justify his belief that *p* to others is explained in terms of his justification for believing that *p*, this view has the effect of reducing all public practices of justification to either secondary or derivative phenomena. Habermas endorses instead a "dialogical" model of justification, in which justification *to others* is taken as the primary phenomenon. The claim that a particular agent's belief might *be* justified is then interpreted in terms of her capacity to justify it to others.

This dialogical conception of justification is roughly equivalent to what has come to be known as "contextualism" in the Anglo-American philosophical tradition. (This has also given rise to some terminological confusion. Habermas often criticizes what he calls "contextualism," when what he really means to criticize is epistemic or moral *relativism*. This is confusing, because moral relativism is more often the product of an underlying foundationalism. When moral judgments are said to derive "ultimately" from culture-specific norms and values, this "ultimately" flags the foundationalist line of thinking. Things are further complicated by the fact that theorists like Richard Rorty are both contextualists and relativists, and often try to blur the distinction. As a result, the term contextualist is not always applied unambiguously. Thus my usage represents something of a regimentation of everyday philosophical use.)

There are two important components to the contextualist/dialogical conception of rational justification, namely, a discursive model of justification and an antirealist response to the regress problem.

5.4.1   A discursive model of justification

Susan Haack identifies the basic characteristic of contextualism as follows:

> It is sometimes felt that contextualism does not really address the same question as the traditionally rival theories, a feeling sometimes expressed in the suggestion that contextualists are focused, not on the explication of "A is justified in believing that *p*" but only the explication of "A can justify his belief that *p* (to the members of C)," or, less charitably, that they have confused the two.[44]

We can refer to the first conception of justification, which attempts to specify the properties that beliefs must possess in order to warrant the attribution of the predicate "is justified," as *criterial*.[45] We can refer to the second conception, which focuses instead on the way beliefs are defended in public practices of justification, as a *discursive* model of justification. Coherentist, foundationalist, and even reliabilist accounts of justification are criterial models, insofar as they attempt to specify necessary and sufficient conditions for the attribution of epistemic properties to beliefs. The foundationalist, for instance, wants to offer something like the following criterion:

Where B is the set of basic beliefs and R the set of valid rules of inference (logical, semantic, evidential, etc.), belief p is justified if and only if:
(1) $p \in$ B, or
(2) p is the conclusion of an argument licensed by a rule belonging to R, which has as its premises only justified beliefs.[46]

The coherentist often has something rather similar in mind, for example, that p is justified iff when compared to any alternative belief, p provides a greater or equivalent level of coherence.

The contextualist radicalizes the discussion by suggesting that there may not be any fact of the matter to this dispute between the foundationalist and the coherentist. To motivate this position, consider the following argument: Let us assume a simple "internalism" constraint, namely, that for an agent to be justified in believing p, she must know what this justification is. To attribute the status of "is justified" to her belief, then we must also attribute to her knowledge of the relevant justification-conditions. Now let us impose the following "use" constraint on the attribution of knowledge, namely, that in order to attribute knowledge to an agent there must be some manner in which the agent can manifest her grasp of this knowledge.[47] But clearly the only way the agent could publicly manifest her grasp of the justification-conditions for her belief would be to actually justify the belief, and for an action to count as "justifying a belief" it must be performed *in a way that is acceptable to others*. Thus the internalism constraint, combined with the requirement that there be a difference between *thinking* one is justified in believing something and actually *being* justified in believing it, implies that our attribution of justification-conditions to beliefs is dependent upon our public practices of justifying beliefs to one another.

In this view, investigation into the structure of justification should begin by examining the way in which agents justify statements to one another, that is, examining the *process* of justification. This suggests that the question "What makes a belief justified?" may not have a simple answer in the way that has traditionally been assumed. There may not be a single (even complex) property that constitutes "being" justified. Naturally, this does not mean that we cannot continue to speak about justification and belief in the way we always have; it just means that we must reconceptualize the relations of explanatory dependence that have dominated the analysis of these terms. The *property* of being justified may only be explicable with reference to the *process* through which a belief can be justified.

5.4.2 An antirealist response to the regress problem

The most important principle underlying the regress argument is the claim that a belief can be justified only through reference to some further belief. Foundationalism is characterized by its rejection of this principle. In the foundationalist view, knowledge is possible only because this regress can be cut short with a terminating judgment that is *known* without being *inferred* from another belief.

Nonfoundationalist models of justification differ in that they accept the claim that beliefs can only be justified by further beliefs. The two dominant nonfoundationalist views are distinguished by the position they take on the need for terminating judgments. *Coherence* theories suggest that, with a few qualifications, the option of repeating an argument is not so bad. In this respect, coherentists claim that justification has a very different structure than had traditionally been assumed. Since an argument is permitted to circle back upon itself, there is no need for terminating judgments. *Contextualist* theories, on the other hand, retain the basic structure of justification from foundationalism, that is, they accept the need for terminating judgments, but introduce the notion of a *background* to take the place of a privileged class of beliefs. The key contextualist idea is that the content of this background changes according to circumstance.

The main difference between foundationalism and contextualism is that the foundationalist maintains that a certain class of beliefs forms a sort of "natural kind" that makes its members uniquely suited to serve as terminating judgments. The contextualist, on the other hand, rejects the idea that there is a particular class of beliefs that, through some built-in epistemic property, is able to serve as the basis for all others. Michael Williams, the most influential proponent of this view, articulates the position in the following way:

Consider Wittgenstein's remark that "My having two hands is, in normal circumstances, as certain as anything that I could produce in evidence for it." Entered in the right setting, a claim to have two hands might function like a foundationalist's basic statement, providing a stopping place for requests for evidence or justification. . . . But in other circumstances *the very same claim* might be contestable and so might stand in need of evidential support. The content of what is claimed does not guarantee a claim some particular epistemic standing.[48]

The status of a belief, in this view, is determined by the context of inquiry, and not by some intrinsic epistemic property. In any discursive context, there will be certain beliefs that are simply taken for granted. These form the background, rather than the subject of inquiry. In a particular context, these beliefs will constitute "the facts" and will serve as regress-stoppers. However, as soon as they become thematized, they immediately lose this status and become problematic claims that may in turn be justified or revised. Thus in the contextualist view, there is no instrinsic property that makes some particular class of beliefs factual. The epistemic status of a belief is determined by the role it plays in actual contexts of justification. In this way, "a fact loses its status as soon as it is no longer used as a possible starting point, but as the conclusion of an argument."[49]

The antirealist response to the regress problem fits well with the discursive conception of justification, because the latter provides a natural interpretation for the notion of "contextually basic beliefs," namely, those beliefs that are taken for granted by the *audience* to whom the justification is addressed. In the case of moral argumentation, for instance, the lifeworld will provide a rich background of moral beliefs that can be taken for granted as the starting point of any moral argument. Thus there is no problem determining what the "input" of any moral argument will be—it will simply be the set of moral beliefs that are shared by all those who are participating in any particular exercise of moral deliberation.

The dialogical component of the contextualist view is, unfortunately, often overlooked. Haack, for instance, suggests that the contextualist is making a proposal something like the following:

Where B is the set of beliefs and R the set of standards or rules of inference that are accepted in the community to which agent a belongs, a is justified in believing p iff:

(1) $p \in$ B, or

(2) p is the conclusion of an argument licensed by a rule belonging to R, which has as its premises only beliefs that a is justified in believing.

What she does here, in effect, is hypostatize the set of contextually basic beliefs and ascribe it to a "community" to which the agent belongs. Since there is presumably a fact of the matter as to which community an agent belongs, there is also then a fact of the matter as to whether any particular one of her beliefs is justified. In setting things up this way, Haack reinterprets contextualism as a monological theory, thereby missing the force of the challenge it presents to the traditional models. Not only does this perpetuate a certain naive realism about the epistemic relations between beliefs, but it assumes that the acceptability of a particular set of beliefs will be fixed by general community standards, rather than by the immediate context of inquiry.

The more legitimate doubts about contextualism concern the extent to which it undermines the normative status of the theory of justification. Criterial conceptions of justification, if they could be articulated in a satisfactory manner, would be powerful normative tools. Not only would they provide a direct specification of the canons of right reasoning, they would also guarantee (granted some minor additional assumptions) the existence of a finite decision procedure that could determine, for any belief, whether or not it was justified. Given an exhaustive characterization of an agent's cognitive states, a criterial model would provide a simple algorithm that would generate a straightforward yes/no answer to any question of the form "Is agent a justified in believing that p?"

A contextualist model cannot make the same sort of claim. Justifying something to others means bringing about a rationally motivated agreement. However, every such rationally achieved agreement will rest upon an antecedent agreement that is itself not rationally achieved, namely, the set of shared beliefs that are taken for granted in the context. This agreement is required in order to fix the terminating judgments. Naturally, in another context these presuppositions can in turn be taken up, questioned, defended, or revised. But since this new context will itself require further presuppositions, a situation that is well-founded in every aspect is precluded in principle. Every explicit agreement achieved in discourse presupposes a broader tacit agreement.

Habermas characterizes the dependence of explicit agreement upon antecedent consensus in the following way:

> There is no "natural" end to the chain of possible substantial reasons; one cannot exclude the possibility that new information and better reasons will be brought forward. Under favorable conditions, we bring argumentation to a *de facto* conclusion only when the reasons solidify against the horizon of unproblematic background assumptions into such a coherent whole that an uncoerced agreement on the acceptability of the disputed validity claim emerges. The expression "rationally motivated agreement" takes this remainder of facticity into account: we attribute to reasons the force to "move" participants, in a nonpsychological sense, to adopt affirmative positions.[50]

As a result, the contextualist cannot regard justification as more basic than agreement. This means that not every agreement factored into the epistemic status of a belief can be de jure, some must be de facto. The conclusion often drawn from this, by both friends and enemies of contextualism, is that an ineradicable element of arbitrariness is thereby introduced into the theory of justification, and so any claim to normative standing must be abandoned. Any procedure designed to determine the epistemic status of a belief would require as "input" not only an account of the cognitive states of the agent, but also a descriptive characterization of what would prompt others to accept the belief. Rorty suggests on this basis that warrant is fundamentally a "sociological matter, to be ascertained by observing the reception of [an agent's] statement by her peers."[51] The only way to avoid this conclusion, he suggests, would be to provide "some way of determining warrant *sub specie aeternitatis*, some natural order of reasons which determines, quite apart from [the agent's] ability to justify *p* to those around her, whether she is *really* justified in holding *p*."[52]

Habermas responds to this dilemma by suggesting that the normative concept of rationality can be scaled down without being entirely abandoned. He first grants that a theory of justification will not provide an "operationalized procedure, adherence to which could be checked like the application of a criterion."[53] Agreement or consensus will have to be admitted as a primitive component of the theory of justification. And certainly, "relativistic consequences are unavoidable if what is collectively valid is conceived only as a social fact."[54] But Habermas thinks these consequences can be avoided if appropriate distinctions are drawn regarding the *quality* of an agreement. He suggests that a particular achieved agreement can be characterized as more or less rational depending on the extent to which the procedure through which it was obtained satisfies certain purely *formal* constraints.

The purpose of these formal or procedural constraints will be to specify what counts as a *rational agreement*, where this is interpreted to mean a consensus that is motivated by the force of the better argument. However, what counts as a good argument cannot be specified criterially. This is why the discourse theory must "explain the peculiar non-coercive compulsion of the better argument in terms of the formal properties of the discourse, and not in terms of something that either lies at the foundation of the context of argumentation, such as the logical consistency of sentences, or, as it were, enters into argumentation from the outside, such as empirical evidence."[55]

Habermas summarizes his line of thinking in the following way:

The foundationalist assumption that there exist basic sentences whose truth is immediately accessible to perception or to intuition has not withstood linguistic arguments for the holistic character of our interpretations, namely, that every justification must at least *proceed from* a pre-understood context or background understanding. This insight tends to support a pragmatic conception of justification as a public practice in which criticizable validity claims can be defended with good reasons. Of course, the criteria of rationality which determine what reasons count as good reasons can themselves be made a matter for discussion. Hence procedural characteristics of the process of argumentation itself must ultimately bear the burden of explaining why results achieved in a procedurally correct manner enjoy the presumption of validity.[56]

Habermas argues that these procedural constraints can be specified as a set of rules: (1) governing the construction of specific argument sequences; (2) imposing procedural constraints on the exchange of arguments; and (3) specifying the overall organizational structure of the interaction. These provide a characterization of the *properties* of rational inference, the *procedures* through which rational argument is conducted, and the *process* through which agreement is achieved.[57] These are elaborated in the following way:

1. Construction of arguments. This set of constraints ensures that claims by participants possess the "general properties of cogent arguments."[58] These include both formal-semantic (inferences must be licensed by standard rules governing natural deduction, introduction and elimination of logical constants, analytic equivalences, etc.) and pragmatic (inferences must follow accepted rules of evidential or casuistic inference, discourse-specific "boundary" rules, pragmatic entailments, etc.). Habermas offers as examples of rules that belong in this category constraints that have the effect of imposing logical and linguistic consistency upon speakers and that ensure uniformity of meaning across individuals.[59]

2. Argumentation procedure. These rules are intended to ensure that arguments are tested in the course of a conversational exchange that exhibits an orderly sequence of topic-relevant argumentative contributions. These are the sorts of rules that Paul Grice investigated in his analysis of conversational implicatures. As Grice put it,

> Out talk exchanges do not normally consist of a succession of disconnected remarks, *and would not be rational if they did.* They are characteristically, to some degree at least, cooperative efforts; and each participant recognizes in them, to some extent, a common purpose or set of purposes, or at least a mutually accepted direction.... [A]t each stage, some possible conversational moves would be excluded as conversationally unsuitable.[60]

The examples Habermas gives of these types of rules are similar to Grice's, requiring that speakers only assert only what they really believe, that they not change topics without good reason, and so on.[61]

3. Interaction structure. These rules specify that the argument, viewed as a sequence of social actions, must satisfy certain symmetry conditions between participants, for example, that opportunities to participate are equally distributed, that the interaction is immunized against repression, force, and so on. The idea is to formalize the intuition that a rational consensus cannot be attained by excluding certain persons, topics, or points of view. Habermas gives as examples rules requiring that all individuals have the freedom and opportunity to participate, to question any assertion, express any attitude, and so on.[62]

In one sense, these rules are just social norms that define a certain sort of practice, namely, rational argumentation. However, they differ from all other types of social norms in that the practice of argumentation is the practice that regiments symbolically mediated interaction in such a way as to permit the emergence of propositionally differentiated speech. It is therefore the practice that fixes the semantic content of our utterances and intentional states. Thus it is one practice that agents, insofar as they retain a broadly communicative orientation, cannot take a hypothetical attitude toward, because it is constitutive of their own reflective competencies. Thus:

The general pragmatic presuppositions that must always be made by participants when they enter into argumentation, whether institutionalized or not, do not have the character of practical obligations at all but that of transcendental constraints. . . . [These presuppositions] have "normative" content *in a broad sense* that cannot be equated with the obligatory force of norms of interaction. Presuppositions of communication do not have regulative force even when they point beyond actually existing conditions in an idealizing fashion. Rather, as *anticipatory* suppositions they are constitutive of a practice that without them could not function and would degenerate at the very least into a surreptitious form of strategic action. Presuppositions of rationality do not impose *obligations* to act rationally; they *make possible* the practice that participants understand as argumentation.[63]

The claim that a particular consensus is rational rests upon the presumption that in the procedure through which it was achieved these idealizing presuppositions were satisfied to an adequate degree. This is how Habermas hopes to split the difference between the criterial and the "sociological" conception of warrant. When we abandon hopes of a criterial conception of rationality, as the contextualist model requires, we admit that it is not possible to determine whether an agreement is warranted by simply checking all the inferences and confirming all the presuppositions (since there can be no fully specifiable procedure for doing so). If, however, we note that the agreement was brought about through a procedure in which every participant had the *opportunity* to question any inference or presupposition, and did not forego this opportunity as the result of any external constraint, then it seems reasonable to say that this agreement is a rational one.

Naturally, in this view a rational consensus is not final. The fact that every participant had the opportunity to question any given presupposition does not mean that they actually did so. That each had the opportunity may create a presumption in favor of the conclusion reached, and may be sufficient to make their consensus a rational one, but it does not preclude the possibility that at some later date this presupposition might be thematized and found inadequate. But this is just to say that justification is defeasible. Thus what Habermas's construction does is preserve the normative force that we intuitively ascribe to the notion of rationality, by permitting a distinction between simply persuading someone that *p* and actually justifying *p* to her, while at the same time acknowledging that what we take to be a rational agreement may still turn out to be mistaken.

Habermas articulates this idea by saying that the practice of justification is one in which agents make "context-transcending validity claims."[64] The suggestion here is not that agents claim that their utterances are warranted in some other, transcendent context, but that their claims are warranted in this epistemic context at this time, and that they will *remain* warranted in other epistemic contexts at future times.[65] This is intended to capture the sense in which we are required to "stand by" our judgments. When we make an assertion we commit ourselves (ceteris paribus) to defending that assertion, in any context and to all persons. The performative force of assertion is not to say that its content is believable this instant, but that it is warranted now, and will remain warranted for the foreseeable future; that it is acceptable to all people in the room, and that it will be acceptable to anyone else who comes along. This is why agents are required to *retract* their claims when contradictory evidence shows up. Similarly, to say "grass is green, but tomorrow we will discover that it is not" is incoherent, because the anticipated discovery is inconsistent with the commitment undertaken in the initial assertion.

So even though justification always occurs in particular contexts, among particular individuals, it is a practice that requires that agents adopt commitments that extend indefinitely beyond the immediate context of inquiry. The "external" observation that none of these commitments is ever fully discharged does nothing to undermine the integrity of the practice from the "inside," because it is simply the commitment to justify one's claims, and the belief that this attempt can be carried along far enough to satisfy all parties, that does the work in securing the conviction that a consensus is rationally motivated. (Similarly, an author's admission in the preface of a book that it contains errors does not eliminate her obligation to defend any given sentence in it.)

Habermas's position has attracted a lot of critical commentary, although most of it quite off topic. However, if one considers both the criterial and "sociological" conceptions of rationality unacceptable, then it is hard to disagree with Habermas's basic idea. Certainly if a particular agreement could be brought about *only* under the condition that one of the rules of discourse was violated, we would not call this agreement rational. It remains possible that there is some agreement that we would not want to call rational but that could be brought about in a way that respects all the rules. But since Habermas does not suggest that his list of rules is exhaustive, new ones could be added to reconstruct the intuitive basis of the counterexample. To demand anything further would simply be to insist upon a criterial conception, and we have independent reasons for believing this to be unobtainable.

5.5 The Discourse Principle

Having rejected the two primary reasons for thinking that agents are incapable of justifying normative claims, Habermas goes on to specify what he takes to be the general structure of moral argumentation. His strategy is to reformulate certain Kantian intuitions about the nature of moral reasoning within the framework of a dialogical conception of justification. Thus he attempts to retain from Kant the basic idea that *universalizability* is a central component of moral justification, while rejecting the criterial conception of rationality that has traditionally accompanied this view.

According to Kant, an action is rational just in case its performance by the agent can be justified. For each action, there is a practical principle that articulates its underlying maxim; this practical principle either does or does not conform to a justifiable hypothetical or categorical imperative. Kant then proceeds to specify what makes a given imperative justifiable, and in so doing, attempts to provide a criterial conception of practical rationality. The first formulation of the categorical imperative, "Act only according to that maxim by which you can at the same time will that it become a universal law,"[66] can be understood as an attempt to specify necessary and sufficient conditions for the moral justification of an action. The problem with this proposal is the same problem that infects all attempts to provide a criterial conception of epistemic rationality—it does not work. Not only does the universalization test procedure proscribe actions that are normally considered moral, or at best neutral, even Kant had to stretch its interpretation to make it prescribe duties that he presented simply by way of illustration.[67]

Habermas suggests that these problems arise because of the underlying view of justification:

Discourse ethics rejects the monological approach of Kant, who assumed that the individual tests his maxims of action *foro interno* or, as Husserl put it, in the loneliness of his soul. The singularity of Kant's transcendental consciousness simply takes for granted a prior understanding among a plurality of empirical egos; their harmony is preestablished. In discourse ethics it is not. Discourse ethics prefers to view shared understanding about the generalizability of interests as the *result* of an intersubjectively mounted *public discourse*. There are no shared structures preceding the individual except the universals of language use.[68]

Kant's universalizability criterion was an attempt to articulate an essentially *contractualist* intuition. In this reading of Kant, the basic idea underlying the three formulations of the categorical imperative is given in the third—that one act as a legislator in the kingdom of ends (although it should be noted that Kant conceived of this as a regulative ideal, i.e., as a condition that we are compelled to seek, but that can never be realized).[69] Kant was attracted by the suggestion that a moral law is justified just in case it can be freely accepted by all those affected. But of course, people can accept and re ject norms for all sorts of reasons. Because Kant required a monological con ception of justifiability, he was led to abstract away all *particular* motives that individuals might have for agreement, leaving behind only their rational motives. This abstraction meant that the scope of the justification for a norm had to extend beyond all those affected to all of humanity. Kant's idea then was to start with an agent's particular desires as "input" and impose a uni versalizability constraint upon them ensuring that all could will a law licens ing the satisfaction of desires of this type.[70] What all can will in common could thereby be transformed into what the individual agent could *consistently* will *on behalf of all*. This could then be represented as a formal property of the agent's maxim.

By rejecting this monological conception of justification, Habermas retrieves the contractualist intuition at the heart of Kant's construction. In Habermas's view, an action is rational if it is licensed by a justifiable norm, and a norm is justifiable if and only if it could be the object of a rational agreement among all those affected. However, Habermas does not have to introduce any special analysis of what it means to be rationally acceptable to all, as this is already provided by the discourse theory of justification. Ratio nal agreement can therefore be understood as the outcome of a procedure presumed to satisfy formal constraints like the ones outlined for theoretical discourse in the previous section. Thus the intuition underlying Kant's third formulation of the categorical imperative is captured by Habermas's dis course principle:

(D) Only those norms can claim to be valid that meet (or could meet) with the approval of all affected in their capacity as participants in a practical discourse.[71]

This principle follows fairly directly from Habermas's analysis of commu nicative action and discourse. The validity of social norms never rests upon their de facto acceptance, in Habermas's view, but is always underwritten by a set of commitments that agents have made to provide discursive justification for the norm upon request. Thus the option to demand the justification for a norm is a built-in feature of linguistically mediated social interaction. However, the only way that justification can be provided is through a process of argumentation that yields a rationally motivated agreement (where the rationality of the agreement is determined by the formal constraints imposed by the rules of discourse). One of these rules requires that no one be excluded from the agreement, so justifying a norm will require that it be made acceptable to everyone with an interest in the matter. Finally, the counterfactual qualification, namely, that the norm *could* meet with the approval of all affected, draws attention to the fact that agents are *committed* to this justificatory procedure when they engage in normatively regulated interaction, even if they are unable to carry out the procedure at some particular point in time.

This last point deserves somewhat greater elaboration, as it has been the source of considerable confusion in the literature. In early work, Habermas made the mistake of referring to the rules of discourse as specifying the structure of an "ideal speech situation." This conception was intended to function as a formal analogue to Kant's "kingdom of ends." Since the latter is a regulative ideal, Habermas operates under the assumption that we will never be in an ideal speech situation, and we can never determine what would be accepted under such conditions.[72] It is simply a way of articulating the task set to us by reason, namely, that to argue rationally, we must be committed to eliminating imperfections in our deliberative conditions as they are uncovered. However, thanks to his use of this expression, many people have taken him to be of the opinion that we can decide whether a particular claim is true or false, right or wrong, by comparing it with what would be agreed to under ideal conditions.[73]

This tendency is exacerbated through confusion of Habermas's discourse ethics with Karl-Otto Apel's, which has a more explicitly Peircean structure. Habermas himself notes that:

[Apel's] formulation could mislead one into thinking the "ideal communication community" has the status of an *ideal* rooted in the universal presuppositions of argumentation and able to be approximately realized. Even the equivalent concept of the "ideal speech situation," though less open to misunderstanding, tempts one to improperly hypostatize the system of validity claims on which speech is based. The counterfactual presuppositions assumed by participants in argumentation indeed open up a perspective allowing them to go beyond local practices of justification and to transcend the provinciality of their spatiotemporal contexts that are inescapable in action and experience. This perspective thus enables them to do justice to the meaning of *context-transcending* validity claims. But with context-transcending validity claims, they are not themselves transported into the beyond of an ideal realm of noumenal beings.[74]

Critics who ignore this warning generally ascribe to Habermas a "consensus" theory of truth according to which he is committed to something like the following as an analysis of truth (or rightness):[75]

(25) *p* is true iff *p* would be agreed to under ideal conditions.

The counterfactual conditional in (D) is then taken to refer to this set of "ideal conditions," and the overall theory of discourse is rejected on the grounds that it tries to derive truth and rightness from the outcome of an entirely hypothetical and in principle unrealizable procedure.[76]

There is a sense in which, even without the explicit disclaimer, this obviously cannot be Habermas's view, since it is inconsistent with the illocutionary-act analysis of the truth predicate (not to mention Schema T).[77] However, the way that Habermas formulates his position has often given rise to this interpretation, so it is worth considering where it comes from. To think that Habermas holds this view, it is necessary to make two mistakes: one concerning his theory of truth, the other concerning his theory of justification. This is, as far as I can tell, how it usually goes.

Habermas starts out saying things like the following:

The point of the discourse theory of truth is that it attempts to show why the question of what it means for the truth-conditions of "p" to be satisfied can only be *answered* by explaining what it means to redeem or ground with arguments the claim that the truth-conditions for "p" are satisfied. *In this way the apparently clear distinction between explicating the meaning of truth and specifying the criteria for ascertaining truth is relativized.*[78]

This just a way of saying that the theory of truth, strictly construed, is not going to tell us anything interesting; only the theory of justification will. What it means is that the question whether "*p* is true" can be addressed only by asking whether *p*. Note, however, that asking whether *p* is not the same thing as asking whether *p* is justified. The former asks a direct question about the state of affairs described by *p*, whereas the latter asks an epistemic question about the status of the claim that *p*.[79] If one confuses these two, it is easy to interpret the passage above as saying that whether or not "*p* is true" is to be determined by asking whether "*p* is justified." This is the first mistake.

The second mistake then arises when an attempt is made to explain what it means to say "p is justified" in Habermas's view. As we have seen, Habermas's theory of justification does not provide specific criteria to determine what is justified and what is not; it simply specifies the rules that agents must conform to if their justificatory procedures are to count as such. As a result, any agreement that is achieved will always be defeasible. Even though all current evidence may suggest a certain conclusion, it is always possible that new information or new doubts could arise to undermine it. This gives rise to the temptation to imagine a state of affairs in which all information is available, all participants are rational, and so on, and to suppose that such conditions provide necessary and sufficient conditions for the ascription of the predicate "is justified" to claims. To do this, of course, is to hypostatize the discourse community in precisely the way that Habermas's dialogical analysis of justification is intended to prevent. Disregarding this results in the second mistake, where one transforms Habermas's discourse theory of justification into a criterial analysis, such as:

(26) p is justified iff p would be agreed to under ideal conditions.

Putting these two mistakes together allows one to infer statement (25). Habermas has attempted to defend his position against this interpretation by stating that the ideal speech situation, like the idea of the unconditioned for Kant, is regulative, not constitutive. Since we can never establish once and for all the epistemic status of a particular claim, we are committed to either defending or retracting our claims in the face of new evidence or challenges. The idea of a limit, in which all evidence is available and all challenges have been met, is a way of illustrating what the principle of reason says we ought to do in the regress. Under no circumstances does it permit or require us to anticipate what the outcome of this regress will be.

The illusion that "truth" is correctly analyzed as some kind of idealization of rational acceptability is further promoted by some of the ways in which the predicate is used in ordinary language. Rorty, for instance, although generally a deflationist, suggests that certain "cautionary" uses of the truth predicate, such as "your belief that S is perfectly justified, but perhaps not true,"[80] express a distinctive feature of the predicate that cannot be assimilated to either the "disquotational" or "approbative" uses. This special use represents a gesture toward the possible "better us" who might later reevaluate what we now consider to be adequate warrant.[81] This suggests that "is justified" might mean "is acceptable to us here and now," whereas "is true" would mean "would be acceptable to us under ideal conditions."

It is easy to see, however, that this is nothing more than a grammatical illusion (albeit one that has caused an enormous amount of mischief). The truth predicate is being used here simply to express the idea that any belief may be mistaken. Many would regard (27) as a reasonable claim:

(27)   Although you may have good reason to believe that snow is white, snow may not be white.

Many would go further, and suggest that statements like (27) can be made about any belief.

(28) $(\forall p)\ M(p$ is justified and $\neg p)$,

otherwise put,

(29)   For all p, it is possible that p is justified, and yet not-p.

To get this into English, given the freestanding occurrence of a propositional variable on the right-hand side of the conjunction, we can insert the truth predicate, then translate as:

(30)   For each proposition, you might be justified in believing it, and yet it is not true.

Here we have the so-called cautionary use of the truth predicate. A surprising number of theorists (including Habermas himself)[82] have failed to notice that the cautionary use provides a textbook example of the deflationary analysis. What this analysis helps to clarify is that the cautionary use of the truth predicate does not express a fact *about truth*; instead, the truth predicate is *used* to express a fact *about justification*, namely, that all justification is defeasible. It is because the expressive role of the truth predicate allows us to say general things about, among other things, relations between sentences, like justification, that it continues to be of service in our language. And this is the insight that is at the heart of the deflationary analysis.

The picture that emerges from this analysis is therefore quite modest. Habermas does not claim that particular moral norms can be evaluated by comparing them against the norms that would be agreed upon under ideal deliberative conditions. Thus his proposal has little in common with various forms of hypothetical contractualism, like Rawls's.[83] All Habermas has committed himself to at this point is the idea that norms are to be considered justified if they can be the object of agreement among all affected, and that this agreement cannot *depend* upon certain procedural constraints having been violated. (This does not mean the agreement must have been achieved under ideal conditions; it simply means there must be no evidence to show that, had the discourse been conducted under improved conditions, the agreement would *not* have been achieved.)

It is worth noting that, even under these very weak conditions, Habermas's conception of practical discourse has significant normative import. According to his view, "openness, equal rights, truthfulness and absence of coercion" represent the "normative content of these suppositions of rationality."[84] Naturally, these are not general social norms, but merely presuppositions that regulate the practice of discourse. While Apel claims that these presuppositions constitute a set of "supernorms" that can be extended to all social interaction, Habermas explicitly rejects this view, claiming that "the moral principle performs the role of a rule of argumentation only for justifying judgments and as such can neither obligate one to engage in moral argumentation nor motivate one to act on moral insights."[85] As a result, the normative content of the rules governing discourse cannot be applied to social interaction in an unmediated fashion:

True as it may be that freedom of opinion, in the sense of freedom from external interference in the process of opinion formation, is one of the inescapable pragmatic presuppositions of every argumentation, the fact remains that what the skeptic is now forced to accept is no more than the notion that as a *participant* in a process of *argumentation* he has implicitly recognized a principle of freedom of opinion. This argument does not go far enough to convince him in his capacity as an *actor* as well. The validity of a norm of action, as for example a publicly guaranteed constitutional right to freedom of expression, cannot be justified in this fashion. It is by no means self-evident that rules that are unavoidable *within* discourse can also claim to be valid for regulating action *outside* of discourses.[86]

Thus the presuppositions of discourse impose constraints on social action only *indirectly*, insofar as they impose limits on the *kind* of norms that can be justified through a rational deliberative procedure. (The link that connects social action with argumentation, in Habermas's view, is the fact that when language is used to coordinate social action, its use carries commitments that can only be redeemed discursively.) For instance, it is part of our understanding of discursively achieved agreement that agents not rely upon threats or force to support their position. The fact that any individual can withhold consent requires that the perspective of each individual be fully accounted for in every proposal. Thus any norm that arbitrarily disregarded the interests of any individual or group, or whose content was inconsistent with their ability to exercise influence over its adoption or implementation, could be claimed to be defective on strictly formal grounds.

Thus even though principle (D) does little more than summarize the idea that agents are committed to a discursive resolution of their differences, it nevertheless captures a number of substantive normative ideas. So although the theory does not specify a set of criteria to pick out what is moral from what is immoral, and it does not prescribe a set of rules that can be applied directly to social interaction, it does guarantee that not just anything can come out of practical discourse as justified. The second stage of the discourse ethics project involves an attempt to specify in more precise terms exactly what kind of outcomes are precluded by the procedure of practical discourse. Habermas therefore attempts to specify a second principle, (U), which places direct constraints on the content of norms that can be discursively endorsed. It is this second stage that produces the most problematic aspect of Habermas's proposal and is the subject of the following chapter.

6

Universalization

The deflationary view of truth, with or without the introduction of "rightness" as a validity claim governing moral utterances, defuses the noncognitivist's claim that moral judgments are not truth-apt, or that this constitutes a defect. The discourse theory of justification undermines the foundationalist picture of justification that sustains subjectivist and relativist theories of moral judgment. It would appear, then, that Habermas's basic theory of language and theory of argumentation successfully defeat the two lines of argument that he takes to be major sources of moral noncognitivism in the modern era. However, defeating arguments for noncognitivism is not the same as establishing moral cognitivism. Habermas's theory of communicative action requires that practical discourse serve as the ultimate source of *social integration*, since it is supposed to provide the mechanism through which the validity claims raised in communicative action are adjudicated. Habermas has shown that there is no reason to think that practical discourses *must* become bogged down in intractable moral disputes, but he has at this point done nothing to show that they will not *in fact* become so. And since he himself describes communicatively achieved agreement as "improbable," he must do something to bolster confidence in the idea that practical discourse can command *convergence*, and hence *resolve* problems of social interaction to the satisfaction of all parties. Otherwise, the idea that communicative action is the basis of social order will begin to appear itself increasingly improbable.

Habermas claims, therefore, that "strict discourses" such as moral argumentation contain rules of inference that make it legitimate to assume that "*in principle* a rationally motivated agreement must always be reachable." His use of the phrase "in principle" here "signifies the counterfactual reservation 'if argumentation were conducted openly and continued long enough.'"[1] The idea is presumably that if all moral questions are resolvable, given world enough and time, then any given failure to reach consensus can be explained away in terms of the limitations imposed by the circumstances under which the discourse was held, for example, lack of time, lack of knowledge, irrationality of participants, and so on. Practical discourse can therefore be expected to exhibit convergence as deliberative conditions are improved and the results of past inquiry are accumulated.

Unfortunately, this line of thinking leads Habermas to adopt a further, entirely unnecessary burden of proof. He claims that to defeat *noncognitivism* he must find "a principle that makes agreement in moral argumentation possible in principle."[2] He thereby ties the cognitive status of moral judgments to an a priori expectation of convergence in moral argumentation. This explains his assumption, mentioned in §5.1, that he must defeat the *relativist* in order to establish moral cognitivism. So far we have seen no reason that these two issues should be connected, and I will argue in the next chapter that they are actually quite distinct. However, the connection that he draws between moral cognitivism and the expectation of convergence is what motivates Habermas to introduce the principle of universalization (U), which occupies a central role in his discourse ethics. It is also what motivates him to distinguish between moral and ethical "employments" of practical reason. Both of these steps have been severely criticized and should, in my view, be retracted. However, since they are both motivated by Habermas's concern to show that practical discourse will exhibit convergence, I will begin by considering the more general question of why he thinks this issue is linked to the cognitive status of moral judgment (§6.1). I will then go on to consider specific problems with the (U) principle (§6.2) and the moral/ethical distinction (§6.3). I conclude by arguing that Habermas's concern to show that agreement is possible in principle leads him to devalue a more robust mechanism for overcoming disagreement, namely, bargaining and compromise (§6.4).

6.1 Why Convergence?

The issue of convergence gets raised in response to what Habermas calls the "first noncognitivist argument," in which the noncognitivist points to the existence of "persistent disagreement" on moral issues as evidence that moral claims lack cognitive content.[3] Habermas states that this objection can be met by showing that even if disagreement persists, agreement is possible in principle. However, his motive for adopting this response is not immediately obvious. As remarked in the previous chapter, it would clearly be erroneous for the noncognitivist to infer from the fact that agreement on some topic has not been achieved to the conclusion that it cannot be achieved. It is therefore unclear why, when the noncognitivist points to instances of disagreement, the cognitivist cannot respond simply by pointing to instances where moral argument does issue in agreement. Habermas clearly wants to go further than simply presenting counterexamples to the noncognitivist's claim; he wants to explain away every instance of disagreement that the noncognitivist presents. This he intends to do by showing that, given *any* particular starting point, it is possible to achieve an agreement that is rationally acceptable to all parties. Even if they fail to achieve it, it is nevertheless in some sense "available." This means that insofar as they conduct themselves rationally, agents can be expected to either reach agreement outright, or at least move toward it.

The question is why this much needs to be shown. Informally, Habermas claims that the need to show that agreement is possible in principle arises when the moral cognitivist is confronted with the "pluralism of ultimate value-orientations."[4] But this way of formulating the problem is already misleading. It is certainly conceivable that agents derive their moral judgments from some set of irreducibly plural "ultimate" value-commitments. But this is certainly not something that can be read off the surface of moral disagreement. An agent's values normally are acquired through internalization of some broader set of social values that are reproduced through cultural traditions and social institutions. These values are both publicly shared (thus open to reinterpretation and challenge by others) and historically variable (thus influenced by a variety of dynamic social processes). It is therefore not clear how they are "ultimate," since they are open to revision in contexts of public argumentation. And if they are open to revision, it is not clear why the pluralism of value-orientations should be irreducible.

On these grounds, for instance, Charles Taylor has argued that we must wait until "the end of the day" to determine whether moral judgments will converge. He grants that moral disagreements may be *harder* to resolve than empirical ones. But he explains this as a mere consequence of the fact that moral disputes involve positions that are usually not fully explicit. This means that moral argumentation will often involve the articulation of implicit premises and commitments:

> Naturally, none of [this] shows that all practical disputes are arbitrable in reason. Above all, it doesn't show that the most worrying cases, those dividing people of very different cultures, can be so arbitrated. . . . And yet I want to argue that these considerations on practical argument show that we shouldn't give up on reason too early. We don't need to be so intimidated by distance and incomprehensibility that we take them as sufficient grounds to adopt relativism. There are resources in argument. These have to be tried in each case, because nothing assures us either that relativism is false. We have to try and see.[5]

Taylor's position draws upon the plausible intuition that the only way to see where an argument ultimately leads is to carry out the argument. To speculate about whether judgments will converge is to presuppose that we have some independent access to where our arguments are leading. But this is highly implausible. Even in formal domains like mathematics, often the only way to show that something is provable is to actually prove it. There is seldom any external guarantee that a particular strategy of proof will be successful. Similarly, we do not have any advance knowledge that physical science will lead to one single account of how the world is. In fact, many philosophers have argued that it will not.[6] But even if this argument were decidable, it is implausible to think that the direction it goes will have any impact on the cognitive status that we attribute to scientific beliefs.

The fact that Habermas does not adopt a "wait and see" attitude is particularly mysterious, given his commitment to a dialogical model of justification. Because there is no fixed set of criteria that determines what is to count as a rationally motivated agreement, only an open-ended set of justificatory practices that are structured by rather broad procedural constraints, one cannot decide "monologically," or *in foro interno* what rational agents would or would not accept; one must actually carry out the attempt to persuade them. This is why Habermas criticizes Rawls for attempting to specify, as a philosophical expert, what social arrangements individuals would accept in a hypothetical original position, rather than simply presenting his proposals "as the *contribution* of a participant in argumentation."[7] But if it is inappropriate for philosophers to make assumptions about what individuals would accept, it is just as inappropriate to make assumptions about what they would reject. The idea that agents' value-commitments are not subject to rational reevaluation would appear to foreclose debate illegitimately in precisely this way.

The claim that moral judgments rest in the end upon ultimate values is normally motivated by a certain style of epistemic foundationalism. Empirical beliefs are thought to be the "ultimate" basis of scientific judgments, because they provide an end to the regress of justification. Values are then thought to be the "ultimate" basis for moral judgments, and because they are not open to rational justification, they are also not open to rational revision. But since Habermas treats discourses as rather open-ended dialogical processes that take place against a background of shared beliefs, norms, values, and so on, he has no need to posit ultimate regress-stoppers. Since any element of this background can be thematized, discussed, and revised, there is no way of specifying in advance that agreements will be achieved, or that disagreements will persist.

In the foundationalist picture, convergence is guaranteed by uniformity of input. Basic beliefs are thought to be the same for all persons, because they hook directly on to the world. But when one eliminates the idea of specifying in advance, for all cases, what the input of a particular argument must be, then in principle one is no longer able to say, in advance, how much agreement can be expected. According to Taylor, it is the role of inquiry to determine to what extent people agree or disagree on fundamental questions of value. This is something that we discover in the process of argumentation, as we strive to provide a more perspicuous articulation of our moral commitments. Thus participants in practical discourse do not *start* with a set of fundamental values; they work out their fundamental values by attempting to articulate the motivation for their particular commitments.

If there is no way of determining in advance the level of convergence that a discourse will exhibit, then it is unclear what relationship the potential for convergence could plausibly be thought to have to the cognitive status of the utterances and arguments that make up that discourse. The real concern is that the positions agents adopt be accepted through valid inferences and motivated by good reasons. Since Habermas argues that there cannot be any criterial specification of what is to count as a good reason, the only thing that appears to be important for the cognitive status of a discourse is that it exhibit sufficient *discipline* to support some pattern of valid inference, and that the conclusions reached through argumentative processes be the result of such inferences.[8]

The important question, then, is whether a lack of convergence in a discourse implies that the discourse is not governed by some pattern of valid inference. Naturally, if agents started out with the same premises and arrived at different conclusions, and no one was making any obvious errors, then one would be inclined to think that the discourse in question lacked the discipline required to sustain a proper logic of inference. But if Taylor's suggestion is correct, then there is no way of determining in advance how far apart the premises that each participant begins with are.[9] This means that there will be no way of getting from the observation that moral argumentation tends not to issue in agreement to the conclusion that the inferences used by participants are invalid.

So why does Habermas that think that convergence is needed for statements in the associated discourse to be considered justifiable? An uncharitable response would be to suggest that Habermas has simply confused the *validity* of an argument with its *soundness*. An agent who holds false beliefs is perfectly capable of making valid inferences from these beliefs to a series of further, equally false conclusions. Such inferences would be valid, but not sound. Observers might agree that the agent in question is entitled to these conclusions—given his background convictions—and yet still reject them. However, Habermas's attempt to define justification in terms of rationally motivated agreement makes it easy to think that an agent is justified in holding a position only if he is able to secure consensus on the actual subject of the claim, as opposed to simply the inferences that took him there. But clearly the latter sort of agreement is the only type that is needed to secure the cognitive status of the associated discourse. To show that a moral claim is justifiable, all one has to show is that a rationally motivated consensus is possible with respect to the inferential moves through which that claim is, or could be, established. There has to be a stable set of rules for the construction of arguments, shared by all. But this does not mean that there has to be a single set of justifiable claims, shared by all. We must leave open the possibility that agents can be perfectly rational, and yet quite mistaken.

Setting aside this uncharitable reading, however, there is one indirect way in which the lack of convergence in a given discourse could be thought to undermine the attribution of a system of valid inference. It is often suggested that whether or not a particular discourse exhibits convergence provides grounds for the adoption of a broadly *realist* stance toward of the object domain of the discourse. The idea here is that if our judgments do converge, the best explanation for this must be that we have in some sense "gotten it right," or described things "as they really are."[10] On the other hand, a lack of convergence can be taken as indication that there is nothing really out there to get right or wrong.

This realist intuition, as we have seen, is often expressed by the claim that there is some "fact of the matter" underlying a given dispute. For instance, someone who is a realist about the past would argue that the question of whether dinosaurs once roamed the earth is settled, ultimately, by whether the state of affairs in question—dinosaurs roaming the earth at time t—obtains. The fossil record is relevant only because it provides us with evidence of this state of affairs, and so reason to endorse the associated claim. An antirealist about the past, on the other hand, would argue that the state of affairs in question is no longer around, and so we cannot do anything to "settle" the question of whether dinosaurs once roamed the earth. The only thing we have access to is the evidence that we use to assess this claim.

One way of formulating this dispute is to say that the realist maintains that "Dinosaurs once roamed the earth" is either true or false, regardless of whether we have any evidence for this claim, whereas the antirealist argues that in the absence of evidence, "Dinosaurs once roamed the earth" simply has no truth-value.[11] (Of course, such a formulation presupposes a nondeflationary theory of truth, and so there are good reasons *not* to adopt this formulation of the realism/antirealism debate. The point is simply to show how one common understanding of this debate could lead a theorist to posit a connection between the level of convergence exhibited by some discourse and the cognitive status of the claims made within it.)

According to this view, to be a "realist" about a particular domain of inquiry is to believe that every sentence in it is in some way determinately true or false. One way of formulating this conviction is to say that the principle of bivalence is satisfied for that domain. Thus (for any p belonging to the domain of inquiry):

(1) p is true or p is false

The principle of bivalence, which states a semantic thesis, should not be confused with the rather similar logical principle, the law of the excluded middle:

(2) p or $\neg p$

In the realist view, the difference between these two principles creates a peculiar tension, since the principle of bivalence must be treated as a substantive claim about the domain of inquiry (even though the law of the excluded middle is a logical truth). The evidence that one would use to assert this substantive claim—that bivalance obtains—is that the discourse in question exhibits convergence. If the relativist is correct, then moral discourse will exhibit little or no tendency toward convergence. As a result, it will not be possible to apply the principle of bivalence to moral judgments. But since the law of the excluded middle can easily be inferred from bivalence and Schema T, in any domain of inquiry where bivalence fails, classical logic will fail as well. Furthermore, without bivalence, one cannot define the logical constants truth-functionally, and so cannot define the notion of valid inference in the usual way. In short, it appears to the realist that in domains of inquiry where bivalence does not hold, there can be no logical inference, and therefore no rational justification.

This means that to show that a particular discourse supports a classical logic of inference, it must be shown that the principle of bivalence holds for all sentences of that discourse.[12] If one could supply reasons for thinking that the discourse will exhibit convergence, this would appear to lend support to the view that bivalence obtains, since the latter provides the best explanation for the former. It is because the realist regards bivalence as an empirical (or metaphysical) claim that entails various truths of logic, that its truth must be demonstrated a priori, or "in principle." It will therefore not be sufficient to adopt a "wait and see" attitude in order to decide whether convergence can be expected in a given domain.

This argument can of course be blocked if one is prepared to give up classical logic.[13] However, less radical consequences follow from the simple observation that the argument is clearly undermined by Habermas's illocutionary-act analysis of truth. If the law of the excluded middle is treated as a primitive axiom, and truth is defined using Schema T, then bivalence will obtain as a truth of logic. This means our intuition that "Dinosaurs once roamed the earth" must be either true or false, regardless of our evidence one way or the other, is not an intuition about how the world is or was, but rather a grammatical intuition that follows from our willingness to embed sentences like "Dinosaurs once roamed the earth" in conditionals, and our belief that "Dinosaurs once roamed the earth" is true just in case dinosaurs once roamed the earth. Since there is no substantive property of sentences called "truth-aptness," there is no underlying fact of the matter that determines whether bivalence obtains in either empirical or moral discourse.

What this analysis does, in effect, is deny that the principle of bivalence expresses the realist intuition regarding the existence of a single "right answer," or an underlying "fact of the matter."[14] Thus the absence of this intuition for a given discourse does nothing to threaten our willingness to apply the law of the excluded middle to statements in the discourse, and so gives us no reason to think that these statements cannot be rationally justified.

With all this in mind, one can only conclude that Habermas's attempt to demonstrate that convergence in moral argumentation is possible "in principle" is unmotivated (insofar as the underlying concern is to establish the cognitive content of moral judgment). Even the rather strained realist argument that convergence is required to sustain classical logic can be easily defused by the illocutionary-act analysis of truth. Nevertheless, comments that Habermas has made suggest that the bivalence intuition did underlie his desire to show that agreement is possible in principle (the idea being to show that there is "one right answer," regardless of whether participants are actually able to find it).[15] The connection with bivalence and excluded middle is the only plausible reason to think that this possibility is in any way connected with the cognitive status of the discourse.

6.2   The Universalization Principle

If the above argument is correct, it shows that Habermas assumes an unnecessarily heavy burden of proof in his attempt to refute moral noncognitivism. Naturally, this is not in itself a problem. If he were able to both assume and discharge this obligation, it would generate a considerable presumption in favor of his view. However, I will argue that he is not able to meet the task that he sets himself, and that a number of ancillary devices he introduces in the course of his attempt to do so generate unnecessary problems for his broader program for a theory of communicative action.

Habermas attempts to establish the expectation of agreement in moral argumentation by introducing a "bridge principle" for moral argument that is intended to function like the principle of induction does for empirical inquiry. This principle specifies that:

(U)   A norm is valid if and only if *all* affected can accept the consequences and the side effects its *general* observance can be expected to have for the satisfaction of *everyone's* interests.[16]

Habermas claims that this principle is a pragmatic rule of inference that is available to participants in practical/moral discourse.[17] In its explicit formulation, it does no more than articulate the way that the generic rules of discourse become operationalized when applied to the topic of which norms are valid. He claims, therefore, that it can be derived from these general rules, along with some additional presuppositions about what it means to justify a norm. (These same rules, when applied to the question of whether a law is valid, generate a different principle.)[18]

This claim is very controversial, but also widely misunderstood. In particular, there is a common tendency to draw too close an analogy between this principle and Kant's categorical imperative. It is important first to remember that (U) is never applied directly to actions, but only to norms. Thus it is not a principle employed in practical deliberation (i.e., at the point of decision, as the categorical imperative is for Kant), but only in practical discourse.[19] Furthermore, (U) is a rule of inference, not a norm. This means that it cannot be used *as a reason* for adopting a particular norm; it is simply a rule that allows agents to use certain kinds of statements to support certain others. In Kant's framework, the categorical imperative can serve as a premise from which particular moral obligations can be deduced. In Habermas's view, the only permissible premises are statements that indicate how a particular norm affects the interests of particular persons affected. The universalization principle shows only how one *gets* from these premises to the more general normative conclusion. Thus it is, like most inference rules, *used* in the process of moral argumentation but seldom *mentioned*.[20]

To see how (U) is supposed to work, it is important to take seriously the analogy with induction. At any given time, each of us experiences the natural world in different, often incompatible ways. Looking at the shape of a coin, one person sees an ellipse, while another sees a circle. Induction allows us to produce general theories that explain both the phenomenon and the difference between these experiences of it, thereby allowing agents to come to an agreement despite discrepancies between their experiences. In the case of morality, each agent begins with different interests and needs. The universalization principle allows them to settle upon a norm that will regulate their interaction in a way that is equally in the interests of all. Since this principle is pragmatic, it cannot be applied deductively to resolve conflicts of interest. It does, however, establish that some agreement is attainable. But it remains up to participants to discover which arrangements will provide a mutually satisfactory resolution to the conflict.

Adopting Stephen Toulmin's argument schema, Habermas presents the analogy as shown in figure 6.1.[21] According to this view, everyday empirical reasoning is governed by a set of material inferences.[22] These allow us to draw specific conclusions directly from specific types of evidence. Discursive moves of this type are licensed by what Toulmin calls "warrants,"[23] for example, "if it rained, then the streets will be wet." In empirical discourse, these warrants are known as "theories." Everyday moral reasoning takes the same form, for example, "if you promised to give it back, then you should do so." In Habermas's view, these warrants are just the set of norms that govern our practices. (Logic, incidentally, allows us to *represent* certain of these inferences using general formulas, with conditionals and so forth, but this does not mean that there is a uniform set of logical principles *underlying* these inferences.)[24]

We always have the option of challenging any one of these warrants. This is how we effect the shift from communicative action to discourse. Once we have done so, we are then faced with the task of redeeming the particular warrant that we have been using. In Habermas's view, we do so in empirical inference by showing that the theory represents an accurate generalization from the facts. This takes the form of an inductive argument: we appeal to a certain number of cases and show that the theory holds better than any other, for example: "given the relevant facts: $\{F_1, F_2, F_3\}$, and given that theory p explains all these facts better than any other, I conclude that p is true." A moral

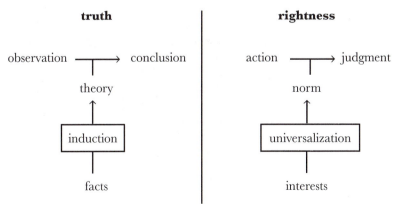

Figure 6.1

argument takes roughly the same form, for example: "given the interests of all those affected: $\{I_1, I_2, I_3\}$, and given that norm n satisfies all these interests better than any other, I conclude that norm n is right." So in the same way that we accept a theory when they see that it accounts for the facts, we accept a norm when we see that it adequately balances the interests of all.

Naturally, it is impossible to consider all interests, just as it is impossible to check all the facts (e.g., ones in the future). Therefore, to generate the presumption that the agreement reached on a particular norm or theory is rational, it will be necessary to suppose that, at the very least, no set of interests or facts has been deliberately excluded from consideration. According to Habermas, this means that the procedural constraints governing the interaction structure of the discourse have to include rules specifying that everyone affected by a norm be allowed to express her opinions, attitudes, desires, and needs, and so forth.[25] These rules ensure that no interests or facts are excluded arbitrarily. If the task of finding a rationally acceptable norm is to find one that all participants can agree upon, and if a norm is to be preferred if it satisfies the interests of all in a way that is better than some other (just as a theory is to be preferred if it explains the facts in a way that is better than some other), then it is easy to see how (U) can be derived. For instance, one might start with some characterization of the qualities that make one norm preferable to another:

(3) Norm n is preferable iff, for any feasible alternative n', n satisfies the interests of everyone affected better than n'.

Assume that rational agents are motivated by the force of the better argument:

(4) Agents will rationally accept a norm iff they find it preferable.

Bring in some version or other of principle (D):

(5) Norm n is valid iff it is rationally acceptable to everyone affected.

From this it is easy to get:

(6) Norm n is valid iff everyone affected can accept that it satisfies the interests of all better than any feasible alternative.

Sentence (6) I take to be more or less equivalent to (U). However, it is fairly clear that this whole "derivation" hinges upon premise (3), which specifies the criteria by which one proposed norm can be deemed superior to another. While this premise clearly articulates what it "means" to justify a norm according to the discourse schema laid out in figure 6.1, Habermas does not provide any independent defense of this analysis of the structure of practical discourse. Most importantly, he does not explain why normative validity is grounded entirely upon the interests of all parties. He usually begins by claiming that norms embody a general *will*, then shifts quickly to the claim that they represent a general *interest*. When he does attempt to justify this transition, he argues that it is simply *analytic*, claiming that it stems from knowledge of "what it means to justify a norm,"[26] or that it "follows with conceptual necessity from the *meaning* of normative validity claims" that normative claims are decidable on the grounds that they express "an interest *common to all* those affected."[27]

But approaching the problem from the standpoint of argumentation theory, there seems to be no reason that agents involved in practical deliberation can appeal only to the interests of all affected in order to defend or criticize a norm. They might just as easily appeal to other norms. (In the same way, it is possible to defend an empirical theory by appealing to other theories, not directly to the facts.) For instance, an agent might criticize a particular norm on the grounds that it promotes dishonorable or shameful conduct. The norm is rejected in this case because it conflicts with another norm. A norm might also be thought necessary in order to protect against dishonor, in which case it would be directly licensed by some other norm. One way of responding to this challenge would be to grant that norms can be inferred from other norms, but claim that they all "ultimately" rest upon some set of interests. To do this, however, it would be necessary to use some kind of epistemic regress argument, which is precisely what the dialogical conception of justification is intended to get around. It appears, then, that Habermas's claim that norms are all derived from interests cannot be defended without reintroducing a certain foundationalist line of reasoning.[28]

There is also considerable ambiguity in Habermas's claim. It is one thing to say that norms represent a "common" or "general" interest. But when conflicts arise that require normative adjudication, it is normally because some sets of individual or group interests have come into conflict. Getting from a set of plural and conflicting interests to a single common interest is notoriously difficult. In standard cases that call for normative regulation, agents are faced with some kind of collective action problem. Thus the "function" of normative regulation is to enable agents to achieve an out-of-equilibrium cooperative outcome that is Pareto-superior to the noncooperative strategic equilibrium. This gives them a "common interest" in finding some sort of cooperative arrangement that everyone can accept. *Any* norm that they adopt can therefore be expected to embody a common interest, but only in the weak sense that the normatively secured outcome is Pareto-superior to the strategic one. This says nothing, however, about which particular outcome should be selected, and there are some outcomes that we would recognize to be unjust, even though they represent a common interest. To illustrate, consider figure 6.2, which shows a standard Prisoner's Dilemma and a graph of the associated payoffs.

The sole strategic equilibrium of this game is (U,L), which gives each player a payoff of 1. Normative regulation allows players to achieve an outcome to

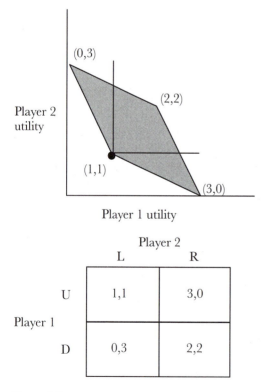

Figure 6.2

the northeast of $(1,1)$ (points in the interior can be achieved using mixed strategies, or over repeated play of the game). However, *any* movement northeast is in the common interest of all players, and so any norm that secures an outcome in this region expresses a common interest. That having been said, it provides absolutely no grounds for preferring one outcome in this set to another. Every norm expresses a common interest, and so no particular norm can be preferred on the grounds that it expresses this interest "better" than some other. And since an enormous number of economic interactions have precisely this structure (given the widespread preference for leisure over labor), it is extremely important that any proposed account of normative regulation be able to handle conflicts of this type. The idea of a common interest therefore provides no guidance in resolving what are probably the vast majority of moral disputes.

Habermas has two responses to this challenge, neither of which is satisfactory. His first is to claim that practical discourse involves a search for "generalizable" interests, or interests that are common to all participants. This might involve eliminating some claims (e.g., on the grounds that they involve harming or depriving others), but also the discovery of new claims through abstraction and reinterpretation. According to this suggestion, participants in practical discourse might come to reconceputalize their conflict when they see that underlying their differences is some kind of common interest stemming from their shared humanity. But none of this is helpful. When people are in conflict, they have a general interest in cooperating, and cooperation is almost always achieved through *compromise*. After all, if they didn't need to compromise, then they wouldn't need to cooperate. All that agents are going to discover at a higher level of abstraction or generalization is that they have an abstract or general interest in compromising. But this does nothing to specify the terms of the compromise, and so does nothing to resolve their specific disagreement.

Perhaps because he sensed this difficulty, Habermas also began to gloss (U) as requiring that normatively prescribed outcomes be "equally in the interest of all."[29] By introducing the idea of an *equal* division of benefits, he thereby provided a principle that could be used to favor particular norms over others. Unfortunately, the notion of equality is notoriously difficult to specify. Even if a commitment to equality could be derived from the rules of discourse, it could not be applied without some decision being made about *what* needs to be equalized (welfare? resources? capabilities?), and this decision will inevitably turn upon what participants regard as the morally salient features of the situation in need of regulation.[30] As a result, general notions of equality can only be operationalized when supplemented with substantive moral norms. This is perhaps why Habermas initially classified Rawls's conception of equality as part of the "substantive" portion of his study, and criticized him for not putting it forward from the standpoint of a *participant* in practical discourse.[31] There is, of course, nothing wrong with the idea that an abstract commitment to equality stemming from the rules of discourse will need to be supplemented with substantive norms in order to be applied to particular practical problems; it just means that glossing (U) in terms of equality does nothing to show that agreement can always be reached in principle.

Given these difficulties, it is worth pausing for a moment to consider why Habermas wants to focus so sharply on interests as the basis of normative justification, and exclude any "thicker" moral considerations. In practical discourse we appear to move easily between reference to principles, guidelines, roles, expectations, entitlements, demands, and so on. It is not necessarily the case that something is to be gained by picking out a particular class and assigning it a privileged role. So why does Habermas attempt to do so? His underlying motivation is quite clear—he wants to banish *values* from the domain of moral argumentation, because he regards differences over questions of value as the primary obstacle to agreement. This is because he understands the term "value" in a broadly Parsonian sense, in which values are considered symbolic elements of the cultural system that have been internalized by agents over the course of primary socialization. This means that agents cannot take an entirely "hypothetical" attitude toward their values, because they have become core components of their personality structure.[32]

One way of doing an end-run around these kind of value-commitments is to restrict moral argumentation to the topic of interests alone. Thus Habermas considers it a central strength of his analysis that "(U) works like a rule that eliminates as nongeneralizable content all those concrete value-orientations with which particular biographies or forms of life are permeated."[33] Having cut values out of the justificatory loop, he can then claim that "it follows directly from (U) that anyone who takes part in argumentation of any sort is in principle able to reach the same judgments on the acceptability of norms of action."[34]

The obvious assumption underlying this view is that whenever a practical discourse is initiated it is always possible to separate out the interests of participants from their values. The type of appeal to values that Habermas intends to preclude here are only those that would issue in the direct prescription of specific institutional patterns. He acknowledges that values will still enter the picture indirectly, insofar as they inform and shape the needs and interests of participants.[35] But the problem, as Thomas McCarthy has pointed out, is that different sets of values can provide incompatible frameworks for the interpretation of needs and interests. This is because values provide agents not only with a way of ranking or evaluating their own needs, but also with a framework for interpreting and assigning priority to the needs of others. This leads to the possibility of conflict. While one person's need to build a temple to his gods may be important relative to his system of values, in someone else's system of values it may show up as a harmful delusion that should be actively discouraged.[36] According to McCarthy, this makes it impossible to cut values out of the loop in the way Habermas suggests:

> Consensus would be achieved only if participants could come to agree on the authentic interpretation of each's needs, and they would have to do so from the very different hermeneutic starting points afforded by a pluralistic and individualistic culture. This would presumably entail criticizing and rejecting value orientations that are too self- or group-centered to permit the proper weighting of other participants' needs, as well as value-orientations imbued with racism, sexism, ethnocentrism, homophobia, or any other less than universalistic outlook.[37]

William Rehg's derivation of (U)—which Habermas has endorsed at various points—assumes that participants in practical discourse will need to use values in order to decide which interests must be accommodated. Thus Rehg appeals to what he calls an "interest-regulating value" that can be used to assign priority to certain classes of interests in the selection of norms.[38] Rehg's view might be thought to provide a template for reversing Habermas's overly strict excision of values from moral discourse. The logic of the position, however, tends to pull in the opposite direction. If values are to be brought back into the picture, what is the point of (U)? If the purpose of introducing (U) was to guarantee agreement in moral argumentation, and values are the source of intractable moral disagreement, then there is no point grounding moral argumentation in those values, for that would defeat the very purpose for which (U) was introduced. The alternative, then, would be to consider the structure of practical discourse in the absence of such principles. If the idea that values are a source of intractable dispute is suspended, it is not clear that there is any point in trying to specify particular moral rules of inference or "bridge principles." However, before pursuing this line of inquiry, I would like to examine in greater detail the strategy that Habermas develops to cut questions of value out of moral deliberation.

6.3   Moral and Ethical Questions

Habermas's final response to the problematic relation between values and interests in practical discourse is to draw a sharp distinction between "moral" and "ethical" uses of practical reason. This becomes an extremely prominent feature of his position in later work, especially *Between Facts and Norms*. The general strategy is to claim that whenever values cannot be eliminated from a particular practical discourse, it is because the issue under dispute is not actually a moral question, strictly construed, but is merely an *ethical* one. For instance, Habermas suggests that the abortion issue, which appears to be a case of intractable moral disagreement, is actually an ethical question, not a moral one. As a result, it is more properly the subject of ethical-evaluative discourse, which has as its primary goal the "clarification of collective identity" rather than the prescription of specific norms of action.[39] As a result, (U) can guarantee consensus in all *moral* discourses because moral discourses are not concerned with evaluative questions.[40]

Sometimes Habermas draws the distinction between moral and ethical questions by appealing to the relatively uncontroversial action-theoretic distinction between deontic and evaluative judgment. In this view, values represent an intersubjectively shared ranking of states of affairs that provide either a standard that agents may adopt in structuring their own preference orderings, or simply an expression of the fact that their individual preferences coincide in a particular domain. Either way, evaluative judgments rank outcomes only in accordance with some shared ordering, whereas deontic judgements go on to specify precisely what actions are to be performed.[41] For this reason values still need to be implemented through instrumental action, while norms can be directly institutionalized. In this usage, the distinction between moral and ethical questions corresponds to the formal distinction between the right and the good.

Habermas sometimes motivates his position using this action-theoretic distinction. Thus he claims:

Norms and values therefore differ, first, in their reference to obligatory rule-following versus teleological action; second, in the binary versus graduated coding of their validity claims; third, in their absolute versus relative bindingness; and fourth, in the coherence criteria that systems of norms and systems of values must respectively satisfy. The fact that norms and values differ in these logical properties yields significant differences for their application as well. Different kinds of action orientation result depending on whether I base my action in a particular case on norms or on values. The question of what I should do in a given situation is posed and answered differently in the two cases. In the light of norms, I can decide what action is commanded; within the horizon of values, which behavior is recommended.[42]

At key points, however, Habermas switches to an alternate usage, in which he *defines* moral questions as simply those that can be resolved through an impartial mediation of interests. Thus the passage cited above continues: "if we start with a system of valid norms, the action is right that is equally good *for all*; on the other hand, in reference to a typical value constellation for our culture or form of life, the behavior is 'best' that, on the whole and in the long run, is good *for us*."[43] The distinction between what is good "for all" and "for us" clearly does not follow from the action-theoretic distinction, and is even inconsistent with Habermas's own claim that norms purport to regulate action only among all those affected, not necessarily all persons.

Habermas sometimes distinguishes the moral from the ethical in a way that is even more tendentious:

The development of the moral point of view goes hand in hand with a differentiation within the practical into *moral questions* and *evaluative questions*. Moral questions can in principle be decided rationally, i.e. in terms of *justice* or the generalizability of interests. Evaluative questions present themselves at the most general level as issues of the *good life* (or of self-realization); they are accessible to rational deliberation only within the unproblematic horizon of a concrete historical form of life or the conduct of an individual life.[44]

This clearly permits him to claim that disagreements that cannot be resolved because of incompatible value-frameworks are in fact concerned only with ethical issues. But having now *defined* moral issues as those that can be decided rationally, he has rendered his "proof" that consensus in moral argumentation is possible in principle entirely tautologous. Any dispute in which agreement cannot be achieved is *eo ipso* reclassified as ethical. And since "it remains an empirical question how far the sphere of strictly generalizable interests extends,"[45] it becomes an empirical question whether a particular issue is moral or ethical. And the only "empirical" evidence that is available to decide this question is simply whether agreement has been reached.

Habermas goes on to claim that the pluralism of values that arises in modern societies tends to "shrink" the sphere of questions that can be answered from the moral point of view, so that what remains are only a "few more sharply focused questions."[46] This reduces the moral to the very narrow field of norms "that are strictly universalizable, i.e., those that are invariable over historical time and across social groups."[47] It is clear from this that the moral/ethical distinction can no longer be mapped onto the deontic/evaluative. For instance, the antiabortion stance, which Habermas treats as an ethical commitment, is almost always given a deontic formulation.

However, the more general problem with this "shrinking" of the moral domain is that it severs the connection between Habermas's account of discourse ethics and his general theory of communicative action. Even after drawing the moral/ethical distinction, Habermas maintains that when "the discourse principle is applied to norms of action that regulate simple interactions for an indefinitely large circle of addressees, questions arise for which a specific type of discourse is appropriate, namely, moral argumentation."[48] But this seems inconsistent with the narrow construal that he gives to moral discourse. Since there will usually be a conventional element in any system of social norms, even if they impose no internal limit on the range of addressees, they will seldom be "invariable over historical time and across social groups." Furthermore, Habermas seems to be implying that social norms that do not apply to an indefinitely large circle of addressees, but apply only to members of particular historical communities, are to be justified in ethical discourses rather than moral. This is inconsistent with the ascription of deontic force to social norms, because it means that agents would then have to be raising evaluative claims in their regulative speech acts.

The problem can be summarized in the following way. Habermas is committed to the view that in making regulative speech acts, agents raise a rightness claim and commit themselves to redeem this claim in the context of a practical discourse. It is because this rightness claim is made with respect to all social norms (e.g., table manners), according to Habermas, that communicative action can serve as a general mechanism for coordinating social interaction. The principle (U) is introduced as a general rule to govern practical discourses that seek to redeem the rightness claim raised in these routine contexts of social interaction. However, if (U) is to be given an ultranarrow construal, as only permitting agreement on the most absolutely general of principles, then no particular social norms could be redeemed as such in the context of practical discourses governed by (U). This means that universalization could not stand to rightness as induction stands to truth, if rightness is still to be understood as the type of validity claim raised by all regulative speech acts. But if regulative speech acts are to be understood as making a weaker sort of claim, one that reflects merely the shared ethical horizon of a particular social group, then they can no longer be understood as raising rightness claims. Their restriction to the domain of shared values would mean that agents were only making claims about what was better or worse *for us*. This teleological construal is inconsistent with the idea that rightness claims are associated with social norms, that is, rules of *action*, since values of this type can just as easily by realized through instrumental action.

However, once it is recognized that Habermas's motivation for attempting to "shrink" the domain of the moral is only to ensure that moral arguments can be resolved in principle, and once we see that there is no need to demonstrate this in order to refute moral noncognitivism, then there is no reason to introduce these modifications. It is possible to retain the strictly action-theoretic distinction between moral and ethical questions and avoid the problematic attempt to distinguish questions of "collective identity" from questions of what is "equally in the interests of all."

Consider a specific example. All parties in the abortion dispute agree that there is a certain value associated with human life. This generates widespread agreement that a state of affairs in which fewer fetuses are terminated is better than a state of affairs in which more are. The value, in this sense, takes the form of an abstract ranking of states of affairs from best to worst with respect to a particular feature that has evaluative salience. However, this abstract ranking has no direct impact on systems of action. To realize such a value, it must in some way be translated into particular motives for particular agents. There are two primary mechanisms through which this can occur. First, the value can become implemented by instantiating particular patterns of preference. In this respect, the value operates as a deliberative consideration in the "desire-rationality" component of the theory of action. Thus one might try to persuade others that they should prefer the use of various forms of birth control over reliance upon abortion to avoid unwanted pregnancy. Similarly, one might attempt to raise one's children in such a way that their ultimate patterns of desire reflect the ordering prescribed by the particular value. Either way, the value is articulated in practice only via systems of instrumental action. The other primary mechanism through which values can be implemented is by adopting a norm that directly prescribes the pattern of action needed to achieve the state of affairs that is ranked highest according to the evaluative standard. Thus one might try to persuade others that abortion should be proscribed. In this case, values would function as deliberative considerations in the "norm-rationality" component of the general theory of action, that is, the theory of practical discourse.

When the issue is framed in this way, it becomes clear that one of the intuitions underlying Habermas's distinction is absolutely correct. When agents engage in ethical deliberation, that is, when they attempt to decide what preferences they should adopt in the light of certain shared values, they may safely disregard the question of how many other individuals share the values in question. Because the value is being "used" only to determine their particular preferences, the direction that the ethical deliberation goes has no direct impact on other persons (only an indirect impact insofar as their preferences then get articulated in particular patterns of instrumental action). In this respect, ethical deliberation affects only those individuals whose preferences are subject to reevaluation. The case of moral deliberation, that is, when agents are trying to decide what social norms should be adopted, is entirely different. Here the number of others who share the value in question must be taken into consideration, because the normative regulation that is ultimately adopted will in turn be enforced.[49] This means that if the value is transformed into a norm, the pattern of action that it prescribes will become sanctioned. As a result, anyone who was not "on board" in the original value-consensus will find themselves subject to coercion. Deriving a norm from a value without considering the question of whether everyone affected by the norm shares that value therefore violates a basic rule of discourse, namely, that consensus must be secured through the force of the better argument. If there are some individuals who cannot be persuaded to accept the value, then they cannot be forced to comply with any norms based upon it, which is to say that the value cannot serve as grounds for normative validity. But if everyone must already accept a value in order for it to be used as a basis for a norm, then everyone's preferences must already reflect the ordering of states that the value prescribes, and as a result, the same norm can be derived by simply looking at the interests of all affected. Thus in moral deliberation, no value can have greater force than the sum of individual preferences that it motivates. In one sense, then, values do not enter into moral discourse per se, only the individual preference orderings that they generate.

To return to the abortion example, there is no problem in having any given individual transform a general respect for the value of life into a desire to avoid having an abortion. No other person need be consulted, because the only consequence of this decision is that the agent in question will make use of the opportunities that are legitimately available to her within the institutional framework of the society to advance these interests through teleological action. This may include not only abstaining from having an abortion herself, but also attempting to discourage others from doing so, through modification of their preferences. The key restriction, however, is that the agent may not legitimately avail herself of the power to sanction others who fail to act in a way that promotes these values, any more than she may sanction those who fail to act in a way that promotes any of her other interests. When sanctioning behavior is motivated by one's preferences, it amounts to nothing more than an unjust exercise of social power. To sanction others legitimately it would be necessary to take the value and transform it into a norm. Doing this, however, requires taking into account all of the other interests at play, precisely because the force of norms stems ultimately from the shared structure of expectations that they provide. But other individuals, even while sharing the same value, may think that it is outweighed by certain other values, such as the importance of reproductive control for securing the social autonomy of women. Thus there is a significant burden of proof incurred when one attempts to move from the claim that some particular outcome is best to the claim that the actions needed to generate this outcome should be mandatory.

For this reason, Habermas's basic intuition—that norms should not directly institutionalize values—makes perfect sense. It reflects the fact that norms are public in a way that preferences are not, and so values are not "trumps" in practical discourse. In deliberating about what I should desire, it is a general characteristic of strong evaluation that I allow values to "trump" the desires that I happen have, forcing me to revise my preferences. However, in deliberating about what norm should regulate our interactions, I cannot use this value to "trump" someone *else's* desires in the same way, since this would effectively allow me to disregard their opinion. This does not mean, however, that it is illegitimate for agents to ground moral arguments in an appeal to shared values. It just means that these values must already be shared in order for the argument to have any force.

In any case, under no circumstances can the distinction between moral and evaluative questions limit the number of issues that are to be regarded as moral. For this reason, Habermas cannot seek to avoid the problem of persistent disagreement by reclassifying a certain class of problems. Ethical questions and moral questions are simply different. The basic moral question, according to this action-theoretical classification, is whether a particular type of action is to be obligatory, forbidden, or permissible. The abortion dispute cannot be regarded as strictly ethical, because the decision to leave abortion a matter of "individual conscience" is simply one way of articulating the moral decision to classify the action as permissible.[50] Naturally, classifying an action as permissible means that agents must go on to weigh the merits of that action with respect to their values and preferences, something that they need not do when it is classified as obligatory or forbidden. But this just means that the initial "deontic pruning" of their decision tree leaves them with some options; it does not mean that the question of how the tree should be deontically pruned has disappeared.[51] The decision not to regulate an action is just as much a moral decision as the decision to regulate.

6.4   Bargaining and Consensus

The moral/ethical distinction, when drawn action-theoretically, is helpful in clarifying the basic reason that values cannot be appealed to as "trumps" in practical discourse to endorse particular norms. However, eliminating this kind of appeal to values from practical discourse cannot be used to reclassify a certain set of problems as "nonmoral," and so cannot help Habermas deal with the problematic cases in which differences over questions of value prevent agents from conferring adequate recognition upon each other's interests. This is the problem that McCarthy raises. If agents adopt a particular preference ordering on the grounds that it is prescribed by a certain class of values, this may lead them to *devalue* the preferences of others who do not share their concerns (e.g., "so what if they don't feel this way, they ought to"). Even if people do not attempt to simply impose these values upon others, they may be unable to agree on how much these other interests "count for" when it comes to deciding the merits of specific moral norms. And this may result in intractable moral disagreement, because no party in the dispute is willing to acknowledge that any one set of interests is "common" or "generalizable."

For Habermas to say that the intransigent party's interests are themselves subject to reappraisal does nothing to resolve the problem. Nor is it plausible to conjure the whole problem away by reclassifying it as an ethical disagreement. Neither of these strategies does anything to dispel the basic conflict that underlies the demand for normative regulation. However, there is a fairly obvious escape route available, which for various reasons Habermas refuses to take. McCarthy's argument presupposes that resolving a particular practical dispute requires that agents make interpersonal comparisons of utility. That is to say, he assumes that agents must come to some agreement about the significance of the different projects that each may be inclined to pursue, in order to decide upon a norm that will regulate them impartially. It is because disagreement over questions of value eliminates the common standard needed to conduct such comparisons that value-pluralism will lead to dissensus, in McCarthy's view. The underlying assumption is certainly correct, insofar as the argument constitutes a criticism of Habermas's view. Since Habermas claims that practical discourse must uncover an interest that is "common" to all, it makes sense to assume that agents must also perceive the significance of this interest in the same way. However, if the notion of a common interest is, at best, unhelpful, then it is not at all clear why interpersonal comparisons are required.

Suppose one characterizes the problem using a purely subjective theory of interest, so that what anyone else thinks about the merits of anyone else's projects will be considered irrelevant to the deliberative proceedings. Clearly, it will then be impossible to resolve the dispute by finding a single interest that all share, because in principle each person's interests will be her own. The obvious recourse is then to resolve the dispute by having agents adopt some kind of reasonable compromise. Under the terms of such a compromise, each agent will give up certain opportunities to pursue her interests. The significance of the foregone opportunities can be calculated simply by determining their significance for the agent who foregoes them. Thus the notion of compromise can be defined subjectively, just like the notion of interest. This means that agents, when confronted with a straightforward conflict of interest, need not simply agree to disagree; they can also agree to split the difference. The normative theory that attempts to specify a set of principles that can pick out a reasonable compromise in the absence of a common metric of value is often referred to as *bargaining theory*. I would like to suggest that bargaining theory offers Habermas an attractive fallback position in support of the view that practical discourse can be expected to yield agreement. (Of course, the bargaining mechanism is not strong enough to show that agreement is possible in principle. But since it has already been shown that such a demand is unmotivated, the goal here is simply to show that the relativist—who predicts intractable disagreement on moral questions—is too pessimistic. There is no reason that reasonable persons should be unable to reach a normative consensus.)

The appeal to bargaining theory should be qualified in several respects. First, note that Habermas explicitly rejects bargaining as a fallback position. I will attempt to show, however, once the basic position has been outlined, that Habermas's reasons for doing so stem from an unwarranted suspicion of the strategic element in bargaining. Second, I do not want to deny that it is best for agents to resolve their moral differences using the "thick" resources of the lifeworld. Clearly, where sets of shared values exist that permit interpersonal comparisons of well-being, it is possible to develop solutions to social interaction and distribution problems that are considerably more satisfactory from the moral point of view.[52] Furthermore, the solution will be significantly better if agents can agree on a framework for "laundering preferences," that is, restricting the interests at play to those that are morally legitimate.[53] Finally, there is no suggestion that the outcome of a bargaining procedure is fixed by merely procedural constraints. Bargaining outcomes are the result of applying a set of norms to a distribution problem. The norms in question are distinguished only by the fact that they can be applied under conditions in which the level of shared information or values is extremely low. Thus the outcomes they prescribe are not ones that agents are rationally *compelled* to accept in any strong sense. What bargaining theory shows is that agents can reach agreements that are acceptable to all given only very weak assumptions about their willingness to compromise and the conditions under which they are prepared to do so. Thus bargaining theory does not guarantee agreement, as (U) is supposed to, but it does suggest that disagreement can be expected to persist only under conditions of very extreme moral or discursive intransigence.

To illustrate, consider the Nash bargaining solution. Nash starts by defining a bargaining situation as one in which individuals "have the opportunity to collaborate for mutual benefit in more than one way."[54] He then defines the problem—significantly—as one of selecting an outcome in the space defined by the agents' utility functions.[55] Thus the bargaining solution does not divide up resources directly; rather, it divides up utility, that is, opportunities to achieve one's preferred outcomes. It then assigns fungible resources to agents to the extent that is needed to provide these opportunities. (This is why the solution does not depend upon the possibility of interpersonal comparisons of well-being.)

Nash begins by defining the bargaining problem. This is constructed by first plotting the set of possible cooperative outcomes in terms of their payoffs. There may not be many outcomes available, but individuals are not forced to select a concrete outcome; they can also agree to a randomization over these outcomes. (Like when we flip a coin to see who gets first possession in a football game, or who gets to keep a contested commodity.) To allow this, we simply allow the expected utility associated with all randomizations over these outcomes into the set of proposals. This gives us the bargaining space. Each point in this space represents a particular allocation of utility to the players.

One of the proposals in the bargaining space is especially important, namely, the one that corresponds to the outcome players will get if they fail to secure agreement. In this context, such an outcome is represented by the expected utility that each player can expect to get from acting strategically, that is, not cooperating. This is referred to as the *disagreement point*, and the associated outcome the *noncooperative outcome*. Together, the bargaining space and the disagreement point specify a bargaining problem (X), which is the set of points belonging to the bargaining space that are Pareto-superior to the disagreement point. (Figure 6.2 illustrates the set of payoffs available in a typical situation where agents can benefit from normative regulation. Here the bargaining problem will be the portion of the shaded region to the northeast of (1,1).)

Nash's proposed solution begins by imposing two intuitive constraints on any acceptable solution to the bargaining problem: (1) efficiency: the solution should not be one in which some agent is worse off and no agent is better off than in some alternative; (2) symmetry: if the bargaining problem is completely symmetric, i.e., $(x,y) \in X \leftrightarrow (y,x) \in X$, then the solution should allocate the same amount to both players. The second constraint articulates a simple "no place-switching" principle. If both players are indistinguishable from one another, and yet one receives more than the other, then the one who receives less will want to switch places with the one that receives more. The only way to prevent this, and thus to secure agreement, is to assign each of them the same amount.

So far not much has been claimed. These two axioms suggest that if one is, for instance, trying to split a pie between two people, each of whom has an equally intense desire to consume pie, then one should split the entire pie evenly between them. Efficiency prevents one from splitting some of the pie and throwing the rest away, while symmetry requires that, since there is no relevant difference between the two players, the solution should not be affected if one of them gets the other's share. These follow fairly directly from simple "role-taking" operations, and the two constraints can arguably be derived from the structure of practical discourse. However, this is not very significant, because all it allows one to do is solve perfectly symmetric distribution problems in which there is no difference between the players. But people are usually in asymmetric positions with respect to particular interactions, and so will have different opportunities and preferences. What Nash does, therefore, is impose an additional constraint that permits him to generalize this solution to any distribution problem.

This axiom is (3) independence of irrelevant alternatives: if some options that are not part of the solution get eliminated as possibilities, it should not change the outcome.[56] The significance of this axiom is that, when satisfied, it implies that for any given distribution problem there will be a perfectly symmetric problem that is equivalent from the moral point of view. Since the two problems are equivalent, the solution that we would pick for the symmetric problem should also be the solution to the asymmetric problem. Thus we can "project" the solution from unproblematic cases onto more problematic ones. (The idea that the two problems are *morally* equivalent is significant, because many critics of the Nash solution point out that eliminating supposedly "irrelevant" alternatives may diminish the bargaining strength of one agent, and therefore reduce the size of the share of the surplus that he might reasonably expect to secure. This objection, however, presupposes that the bargaining process is conducted strategically, which is inconsistent with Nash's axiomatic approach. The only question at stake is whether, from the moral point of view, differences in strategic position should be relevant to the solution. Here there is a widespread intuition that they should not.)

It turns out that there is exactly one outcome in every bargaining problem at which all three axioms are satisfied, and this is the one that maximizes the *product* of the utility assigned to each player.[57] This outcome can be found by drawing the largest rectangle that can fit inside the bargaining problem, that is, with the southwest corner at the disagreement point and the northeast corner on the Pareto-frontier. The northeast corner of this rectangle is, then, the Nash bargaining solution.

The Nash axioms allow one to take any given distribution problem and construct a "larger" problem (by adding "irrelevant alternatives") that is equivalent, from the moral point of view, and perfectly symmetric. This provides a mechanism through which, in effect, the symmetry axiom can be applied to any distribution problem. However, other mechanisms have been proposed. The other primary solution concept, known as the Kalai-Smorodinsky bargaining solution, replaces the "independence of irrelevant alternatives" axiom with a "monotonicity" constraint, which states that if the bargaining problem is transformed in such a way that both players' feasible utility level is higher, and the solution assigns one player a higher payoff, then the other should not receive a payoff lower than the one received in the original problem.[58] This reflects the moral intuition that when increased benefits become available to both players, this should not result in one of the players being disadvantaged.

These two bargaining solutions sometimes produce different answers depending on the context, and so deciding between them is often a matter of balancing morally salient features of the specific cases under consideration. What both solutions allow us to do is project the solutions to easy distribution problems onto more difficult ones. The potential stumbling block therefore arises in trying to decide exactly *which* easy problem any particular difficult one is equivalent to. It is therefore no surprise that the rules that effect this transition—independence of irrelevant alternatives, monotonicity—are the ones that have attracted controversy. The axioms that solve the easy cases, however, are extremely intuitive, and it would not be implausible to suggest that they arise from the structure of practical discourse itself. The combination of efficiency and symmetry pick out outcomes that no one has any particular reason to reject. No agent could do any better by changing places with any other, and there is no way of improving any agent's position without harming another, thereby giving the latter a reason to reject the arrangement. Even though the outcome is not a strategic equilibrium (since each agent still has an instrumental incentive to defect), it forms something of a *discursive* equilibrium, because any proposal to deviate from this outcome would automatically generate an objection from someone.

Given that bargaining theory models have these attractive properties, the question is why Habermas does not point to bargaining theory as evidence that practical discourse is unlikely to result in intractable disagreement. The answer is that he thinks incorporating bargaining and compromise as part of the procedure of practical discourse would undermine the cognitivism of discourse ethics. This concern, however, is based on two misunderstandings.

6.4.1 Bargaining as strategic action

The first problem is that Habermas treats bargaining as a form of strategic action. Thus he grants that, in democratic deliberation, "whenever it turns out that all the proposed regulations touch on the diverse interests in respectively different ways without any generalizable interest or clear priority of some one value being able to vindicate itself . . . there remains the alternative of bargaining, that is, negotiation between success-oriented parties who are willing to cooperate."[59]

The problematic assumption here is that when agents are unable to achieve consensus on a common interest or value, they have no choice but to drop the performative stance and adopt a strategic orientation. It is certainly true that many real-life bargaining procedures are institutionally regulated strategic interactions. And there are game-theoretic bargaining models in which theorists attempt to characterize the process through which alternating offers are made, threats exchanged, and so forth, leading to a final outcome.[60] However, these "noncooperative" models of bargaining are entirely distinct from the axiomatic models outlined above. What the axiomatic bargaining solutions show is that, even when agents are unable to agree on a common interest, or a shared metric of value, they can still achieve consensus through discursive procedures. Their acceptance of the relevant set of axioms gives them good reason to accept the solution that uniquely satisfies these constraints. Thus Habermas's assumption that disagreement over values forces agents to adopt a strategic orientation is entirely unmotivated.

Habermas is correct in saying that the outcomes generated by *noncooperative* bargaining procedures lack cognitive content, because these outcomes are selected for instrumental and not communicative reasons. As a result, they have no more validity than an empirical belief adopted on the basis of wishful thinking. However, in axiomatic bargaining theory, the model itself provides agents with absolutely no instrumental reason for adopting the bargaining outcome— its sole merit is that it is the only outcome that satisfies a set of plausible discursive and moral constraints on acceptable distributions. Furthermore, in almost every distribution problem, each of the agents will generally have *some* outcome that they prefer to the bargaining solution. Since they will each have an instrumental incentive to pursue this outcome, insofar as they do accept the bargaining solution, it cannot be for instrumental reasons. Thus the suggestion that agents are acting strategically is inconsistent with the axiomatic approach.

Of course, the fact that the Nash and Kalai-Smorodinsky bargaining solutions lack strategic microfoundations has been significantly obscured by game theorists, who for a long time tried to correct what they regarded as a deficiency in that regard.[61] However, it is now generally acknowledged that what these "cooperative" models really show is how one can apply moral norms to particular distribution problems, and that they say nothing whatsoever about which outcomes would follow from interactions conducted according to the usual principles of individual utility-maximization.[62] A lot of the confusion here arises from the fact that bargaining theory uses agents' utility functions to represent the bargaining problem. This naturally leads to the assumption that agents approach the bargaining problem with an eye toward maximizing their expected utility. But this is incorrect. The reason for using utility functions is simply to represent what *interests* are at stake for each agent in the deliberation. The reason these are defined individualistically is twofold. First, utility functions represent a very weak information source, because they do not support interpersonal comparisons. This is what motivates the selection of a bargaining approach in the first place—in cases where disagreement over the set of values makes it impossible to establish a shared metric. The second reason is slightly more subtle. In fixing the terms of a compromise it is necessary to fix the interests at stake in as stark a manner as possible, in order to ensure that no agent is disadvantaged by virtue of having an altruistic or compliant disposition. If interests are not characterized in this way, certain classic difficulties arise, which are best illustrated with an old Talmudic example. One person sees a pie and says, "I want it all." A second person comes along and says, "Why don't we each take half?" An impartial mediator comes along and says, "Okay, split it 75–25." The problem here is that the second agent's *offer* is being mistaken for her *demand*. By taking a proposed compromise as a statement of the agent's interest, the arbitrator thereby penalizes the agent for being more reasonable. Because of this, the fairness of a compromise can only be determined by finding out what the underlying interests are, prior to the moderation of these interests to accommodate the interests of others. This is precisely the information that a utility-function conveys. Thus the fact that bargaining theory defines the distribution problem over a utility space does not mean that agents are assumed to act in an individualistic manner. It simply means that their interests must be characterized in an individualistic manner in order to determine whether they are being treated fairly by any proposed bargaining solution.

Even if agents are not acting strategically, a more general way of formulating the concern would be to say that bargaining produces only a *modus vivendi*, not a genuine agreement. Because the extent of each agent's compromise is determined by its "distance" from the disagreement point, and the location of the disagreement point is determined by each agent's strategic position, any agreement reached will merely reflect the background constellation of social power and interests. Furthermore, every time the relative strategic strength of the parties changes, there will be a call to renegotiate the agreement. This conclusion can be avoided, however, if we note that the location of the disagreement point may be normatively specified. It would usually be the case that even if there is a failure to reach consensus on a particular norm, agents will remain constrained in their strategic options by the rest of the norms that remain unproblematic components of their lifeworld. For instance, it is reasonable to suppose that the disagreement point should not be affected by threats.[63] Furthermore, agents who disagree over which specific norm should regulate their interactions may nevertheless agree on a default norm that should apply in case they fail. In this case, the disagreement point is normatively fixed, and so would be insensitive to changes in the relative strength of the parties.

Finally, there is Rawls's important observation that even if an agreement does begin as a mere *modus vivendi*, it may acquire stability over time simply because regular cooperation builds a level of trust and goodwill, which in turn makes agents less likely to press any strategic advantage that they may acquire.[64]

6.4.2 Bargaining as will-formation

The second objection Habermas makes is that even if agents are not adopting a bargaining proposal for the wrong kind of reason, they will still each be adopting it for a different reason, namely, the satisfaction that it provides for their particular interests:

The compromises achieved by such bargaining contain a negotiated agreement that balances conflicting interests. Whereas a rationally motivated consensus rests on reasons that convince all the parties *in the same way*, a compromise can be accepted by the different parties each for its own different reasons.[65]

On this basis, Habermas claims that bargaining is a procedure that results in *will-formation*, as opposed to discourse, which involves *opinion-formation*. Unfortunately, he has a tendency to conflate this distinction with the action-theoretic one, thereby assuming that will-formation involves regulated strategic action, and opinion-formation communicative. This becomes problematic when it comes to handling cases like Rawls's "overlapping consensus" model, in which agents agree on a shared conception of justice for different communicative reasons (each finding justification for the theory in some component of their rival comprehensive doctrines).[66] There is, of course, no reason to think that simply because different agents find different arguments compelling, there is some strategic dimension to their actions. To keep the relevant issues distinct, I will therefore restrict the term "will-formation" to a sequence of linguistic—not strategic—actions that leads agents to accept a particular proposal for *different* justificatory reasons. It has already been shown that bargaining procedures need not involve any element of strategic action. The question now is whether bargaining and compromise counts as an opinion- or a will-formation process.

At first glance, it seems obvious that axiomatic bargaining theory models an opinion-formation process. Under the Nash bargaining solution, every agent accepts the outcome for the same reason, namely, that it is the only outcome that satisfies the axioms that they regard as providing reasonable constraints on a cooperative solution. More generally, everyone accepts the solution because it represents, roughly speaking, a fair compromise. They can see this by engaging in a process of "ideal role taking," to confirm that any other proposal would generate reasonable objections from some quarters. Habermas's suggestion that compromises can be accepted for different reasons actually represents a deep confusion about the nature of compromise. The only reason for accepting a compromise is precisely that it is a compromise (which is partly why it is so difficult to get people to accept them—there are usually a thousand and one reasons to say no, and only one reason to say yes). Under any compromise proposal there will always be other possibilities under which one's own party does better, and the only reason for rejecting these and going with the compromise is precisely that one can see that these alternatives will be unacceptable *to the other parties*. Common knowledge that all parties are in the same position is precisely what serves to recommend the compromise, and so the reasons that each side has for adopting it will of necessity be identical. Naturally, this does not change the underlying interest structure of the interaction that is being regulated, but this interest structure is not what provides agents with their reasons for accepting the compromise. The interests are what make the compromise reasonable; they are not what make it reasonable to accept the compromise. It is the rational insight that the compromise is reasonable that provides the agent with a reason to accept it.

However, upon closer examination, it is not so clear that the distinction between opinion and will-formation is as clear-cut as Habermas's account suggests. The action-theoretic distinction between saying "yes" for instrumental reasons and saying it for communicative ones is unproblematic. But it is not clear at all that there is a sharp distinction between saying "yes" for the same communicative reasons and saying it for different ones. With any complex issue, there will inevitably be a large number of deliberative considerations that support or detract from a particular view, and agents will inevitably weigh these considerations differently. It is deeply implausible to think that even the mostly widely endorsed scientific theories, for instance, are all accepted by scientists for exactly the same reasons. But even more importantly, since no chain of justification is ever rendered explicit, but each is grounded in a background consensus that is, at best, overlapping, there will be no fact of the matter as to what reasons "ultimately" led agents to accept a particular claim. Thus the distinction between opinion- and will-formation presupposes an illegitimate reification of justificatory relations.

Finally, it should be noted that agents always have the option of unanimously adopting warrants that will allow them to "externalize" disagreement. For instance, they may all simply agree that "in cases of disagreement, it is acceptable to adopt the outcome of procedure x," where x indicates some nondiscursive procedure such as majority-rule voting.[67] In such cases, when agents give up on argumentation and decide to vote, it can still be said that they accept the final outcome for the same reason, because they are all motivated by the same inference from the same facts. This is perhaps an extreme example, but the point is to show that agents can very easily adapt the criteria that determine what is to count as rational acceptability in order to accommodate varying degrees of disagreement. And there is no doubt that similar management techniques are used throughout scientific-empirical discourse, for example, referral to authoritative sources, and so on. It is therefore unreasonable to expect that agents in practical discourse must always follow the same line of reasoning, all the way along, in order for the discourse to count as "cognitive."

It has been pointed out repeatedly that bargaining solutions are fairly low-powered, both from a moral and a practical point of view. The point of bringing them in here is simply to show that agents would have to be extremely disagreeable to get themselves into a situation in which they are incapable of deciding upon some norm acceptable to all through practical discourse. This of course does not do justice to Habermas's intuition that moral questions make a "strong" claim to validity, that is, that they must be resolvable in principle. I have tried to show that there is no reason to think that this kind of strong claim is needed to guarantee the cognitive status of moral judgment, and that Habermas's attempts to provide this guarantee lead him into all sorts of unnecessary difficulties. My goal in bringing in bargaining theory has been to show that there is no special reason to think that practical questions are not resolvable. The lack of shared values does not impede the ability of agents to achieve agreement on normative questions, and so there is no need to impose a universalization principle on practical discourse, or to relocate "ethical" questions into a separate discursive domain. This still leaves unexplained, however, the intuition that moral questions are not ones over which we can "agree to disagree." Habermas claims that this intuition reflects a structural feature of practical discourse; in the next chapter, however, I will attempt to argue that it derives its impetus from the pragmatic role that social norms play in the regulation of social interaction. This argument is intended to relieve any residual discomfort that may have been produced by the "wait and see" attitude that I adopt toward the outcome of practical discourse.

7
Cognitivism and Convergence

According to the theory of meaning that Habermas develops, all language has a built-in "telos" of mutual understanding/agreement. This is because understanding the meaning of a sentence consists in knowing the conditions under which it could be discursively redeemed, and the discursive redemption of a validity claim involves securing a rationally motivated agreement on its behalf. Accepting an utterance involves not only knowing what these conditions are, but also believing that they obtain, or could be brought to obtain by the speaker. In standard cases, the speaker will not be deploying the speech act with strategic intent, but will be incurring a commitment to discursively redeem the utterance if called upon to do so. As a result, successful performance of the speech act will require that this commitment be accepted, and so will generate not only understanding, but also agreement between speaker and hearer.

Because of the compositional structure of language, the meaning of any single expression is determined by its relation to a large number of other semantic expressions, which the hearer will have to grasp in order to understand it. However, these relations are not purely linguistic, but epistemic, because they include an understanding of the practical contexts in which these expressions can be used. Since the validity of epistemic relations is determined, in Habermas's view, by their ability to motivate a rational consensus, persistent and intractable disagreement among agents suggests they have not correctly situated each other's utterances in the right set of epistemic relations—which is to say, that they have not correctly understood one another. As a result, the theory of meaning guarantees that all linguistic communication systems will exhibit a certain level of convergence with respect to their *content*, because it is possible for agents to disagree only so much before it becomes uncertain that they mean the same thing by their expressions.

One way of articulating this feature of language use is to say that the "goal" of assertion is to state the truth. The significant point is that assertion cannot be understood merely as an attempt to present something intelligible to others; it is also an attempt to present something that will be acceptable to them. The use of the truth predicate in formulating this thesis can be misleading, since it appears to suggest that all assertions have as their goal the attempt to state that a sentence possesses some special property. On these grounds, it is sometimes thought that the goal of all inquiry is to determine whether or not a certain class of sentences possesses this same property. Thus the idea that truth is the "goal of inquiry" is interpreted to mean that the goal of inquiring into whether snow is white is to determine whether "snow is white" is true or false. But of course the point of investigating whether snow is white is to determine whether snow is white, just as the point of investigating whether $E = mc^2$ is to determine whether $E = mc^2$. The truth predicate is merely *used* to state this fact about inquiry in its full generality.

Unfortunately, this misleading use of the truth predicate has given rise to the suggestion that unless we know whether or not a particular class of statements is capable of truth or falsity, there is "no point" in investigating any of them. The problem arises here from a confusion of truth with an ordinary empirical property, like "yellow." Certainly, before we conduct an inquiry into whether or not something is yellow, we would want to know whether it is the type of thing that is capable of being colored. But it is often inferred, on the basis of this analogy, that before investigating the truth-value of a given statement we should determine whether the class of statements to which it belongs is truth-apt. The deflationary analysis of the truth predicate reveals the error underlying this analogy, and so removes the need to ascertain, in advance, what level of convergence we expect to obtain in a given discourse before engaging in it.

Nevertheless, we are still faced with the fact that different types of discourse exhibit different levels of convergence, and that some arguments are likely to be more productive than others. Arguing about whether or not something is funny, or about whether or not something tastes good, quickly becomes a waste of time. Arguing about what happened in the distant past, or what will happen in the future, is perhaps somewhat more productive. In all of these cases, however, there appear to be limits on the amount that can be achieved through argument. Habermas attempts to explain this phenomenon by distinguishing between different types of validity claims that are raised in different types of speech acts. Each validity claim is indexed to a particular form of discourse, which is governed by its own set of inference rules. Some of these discourses, namely, the moral and the theoretical, contain special "bridge principles" that guarantee consensus, while others, namely, the expressive and the evaluative, do not. Thus Habermas claims that agents making evaluative judgments claim only "relative validity" for their utterances.[1] In this way, constructive principles built into the structure of particular discourses provide the guarantee of convergence. As a result, whether there is any "point" to pursuing a particular argument will be determined by how far the associated validity claim permits agreement.

Apart from the more general difficulties that this attempt to distinguish between types of validity claims creates for Habermas's view, this particular strategy for explaining variations in the level of convergence generates its own special problems. Most importantly, the analysis retains an adherence to the idea that the level of convergence exhibited in a discourse is ultimately determined by its topic. In moral discourse, for instance, since the universalization principle is derived simply from the general rules of discourse and the "meaning" of normative validity, the suggestion is that something intrinsic to the nature of social norms gives their associated discourses the potential for convergence. Apart from the fact that the claim about the "meaning" of normative validity is presented dogmatically, this position is disconcertingly close to the traditional view that there is something special about "truth," and statements that admit of truth or falsity, that guarantees convergence. The deflationary analysis of the truth predicate clearly precludes this line of thinking.

However, if the convergence potential of a discourse is not determined by the alleged "nature" of its associated validity claim, then it remains to be explained why we sometimes approach arguments with the expectation that there is a single correct answer, and sometimes do not. In particular, insofar as one shares Habermas's intuition that agents enter into moral argumentation with the strong presumption that there is a single correct answer to be found, some defense of this intuition must be provided. Having denied the universalization principle, which Habermas introduced to defend precisely this claim, it is necessary to provide some alternative account that explains why moral questions should be thought more tractable than, say, questions of taste or humor.

To meet this challenge, I would like to develop what I consider to be a more consistently pragmatist account of the variation that discourses exhibit in their levels of convergence. I will argue that the issue of convergence should not be addressed by looking at intrinsic features of different types of judgment or intentional states (§7.1), but rather by considering the consequences that agents will face if they *fail* to secure agreement. To establish this claim, I begin (§7.2) by showing that differences in the level of convergence exhibited between beliefs and desires can be explained without reference to the representational nature of beliefs, but entirely through the pragmatic structure of social interaction. The primary advantage of this analysis is that it is able to account for the fact that different discourses exhibit varying *degrees* of convergence, without having to posit a variety of kinds of validity claims. I conclude (§7.3) by showing how these different types of judgment can be classified from an action-theoretic point of view, and the levels of convergence explained by the pragmatic requirements of social interaction. The most important consequence of this analysis is that it is able to show how the relatively high level of convergence that we expect in moral argumentation can be explained, given the "nonfactual" character of the relevant judgments.

7.1. Convergence and Representation

The multidimensional theory of action that I have outlined assigns to each agent three kinds of intentional states that may be brought to bear upon an interaction problem—beliefs, desire, and principles. To act rationally, it is necessary only to put these components together in the right way. However, the question of where the agent gets her beliefs, desires, and principles from is not entirely irrelevant to the question of whether her action is rational. In a strict sense, it is possible to act quite rationally on the basis of crazy beliefs. But in a somewhat broader sense, rationality requires that the agent act on the basis of intentional states that are also, in some sense, rational. This is why I suggested that the basic theory of action should be supplemented by a theory of belief-rationality, desire-rationality, and norm-rationality that would explain how a rational agent acquires the relevant states. (Some form of discourse ethics, in my view, can provide the norm-rationality component of this theory.)

In all three cases, the fact that the intentional state is a propositional attitude means that it is necessarily susceptible to *inferential articulation*. It is only because the intentional state is licensed by, and in turn licenses, other intentional states, that it can be said to have propositional content. For example, a desire to go for a walk entitles others, in standard circumstances, to infer a desire to go outdoors. If there are no systematic connections of this type between an agent's desires, it is impossible to say that her desires have the content that would normally be assigned to them. Because of this, agents can always be held accountable for their intentional states—"you say you want to go for a walk, but. . . ." Rendering the intentional states intelligible requires showing how they can be deployed in argumentative practice. (For example, the requirement that rational preferences form a transitive ordering over possible outcomes can be seen to stem from this requirement.) As a result, it can always be said that an agents' intentional states are "rational" in a weak sense.

However, it is obvious that the standards we employ in determining what is rational—or, to use Habermas's term, valid—differ enormously, depending upon the type of intentional state that is at issue. Consider Habermas's discourse principle:

(D)   Only those norms are valid that meet (or could meet) with the discursive approval of all affected.

In the case of beliefs, we would be inclined to subscribe to a somewhat stronger constraint, for example:

(B)   Only those beliefs are valid that meet (or could meet) with the discursive approval of all.

But with desires we are inclined to think that they need not be "acceptable" to anyone other than the agent who holds them:

(V)   Only those desires are valid that meet (or could meet) with the reflective endorsement of the agent.

What appears to change in each case is the scope of the relevant discursive consensus—from the agent herself in the case of desires, to all those affected in the case of norms, to anyone at all in the case of beliefs. Thus discourse about beliefs is expected to command convergence among all persons, norms among all those affected, and desires among no one at all. But this creates a prima facie problem for discourse ethics. When agents are questioned about their desires, the intuition that motivated principle (V) suggests that agents are entitled to refuse certain kinds of justificatory demands. Ultimately, one can say, "this is what I want, and if you don't like it, too bad." *De gustibus non disputandum est.* With beliefs there is no point at which this is an acceptable argumentative move. Norms, however, seem to fall somewhere in between. Habermas's formulation of (D) suggests the agents are committed to justifying their norms only to all those affected. Thus they might, under certain circumstances, be entitled to turn back a demand for justification by saying, "it's none of your business, if we choose to do things this way." Habermas, however, does not have an argument that would explain the differences in the scope of the consensus required in these different domains. He simply treats the intuitions underlying (D) as first principles, or as analytic truths.

To provide the needed argument, it is helpful to begin with some account of why agents are held to a higher standard of accountability in the case of their beliefs than they are in the case of their desires. Once this has been established, it will be much easier to see why norms are situated somewhere in the middle. The standard approach to this problem has been to look for intrinsic epistemic features of beliefs and desires that make argumentation over the former more likely to converge than argumentation over the latter. This approach to the problem is, in my view, seriously misleading, and must be set aside before any clear analysis of the issues can be developed.

The story that is usually told about convergence appeals to the representational character of beliefs. There are two components to this view. First, there is the claim that cognition is fundamentally representational—what it produces as output in some way reproduces or "mirrors" what it gets as input. Whether or not cognitive systems of this type are functioning correctly is to be assessed in terms of the fidelity of this process. Thus the ideal governing the operation of such systems is one of transparency. If the input is thought of as a bundle of information, cognition may produce a computational or notational transformation as output, but all of the information will be preserved. When this is done successfully, it will be possible to run the same process in reverse, and reconstruct the original input from the copy made through cognition.[2]

In this view, it is helpful to distinguish between intentional states, which are merely *about* something, and cognitive states, which *represent* something. The latter will be a subset of the former. All by ourselves, we may be unable to tell which of our intentional states are genuinely cognitive.[3] However, social inter-action affords us the opportunity to communicate our intentional states to one another, and so to compare and contrast. We find that while many of our intentional states are different, many are the same (or equivalent). The most obvious explanation is that, in cases where the output of our cognitive processes is the same, it is because the input was the same.

The second major component of the view concerns the explanation of how we could each have received the same input. The most obvious hypothesis is that it all came from the same source. Thus it is reasonable to suppose that there is a single world, external to us all, that provides us with sensory infor-mation, and so on. This is commonly expressed by the idea that a unified physical world provides the "best explanation" for the convergence that our cognitive states exhibit (as opposed to, e.g., a plurality of virtual environments synchronized to provide us all with identical sensations). In cases where our intentional states are not the same or equivalent, two explanations are avail-able. There is the possibility that the states are cognitive, but the input that they process is private, that is, has its source in the individual's own body. It is often thought that desires are intentional states of this type. In this view, they would be representations of private phenomenal states of affect or disposition. Finally, there could be intentional states that are not representational at all, but perhaps constructive, such as works of imagination.

This analysis has the effect of dividing all of our judgments into two classes: those that are "objective" and those that are "subjective." Objective judgments are the same for all, because their source lies outside the mind, in something that is accessible to all. Subjective judgments, on the other hand, have their source in something private, and therefore can be expected to vary from indi-vidual to individual. One of the peculiarities of this view, incidentally, is that because all cognition is considered representational, the objective/subjective distinction becomes an exclusive dichotomy—there can be nothing in between. As a result, many philosophers have felt that refuting moral relativism requires showing that moral judgments are "objective," which then puts them in the awkward position of trying to show that moral properties are somehow instan-tiated in the physical structure of events.[4]

Despite these unfortunate consequences for morality, the representational-ist view does have considerable intuitive plausibility. However, there are several respects in which it does not do the job that it is called upon to perform. One of the characteristic features of our dealings with the external world is not just that we "happen" to converge in our beliefs, but that we "expect" to find such convergence. The expectation is not of the weak inductive variety ("I wouldn't be surprised if . . ."); it is of the sanctionable normative variety ("There's something wrong with you unless . . ."). When two people disagree in their beliefs about the physical world, we automatically suppose that one of them is mistaken. Crispin Wright articulates this idea by saying that discourse about the physical world exhibits what he calls *cognitive command*. A discourse exhibits cognitive command if and only if it is a priori that differences of opinion arising within it can be satisfactorily explained only in terms of divergent input, unsuitable conditions, or malfunction.[5] It is the a priori status of this presumption that signals its normative force.

In the "best explanation" account of convergence outlined above, it is unclear where this normative force would come from. One might suppose that, having provided an explanation for the level of convergence exhibited by some of our cognitive states, it is then possible to anticipate that inquiries that seek to extend our knowledge of the physical world will also result in high levels of agreement. This might be what licenses our expectation of convergence in scientific inquiry, and our willingness to accept disagreement in many other nonscientific domains. But the standard objection to this line of reasoning is that the "unified" physical world switches from being an empirical hypothesis to a normative ideal when the transition is made from explaining convergence to licensing the expectation of convergence. The physical world posited to explain the similarity between our representations is one that transcends our recognitional capacities, which is why it can supply a norm for our expectations. But it is unclear how such an object could ever be posited on the basis of finite evidence—thus the standard objection to realism, namely, that it is metaphysical in the pejorative sense.

This problem is symptomatic of deeper difficulties. The idea that our beliefs happen to converge, and that our other intentional states happen not to— leading us to seek an explanation for the difference—is a deeply unrealistic account of how our discursive practices operate. Sociological analyses of the practices of "mundane reasoning" have shown that agents consistently *use* the assumption that beliefs must converge in order to determine "what really happened" at a particular place and time. Melvin Pollner, for instance, has studied the way in which the line of questioning pursued by judges in traffic court is governed by the goal of constructing a coherent, "objective" account of events.[6] The definitive temporal sequence of events, for instance, is constructed subject to the constraint that incompatible events not occur simultaneously. Contradictory testimony from witnesses is interpreted as the result of error, or hidden motives, and so on. The idea that there is a single, correct story about what occurred is an assumption that is, on the one hand, completely unfalsifiable, but on the other hand, an essential inferential component of any narrative that might eventually be settled upon.

The conclusion of Pollner's research is that the level of convergence exhibited in our beliefs about the physical world is not something that we happen to discover; rather it is a *practical accomplishment*. Furthermore, it is a practical accomplishment that agents often use extraordinary ingenuity to achieve, developing complex and sometimes unlikely stories to account for divergence. This is not a new idea. Kant argued that the expectation of an unified, coherent, shared physical world was a regulative ideal governing our cognitive activity.[7] Such a regulative ideal could never come from experience, so it cannot be the world, qua phenomenon, that explains the level of convergence exhibited by our systems of belief. What we need, as Kant recognized, is some story that explains where the normative expectation of convergence comes from.

In this respect, the fact that the expectation of convergence is a nonfalsifiable assumption acquires significance. The fact that people disagree about "what happened" can always be explained in terms of differences in perspective, error, improper motivation, and so on. The ideal of convergent beliefs says, in effect, that "all things being equal," agents exposed to the same stimulus will form the same beliefs. Whenever they fail to do so, this is simply proof that all things were not equal. Examples of how generously this principle can be applied abound. For instance, it has become something of joke among economists that, whenever they encounter an activity that should not occur according to their models (like most of the buying and selling on stock markets, or currency exchanges), they reply that "it must be some kind of asymmetric information."[8] The underlying point is a serious one. Whenever one encounters putatively rational agents holding inconsistent beliefs (speculative trading implies that the buyer thinks the price will go up, while the seller thinks it will go down), it is always possible to iron out the inconsistency by supposing that they assign the same prior probabilities to events, but have subsequently been exposed to different information. Thus any superficial disagreement in belief can be explained as the product of underlying agreement plus asymmetric information.

The important point is that these strategies are not specific to the case of beliefs about the physical world, but can be applied to any intentional state. Gary Becker, for instance, has argued influentially that just as agents' beliefs are convergent, so are their desires. He claimed that differences in manifest preference for particular market goods can be explained without positing differences in taste.[9] Instead, he suggested that agents have a uniform desire to consume the same "commodities," which they manufacture internally using market goods as inputs. In this view, each agent can be characterized by some production function, that takes market goods, along with the agent's own time and "consumption capital" as inputs. Agents all start out with the same basic tastes, but accumulate different levels of consumption capital. This makes them capable of converting goods into commodities at different rates. For example, they acquire the capacity to convert good music into listening enjoyment through repeated exposure. Becker argues that a model of this type, combined with asymmetric information about the productive capacity of various market goods, is more than sufficient to explain any observed differences in demand for market goods.

What Becker claims, in effect, is that "all things being equal" people will have the same desires. In cases where they exhibit differences in their choices, it is because all things are not equal, but there exists some asymmetry in the distribution of consumption capital or information. The implication of this argument is that *discourse about what is desirable will satisfy Wright's cognitive command constraint.* And for those who think this obtains only because Becker makes unduly generous use of the ceteris paribus clause, it should be noted that his framework does have considerable explanatory value, particularly for the analysis of advertising on consumption patterns. Becker presents his uniformity of desire hypothesis as the "best explanation" of a variety of significant economic phenomena.[10] (Less esoterically, some eudaemonistic theories in ethics play upon the same idea—"Everyone wants the same thing, to be happy. People just have different beliefs about what will make them happy.")

I am inclined to view Becker's position as a reductio of its own basic strategy. It shows that whether or not a particular discourse can be characterized as convergent is ultimately not an empirical question. Any discourse can be characterized as convergent—there is a generic mechanism available for doing so. Surface disagreement can be explained away by positing a deeper underlying agreement, coupled with some asymmetry in subsequent experience. One can then claim that had agents been exposed to the same set of subsequent events, they would still agree. Thus explanatory strategies that attempt to get at the underlying source of agreement or disagreement, like Becker's analysis of taste, or the representationalist analysis of cognition and the physical world, are guaranteed to succeed. For that reason, they are devoid of analytic value.

In my view, this approach goes wrong when it attempts to posit deep structures to explain surface patterns of agreement and disagreement. The level of surface agreement on a given topic should be explained by surface features of the discourse. It should be understood as a direct result of the level of *discipline* imposed by that discourse upon its participants. The rules governing any discursive practice impose constraints on the level of convergence that it must exhibit, because these rules fix the criteria of warranted assertibility for that discourse, and so indirectly determine the intelligibility of statements made within it. High levels of convergence can be obtained by placing extremely narrow constraints on the "entry moves" available to participants (i.e., what counts as good evidence, or reasonable grounds to initiate a claim). In the case of formalized languages like mathematics, disagreement is excluded by making it impossible to have an asymmetric distribution of language entry moves. The only way to start out an argument is with an axiom, and an axiom is always available to everyone playing the game. On the other hand, discourse that describes the physical world may have entry rules that allow asymmetric opportunities to make claims. One person may "see it happen," another may not. These may result in disagreements, since the second agent may not accept the reliability of the first, and so on. Some specialized subdiscourses, like certain kinds of empirical science, attempt to minimize these asymmetries by requiring that all experimental findings be reproducible. This has the effect of lowering the level of disagreement. Other discourses, such as the aesthetic, make a point of allowing entirely private experiences to count as warranted entry moves.

The consequence of this view is that the level of convergence exhibited by a given discourse will be a product of the inference-licenses that pertain to its specific content. To speak in a slightly misleading fashion: "society" has the discretion to require as much or as little agreement as it likes (although as the level of tolerable disagreement increases, the level of intelligibility begins to fray). The question that must then be asked is why the different discursive practices that we participate in institutionalize different levels of convergence.

In my view, the traditional theory goes wrong in taking agreement, rather than disagreement, to be the *explanandum*. The older view makes sense from the perspective of the "philosophy of consciousness"—if agents formulate their ideas independently, each in their own heads, then agreement certainly seems more mysterious than disagreement. The linguistic turn, however, suggests that agents formulate their thoughts using the public medium of language, whose appropriate use is pinned down by an underlying uniformity of linguistic practice. From this perspective, it is actually disagreement that starts to seem mysterious. When Wittgenstein says, for instance, that he is justified in asserting "this is red" *because he speaks English*, it suggests that anyone who disagrees with the assertion is simply not using the words correctly.[11] For this reason, I would argue that devices like first-person authority, which weaken the kind of discursive commitment that agents incur through their utterances, are important because they *permit disagreement*. The extent to which different discourses exhibit convergence, I would then argue, is determined inversely by the extent to which they incorporate devices, such as first-person authority, that allow disagreements to develop and persist. The level of disagreement that they permit is, in turn, determined by the pragmatic consequences that follow from "agreeing to disagree" in that domain. This thesis can be illustrated by considering some differences in the consequences that follow from disagreement about belief and disagreement about desire.

7.2 A Pragmatist Theory of Convergence

To motivate this position, I would like to divert the discussion briefly in order to articulate the more general pragmatist strategy that informs my response. Here I take Charles Sanders Peirce's analysis of how we come to "fix" our beliefs as paradigmatic. In the standard representationalist view, we form beliefs because the world in a certain sense imposes itself upon us. Our environment impinges upon our senses, causing us to form impressions of the world around us. Peirce's view constitutes a clever inversion of this picture. He claimed that belief-formation is not a passive response to the world, but is an active process in which we pick out the information that we need in order to conduct our activities. Our system of beliefs is formed as a sedimentary by-product of our actions. In Peirce's view, we get along just fine not having any beliefs at all about innumerable features of our environment—because we do not need them. There is nothing in the world in general that compels us to have one or another conviction about which road leads to which town. But when we are trying to get to one of these towns, and encounter a fork in the road, we are forced to make a choice.[12] Peirce defines a belief as simply the policy that one is willing to act upon in such situations.

To modify Peirce's example slightly, I have noticed that of the people who live in my neighborhood, those who own cars generally know which direction the various one-way streets run. People who don't own cars, but get around on foot, usually have no idea. Of course, walking through the neighborhood, it is as plain as day which direction the traffic flows. But pedestrians don't need to know this to get where they are going, and so simply have no beliefs about it. This feature of their environment is not *salient*, because it is not needed for any practical purpose.

Thus Peirce's answer to the question of why we develop beliefs about the world is that we *need to for practical purposes*. I would like to propose a similar account of convergence. The reason that we work so hard to achieve agreement in our beliefs about the physical world is that we need to for practical purposes. The reason that we do not strive as hard to achieve agreement in our desires is that we can get along just fine without it. Thus what I propose is something like an intersubjective generalization of the Peircean account of belief-formation. My task is then to show why, and in what sense, we need to have agreement in belief but not desire. The answer lies, I will argue, in the demanding epistemic requirements for fixing stable expectations in contexts of social interaction.

Both the Peircean point and my own can be formulated more precisely by situating them within the decision-theoretic model of action. As we have seen, when reasoning instrumentally, the agent is not interested in performing any actions "for their own sake," but is instead interested in the outcomes that can be achieved. However, the agent is unable to pick an outcome directly; she can only choose an action. And once an action is selected, the outcome that results is entirely a function of which state obtains. This means that unless the agent has some knowledge, or at least some estimate, of which state will obtain, her preference ordering is completely useless as a guide to instrumental action. To reason back from outcomes to actions, the agent must assign some probability to the occurrence of the relevant states. Once this is done, she can select the action that produces the highest probability-weighted satisfaction of her desires, as expressed by her preference ordering over these outcomes.

Because instrumental reasoning depends upon the use of beliefs about states to project preferences over outcomes onto the set of actions, decision theorists draw a sharp distinction between certainty, risk, and uncertainty. When the agent is certain that a given state will obtain, her preference ordering over actions will directly mirror her preference ordering over outcomes. In cases where there is some risk, that is, where she does not know with certainty which state will obtain, but knows the relative likelihood of every state, then her preference ordering over actions will be a slightly refracted version of the ordering over outcomes. However, if she does not know *at all* which state will obtain, then her preference ordering over actions will simply be undefined. Thus when it comes time to act, agents need to have some expectation about which state will obtain. Even if it is completely wrong, some belief is better than none, because it gives the agent some basis for action.

If one adopts Davidson's view of decision theory, according to which the theory is treated as an interpretive structure used to analyze action into the twin components of belief and desire, then the Peircean view of belief-formation is an immediate consequence.[13] The impossibility of rational action under uncertainty guarantees that any action can be interpreted as the product of some determinate set of beliefs. And since the only evidence one ever has that an agent has a given belief is that she acts in a certain way, if one adopts a broadly antirealist stance toward these beliefs then they become simply policies that agents act upon.

In game-theoretic contexts, as we have seen, the question of how agents are to develop beliefs is more complicated. Because they are unable to simply parameterize their environment, they must find a set of beliefs that is in equilibrium. However, to get a stable equilibrium, it is not sufficient for agents simply to develop *some* system of beliefs. They must achieve what game theorists call "consistent alignment of beliefs" (CAB).[14] This requirement reflects two constraints: not only must each agent develop a set of expectations that is internally consistent, but these expectations must also be "aligned," which means that each player must ascribe to all the others a set of intentions that corresponds to his own expectations, and a set of expectations that correspond to his own intentions. Each player must, in effect, believe that everyone has the same beliefs, and that these beliefs are correct. And in order to successfully coordinate upon an equilibrium, everyone must *in fact* have the *same* correct beliefs. Thus agents, in order to select a purely utility-maximizing course of action in contexts of social interaction, must presuppose that the belief sets of all players converge, and for these actions to produce the out-comes that they were intended to produce, the belief sets of all players must actually converge.

The more surprising consequence is that not only must players assign a convergent set of beliefs to one another about how each intends to play, but they must also assign the same set of beliefs to one another about the probability of every state of nature that might occur. This is one version of the so-called Harsanyi doctrine, which states that the prior probability of all relevant states of nature must be common knowledge among all players.[15] Thus it will not be adequate for players to assign any old subjective probabilities to the natural states that form the parameters of the game; they must all assign the same probabilities, believe that they have all assigned the same probabilities, and so on. This assumption is often rendered implicit in game theory models by having "nature" represented as a pseudo-player who moves with fixed probability (e.g., as was done in figure 2.5). This has the effect of treating nature's move as part of the equilibrium, and so slips the common prior assumption in under the CAB constraint.

At a strictly intuitive level, the reason that players' beliefs must converge in this way is that they are only able to get to a stable set of strategic expectations by "mirroring" each other's reasoning processes. They cannot just assign subjective probabilities to the occurrence of each other's actions, because they must treat these actions as the product of a set of rational beliefs about the anticipated interaction. Thus they must develop beliefs about each other's beliefs, beliefs about each other's beliefs about each other's beliefs, and so on. But this requires them to take an interest in the way that their own beliefs "fit" with the system of beliefs that they are ascribing to others. A system of beliefs determined in this way will only be internally consistent if it is possible to hit upon a set of expectations that would be self-enforcing; that is, if everyone adopted them, then no one would have any reason to do anything that would falsify them. This is what generates the CAB constraint. In cases where players succeed in coordinating upon a Nash equilibrium, their beliefs will be the same. Player 1 does a_1 because he expects player 2 to do a_2, player 2 does a_2 because she expects player 1 to do a_1 (and he expects her to do a_2 because he expects her to expect him to do a_1, she expects him to do a_1 because she expects him to expect her to do a_2, etc.). In cases where they fail to coordinate upon an equilibrium, they will each believe that their beliefs are the same, but this expectation will turn out to be mistaken. But if either of them thought that there was any disagreement about what each expected the other to do, this would give them each a reason to change what they intended to do, and so the equilibrium would unravel.

This is already an interesting result. It suggests that in order to act successfully in strategic interactions, agents need to come up with not just *a* set of beliefs about how others will act, but the *same* set of beliefs about how all of them will act. The fact that agents also need to assume that they all assign the same probability to all natural events follows from a straightforward extension of the logic that generated the CAB constraint. They get to an equilibrium by mirroring each other's reasoning processes. If player 1's choice of action is governed both by expectations about how player 2 will act, and by information about some state of nature, player 2 needs to know what player 1's beliefs are about this state of nature in order to anticipate his move. Player 1 also needs to know what player 2's beliefs are about his beliefs about this state of nature in order to anticipate her move, in order to plan his own move, and so on. If they disagree about what the probability of this state is, it will dramatically multiply the number of possible equilibria.

Take the following example. Suppose a friend and I both want to go on a picnic, but will not enjoy it nearly as much if it rains. If I think it is going to rain with a probability of 30 percent, and my friend thinks it is going to rain with a probability of 70 percent, then we have a problem. What should I suppose she will do: act on the basis of her expectation of what I will do, based on my expectation that it probably will not rain; or act on the basis of my expectation of what she will do, based on her expectation that it probably will rain? Whereas the original interaction may have had only one equilibrium, our disagreement over the probability of rain creates at least two. My friend may decide not to go, because she expects it to rain, and expect me not to go, because she figures that I will expect her not to go. She might, on the other hand, expect me to go, because I do not expect it to rain. And so she might choose to go despite her anticipation of rain, because she expects me to be there. The general point is that common knowledge of belief is not enough to generate a determinate outcome. There must be actual agreement in belief.

To get around this difficulty, game theorists eliminate disagreement about natural events by introducing a common prior and asymmetric information states. The solution suggested by Harsanyi is to construct a game in which we both start out assigning the same prior probability to the chance of rain—say

30 percent—but then my friend acquires information that leads her to update her prior—say she looks out the window and sees clouds.[16] If she has no chance to signal me, then we work off the common prior in order to fix the equilibrium. If she can perform some action that I can observe after acquiring this information, then I will update my prior based upon what I see her do, and we will fix the equilibrium based on our jointly updated priors. Either way, we will act on the basis of an estimate of the probability of rain that is common knowledge, and so will not "agree to disagree."[17]

It should be noted that neither the CAB constraint nor the Harsanyi doctrine follow directly from the instrumental conception of rationality. They are additional assumptions, both of which many game theorists regard as problematic. However, game theorists persist in making them, because without these assumptions it is impossible to define a solution concept that places any meaningful constraints on the strategies that the players may adopt.[18] This means that without these assumptions, instrumental rationality would underdetermine the choice of action even in social interactions that contain only one "strategic" equilibrium. In its defense, it is often pointed out that if players fail to achieve CAB, that is, if they make a mistake as to which equilibrium will be played, they will immediately adjust their belief systems in order to achieve it as soon as the error is discovered.

In any case, I would like to suggest that rather than being a problematic modeling assumptions, the CAB constraint and the Harsanyi doctrine show that convergence in empirical belief has an enormous pragmatic significance for social interaction. Just as we need to assign some probability to events in order to act in decision theoretic contexts, we need to assign some potentially convergent system of beliefs to all persons in order to act in strategic contexts. Thus convergence in empirical beliefs is not a metaphysical necessity, but it is a pragmatic necessity insofar as we want to pursue projects that require instrumental reasoning in contexts of interdependent choice. If we fail to develop a set of convergent beliefs, the price we pay is that our actions will fail to achieve the desired outcomes. Thus, to act successfully in strategic contexts, we must actually align our beliefs in such a way as to satisfy this reciprocally imputed system of consistent beliefs. We need agreement in order to carry out our plans, *even if these plans are formulated and pursued in an entirely individualistic manner.*

This analysis, in my view, provides a clue as to where the "regulative ideal" that governs the notion of representation and cognitive command comes from.

The requirement that we think of one another as working off a common prior, responding in the same way to the same information, is imposed by the structure of social interaction as a practical postulate. It is necessary in order to construct the cognitive framework needed to interact instrumentally. It is only by expecting our belief systems to converge, and expecting one another to expect our belief systems to converge, that we are able to develop even halfway determinate expectations about how each of us will behave. We are capable of relinquishing this assumption, but the cost will be a complete inability to act instrumentally in contexts of social interaction. (Although in cases where it happens not to matter, e.g., the existence of aliens, a transcendent God, etc., we are more willing to live with persistent disagreement.)

The difference between belief and desire is significant in this context. There is no particular reason for agents to have a "consistent alignment of preferences." Preferences are in general not interdependent; that is, it is seldom the case that what I prefer depends upon what someone else prefers *and* what that other person prefers depends upon what I prefer. As a result, there is usually no regress of preference, and so no need for consistent alignment to sort things out. Agents can therefore be in complete disagreement over which outcomes are better or worse without it providing any significant interference with their ability to plan a course of action. So even though we are capable of treating one another's preferences as merely the surface expression of an underlying set of identical tastes, as Becker has shown, there is no practical reason for us to do so. Failure to think of our preferences in these terms does not in any way compromise our ability to plan and execute instrumental actions.

7.3 Convergence and Social Norms

I stated at the outset that one of the advantages of this approach is that it is able to explain the fact that certain discourses exhibit levels of convergence that are somewhere in the middle range between, say, mathematics and gastronomy. My primary concern in this section will be to explain the level of convergence exhibited by moral discourse, which I take to be, despite the tenor of much recent popular discussion, actually quite high.[19]

The argument developed above suggests that instrumental rationality imposes a strong convergence constraint on agents' empirical beliefs. However, as we have seen, strategic rationality is itself often indeterminate in generating solutions to concrete social interaction problems. One of the facts that I repeatedly glossed over in the previous section is that even though strategic reasoning requires that agents develop a system of internally consistent beliefs, very few interaction problems present agents with a single set of beliefs that could satisfy this constraint. But even though instrumental rationality alone does not provide a mechanism that would allow agents to hit upon the same set of beliefs, having internal consistency and a common prior significantly reduces the number of equilibria.

These indeterminacy problems are what motivated the introduction of a multidimensional theory of rational action, in which practical deliberation is taken to involve the application of both normative and instrumental reasons for action. According to this view, social norms act as deontic constraints that effectively limit the range of actions that are subject to instrumental deliberation. Norms are thus able to provide a massive reduction in the complexity of social interaction, by directly motivating conformity to particular institutional patterns.

As a result, the same considerations that were invoked to explain convergence of belief systems can be used to explain the convergence exhibited by systems of social norms. There will be strong pragmatic reasons for maintaining agreement on a set of shared norms, since the indeterminacy of strategic reasoning ensures that the stability and predictability of social interaction will break down in their absence. Persistent disagreement over normative questions leaves agents unable to coordinate their interactions through institutional mechanisms. This leaves them only strategic action to fall back upon, an option that is often unattractive from both a moral and an instrumental point of view. Not only is strategic action usually indeterminate, as the problem of multiple-equilibrium games shows, but it also harbors significant potential to produce suboptimal interactions. When this is likely to occur, agents are in a position to recognize that they would all be better off if they could come to some agreement.

Habermas himself makes a similar suggestion when he says: "Political disputes would forfeit their deliberative character and degenerate into purely strategic struggles for power if participants did not assume—to be surely fallibilistically, in the awareness that we can always err—that controversial political and legal problems have a correct solution."[20] However, he draws from this the illegitimate conclusion that practical discourse must have some built-in structure that guarantees convergence on some particular outcome. The pragmatist analysis developed here suggests that this convergence is not guaranteed in advance. Moral discourse can be expected to yield a high level of agreement only because we cannot agree to disagree in this domain without seriously impairing our practical efficacy in contexts of social interaction. Thus agents will pursue moral arguments to the limit, not because they have some reason to believe that the answer is out there, but simply because giving up is an extremely unattractive option.

Naturally, there is a conventional element in the system of norms that is absent in the case of beliefs about the world. A norm will be pragmatically successful as long as it prescribes *some* set of actions, regardless of *which* particular set it prescribes.[21] The same is not true of the common prior in belief systems. It is important for agents to have the same beliefs, but it is also important that things in the world turn out the way that they were supposed to. Normatively prescribed expectations, on the other hand, are self-fulfilling, insofar as the adoption of a particular expectation provides each agent with a reason to behave in a way that conforms to the normative pattern. It is therefore important that agents share the same norm, but it often does not matter which particular norm they share. As long as they agree, things in the world (i.e., one another's actions) will turn out the way that they were supposed to. This means that the pragmatic value of a normative consensus extends only as far as the sphere of individuals for whom the norm can serve as a coordination mechanism, and that other individuals, within a different sphere of interaction, are able to get along just as well with an entirely different norm (this is what motivates, in my view, the intuition that the consensus requirement on practical discourse extends only to all those affected by the norm, whereas consensus on empirical questions extends to all persons).

In large measure, it is this conventional element that explains the enormous cultural variation in the set of normatively prescribed social obligations that individuals uphold. This helps to eliminate the tension in Habermas's view that arose from his claim that the social norms which regulate day-to-day interactions in the lifeworld can be redeemed in moral discourse. When Habermas maintains that there is "one right answer" to all moral questions, secured by a strict universalization procedure, he is just a short step away from the absurd conclusion that there is only one right set of social norms for all societies. So when he says that "in moral discourse, the ethnocentric perspective of a particular collectivity expands into the comprehensive perspective of an unlimited communication community, all of whose members put themselves in each individual's situation, worldview, and self-understanding,"[22] the implication is that we should expect to see convergence not just at the level of abstract principles, but also in the institutional structure of every concrete form of life. This problem stems directly from Habermas's attempt to guarantee convergence in principle. This is what leads him to build a strict universalizability criterion into moral discourse, which in turn threatens to make moral discourse useless as a device for resolving disputes over particular social norms in particular cultural contexts. The whole issue can by avoided simply by leaving open the question of how much convergence can be expected in principle, but then providing a set of pragmatic reasons that justify the expectation of high levels of convergence among parties who interact with one another on a routine basis.

In this context, it is significant to note that the large-scale differences in social institutions between different cultures coincide to a significant degree with geographic and linguistic boundaries that have traditionally limited the amount of social interaction that could occur between members of the different cultural groups. Once social interaction becomes more common, either as the result of migration or through improvements in transport and communication, it tends to generate enormous pressure for the standardization of social practices (starting with the basic rules governing respect for persons, extending then to economic and political decision-making, language-use, and finally social and family routines). This built-in tendency toward convergence is such a striking characteristic of polyethnic societies that national minority groups often seek to defend their cultural particularity by limiting the level of social interaction that can occur among cultural groups, primarily through developing autonomous institutions.[23]

The important point is that the expectation of convergence in moral discourse is not to be grounded in some special characteristic of moral convictions. In the end, it is the "sociological" conception of morality that does all the work in licensing the expectation of convergence. As Durkheim put it:

One must not conceive of morality as something extremely general, which becomes determinate only insofar as is necessary. On the contrary, it is a set of very definite rules, like so many molds, with firm contours into which we are forced to fit our actions. We do not have to construct these rules at the point when we must act, by deducing them from higher principles. They are already made, they exist, live and function all around us. They are moral reality in its concrete form. . . . This shows, in effect, that the role of morality is, first and foremost, to regulate action, to fix it, to eliminate the element of individual arbitrariness.[24]

If all social norms have an implicitly moral character, relying as they do upon an irreducible element of commitment and trust, then the pragmatic pressures that lead agents to develop a uniform system of social norms to regulate their day-to-day interactions will induce convergence in the more abstract theories that they use to articulate the latent moral structure of this norm system. To think otherwise is, in Durkheim's view, to succumb to an inverted picture of morality, "to take for the base of morality that which is only the summit."[25]

While this analysis suggests that we should expect high levels of convergence in the normative rules governing conduct among agents who interact on a sufficiently regular basis, individuals who interact infrequently, and so have no opportunity or need to develop institutions to regularize these exchanges, will often adopt a broadly instrumental stance toward one another. This means that in these cases the pressure toward convergence in the domain of norms will be low, but because they are interacting strategically, there will still be a powerful incentive to develop a system of shared beliefs. This explains why there are greater transcultural pressures toward agreement in empirical belief systems than there are in moral rules. But this is also something that we should expect to see change, as the development of communication and transportation technology continues to remove the barriers that have traditionally limited the amount of social interaction among members of different national and cultural groups.

Note that, according to this view, increased social interaction will not generate any significant tendency to level out differences in the *values* to which agents adhere (where these are understood as culturally shared standards that agents employ in reflecting upon and revising their "first-order" desires). Evaluative judgments consist in a ranking of outcomes, not according to personal preferences, but according to socially shared standards for ranking alternative states. Clearly, in the context of strategic interaction, agents' preferences and desires can vary to an arbitrary degree without generating any pragmatic difficulties. This means that the differentiation of system and lifeworld, which produces spheres of interaction in which agents are released from any direct normative obligations, dramatically reduces the need for value-consensus. But even in norm-governed interactions, the precise reason for which agents conform to normatively prescribed expectations is not always pragmatically significant. So although shared values may be helpful in some ways, for example, by simplifying the task of justifying certain social practices by providing a basis for interpersonal comparisons of utility, etc., the lack of shared values does not generate any pragmatic problems in the Peircean sense. Thus there is no reason to think that peoples' values will converge in the long run, but also no reason to think that this will reduce the overall level of social integration, or impair our ability to achieve consensus on matters of moral principle.

7.4　Constructing Convergence

According to the view that I have been developing, the mistake that traditional accounts of convergence make is to think that our empirical beliefs exhibit high levels of convergence because they are "about" the physical world. Aesthetic judgments are just as much "about" the world, but they leave much more room for persistent disagreement.[26] To understand the difference between these cases, it is important to look at the structure of the discourse in question, in order to see where the opportunities for disagreement arise. I suggested earlier that the rules governing language entry moves provide a mechanism that regulates the level of acceptable disagreement. Mathematics, even though it is not "about" the physical world at all, is able to minimize disagreement by stipulating that any entry-move or inference that is available to one participant must also be available to all others. This has the effect of eliminating, among other things, all first-person authority. Scientific discourse can be understood as a regimentation of "mundane" discourse about the world, which also eliminates certain forms of first-person authority. If I claim to have seen one car swerve just before the accident, this assertion enjoys considerable prima facie warrant. If I claim to have seen cold fusion in a beaker, this assertion has no "scientific" warrant until it has been reproduced by others.

What this shows is that we are capable of constructing language games that permit considerable variation in the level of expected convergence. Rawls's "constructive" political philosophy, for instance, can be seen as a proposal for a regimented version of our everyday discourse about norms. The framework guarantees high levels of agreement about a basic institutional structure by imposing limits on the entry-moves available to participants. This is captured by the notion of a "public use of reason," which eliminates the opportunity to make valid entry-moves based on controversial metaphysical or religious views ("private comprehensive doctrines"). The requirement that any proposal for a conception of justice be freestanding guarantees a symmetric distribution of opportunities to make any particular entry move, and so vastly increases the potential for convergence in outcome.

The pragmatic reason for developing a discourse of this type is perfectly explicit in Rawls's work.[27] The facts of cultural pluralism in modern societies make it harder to get to consensus on the basis of shared values, because no one set of them is sufficiently widely shared. Our traditional forms of normative and political discourse permitted claims based on substantive value judgments, because these institutions arose in the context of culturally homogenous societies. So although there was always a latent potential for disagreement in the structure of our political discourse, it seldom surfaced because of an underlying consensus on questions of value. With the development of culturally plural societies, this latent potential began to be actualized, and so the "loophole" needed to be closed.

Habermas recognizes this, but thinks that the rules of discourse are anchored in some feature of the topic, such as the type of validity claim at issue. The pragmatist theory that I have outlined offers an alternative account of why these discourses are structured in the way they are, one that does not refer to any intrinsic epistemic feature of the discourse topic. Instead, it provides an action-theoretic analysis of the reasons that highly regimented discourses should be favored in particular domains. We have a discourse about the physical world in which we try to limit disagreement, which provides us with the "official" beliefs that we use to coordinate social interactions. We also have a set of procedures for fixing authoritative norms to govern social interaction (which include, e.g., basic principles of arbitration and bargaining). In both cases, there is no pragmatic alternative to having discourses of this type, since without some set of shared beliefs and norms, our capacity to engage in successful social interaction is dramatically impaired. Ultimately, the level of convergence exhibited by any particular discourse is determined by the rules of that discourse, but these are constrained only by the level of inconvenience that would flow from having to agree to disagree in the associated domain.

An instructive example can be drawn from Habermas's analysis of the rationality of legal adjudication. Here as elsewhere Habermas claims that the cognitive character of judicial deliberation would be compromised unless there were reason to believe that all cases admit of a single correct decision.[28] If the idea is to show that the correct solution is always "out there" waiting to be found, then this claim extends far beyond the bounds of plausibility. The prima facie difficulty is that laws are enacted at different times, by different people, and so there is simply no reason to think that they can be put together to form a coherent whole. As a result, the idea that there is a single right answer in cases where laws or precedents conflict is completely unmotivated. Habermas tries to finesse this problem by associating his view with Ronald Dworkin's theory of legal adjudication, which does carry with it the suggestion that there is a single correct answer to every case. But Dworkin's view cannot be used to support Habermas's case, because it rests upon a "constructive" conception of legal interpretation that overcomes the "rationality deficit" in adjudication by supplementing statutory law with explicitly teleological components. Thus judges are invited, in hard cases, to regard the practice of law "as if this were the product of a decision to pursue one set of themes or visions or purposes, one 'point' rather than another."[29] Habermas, on the other hand, requires that judges restrict themselves to the use of pragmatic, ethical, and moral considerations that were considered in the original legislative process. This restriction directly reintroduces the problem of incoherence. Judges cannot interpret the law "as if" it had some particular point, and so are constrained in their ability to iron out conflicts between the objectives that different legislatures may have been pursuing at different times.

What this problem shows is that the idealization of a single correct decision cannot possibly come from an analysis of the underlying material or topic of legal discourse, because there is simply no reason to think that "black-letter" law is coherent. Legal discourse is, however, structured by an enormously complex set of rules that regulate the set of legitimate entry-moves and inferences, and a set of formal procedures for reviewing past decisions. This dramatically improves the capacity of this discourse to produce authoritative agreements. However, these rules should not be seen to be legitimated by some underlying idealizations that stem from the nature of the legal medium. They are justified by the mere fact that disagreement in legal interpretation is highly undesirable, from a pragmatic point of view. This allows one to acknowledge Dworkin's rather realistic observation that the interpretive devices used to secure agreement often have an overtly fictitious character, without thinking that this introduces a decisionistic element into the practice of adjudication.

I therefore take Habermas's basic idea—that the level of convergence stems from the rules governing the discursive practice—to be correct. However, I do not endorse the claim that these rules reflect any deep fact about the nature of "normative validity," or any other aspect of the discourse topic. As a result, I do not consider it necessary to show that moral argumentation will generate convergence in principle. It can simply be shown that there is no pragmatic alternative to the normative regulation of social interaction, and as a result, there is a powerful incentive for agents to pursue moral argumentation until they reach some agreement—if need be, through compromise or bargaining.

8

Transcendental Pragmatics

Habermas's discourse ethics takes as its point of departure the simple observation that, when faced with a conflict of interest, people have the option of either "fighting it out" or "talking it out." In the former case, agents adopt a strategic orientation and seek to influence each other's actions through external incentives and sanctions. In the latter case, agents adopt a performative stance, and seek to influence one another through the force of the better argument. The limitative results of game theory show that strategic action is unable to generate a stable social order, and so agents will sooner or later have to fall back upon the general resources of communication in order to achieve a fully institutionalized interaction pattern. Habermas's more general point, which he attempts to establish through his analysis of the structure of practical discourse, is that the decision to "talk it out" is not normatively neutral. The medium of talk itself constrains the range of discursively obtainable outcomes in a way that we can recognize, post hoc, as morally significant. Argumentation, which is the background practice that secures the intelligibility of talk, imposes a set of constraints that are captured in the familiar moral ideas of symmetry, reciprocity, recognition, and so forth. Thus the decision to "talk it out" already commits participants to a specifically moral resolution of their differences. Formal moral principles—from the golden rule to the categorical imperative—reflect different attempts to articulate this latent moral content of the practice of argumentation.

Habermas can therefore be said to "ground" morality in argumentation. The action theory attempts to establish this link by showing how social order is underwritten by a set of tacit commitments to discursively redeem the validity claims associated with the set of operative social norms. The theory of meaning attempts to render the link more plausible by showing how the practice of argumentation is constitutive of the meaning of all the linguistic expressions that are used in the communicative regulation of everyday practice. The discourse theory then attempts to reconstruct argumentation, characterizing it not as a set of logico-semantic relations between linguistic expressions, but as a social practice structured by procedural commitments to open participation, free expression, immunization against force, and so on. These procedural constraints leave their "imprint" on each set of norms that is subjected to thematization and discursive testing. In this way, the "morality" of argumentation wends its way from the abstract realm of discourse into the real world of communicatively mediated interaction.

But even if it were possible to ground morality in argumentation in this way, it is not clear how much has been accomplished. In particular, there is the obvious question of what argumentation is supposed to be grounded in. What stops us from deciding to adopt some other practice—one that permits an unrestricted use of force and fraud—in lieu of argumentation? The final component of Habermas's view consists in his answer to this question. What he claims, in effect, is that our existing practice of argumentation does not need to be justified or grounded, because it has a transcendental status with respect to all practices of inquiry. Argumentation is, as he puts it, *nicht-hintergehbar*—"non-get-behindable."[1]

This claim needs to be approached carefully, because it is perhaps the most widely abused component of Habermas's theory. I will therefore provide a brief analysis of the status of transcendental arguments (§8.1) before going on to show how Habermas uses this justificatory strategy to defend the status of argumentation against three kinds of objections. It is often suggested that the rules of argumentation vary from context to context, and so there can be no general ethic of discourse, because there is no invariant practice of discourse. Habermas must therefore show that agents cannot simply choose to revise particular rules governing practical discourse (§8.2), and that different groups cannot have entirely different conceptions of what counts as rational argumentation (§8.3). If either of these arguments fails, it will have relativistic consequences that undermine Habermas's most basic theoretical ambitions. Finally, Habermas must defend his position against the more radical objection that the focus on argumentation is an entirely Western preoccupation—that other cultures have entirely different mechanisms for resolving disputes (§8.4) and are therefore able to opt out of discourse entirely.

8.1 Transcendental Arguments

The term "transcendental" has acquired somewhat pejorative connotations in contemporary philosophy, so that it is more often used as a term of abuse than as a philosophical term of art. This is in part owing to an unfortunate tendency to ignore the technical meaning of the term, and to use it in a way that makes it roughly equivalent to "metaphysical." (In Kantian terms, this is to confuse "transcendental" with "transcendent" claims.) No doubt this tendency is exacerbated by the way that the word is used in popular culture, in expressions like "transcendental meditation" and so forth. In the Kantian sense, transcendental inquiry denotes nothing more than an attempt to investigate the *conditions of possibility* of some particular phenomenon.

In the weakest sense of the term, transcendental does not mean much beyond the following: When faced with a somewhat mysterious process or capacity, it is often difficult to know where to begin in constructing an explanation. So instead of attempting to determine straight away how something is done, or how it came about, it may be helpful to investigate what must be the case for it even to be possible. Answering this kind of question has the effect of narrowing the range of possible explanations. In this sense, transcendental conditions are nothing more than *conditio sine qua non*. Transcendental inquiry will therefore yield facts of the following form:

(1) $\neg x \rightarrow \neg My$

This just says that y would not be possible without x. As a result, x can be referred to as a "transcendental condition" of y. Transcendental conditions, once established, can be used as the basis for valid transcendental arguments, which take the following form. Suppose one discovers that y is true. Then:

(2) $\neg x \rightarrow N\neg y$ (substituting $\neg N\neg/M$ in 1)

(3) $N\neg y \rightarrow \neg y$ (axiomatic)

(4) $\neg N\neg y$ (modus tollens from 3 and the fact that y)

(5) x (modus tollens from 4 and 2)

Summed up, this argument says: "*y* cannot occur unless *x*; *y* does occur; therefore *x*." A famous example of this kind of argument in contemporary philosophy is Donald Davidson's claim that speech is intrinsically veridical. Schematized somewhat, his argument goes as follows: "interpretation is impossible unless most of what the informant says is true; interpretation actually occurs; therefore most of what the informant says is true."[2]

All of this is quite unproblematic. Where transcendental arguments become controversial is when they are used to introduce the more robust notion of *transcendental necessity*. The idea that certain facts may be transcendentally necessary emerges as soon as one abandons the picture of human cognition as a kind of purely detached "mirror of nature." If there is no such thing as a God's-eye point of view, then the representations of the world that are generated through cognition are the product of a set of material processes, and the specific character of these processes will probably have some impact upon the structure or content of these representations. If it is possible to establish any facts about the kind of processes that could give rise to the representations that we experience, then these facts will be transcendental conditions of any state of the world that we may posit. However, if necessity is simply truth at all possible worlds, then these transcendental conditions will also be necessary conditions (in some sense), since they will be true in every world that could be experienced by creatures with our particular mode of cognition.[3]

In this sense, transcendental necessity occurs when *y* picks out some basic feature of our own cognitive activity. If *x* can be shown to be a transcendental condition of *y*, it follows that *x* will be true in all states of the world that could be posited through cognition. The "necessity" operator is simply a restricted universal quantifier over possible worlds—to say that something is necessary is to say that it is true at all possible worlds that satisfy a certain restriction.[4] The worlds that satisfy this restriction are said to be *accessible* to our own. Thus transcendental necessity can be defined as truth at all possible worlds that are cognitively accessible from our own (i.e., in which conditions of possible experience are satisfied). Insofar as the world is constituted through cognition, the conditions of possibility of cognition will be true in all states of the world. Transcendental necessity is therefore stronger than logical necessity (true at all possible worlds logically accessible from our own, i.e., having the same laws of logic as ours), but weaker than physical necessity (true at all possible worlds physically accessible from our own, i.e., with the same laws of physics).[5]

As Kant saw quite clearly, the only way to avoid the conclusion that certain facts are transcendentally necessary is to posit a "God's-eye point of view," or some form of intelligence that is able to grasp things as they are in themselves. (And even in this case, transcendental necessity would merely become equivalent to logical necessity.) There would be no transcendentally necessary truths only if the world were not in any way constituted by our own cognitive faculties. This is the point most often missed by critics of transcendental philosophy—the idea of transcendental necessity arises directly from the recognition of the *embodied* character of human rationality and cognition. It is precisely because our knowledge always arises in specific biopsychosocial contexts that aspects of this context acquire a transcendental status with respect to the world as the object of this knowledge. As a result, the only world in which there is no transcendental necessity is the world of the metaphysical realist (and this is, as Richard Rorty put it, "a world well lost").[6]

Once the idea of transcendental necessity is introduced, it opens up the possibility of a new strategy for rejecting skeptical doubts about the status of human knowledge. It is possible to offer a *transcendental justification*. Broadly speaking, one constructs such a justification by showing that although a particular belief may be contingent from a logical point of view, it is transcendentally necessary. This strategy takes its classic form in Kant's response to Hume. Hume argued, famously, that causal relations are not something that we find in the world, but reflect mere habits of mind that we develop from observing constantly conjoined events. Because it is a contingent fact about humans that we develop associations of this type, it shows that our belief in causal relations is ultimately unjustified. However, Hume assumes that what is contingent from a "God's-eye" perspective is also contingent from our perspective (this is what makes his solution to skepticism a "skeptical solution"). What Kant's transcendental deduction tries to show is that our propensity to connect chains of experience together using the concept of causal relation is constitutive of our capacity to organize any perceptual experience. So even though the concept of causality is "contributed" by the mind and not "the world," without this contribution there would be no world. As a result, the idea that we could organize our experience otherwise, although a logical possibility, can only be conceived of from the standpoint of a purely discursive intellect, that is, God. Because the structure of our cognitive faculties constitutes the world we live in, we cannot imagine living in the world with a different set of faculties. As a result, causal relations between appearances are transcendentally necessary.

The validity of Kant's argument in the transcendental deduction is not at issue here, but merely the form. What is important to note is that Kant provides no positive justification for the concept of causal relation. We just happen to be the type of creatures who organize the material in our environment in this way, and God could have made us otherwise. However, because we cannot conceive of any alternative consistent with the conditions of possible experience, we can only regard this contingency as a defect if we are willing to take seriously a number of metaphysical hypotheses. What is wrong with Hume's view, from Kant's perspective, is not that he regards causality as mind-dependent, but that his metaphysical presuppositions (what we would now call his realism), leads him to ignore the possibility that the relations the mind "reads into" the world could also be necessary with respect to that world. Thus what transcendental justification amounts to is a way of granting that certain structures of human cognition are contingent from the standpoint of logical possibility, without allowing this to introduce an element of arbitrariness or decisionism into any conclusions generated by the exercise of these cognitive structures.

Kant's argument is formulated entirely within the framework of what Habermas calls the "philosophy of consciousness." With the linguistic turn, transcendental inquiry becomes less interested in structures of consciousness, characterized in terms of the dominant perceptual paradigm, and becomes more interested in the structure of language. For a long time, philosophers had noted that both consciousness and language share the property of intentionality, or "aboutness." In the early modern period, it was simply assumed that the intentional structure of consciousness was to be taken as primitive, and the intentional structure of language as derived. With the linguistic turn, this explanatory order is reversed. As a result, since all of the "representations" that epistemologists have traditionally been interested in are propositional attitudes, the linguistic medium in which these attitudes are formed will occupy a transcendental status with respect to the content of any representation.

For example, it has often been noted that our commonsense ontology involves a commitment to the existence of "objects," which are configured in various ways and undergo various transformations. In principle, we could just as easily posit the configurations as basic, or the transformations. We might choose to set aside what Quine calls our "tiresome bias" in the treatment of time, and adopt an "event" or "process" ontology instead of our usual "object" ontology.[7] Some philosophers have rejected this proposal, however, on the grounds that the object ontology is dictated by the subject-predicate structure of language, and that a language lacking this structure would be defective in various ways.[8] As a result, the object ontology is transcendentally necessary—not because a possible world lacking this feature cannot be coherently imagined, but because it cannot be coherently articulated.

One way to understand the shift in transcendental philosophy effected by the linguistic turn is to see it as a disagreement over which possible worlds are cognitively *accessible* from our own. (This is often somewhat misleadingly expressed as a question of where the "limits" of the world lie.) For Kant, all cognition had to arise through sensibility, and so the only worlds cognitively accessible from our own were those that satisfied the conditions of possible experience. This is what produced the broadly verificationist constraint that was at the heart of his critique of metaphysics. The "phenomenal realm" is, in effect, the set of possible worlds cognitively accessible from our own. The "noumenal realm" is the set of possible worlds logically accessible from our own, but not cognitively accessible.[9] The fact that statements true of phenomena may not be true of noumena is, from this point of view, cognitively idle. Philosophical error arises when we try to show that some particular claim is true at all worlds, not just those cognitively accessible from ours.

In the *Tractatus Logico-Philosophicus*, Wittgenstein in many ways just reformulates this Kantian idea. Confident that Frege's logicist program would succeed—that geometry and arithmetic would be reduced to logic—Wittgenstein eliminates the distinction between sensibility and understanding. He is then in a position to claim that the conditions of the discursive intellect, that is, language itself, constitute the only transcendentally necessary structure. "*The limits of my language*," he claims, "mean the limits of my world."[10] This sets up a distinction between that which can be said (which determines the set of cognitively accessible worlds) and that which can only "show itself." Any statement or question pertaining to areas "whereof we cannot speak" is at worst misleading, at best cognitively idle. Philosophical error arises, again, when we try to show that some claim is true not just at worlds cognitively accessible from our own, but at all possible worlds.

Wittgenstein's attempt to absorb sensibility into understanding was ultimately unconvincing (largely owing to the declining fortunes of logicism). This generated a new interest in Kantian verificationism, except this time within the linguistic paradigm. Theorists like Dummett and Ayer, for instance, retain from Wittgenstein the idea that language determines the cognitive accessibility relation, but suggest instead that the conditions of possible experience impose a verificationist constraint on the expressive power of language. They agree, in effect, that the set of cognitively accessible possible worlds is limited only to "that which can be said," but they argue that "that which can be said" is in some ways limited by "that which can be experienced"—seen, heard, felt, and so on. While Ayer takes this in a broadly Humean direction, with Dummett it leads to a revitalized version of transcendental philosophy. His primary objective is to show that there are *substantive* limits on "what can be said." As a result, in his view, statements are made true by the world, but "the world" is epistemically constrained. Philosophical error, exemplified for Dummett by the principle of bivalence, occurs when one attempts to establish claims that violate these epistemic constraints.

Habermas takes this shift to the philosophy of language one step further. Language occupies a transcendental position with respect to the world it is used to represent. But language itself is grounded in certain types of social practices. The inferential rules that provide it with compositional structure, for instance, are grounded in social practices of argumentation. If a particular set of social practices confers semantic content upon our utterances, and if language is the vehicle of thought, then these practices are just as constitutive of our cognitive capacities as the symbolic systems that they support. This means that not only will certain features of language be transcendentally necessary, but certain social practices will as well. (This is why Habermas sometimes refers to this aspect of his theory as a "transcendental-pragmatic" claim.[11] He is less interested in the set of worlds cognitively accessible from our own than the set of worlds pragmatically accessible from our own.)

This strategy, incidentally, informs Habermas's work from the very beginning. In *Knowledge and Human Interests*, which is in many ways a response to Mannheim's *Ideology and Utopia*, he grants the basic idea underlying Mannheim's "sociology of knowledge"—that material interests do not just bias inquiry, but are in many ways consitutive of its outcome.[12] All knowledge is therefore "ideological" in the Marxian sense. However, Habermas attempts to defuse the skeptical implications of this claim by, in effect, transcendentalizing a certain class of material interests. He argues that although many interests are involved in inquiry, there is a particular set of interests that *must* be involved in order for the inquiry to produce something that we can even recognize as knowledge. These he refers to as "knowledge-constitutive human interests"—they are the material, pragmatic *conditio sine qua non* of knowledge. So in the same way that Kant responds to Hume's psychologism by transcendentalizing a certain number of mental operations (the "categories"), Habermas responds to Mannheim's sociologism by transcendentalizing a certain class of practical interests. In his later work, Habermas simply presents a linguistically remodulated version of the same argumentation strategy.

Language determines the limits of the world. For Dummett, not just anything can be said. For Habermas, things cannot be said under just any social conditions. Certain practices have to be in place in order to sustain communication. These practices are transcendentally necessary, *nicht-hintergehbar*. As a result, the structure of these practices does not stand in need of justification, because any proposal to change them is cognitively idle.

8.2 Revising the Rules of Discourse

With this analysis of transcendental arguments in hand, it is now possible to see why Habermas does not think that the rules of discourse require the usual sort of justification. In one sense, it is fairly obvious that the rules of argumentation are going to present special problems from the standpoint of justification. Everyday social norms are open to discursive thematization in a fairly straightforward way. We can simply ask ourselves whether this is the way we want to do things, entertain various alternative proposals, argue about their relative merits, and come to a decision. However, it is clearly not going to be so simple when it comes to the rules of argumentation, because we need to use these rules in order to evaluate the merits of different proposals. Thus we cannot assume an entirely hypothetical stance toward them, the way we can with rules that lie "outside" the practice of discourse. This suggests that the rules of discourse cannot be justified without circularity, because anyone attempting to construct such a justification would be tacitly using these rules in order to justify them.

This is in fact just a pragmatic version of an old philosophical question concerning the status of logic. The problem was dramatized by Lewis Carroll, who showed that, within a deductive system, one cannot transform the rules of inference into axioms, that is, sentences in the calculus, in order to test them, because one needs to use them to construct any justification that one might care to provide.[13] If one treats rules of inference as if they were "theories," or things that could be true or false, then one can no longer use them, and as a result, one cannot *do* anything with the corresponding formal system.

As a result, there appears to be circularity in the attempt to justify a logico-semantic rule of inference. Whether or not this circularity is problematic, however, depends upon how the relationship between meaning and inference is construed. If the meaning of sentences is given independently of their inferential relations, then there will be an external standard against which the "validity" of any particular rule of inference can be checked. A bad rule of inference will be one that permits us to conclude that a particular statement is true when it is in fact false. But to say that the sentence is "in fact" false, it would have to be the case that the meaning of the sentence is determined by something other than its inferential relations. If the meaning of sentences is *given* by their inferential relations, then there can be no external check on the validity of a rule of inference, because any sentence licensed as true will of necessity be so, because its meaning will be determined by its relationship to other sentences *via* that rule of inference. If the sentence appears to be correctly derived, but false, this only provides evidence that the sentence has been misinterpreted.

The inferentialist view in semantics therefore suggests that the circularity in the justification of inference rules is unproblematic. Dummett describes the inferentialist position as follows:

> We speak as we choose to speak, and our practice, in respect to the whole of language, determines the meaning of each sentence belonging to it. Forms of deductive inference do not need to be faithful to the individual contents of the sentences which figure in the inference, because there is no individual content other than that determined by the language as a whole, of which those forms of inference are a feature. It is not, therefore, that there is something which must hold good of deductive inference, if it is to be justified, but which, because we should thereby be trapped in a vicious circle, we are unable to demonstrate, but must simply assume: rather, there is no condition whatever which a form of inference can be required to satisfy, and therefore nothing to be shown.[14]

A pragmatist version of this argument would be as follows. To know the meaning of an expression is to know how it can be discusively redeemed, which is equivalent to knowing its *use* in the practice of argumentative discourse. This means that the structure of this practice is what confers semantic content upon these utterances. As a result, the rules governing this practice will always be discursively redeemable, but this result is entirely trivial, insofar as their validity is presupposed in the action of discursive thematization and investigation. Of course, Habermas is not saying that his own *theory* of practical discourse does not require justification. The rules of discourse are trivially valid. But Habermas's theory of practical discourse is merely an attempt to articulate the content of these rules, and any such attempt will always be fallible.[15] The fact that any proposed reconstruction could prove false does not mean that the underlying rules could turn out to be invalid.

As a result, Habermas does not seek to provide a positive justification for the rules of discourse. Instead, he tries to show that they are transcendentally necessary. He sets up the argument in the following way:

> Just as someone interested in a theory of knowledge cannot adopt a standpoint outside his own cognitive acts (and thus remains caught in the self-referentiality of the subject of cognition), so too a person engaged in developing a theory of moral argumentation cannot adopt a standpoint outside the situation defined by the fact that he is taking part in a process of argumentation (e.g. with a skeptic who is following his every move like a shadow). For him, the situation of argumentation is just as inescapable as the process of cognition is for the transcendental philosopher. The theorist of argumentation becomes aware of the self-referentiality of his argument as the epistemologist becomes aware of the self-referentiality of his knowledge. Such awareness means giving up futile attempts at a deductive grounding of "ultimate" principles and returning to the explication of "unavoidable" (i.e. universal and necessary) presuppositions.[16]

Habermas therefore presents an imaginary argument with a skeptic who demands justification for a particular rule of discourse. According to Habermas's dialogical conception of justification, this demand generates a regress that ends only when the controversial claim has been grounded in something that is accepted by all participants in the discourse, thereby generating a rationally motivated agreement. However, when the controversial claim is a rule of discourse, the argument simply ends the moment it has begun. Empirically, each interlocutor must already share a commitment to this rule, and so there is nothing to justify. This empirical fact can be established by a transcendental argument: if accepting the rules of discourse is what makes it possible to interpret utterances, and participants understand one another, then they must all accept the rules of discourse. It is not that we would not know how to justify the rules of discourse to someone who does not already accept them; it is that we would not know how to *speak* to him. As a result, the only option for the skeptic who wants to opt out of discourse is to opt out of language entirely. But since language is the vehicle of thought, this is to opt out of sapience in general.

The structure of this argument directly parallels Kant's. For Kant, the fact that we interpret events in terms of causal relations is at some level contingent. As a result, Kant does not provide any positive justification for the idea of nature as a causal nexus. This just happens to be the way we see things. Another species could see things another way. What his argument attempts to show is that this kind of speculation is cognitively idle, from our standpoint, because we do not have the option of seeing things any other way. Trying to offer a justification that extends beyond our standpoint generates "dialectical illusion." Every world that is cognitively accessible from our own is one in which natural events are interpreted as causally linked. Habermas follows this strategy in conceding that the rules of discourse are also, from a certain standpoint, contingent. We just happen to be a species that uses communicative utterances to organize interactions, and the content of these utterances is fixed by a certain kind of practice. But not only is a world without such a practice not pragmatically accessible from our own, because language is also the vehicle of thought, such a world is also not cognitively accessible. As a result, skeptical doubts about the rules of discourse are also cognitively idle.

The key to this argument is the idea that language does not just "fall out of the sky," but arises out of a particular social practice. Once it has arisen, it functions as an all-purpose mechanism that can be used to generate new practices. It allows agents to *state* what they want to do, and in Habermas's view, generate the commitments to do it. All practices generated through linguistically achieved consensus are therefore rationally revisable, as they are undergirded by a commitment to discursive redeemability. However, it is important not to confuse these practices with the proto-practice that permits the initial development of propositionally differentiated speech. This is not revisable, because one must already be playing this game in order to engage in the activity of discursively testing norms. Thus there is a hierarchical organization of our practices, as some of the more complex ones are built using resources provided only by "lower" ones.

This argumentative strategy has encountered a certain amount of resistance from theorists who are suspicious of claims to universality. Since Habermas's rules of discourse define what it is to participate in a rational deliberative process, it appears that they could be used to exclude or marginalize those who happen not to share this particular conception of rationality. If one claims that there are certain universal structures that are constitutive of cognition, then the way these universal structures get characterized is neither normatively nor politically neutral. As a result, the question "Who gets to decide what these universals are?" acquires particular salience. Many critics argue that the decision inevitably falls to those who have power, or who have voice, and so the supposedly "universal" characteristics will simply reflect the practices and preferences of privileged groups.

The problem with this objection is that it confuses the rules of discourse with the particular theories that attempt to articulate these rules. A particular reconstruction of the rules could be exclusionary, in the sense that it might not recognize the discursive practices of some people. But the mere fact that the proposed reconstruction excludes some people directly falsifies that reconstruction. This is because the theory represents an attempt to reconstruct a set of transcendentally necessary conditions, and transcendentally necessary conditions, in principle, cannot be exclusionary (this follows from the definition of transcendental necessity). If one were to discover that a particular reconstruction excluded some person, one would have to immediately discard that reconstruction, and start figuring out what rules all these people *do* share that allows them to understand one another.

The irony is that this line of criticism derives its normative force from precisely the same moral intuitions that Habermas is attempting to articulate. What the concern about who gets to determine the content of the universals really shows is that every discourse, *including the discourse about what the rules of discourse are*, is subject to the same discursive rules, requiring open participation, symmetry, reciprocity, and so on. The assumption that marginalizing or excluding people is a bad thing, or that a theory produced through collusion of the powerful is defective, follows directly from the idealizing presuppositions upon which every discursively achieved consensus tacitly rests. If anything, the criticism *illustrates* the universality of the rules of discourse—they must be respected, even when the topic of discourse is the rules themselves. The difference between Habermas and his critics is that Habermas attempts to articulate these normative intuitions and determine their philosophical status, whereas his critics often attempt to deny that they have adopted a normative stance at all. As a result, they apply the principles unreflectively, relying upon normative vocabulary ("exclusion," "marginalization," "the other," and so forth) to block the attempt to articulate these very same principles. The result is a sort of self-imposed inarticulacy, in which theorists refuse to acknowledge or disclose their underlying moral concerns—a position Habermas refers to as "cryptonormativism."[17]

It should also be noted that for all the criticism that has been directed at Habermas's attempt to reconstruct the universal presuppositions of discourse, no one has challenged any of the specific rules that he has presented. To my knowledge, none of Habermas's critics has ever argued that coercion is a perfectly acceptable way of securing a rational agreement, and that his commitment to free and open discussion reflects merely a parochial bias. Instead, the criticism has tended to focus on the metaphilosophical status of the reconstruction, rather than the reconstruction itself. As a result, there has been no counterevidence presented to Habermas's claim that these rules are universal, just a general critique of the transcendental status that he assigns to them. But transcendental inquiry can be ruled out in principle only if we are willing to treat persons as literally disembodied intellects. As long as our cognitive processes have a material, pragmatic dimension, then the attempt to discover transcendental conditions of cognition is a legitimate endeavor. Whether or not these transcendental conditions are also universal is then simply an empirical question. In the absence of counterevidence, there can be no presumption against any proposed reconstruction.

A second major source of criticism of Habermas's view involves his use of so-called performative contradiction arguments. The simplest type of performative contradiction is the class of utterances referred to in the Anglo-American literature as "Moorean paradoxes." Consider someone who says, "It's going to rain, but I don't believe it." There is something incoherent about this utterance, even though there is no semantic contradiction. The problem involves some unhappy interaction between the semantic and the pragmatic components of the utterance. To assert that "p and q" is to assert that p and to assert that q. The above sentence therefore asserts that it is going to rain, and so the speaker commits herself to this claim. However, the second half of the sentence says that the speaker retracts this commitment, and therefore contradicts the performative force of the utterance as a whole. This makes the utterance a "performative" contradiction.

The idea that these type of sentences involve some kind of incoherence is not especially controversial. The issue became more controversial, however, when Karl-Otto Apel pointed out that anyone who attempted to deny a rule of discourse would become embroiled in the same sort of self-contradiction.[18] Consider a person who tries to defend a statement like the following: "Having excluded persons A, B and C from the discussion, we were able to establish that N is warranted."[19] In uttering this statement, the speaker is making a certain kind of move in the language game of assertion. This involves a set of pragmatic claims—first and foremost, that the assertion is warranted. However, for this assertion to be warranted, it must be acceptable not only to the immediate circle of listeners, but to anyone else who comes along. The content of the utterance, however, suggests that assertions can be warranted even if they are not acceptable to all persons, so long as those person can be excluded from participating in the discussion. The content of the utterance is clearly in tension with the kinds of discursive commitments that the agent incurs through the act of uttering it, and so generates a "performative contradiction."

What made people uneasy about Apel's claim was the conclusion, which he was quick to draw, that anyone who challenged his particular theory of what the correct rules of discourse were would automatically embroil himself in a performative contradiction. This would allow Apel to dismiss any objection to his theory as incoherent. But such an argumentation strategy makes the analysis of performative contradictions look like nothing more than a way of illegitimately closing down discussion of what the correct conception of practice discourse should be. Apel tried to use the performative contradiction argument to provide "ultimate" foundations for his version of discourse ethics, thereby immunizing his own philosophical theory against precisely the kind of discursive testing that he prescribed for everyone else.

Habermas, on the other hand, rejects this argumentation strategy entirely. While he agrees with Apel that denying certain rules of discourse generates performative contradictions, he does not think that an appeal to these contradictions can in any way justify the rules. This is because the rules themselves, in Habermas's view, do not need to be justified:

Demonstrating the existence of performative contradictions helps to identify the rules necessary for any argumentation game to work; if one is to argue at all, there are no substitutes. The fact that there are no alternatives to these rules of argumentation is what is being proved; the rules themselves are not being justified. True, the participants must have accepted them as a "fact of reason" in setting out to argue. But this kind of argument cannot accomplish a transcendental deduction in the Kantian sense.[20]

Apel's argument also involves a confusion between the rules of discourse, which do not stand in need of justification, and his particular reconstruction of these rules, which does stand in need of justification. This allows him to draw the illegitimate conclusion that because one cannot reject the rules without contradiction, one cannot reject his reconstruction of these rules without contradiction. For Habermas, on the other hand, any proposed reconstruction is an empirical theory like any other:

> The description we employ to pass from knowing how to knowing that is a hypothetical reconstruction that can provide only a more or less correct rendering of intuitions. ... To be sure, the intuitive knowledge of rules that subjects capable of speech and action must use if they are to be able to participate in argumentation is in a certain sense not fallible. But this is not true of our reconstruction of this pretheoretical knowledge and the claim to universality that we connect with it. The certainty with which we put our knowledge of rules into practice does not extend to the truth of proposed reconstructions of presuppositions hypothesized to be general, for we have to put our reconstructions up for discussion in the same way in which the logician or the linguist, for example, presents his theoretical descriptions.[21]

What performative contradictions can do, in Habermas's view, is serve as a guide, helping us to identify the rules of discourse. When a performative contradiction occurs, the utterance will intuitively strike us as anomalous or incoherent. We will be inclined to say things like: "then you're not really saying that it's going to rain," or, "then you didn't really establish that N is warranted." According to this view, performative contradictions play a *maeutic* role in helping us to discover what the rules of argumentation are.

In the earlier "philosophy of consciousness" tradition, the imagination played a central role in the attempt to uncover transcendental conditions of possible experience. For Kant, the way to uncover the conditions of possible experience was to see which components of our intuitions cannot be "imagined away." So he argued, for instance, that space is a pure form of intuition because, although we can imagine the absence of objects in space, we cannot imagine the absence of space itself.[22] Husserl referred to this method as one of "free variation"—whatever stood fast throughout imaginative variation, he thought, would be the transcendental condition of the experience.[23] Through this method of inquiry, it was thought, the philosopher could discern the limits of thought "from the inside." With the shift from the philosophy of consciousness to the philosophy of language, transcendental philosophy becomes less interested in what can be imagined than in what can be said. In this view, the way to discover the transcendental conditions of experience is not to uncover what we are mentally incapable of imagining, but to determine what cannot be said without semantic or pragmatic anomaly. So for Habermas, the search for performative contradictions plays a role similar to what "imaginative variation" did for Kant and Husserl.

Thus Habermas's real "defense" of the rules of discourse does not come from his analysis of performative contradictions, but from the connection that he draws between language and argumentation. The norms that govern practices of argumentation are the norms that *enable* communication. This conclusion allows him to make the following, "universal-pragmatic" argument: since all communication must presuppose the norms governing our practices of justification, these norms are effectively unrevisable. The norms governing discourse "are not mere *conventions*; rather, they are inescapable presuppositions."[24] Since these norms must be *used* to conduct an argument, we cannot suspend them in the course of a discussion, or treat them hypothetically. Not everything can be up for grabs at the same time, and since the intelligibility of linguistic interactions depends upon certain sorts of practices being in place, those practices cannot be up for grabs while we are engaged in linguistic interaction.

If someone proposes a change to one of the rules of discourse—not the philosopher's reconstruction, but the actual rule—they put themselves in a peculiar position. Since their attempt to justify this claim itself presupposes an antecedent understanding of what it is for an agreement to be rational, any justification they could offer for the new rule would presuppose the validity of the old one, and so could not possibly replace it.[25] As a result, Habermas adopts a straightforwardly "quietist" position in response to such proposals. Unlike Apel, he does not think that attempts to revise the rules of discourse require any philosophical response, any more than for Kant, a proposal to start seeing things in four dimensions requires a response (the fact that our perceptual system is "inside" our brains and the social practices are "outside" makes no difference). As a result, Habermas argues that moral philosophy should not be in the business of justifying morality:

In this case the therapeutic self-understanding of philosophy initiated by Wittgenstein is for once, I think, appropriate. Moral philosophy does have an enlightening or clarificatory role to play vis-à-vis the confusions that it has created in the minds of the educated, that is, to the extent to which value skepticism and legal positivism have established themselves as professional ideologies and have infiltrated everyday consiousness by way of the educational system. Together skepticism and positivism have misinterpreted and thus neutralized the intuitions people acquire in a quasi-natural manner through socialization. Under extreme conditions they can contribute to the moral disarmament of academics already in the grip of a cultivated skepticism.[26]

8.3 Cultural Relativity

What Habermas's transcendental-pragmatic argument shows is that the rules of discourse will be reflectively stable. Agents acquire through socialization the basic capacity to engage in argumentation. Mastery of this practice allows them to develop more complex linguistic abilities, including mastery of propositionally differentiated speech. This means that they cannot later, through the exercise of this linguistic capacity, question and revise the practice that serves as its necessary precondition. Furthermore, since the exercise of this linguistic capacity generates the dense web of social relations and practices in which agents are always immersed and in which personality structures are formed, opting out of language use entirely is only possible for those "willing to take refuge in suicide or serious mental illness."[27]

However, all that this argument shows is that we who share roughly the same practice of argumentation are, in a sense, "locked in" to this way of doing things. It has not yet been shown that other people, in other cultural contexts, must employ the *same* practice as us. At best, it shows only that the *functionally equivalent* practice in their society will be one that they too are locked in to. As a result, Habermas may have shown that discourse is transcendentally necessary *for us* (once we are fully socialized into our way of life), but he has not shown that it is universal (and so he has not eliminated the possibility that we could be socialized in some other way).

Habermas's response to this argument is basically to grant the point, but subject to one major caveat. He acknowledges that "the assertion that there is no alternative to a given presupposition, that it is one of the inescapable (i.e. necessary and general) presuppositions, has the status of an assumption. Like a lawlike hypothesis, it must be checked against individual cases."[28] But although this may appear to be a major concession to the relativist, it is much less significant than it seems. The transcendental argument shows that the rules of discourse are a presupposition of our capacity to interpret linguistic utterances. This means that the same rules of discourse must by shared by all those who speak our language, *and any language intertranslatable with our own.* This means that, as a point of empirical fact, there may be people somewhere who have completely different ideas than we do about what constitutes a rational argument, but if there are, we would not be able to understand their language. Thus genuine incommensurability in standards of rationality would generate incommensurability in translation. And since we have yet to encounter a human language that is genuinely untranslatable, there is no evidence that the basic standards of rational argumentation are not universally shared.

This connection between translation and rationality is one of the most important ideas to come out of the debate over incommensurability and relativism that occupied many philosophers, including Habermas, in the 1970s and early '80s. The classic version of the argument is given in Davidson's "On the Very Idea of a Conceptual Scheme," but the same idea is also presented forcefully by Hilary Putnam.[29] The argument follows fairly directly from the rejection of semantic realism. According to the antirealist view, there is no simple "fact of the matter" as to what a particular speaker's utterance means. The meaning of the utterance is the meaning that is conferred upon it by the best interpretation. This suggests, however, that there is no "external" way of checking an interpretation to see if it is correct, because there is no independent category of semantic facts against which it can be checked. As a result, the only constraints on the correctness of an interpretation are *internal*. What kind of internal constraints might these be? Davidson suggests that the best interpretation will be the one that makes the speaker come out sounding the most reasonable, that is, the interpretation that is most restrained in the ascription of error to the speaker.

This position can be illustrated by considering the famous ethnographic studies in which certain early anthropologists claimed to have discovered "prelogical" cultures.[30] Unable to make sense of certain aspects of Nuer religion, for example, they concluded that the rules of inference in this society simply did not respect the same consistency requirements as our own. Naturally, what then happened was that subsequent generations of ethnographers came along and suggested a variety of more charitable interpretations, ones that paid greater attention to expressive or metaphorical uses of language.[31] These later interpretations had the merit of making the Nuer come out looking much more rational, but rational *according to our standards*. What Davidson's argument suggests is that these subsequent interpretions are superior precisely because they make the Nuer come out sounding more rational, not because they get closer to what the Nuer "really" mean. Because there are no external facts about what people really mean, there is nothing that could serve to favor one interpretation over another, other than how reasonable it makes them sound.

For one interpretation to be judged better than another, there must be something internal to language that stands fixed, so that it can serve as a basis for comparing the two. Rationality is precisely this fixed point. If one attempts to distinguish between rational-for-us and rational-for-them, as these early anthropologists did, one eliminates the standards according to which the relative merits of rival interpretations can be assessed. If one suspends the assumption of rationality, then there are no limits on the range of interpretations that can be given to people's speech. Naturally, we can still ascribe meaning to their utterances, but because we can ascribe almost any meaning to them, there is no sense in which what we are doing counts as an *interpretation*.

Again, it is worth emphasizing that what is rational is not equivalent to any particular conception that we may have of what is rational. What Davidson's argument shows is not that our particular theory of rationality must be shared by everyone, but that among intertranslatable languages there must be a common core of epistemic standards. Our understanding of what these standards are may change through an encounter with different cultures. But the view that the norms governing our epistemic practices could themselves be culturally variable rests upon the mistaken idea that we could understand each sentence of a language without grasping any of the epistemic relations, real or potential, between them. This would require that the meaning of an utterance be quite dramatically divorced from aspects of its use. If we reject this picture, then we are forced to acknowledge the existence of hierarchical relations between our various norms and practices. Certain practices are structurally basic in that they provide the competences and resources that we rely upon in our construction of other practices. The practice of rational justification that underlies our ability to speak and understand a shared language is basic in precisely this sense, and so it must be shared by all speakers of intertranslatable languages.

To illustrate, imagine a society that does not recognize the idea that a rationally motivated agreement must be brought about by the force of the better argument. Suppose instead that there was some kind of agency whose power was so deeply entrenched that its use of coercion came to be regarded as perfectly permissible in practical discourse. On the surface this seems plausible, and it would appear to show that, in this case, what agents would agree to in the context of practical discourse has no moral authority. But in the same way, the idea of a language in which there is no convention of truth-telling also seems plausible, until one realizes that such a language could never be learned or interpreted. An assertoric practice in which coercion played a prominent role is quite different from our own, and it is not obvious that it provides the resources needed to support language. For instance, if backed by coercion alone, assertoric warrant would not be interpersonally transferable (the fact that one person is entitled to a claim does not mean that anyone else is entitled to it). As a result, the inferential role of a statement would differ across individuals. This makes it difficult to see how words could come to mean the same thing when spoken by different people. This is not a decisive objection to the thought experiment, but it does suggest that a significant burden of proof lies with those who would claim that language could function with a different set of underlying argumentative practices.

Seen in this light, the view that standards of rationality could be culturally relative rests upon a rather controversial presupposition. What it suggests, in effect, is that epistemic incommensurability could be consistent with linguistic commensurability. This suggestion follows easily from the earlier "philosophy of consciousness" view, in which language is seen as just a device used to communicate "ideas" that are independently formulated in the minds of speakers. According to this view, people could have completely different ways of forming ideas, but then use very similar techniques to communicate them, once formed. However, when sufficient attention is paid to the compositional structure of language, it becomes clear that the operations used to form complex ideas are *the same* as the linguistic operations used to communicate them. Figuring out how people communicate will therefore amount to figuring out how they think; thus rendering their speech commensurable (i.e., mapping expressions in their language onto equivalent expressions in our own) will require rendering their epistemic standards commensurable (i.e., mapping their standards onto equivalent standards of our own).

Of course, the claim that standards of rationality may be culturally variable is not usually motivated by empirical evidence. The majority of the proponents of such views are motivated by moral rather than theoretical considerations. It is widely felt that in order to show proper respect for other cultures, one must attempt to understand them "on their own terms." [32] The suggestion that any of the structures internal to our own conceptual scheme are universal can lead to nothing other than a biased and possibly condescending view of others. When formulated in these terms, of course, the debate is unresolvable, because it is really just a proxy for another set of issues. To make any progress, we need to set aside the desire to denounce—yet again—European colonialism, and focus on the question of how intercultural dialogue actually occurs. On this narrower question, we can see that it would be a straightfor-ward compositional fallacy to think that because *some* elements of a culture must be understood according to the internal standards of that culture, *every-thing* in the culture must be so understood. If everything is internal, then the interpreter would have no point of entry—she would not be able to begin the task of interpretation.

It is sometimes argued that Habermas's conception of practical discourse merely articulates or reflects a particular set of values that have acquired cur-rency in the West. As a result, trying to understand moral reasoning in other cultures using this framework amounts to nothing more than an imposition of "our" values on them. Once it becomes clear that the existence of shared struc-tures of reasoning between cultures cannot be precluded in principle, it becomes clear that this objection directly begs the question against Habermas's theory. Accepting the rules of discourse clearly does not involve endorsing a particular "Western" vision of the good life, since the latter would presumably need to be linguistically formulated (e.g., it would need to refer to possible states of affairs). The fact that we consider, for instance, lying to be morally wrong does not mean that the norm of truth-telling that governs assertoric discourse reflects merely a particular value. Since languages would be unlearnable if that norm was not generally respected, it must already be in place for us to be capable of articulating and debating rival visions of the good life. Thus the mere fact that discourse ethics has normative implications does not mean that it merely represents a particular set of values.

What lends plausibility to the relativist's moral reservations about claims to universality is the (seemingly universal) tendency of people from culturally homogenous societies to view their own values and way of life as superior to every other.[33] This suggests that even if relativism is false, we would all be better off believing that it is true. Unfortunately, it is unlikely that we will ever find a *philosophical* cure for insensitivity and ignorance. In their search for truth, people have often made mistakes, many of these disastrous. But it is not because they had a bad philosophical *theory* of truth that they made these mis-takes; it is because they were human. It is sheer delusion to think that decon-structing "truth" at a philosophical level will do anything to prevent people from making further mistakes. Similarly, people have been insensitive to cultural dif-ferences, but adopting relativism at a philosophical level is not likely to make this any less likely to occur. The only option we have is to do what people have always done, which is to engage in substantive criticism aimed at revealing particular mistakes, or particular insensitivies as they arise. And the best way to promote this kind of substantive criticism is to eliminate the barriers and restrictions that make existing critical discourses fall short of the ideal of free and open inquiry.

8.4 Why Argumentation?

Even if the initial charge of ethnocentrism against Habermas's discourse ethics is dismissed, something still needs to be said about that *fact* that argumentation plays a much less important public role in some societies than it does in others. Democratic societies generally cultivate a disputatious public sphere in which citizens are encouraged to "have their say" on any issue that arises. In nondemocratic societies, many people have a principled opposition to these sorts of "messy" public debates, and seek to rely upon other institutional structures—religious, military, familial, and so on—to resolve questions of public policy. This suggests that, even if every society shares the same general practice of argumentation and rules of discourse, they may choose not to use this practice to resolve all of their problems.

Habermas's explanation for these empirical differences in the extent to which different societies depend upon explicitly discursive procedures to secure social integration draws upon his theory of modernization. Modernization processes, in his view, are driven by increases in social complexity. As people begin to experiment with more advanced techniques of production and forms of social organization, increasing demands are placed upon agents to coordinate these more complex activities. This means that they are called upon to employ more sophisticated communicative competencies. They must take greater care to distinguish between the various validity-dimensions of their speech acts, so that, for instance, they make it clear whether a particular proposal is being rejected because it is impractical, impermissible, or insincere. This increasing attention to illocutionary modalities leads to a steady differentation of the natural, social, and inner-personal worlds. Habermas refers to this process as the *rationalization of the lifeworld.*[34]

At the same time, communicative competences may become overtaxed by modernization pressures. The organizational demands placed upon agents may simply be too complex to permit integration through explicitly discursive procedures. However, it may be possible to resolve such problems by drawing upon the resources of instrumental action. It may prove advantageous to release agents from direct normative control in specific domains of interaction, permitting them to adopt a broadly instrumental orientation. Since the outcome of instrumental actions is often predictable, it may be possible to adopt a minimal regulatory apparatus that simply defines the "rules of play" in such a way as to produce coordinated outcomes. Habermas calls domains of interaction of this type *systems* (taking markets as the paradigmatic example).[35] Thus the second aspect of modernization processes involves the differentiation of system and lifeworld.

In Habermas's view, both of the these aspects of modernization tend to increase the role of argumentation in society. The rationalization of the lifeworld, which takes the form of an increasing differentiation between natural, social, and inner-personal worlds, means that existing forms of social organization lose their quasi-natural character and come to be seen as artificial, historically contingent, and hence alterable structures. As Habermas puts it:

One of the features of Western rationalism is the creation in Europe of expert cultures that deal with cultural traditions reflectively and in so doing isolate the cognitive, aesthetic-expressive, and moral-practical components from one another. These cultures specialize in questions of truth, questions of taste, or questions of justice. With the internal differentiation into what Weber calls "spheres of value" (i.e., scientific production, art and art criticism and law and morality), the elements that make up an almost indissoluble syndrome in the lifeworld are dissociated at the cultural level. With these value spheres there appear for the first time the reflective perspectives from which the lifeworld appears as "practice" with which theory is to be mediated, as "life" with which art is to be reconciled . . . , or as "mores" to which morality must be related.[36]

This leads to a steady decline in the authority of tradition, which in turn reduces the level of background consensus on normative questions. This makes it *harder* to secure agreement, and so practices of argumentation assume a higher public profile. The underlying role of discourse has not changed; it is just that the specific discourses must be conducted more intensively, and at greater length, in order to generate outcomes acceptable to all.

The differentiation of system and lifeworld also increases the profile of argumentation, because of the peculiar regulatory demands that the system places upon society. When agents adopt an instrumental orientation, they are no longer directly accountable for their actions. As a result, systems of instrumental action cannot be culturally "patterned" or regulated in the way that the lifeworld can. Agents acting instrumentally respond only to incentives. This means that legal regulation of the system must take the form of what Habermas calls *positive law*. The specific character of this form of law, in Habermas's view, is that it is enforced mechanically, so that it can leave open to agents the option of conforming to it for purely instrumental reasons. But once law is "positivized" in this way, it forfeits its claim to direct moral authority. The norms that one would adopt under the assumption of full compliance are simply different from the norms that one would adopt to regulate a group of actors seeking to avoid compliance. As a result, the law is no longer subject to direct moral justification, but must acquire its legitimacy at a somewhat higher level of abstraction. Habermas argues that what democratic institutions do is provide precisely this more abstract procedural justification for positive law.

The significance of this analysis for the issue at hand is that the development of positive law calls for the direct institutionalization of discursive practices, because it can no longer draw directly upon background moral or ethical agreement to redeem its claim to validity. As a result, Habermas thinks that the high profile that argumentation enjoys in Western societies is an adaptation to the specific demands of social modernization.

> The positive law that we find in modernity as the outcome of a societal learning process has formal properties that recommend it as a suitable instrument for stabilizing behavioral expectations; there does not seem to be any functional equivalent for this in complex societies. Philosophy makes *unnecessary* work for itself when it seeks to demonstrate that it is not simply functionally recommended but also morally required that we organize our common life by means of positive law, and thus that we form legal communities. The philosopher should be satisfied with the insight that in complex societies, law is the only medium in which it is possible reliably to establish morally obligated relationships of mutual respect even among strangers.[37]

This is why he makes the somewhat surprising claim that human rights are not culturally universal, but represent a specific legal idea that arises in response to particular historical circumstances.[38] Although these rights *activate* a particular constellation of normative ideas that is present in every culture, they provide an appropriate mechanism for institutionalizing these ideas only in the context of a society that has highly differentiated systemic elements. The universality of democratic deliberation and the system of public autonomy rights through which it is entrenched are not to be determined by normative considerations. The question is simply whether or not the kinds of differentiation processes that Western societies have undergone represent an inevitable, or merely an optional, development—whether or not there can be different trajectories of modernization.

This having been said, there is another current in Habermas's thought that tends to favor a somewhat stronger account of the status of argumentation. There is throughout Habermas's development of the theory of communicative action an attempt to show that merely by using the medium of language to coordinate their interactions, agents commit themselves to an explicitly discursive redemption of the validity claims associated with their utterances. Habermas attempts to show, as we have seen, that this commitment extends to include all of the social norms that govern their practices. This argument is intended to demonstrate that agents, no matter what society they live in, are "always already" committed to a discursive redemption of their practices. In chapter 3, I argued that this portion of Habermas's program does not go through, and that agents are in no sense "already" committed to discourse. In any case, the point is somewhat idle, in the sense that even agents "already" committed to discourse can always opt out by adopting a strategic orientation. As a result, even Habermas's argument does not show that agents *must* enter discourse, only that they *ought* to.

In my view, this line of thinking should be rejected in favor of the more pragmatic argument that Habermas adopts in his discussion of rights. The question is whether, when agents shift from communicative action to discourse, they are initiating something new, or simply activating commitments that were already incurred over the course of their previous interaction. I have argued that they are initiating something new. As a result, they are free to avail themselves of any conflict-resolution procedure that is available to them, including adjudication, counseling, oracles, and of course rational argumentation. Naturally, any procedure that they do employ will need to make significant use of linguistic communication, because only language has the expressive resources that agents need to deliberate *about* their practices.

What makes rational argument special is that it provides a resource that cannot break down in the way that all of these other practices can. The impartiality of a judge can be questioned, as can the reliability of an oracle. Once this occurs, then the institution of adjudication, or revelation, can no longer be drawn upon to reestablish the authority of the judge, or the oracle. But precisely because of their transcendental status, the rules of discourse cannot be undermined in this way. This means that as long as the language itself does not break down, the underlying practice of argumentation will always be available as a mechanism for resolving disputes.

In a sense, discourse is something like the "gold standard" of conflict-resolution practices. But this should not be taken to mean that all other practices "ultimately" depend upon discourse for their value. It just means that discourse, unlike the other practices, always retains its value. It is always around, but not "always already" around. This means that in many cultures, discourse may not be the central mechanism of conflict resolution. People may use all kinds of other "thick" practices to resolve disputes, and there is no particular reason that they must select argumentation ex ante. However, each of these practices is vulnerable to criticism in a way that discourse is not. This means that as the level of substantive value-consensus declines through increasing complexity and cultural pluralism, the society could be expected to rely increasingly upon purely discursive modes of conflict-resolution.

8.5 Summary of Conclusions

The position that I have been developing weakens Habermas's theory at several points:

• I have argued that the accountability of social action cannot be explained as a consequence of the fact that it is linguistically coordinated, because speech acts do not generate the type of extradiscursive commitments that Habermas claims. Because the compositional component of the speech act provides it with essentially descriptive content, the only inferential consequences of the speech act that the speaker and hearer must know are those that would be needed to demonstrate that the relevant state of affairs obtains. That information, combined with a general understanding of the practice of issuing orders, is all that is needed to understand imperative speech acts. The reasons that could be given for or against the social norms that license such imperatives do not need to be known in order to grasp the meaning of the utterance. As a result, the speaker makes no commitment to the justification of these norms through performance of the speech act, nor does the hearer tacitly accept these reasons.

• I also argued that there is no such thing as a specifically "practical" form of discourse governed by its own distinct inference rules. Habermas's suggestion that there are three types of validity claims raised in speech acts, each of which must be discursively redeemed, was already in tension with various considerations arising from the analysis of theories of meaning. I tried to show that with a dialogical conception of justification and a deflationary theory of truth, it is possible to claim that moral judgments admit of straightforward truth. "Rightness," I argued, should not be treated as a special kind of validity claim, but rather interpreted in terms of a set of deontic modalities. Moral arguments could then be decided using precisely the same discursive procedures that are used to decide any other kind of argument. Practical discourse, I then claimed, should be distinguished simply by its topic, not its structure. (Of course, if understanding speech acts does not require understanding how a special kind of "rightness claim" can be discursively redeemed, it also eliminates the need to posit a structurally distinct kind of practical discourse.)

• Finally, I argued that there is no reason to think that moral argumentation must exhibit convergence "in principle." I criticized Habermas's attempt to establish this with his universalization principle, and tried to show instead simply that there is no reason that a group of agents intent on resolving their differences should be incapable of reaching agreement. I then argued that the pressure to find a "single correct answer" in moral questions stems not from any intrinsic characteristic of norms, but simply from the pragmatic consequences of accepting disagreement in this domain.

The alternative that I have been proposing takes accountability to be a basic feature of norm-governed social action. Normative reasons for action, I argued, are characterized by the fact that they specify actions directly, without reference to the anticipated outcome. Agents are socialized in such a way that they develop a higher-order disposition to assign normative reasons priority over instrumental ones in their practical deliberations. Speech is a form of norm-governed action—the meaning of the utterance is determined by the changes in the agent's deontic status that it effects. This is why language cannot be sustained except among agents who can subordinate their instrumental goals to their normative commitments.

Normative integration, in this view, requires that there be a set of shared rules of action that is common knowledge among all participants in the interaction. This makes it vulnerable to both individual defection and dissent. Some amount of deviation from the norm can be controlled through sanctions, but ultimately the system of norms will be stable only if it is endorsed by all. As a result, problematization of the existing norms by any participant presents everyone with the practical challenge of repairing the disrupted normative order. The only "foolproof" way of doing this is to argue about what the norms should be and reach a rationally motivated agreement, drawing upon whatever background resources and consensus is available. As a result, various practical constraints that determine what can count as a "rationally" motivated agreement will find their way into the system of norms. In this way, the ethic of discourse gradually becomes a societal ethic.

I ended with a discussion of Habermas's transcendental pragmatics because the general strategy of transcendental argument is needed by my proposal at two points. First, I need it to show that the rules of discourse are reflectively stable, and so the decision to resolve our differences through argumentation does not have arbitrary moral consequences. Second, I need this argument to explain why the agent's higher-order disposition is reflectively stable. Even though this particular structure of agency is produced through socialization, it becomes effectively unrevisable because it provides agents with the competences required to participate in linguistic communication. Since rational reflection involves an exercise of this linguistic competence, the underlying choice disposition will be a transcendental-pragmatic necessity. As a result, there is no ultimate justification required for a higher-order choice disposition that assigns priority to normative reasons for action, just as there is no ultimate justification required for the rules of discourse.

Finally, since I have argued that there is no antecedent commitment to discursive resolution of conflict, I need to provide some account of why agents should ever bother to seek a consensual resolution of their differences. I have argued that normative integration can only be secured through consensus, but unlike Habermas, I do not consider agents to be already committed to normative integration. As a result, I have tried to draw upon more general pragmatic considerations to explain why agents should seek to restore a disrupted normative order. A more vivid sense of the potential suboptimality and indeterminacy of strategic interaction helps us to understand why agents would be motivated to seek normative regulation, even if they are not "already" committed to doing so. Normative regulation serves to counteract the general tendency of human affairs to go very badly when left to self-interest, but it also allows agents to eliminate a vast number of unnecessary coordination failures that can arise from the inability of strategic reasoning to focus expectations on a single set of equilibrium beliefs. (I argued that the same set of considerations will motivate agents to structure their moral arguments in such a way as to promote high levels of convergence.) From this point of view, it is Habermas this time who makes "unnecessary work" for himself, in attempting to show that the transition to discourse and the expectation of convergence is required as a matter of principle, as opposed to being "simply functionally recommended."

The theory that results is more consistently pragmatist that Habermas's own. The reason for this, I believe, is that Habermas consistently overestimates the robustness of the instrumental model of action. In particular, he tends to treat instrumental rationality as if it were always a matter of solving parametric decision problems, rather than strategic interactions. Decision problems, however, always have solutions, and so it is difficult to find the "limits" of an instrumental model of this type. Strategic interactions, however, are frequently indeterminate, since agents who are reasoning strategically must solve equations with at least two variables, not just one. This means that for any given strategic interaction, there should be absolutely no presumption that the problem can be resolved through instrumental reasoning. To demonstrate the applicability of the instrumental model, one must provide a game-theoretic solution concept. This means that instrumental rationality is often "self-limiting," in cases where it can be shown that no such solution concept is available. Because Habermas fails to exploit this feature of the instrumental model, he often assumes an unnecessarily heavy burden of proof, which in turn leads him to develop positions that are much stronger than they need be.[39]

The major advantage of studying game theory more carefully, I have tried to show, is that it helps to distribute the burden of proof somewhat more evenly among the different conceptions of rational action. To prize agents out of their instrumental orientations, Habermas claims that the mere act of speaking automatically locks them into a commitment to discursive redemption of their validity claims. Once it becomes clear that instrumental action sometimes is just not feasible, it seems reasonable to suppose that agents will enter into discourse just because normatively regulated interaction works better than strategic action, and practical discourse is the best way to fix the content of the normative system. Similarly, Habermas suggests that unless agents are already committed to the idea of a single correct answer when they enter moral discourse, they may throw up their arms and "revert" to a strategic orientation. But again, if the strategic orientation is simply not feasible, agents may have no option but to work out their differences discursively, in which case it does not matter what they believe, in their heart of hearts, about where their arguments are ultimately leading. In both cases, a clearer picture of the limits of the instrumental conception of rationality eases the burden of philosophical demonstration for those committed to articulating the other "dimensions" of rational action. This is ultimately the payoff that comes from developing a dialogue between Habermas's theory of communicative action and the theory of rational choice.

Abbreviations of Works by Habermas

BFN   *Between Facts and Norms.* Trans. William Rehg (Cambridge, MA: MIT Press, 1996).

IO   *The Inclusion of the Other.* Ed. C. Cronin and P. De Greiff (Cambridge, MA: MIT Press, 1998).

JA   *Justification and Application.* Trans. C. Cronin (Cambridge, MA: MIT Press, 1993).

MCCA   *Moral Consciousness and Communicative Action.* Trans. C. Lenhardt and S. Weber Nicholsen (Cambridge, MA: MIT Press, 1990).

OPC   *On the Pragmatics of Communication.* Ed. Maeve Cooke (Cambridge, MA: MIT Press, 1998).

PMT   *Postmetaphysical Thinking.* Trans. W. M. Hohengarten (Cambridge, MA: MIT Press, 1992).

TCA   *The Theory of Communicative Action.* 2 vols. Trans. T. McCarthy (Boston: Beacon Press, 1984–87).

Symbols Used in the Text

Logical

$\forall$	universal quantification
$\neg$	negation
$\rightarrow$	implication
$\leftrightarrow$, iff	biconditional ("if and only if")

Modal

$\mathcal{N}$	it is necessary that
M	it is possible that
I	it is impossible that
F	it is forbidden that
P	it is permitted that
O	it is obligatory that

Mathematical

$\in$	is an element of
$\subseteq$	is a subset of
$\times$	Cartesian product
$\succ$	is preferred to

Notes

Introduction

1. See Quentin Skinner (ed.), *The Return of Grand Theory in the Human Sciences* (Cambridge: Cambridge University Press, 1985). There is no doubt an element of "sour grapes" in this reaction, since there is no real reason to think that, in principle, we should be incapable of developing a general theory about how people decide what to do.

2. This is a point that has been emphasized by Harold Garfinkel, *Studies in Ethnomethodology* (Oxford: Polity Press,1967).

3. See Jeffrey Alexander (ed.), *The Micro-Macro Link*, (Berkeley: University of California Press, 1987). Methodological individualism, strictly speaking, is just the view that explanations of social phenomena are incomplete until some account of their action-theoretic underpinnings has been supplied. It becomes controversial only when paired with the further claim that these action-theoretic explanations must be instrumental in form.

4. This is explained at greater length in §5.3. See also Joseph Heath, "Foundationalism and Practical Reason," *Mind* 106 (1997): 451–474.

5. On the linguistic turn, see Michael Dummett, *The Origins of Analytical Philosophy* (Cambridge, MA: Harvard University Press, 1993).

6. This is one of the defining characteristics of "noncooperative" game theory. See John Nash, "Noncooperative Games," *Annals of Mathematics*, 54 (1951): 289–295. Anyone who uses the Nash solution concept is assuming that the interaction is noncooperative. For further discussion, see §2.4.

7. See, e.g., Joel M. Charon, *Symbolic Interactionism*, 3rd ed. (Old Tappan, NJ: Prentice Hall, 1989).

8. On speech act theory, see John Searle, *Speech Acts* (Cambridge: Cambridge University Press, 1969).

9. James Johnson, "Is Talk Really Cheap? Prompting Conversation Between Critical Theory and Rational Choice," *American Political Science Review*, 87 (1993): 74–86.

10. Jon Elster, "The Scope and Nature of Rational Choice Explanations," in B. McLoughlin and E. LePore, *Actions and Events* (New York: Blackwell, 1986): 60–72.

11. J. L. Austin, *How to Do Things with Words*, 2nd ed., eds. J. O. Urmson and M. Sbizà (Cambridge, MA: Harvard University Press, 1975).

12. On the problem of order, see Talcott Parsons, *The Structure of Social Action*, 2 vols. (New York: Free Press, 1968), 1: 89–94.

13. Michael Smith offers a precise account in *The Moral Problem* (Oxford: Blackwell, 1994).

14. David Hume, *A Treatise of Human Nature*, ed. L. A. Selby-Bigge, 2nd ed. (Oxford: Clarendon Press, 1978), 416.

15. Bernard Williams, "Ought and Moral Obligation," *Moral Luck* (Cambridge: Cambridge University Press, 1981), 122.

16. MCCA, 164.

Chapter 1

1. This is most explicit in Immanuel Kant, *Religion within the Limits of Reasons Alone*, trans. T. M. Greene and H. H. Hudson (New York: Harper & Row, 1960).

2. Max Weber, *Economy and Society*, 2 vols., eds. G. Roth and C. Wittich (Berkeley: University of California Press, 1978), 1: 24.

3. Max Weber, *The Protestant Ethic and the Spirit of Capitalism*, trans. T. Parsons (New York: Charles Scribner's Sons, 1958).

4. Talcott Parsons, *The Structure of Social Action*, 2 vols. (New York: Free Press, 1968).

5. Talcott Parsons, *The Social System* (New York: The Free Press, 1951).

6. Bernard Williams, "Ought and Moral Obligation," *Moral Luck* (Cambridge: Cambridge University Press, 1981), 122.

7. The fact that this expectation can be suspended explicitly suggests that it is latent.

8. For an argument of this type, see Michael Smith, *The Moral Problem* (Oxford: Blackwell, 1994), 111–125.

9. See Philip Pettit and Michael Smith, "Freedom in Belief and Desire," *The Journal of Philosophy* 93 (1996): 429–449.

10. Immanuel Kant, *Foundations of the Metaphysics of Morals*. 2nd ed., trans. L. White Beck (New York: MacMillan, 1990), 49 [432].

11. Talcott Parsons, *The Structure of Social Action*, 89–94.

12. For an overview of these problems, see Jon Elster, *The Cement of Society* (Cambridge: Cambridge University Press, 1989).

Notes

13. Aaron Cicourel, *Cognitive Sociology* (Harmondsworth: Penguin, 1973), 21 (my emphasis).

14. Donald Davidson, "Toward a Unified Theory of Meaning and Action," *Grazer Philosophiche Studien* 2 (1980): 1–12.

15. Jürgen Habermas, "Actions, Speech Acts, Linguistically Mediated Interactions, and the Life-world," in his *On the Pragmatics of Communication* (Cambridge, MA: MIT Press, 1998): 215–256 (hereafter OPC).

16. Donald Davidson, "The Folly of Trying to Define Truth," *Journal of Philosophy* 93 (1996): 263–278.

17. Donald Davidson, "The Structure and Content of Truth," *Journal of Philosophy* 87 (1990): 279–328.

18. Donald Davidson, "Truth and Meaning," in *Inquiries into Truth and Interpretation* (Oxford: Clarendon, 1984): 17–36.

19. Naturally, they would still have some underlying cognitive state that impelled them to action. Davidson's point is that we would have no reason to call such states desires. The same sorts of considerations are what tell against the ascription of beliefs and desires to animals.

20. This is the claim made by Habermas and Davidson that is most often rejected by critics. The underlying intuition, however, seems eminently plausible. If we didn't presuppose that for the most part people mean what they say (Habermas), or try to tell the truth (Davidson), we would never be able to figure out what they were saying. Imagine trying to learn a language in which the norm of honesty was entirely absent! These considerations suggest that many critics who reject Habermas's "mutual understanding" thesis do so only because they presuppose what needs to be shown, i.e., they assume that speakers have a primitive grasp of linguistic meaning, and so need not learn it from participating in linguistic practice.

21. Parsons, *The Social System*, 10–11. The structure of these anticipations will be outlined with greater precision in §2.2.

22. OPC, 221. This does not refer to a coordination problem in the game-theoretic sense, i.e., with multiple equilibria. The problem identified is what game theory treats as "the regress of anticipations."

23. OPC, 221.

24. For an overview of these epistemic requirements, see Adam Brandenburger, "Knowledge and Equilibrium in Games," *Journal of Economic Perspectives* 6 (1992): 83–101.

25. Habermas, *Between Facts and Norms*, trans. William Rehg. (Cambridge, MA: MIT Press, 1996), 8 (hereafter BFN).

26. OPC, 223.

27. BFN, 3.

28. It should be noted that sociologists have often attempted to set the problem aside by declaring that norms are "nonrational." This strategy only makes sense if one treats "reason" in the eighteenth-century sense, as a specific mental faculty. From a modern standpoint, insofar as the

mental states underlying norm-conformative action are to be treated as propositional attitudes, familiar Davidsonian arguments require that the action be treated as rational. See Donald Davidson, "Radical Interpretation," in *Inquiries into Truth and Interpretation* (Oxford: Clarendon Press, 1984): 125–140.

29. See Edmund Husserl, *Logical Investigations*, 2 vols., trans. J. D. Findlay (London: Routledge, 1970), 1: 53–247.

30. The term "validity claim" is unfortunate, since it is characteristic to distinguish between the validity of an argument and the truth of its conclusion. Not only does it sound strange to claim validity for a *statement*, but the terminology creates a temptation to introduce an epistemically constrained notion of truth on the sly. These issues will be discussed in greater detail in chapter 5.

31. For an overview of this strategy, see Robert Brandom, *Making It Explicit* (Cambridge, MA: Harvard University Press, 1994), 67–140. For Habermas, the most important theorist in this tradition is Michael Dummett.

32. Habermas, *The Theory of Communicative Action.* 2 vols., trans. T. McCarthy (Boston: Beacon Press, 1984–87), 1: 115–116 (hereafter TCA).

33. See W. V. O. Quine, "Two Dogmas of Empiricism," in *From a Logical Point of View* (New York: Harper & Row, 1963): 20–46, and Donald Davidson, "On The Very Idea of a Conceptual Scheme," in *Inquiries into Truth and Interpretation* (Oxford: Clarendon Press, 1984): 183–198.

34. OPC, 232–233.

35. Habermas, "Some Further Clarifications of the Concept of Communicative Rationality," in OPC, 327.

36. Habermas, *Postmetaphysical Thinking*, trans. W. M. Hohengarten (Cambridge, MA: MIT Press, 1992), 57 (hereafter PMT).

37. TCA, 1: 319–328.

38. TCA, 1: 117–128.

39. OPC, 217.

40. TCA, 1: 293.

41. TCA, 1: 293.

42. Some commentators lament the fact that the German term *Verständigung* is ambiguous between understanding and agreement (see William Mark Hohengarten, *Language Games versus Communicative Action: Wittgenstein and Habermas on Language and Reason* [Ph.D. dissertation, Northwestern University, 1991], 259). Many regard the claim that language use is oriented toward understanding as unproblematic, but reject the thesis that language use is oriented toward bringing about agreement. This line of criticism fails to appreciate the significance of Habermas's claims regarding the internal relation between understanding and evaluation. Far from being an ambiguity, the fact that *Verständigung* suggests both understanding and agreement is precisely the point. If understanding can be achieved only through grasp of epistemic relations, and valid epistemic relations are expected to command assent, then trying to bring about understanding will also require trying to bring about agreement. (This is a variation on the idea that Davidson presents in "On The Very Idea of a Conceptual Scheme," *Inquiries into Truth and Interpretation*, 196–197.)

43. Jürgen Habermas, "Communicative Rationality and the Theories of Meaning and Action," in OPC, 198.

44. TCA, 2: 39.

45. For the latter, see MCCA, 116–194.

46. George Herbert Mead, *Mind, Self, and Society* (Chicago: University of Chicago Press, 1934), 13–18.

47. TCA, 2: 14.

48. TCA, 2: 22.

49. TCA, 2: 219.

50. TCA, 2: 6.

51. TCA, 2: 30.

52. TCA, 2: 30.

53. TCA, 2: 54.

54. TCA, 2: 56.

55. TCA, 2: 89–90.

56. See Jürgen Habermas, "Toward a Reconstruction of Historical Materialism," in *Communication and the Evolution of Society*, trans. T. McCarthy (Boston: Beacon Press, 1979): 130–177.

57. BFN, 36.

58. This three-level framework is widely used. For instance, Carol Gilligan, one of Kohlberg's most influential critics, develops her account of the "ethics of care" using the same three levels. See Lawrence Kohlberg, *The Philosophy of Moral Development: Moral Stages and the Idea of Justice* (San Francisco: Harper & Row, 1981), and Carol Gilligan, *In a Different Voice: Psychological Theory and Women's Development* (Cambridge, MA: Harvard University Press, 1982).

Chapter 2

1. TCA, 1: 286.

2. OPC, 218.

3. OPC, 218–219.

4. David Lewis, *Convention* (Cambridge, Mass.: Harvard University Press 1969), 122–159 presents the game informally. Formal models of the same game are available at various locations, including Drew Fudenberg and Jean Tirole, *Game Theory* (Cambridge, MA: MIT Press, 1991), 324–331, and J. S. Banks and J. Sobel, "Equilibrium Selection in Signalling Games," *Econometrica* 55 (1988): 647–661.

5. This "chain" of events is represented, for simplicity, by a single event—the outcome. This can be justified by thinking of the outcome as either a very long event, or as the segment of consequences that are relevant, in some sense, to the agent.

6. Proof that a simple ranking can be represented on an intensity scale is given by the standard derivation of a *cardinal utility function* for the agent. See, e.g., R. Duncan Luce and Howard Raiffa, *Games and Decisions* (Wiley: New York, 1957). Use of the matrix representation shows why a cardinal utility function for an agent remains unique through any positive linear transformation.

7. H. Paul Grice, "Meaning," in *Studies in the Ways of Words* (Cambridge, MA: Harvard University Press, 1989).

8. Natural events can still be included by treating nature as one more "player," the probability of whose moves are fixed in advance and common knowledge among the players.

9. John von Neumann and Oskar Morgenstern, *The Theory of Games and Economic Behavior*, 3rd ed. (New York: John Wiley & Sons, 1953), 11.

10. This was first shown by John Nash, "Noncooperative Games," *Annals of Mathematics* 54 (1951): 289–295. For a more accessible proof, see Fudenberg and Tirole, *Game Theory*, 29–33.

11. Thomas Schelling, *The Strategy of Conflict* (New York: Oxford University Press, 1963).

12. Lewis, *Convention*, 5–6.

13. If meanings were determined exogenously, then one would have to treat meaningful and non-meaningful actions differently, which by definition would transform the model into a cooperative game. Cooperative games need to handled with care, and so discussion of them will be deferred until the next section.

14. I am following the convention of using male pronouns to refer to odd players and female pronouns for even.

15. David M. Kreps and Robert Wilson, "Sequential Equilibria," in *Econometrica* 50 (1982): 871–889 at 871.

16. John Harsanyi, "Games with Incomplete Information Played by 'Bayesian' Players," 3 parts, *Management Science* 14 (1967–68) 159–182, 320–334, 486–502.

17. To make this situation tractable, the complete set of types, along with the prior probability distribution over this set, is taken to be common knowledge among all players. Note the implication: every player must know, in advance, the probability of every possible state of the world that could in any way affect the game. This assumption is heroic, but its precise significance is debatable—as will be seen in chapter 7.

18. For a clear presentation of the model, see Banks and Sobel, "Equilibrium Selection in Signalling Games," 647–661, or Vincent P. Crawford and Joel Sobel, "Strategic Information Transmission," *Econometrica* 50 (1982): 1431–1451.

19. This type of game tree diagram can be hard to read at first. The origin is in the center, and nature starts the game by moving left or right, thereby determining player 1's type. From either 1.a or 1.b, player 1 then moves up by shouting "block" or moves down by shouting "slab." If Player 2 hears "block" then she is at information set 2.a, and is at 2.b if she hears "slab."

She then passes either a block or a slab, ending the game. This is essentially a formalized version of the signaling game that Lewis presents. Lewis uses an example that involves Paul Revere hanging lanterns in the belfry (*Convention*, 122–123). The structure of the game shown in figure 2.5 is the same, except that it has only two messages instead of three. One could add more types to the above game, e.g., pillars and beams, but it would make the diagram even harder to read.

20. Lewis adds a clever mechanism for determining whether the utterance is an assertion or an imperative, which need not concern us here. Lewis, *Convention*, 144.

21. Roger B. Myerson, *Game Theory: Analysis of Conflict* (Cambridge, MA: Harvard University Press, 1991), 373–374.

22. For example, Lewis, *Convention*, 115.

23. Joseph Farrell, "Meaning and Credibility in Cheap-Talk Games," *Games and Economic Behavior* 5 (1993): 514–531 at §1.

24. Crawford and Sobel, "Stategic Information Transmission," 1450. A *cheap-talk* game is one in which there are no costs or benefits *directly* associated with the signal selected.

25. Lewis, *Convention*, 160.

26. Nash, "Noncooperative Games," 286. See also John Eatwell et al., eds., *The New Palgrave: Game Theory* (New York: W. W. Norton, 1989), 95.

27. Farrell, "Meaning and Credibility in Cheap-Talk Games." The example below follows Farrell quite closely.

28. Technically, this is because beliefs are updated over the course of a sequential-move game using Bayesian conditionalization. Any neologism is a zero-probability event, and because Bayes's rule places no constraints on what beliefs an agent may form in response to zero-probability events, it does not place any constraints on the interpretation that players can give to neologisms.

29. The only problem with neologisms is that they multiply the set of equilibria enormously; e.g., R could take "pillar" to reveal type need-a-block, and then there would be all sorts of new equilibria in which S randomized in various ways between "block" and "pillar" every time he was of type need-a-block. But other than creating this annoying proliferation of equilibria, neologisms do not create fundamental problems for any of the traditional noncooperative solution concepts.

30. This analysis may seem counterintuitive. For more extensive discussion, see Farrell, "Meaning and Credibility in Cheap-Talk Games," §7.

31. See, e.g., Roger B. Myerson, "Credible Negotiation Statements and Coherent Plans," *Journal of Economic Theory* 48 (1989) 264–303 at 287.

32. Myerson, "Credible Negotiation Statements and Coherent Plans," 266.

33. See, for instance, Jürgen Habermas, "Reply to Skjei," *Inquiry* 28 (1985): 105–112 at 108.

Chapter 3

1. PMT, 77.

2. If we think of beliefs as internalized assertions, then this is just the same norm.

3. Commentators frequently overlook the fact that Habermas relies specifically on Dummett to provide the crucial argument in the elaboration of his own view. See OPC, 197.

4. PMT, 80.

5. Thomas Hobbes, *Leviathan*, ed. Richard Tuck (Cambridge: Cambridge University Press, 1991), 184.

6. Naturally, it can be transformed into a reason for action if the announcement prompted other people to adopt strategies based upon it. They might, for instance, plan to punish the agent if she does not do what she said she would do. But this does not change the essential point. The past is never intrinsically relevant to decision; it becomes relevant indirectly by influencing the actions of others in the future.

7. Reinhard Selten, "Reexamination of the Perfectness Concept for Equilibrium Points in Extensive Games," *International Journal of Game Theory* 4 (1975): 25–55. This is his clearest presentation. For reasons that need not concern us here, his purpose in this paper is to introduce *trembling-hand perfect equilibrium*, which restricts the set of equilibria to those that are Nash in a slightly "perturbed" game whose strategies are such that every node is reached with positive probability.

8. What it actually does is systematically eliminate false counterfactual beliefs from each player's belief set, on the plausible grounds that an equilibrium belief set should not contain any demonstrably false beliefs. See Cristina Bicchieri, "Strategic Behavior and Counterfactuals," *Synthese* 76 (1988): 135–169.

9. This illustrates a point long familiar to game theorists, which is that threats and promises have a similar action-theoretic structure, and that both are (in the instrumental model) by definition irrational. Thomas Schelling, *The Strategy of Conflict* (Cambridge, MA: Harvard University Press, 1960): "Threats," 123–30, "Promises," 131–137.

10. Excepting certain types of Newcomb problems, which are not really decision problems. See Richmond Campbell and Lanning Sowden (eds.), *Paradoxes of Rationality and Cooperation* (Vancouver: University of British Columbia Press, 1985).

11. See David Braybrooke, "The Insoluble Problem of the Social Contract," in *Paradoxes of Rationality and Cooperation*: 277–305.

12. I discuss this feature of the instrumental view at greater length in §4.2.

13. Nicholas Rowe, *Rules and Institutions* (Ann Arbor: University of Michigan Press, 1989).

14. David Gauthier, "Assure and Threaten," *Ethics* 104 (1994): 690–721.

15. See Kenneth Binmore, "Bargaining and Justice," in *Rationality, Justice, and the Social Contract*, eds. David Gauthier and Robert Sugden (Hemel Hempstead: Harvester Wheatsheaf, 1993): 131–156.

Notes

16. Hence Gauthier's need to introduce the assumption that agents are "translucent" to one another. David Gauthier, *Morals by Agreement* (Oxford: Clarendon Press, 1986), 174–177. There has been little commentary in the literature on the impact that these sorts of solutions would have on game theory.

17. I have criticized the usual set of justifications in Joseph Heath, "Foundationalism and Practical Reason, " *Mind* 106 (1997): 451–474.

18. TCA, 2:210–211; BFN, 336.

19. TCA, 1:8–9.

20. For an analysis of belief and desire as doxastic and practical commitments, see Robert Brandom, *Making It Explicit* (Cambridge, MA: Harvard University Press, 1994), 229–243.

21. TCA, 1:9.

22. For example, David Hoy claims that there is "no real argument for the Habermasian axiom that reaching agreement and understanding is so essential to all language," in David Couzens Hoy and Thomas McCarthy, *Critical Theory* (Oxford: Blackwell, 1994), 183.

23. TCA 1:317.

24. PMT, 67–68.

25. Jürgen Habermas, "Wahrheitstheorien," *Vorstudien und Ergänzungen zur Theorie des kommunikativen Handelns* (Frankfurt: Suhrkamp, 1984): 127–183, at 161–162.

26. This is why talk of other animals having a "language" is usually misleading. A better term would be "signaling system," or something that more precisely captures the idea that the system has finite expressive potential. See Terrence W. Deacon, *The Symbolic Species* (New York: W. W. Norton, 1997).

27. On the consequences of lifting this constraint, see Donald Davidson, "Theories of Meaning and Learnable Languages," in *Inquiries into Truth and Interpretation* (Oxford: Clarendon, 1984): 3–17.

28. With Kant, this is expressed in the idea that concepts are the contents of possible judgments. Frege carries this through with the analysis of predicates as functions.

29. Gottlob Frege, *The Foundations of Arithmatic*, 2nd ed., trans. J. L. Austin (Oxford: Blackwell, 1968), x^e.

30. Michael Dummett, "The Philosophical Basis of Intuitionistic Logic," in *Truth and Other Enigmas* (Cambridge, MA: Harvard University Press, 1978): 215–247.

31. Many of the "insights" of deconstructionism regarding the looseness of fit between signifier and signifed are a trivial consequence of this basic fact about language. They appear surprising to theorists of a broadly post-structuralist orientation only because the tradition of semiotics that has dominated continental philosophy this century retains an essentially atomistic approach to the theory of meaning (focusing as it does upon "the sign" as the basic unit of meaning).

32. To extend the analogy, a molecular cake theory would be one in which he became acquainted with the taste of various ingredients strictly by eating cakes in which they do and do not appear,

while an atomistic theory would be one in which he began by tasting each ingredient individually, then applied this knowledge to the cakes as they are produced.

33. Here I am thinking of J. L. Austin above all. John Searle, in later work, essentially abandons the speech-act project when he grants that truth-conditions will be needed to establish the propositional content of an utterance.

34. Donald Davidson, "Moods and Performances," *Inquiries into Truth and Interpretation* (Oxford: Clarendon, 1984): 109–122, at 113.

35. Ludwig Wittgenstein, *Tractatus Logico-Philosophicus*, trans. D. F. Pears and B. F. McGuiness (London: Routledge, 1961).

36. Crispin Wright, "Strict Finitism," *Realism, Meaning, and Truth*, 2nd ed. (Oxford: Blackwell, 1993): 107–175 at 121–122.

37. This is the view that Dummett develops in *The Logical Basis of Metaphysics* (Cambridge, MA: Harvard University Press, 1991).

38. See Brandom, *Making It Explicit*.

39. Stephen Toulmin, *The Uses of Argument* (Cambridge: Cambridge University Press, 1964).

40. "Langue entry move" is an expression used by Wilfrid Sellars to designate an action through which an agent comes to occupy a position in a language game that is not based on a transition from some other point in the game. See Wilfrid Sellars, "Some Reflections on Language Games," *Science, Perception, and Reality* (New York: Routledge & Kegan Paul, 1963), 329. See also Brandom, *Making It Explicit*, 221–222.

41. Brandom, *Making It Explicit*, 474.

42. OPC, 232.

43. BFN, 34.

44. TCA, 1:278.

45. BFN, 17 (translation modified).

46. OPC, 198.

47. OPC, 329. Habermas writes: "a cognitive agreement about facts requires the participants in communication only to take these agreed-upon facts into consideration in the subsequent course of their interaction. In contrast to a normative agreement, a cognitive agreement does not affect the way in which the actors select and pursue their action goals; it does not affect whether they are guided exclusively by their personal preferences or whether they are also guided by binding norms (and values held in esteem by all members)."

48. Habermas sharply separates questions of justification from questions of motivation, what he calls "an uncoupling of moral judgment from moral action," JA, 34. Motivational questions, in his view, are to be handled by socialization, not argumentation.

49. *Moral Consciousness and Communicative Action*, trans. C. Lenhardt and S. Weber Nicholsen (Cambridge, MA: MIT Press, 1990; hereafter MCCA). Later, Habermas distinguishes between

three types of practical discourse: moral, ethical, and pragmatic. The latter two, however, influence action only indirectly, insofar as they change some of the input that goes into instrumental deliberation. Only moral discourses generate genuinely noninstrumental reasons for action. These issues will be discussed in greater detail in chapter 6.

50. PMT, 75.

51. For a detailed analysis of this attempt, and its ultimate failure, see Cristina Lafont, *The Linguistic Turn in Hermeneutic Philosophy*, trans. José Medina (Cambridge, MA: MIT Press, 1999), ch. 4. However, Lafont's somewhat quixotic conclusion—that we must adopt a theory of direct reference to account for the cognitive content of speech acts—is severely underargued in the text. In particular, despite occasional references to Brandom, Lafont does not discuss his claim that *anaphora* can be used to explain the so-called referential use of singular terms.

52. See, e.g., Maeve Cooke, *Language and Reason* (Cambridge, MA: MIT Press, 1994), 59, or William Outhwaite, *Habermas: A Critical Introduction* (Cambridge: Polity Press, 1994), 40.

53. Jürgen Habermas, "What Is Universal Pragmatics?" *Communication and the Evolution of Society*, trans. Thomas McCarthy (Boston: Beacon Press, 1979), 66.

54. PMT, 58–64.

55. TCA, 1:306.

56. TCA, 1:307.

57. TCA, 1:307 (my emphasis).

58. This is a point also emphasized by Lafont, *The Linguistic Turn in Hermeneutic Philosophy*, 200–201. However, Lafont then proceeds to an overly hasty dismissal of Habermas's view (as the discussion in §3.4 should reveal).

59. Note that Habermas claims that we have to understand both the justification for the action *and* for the norm that legitimates it. Since the direct extension of this principle from the former to the latter is an obvious non sequitur, and given the conspicuous absence of any argument to justify this transition in Habermas's work, I will simply ignore it in the discussion.

60. In *The Theory of Communicative Action*, Habermas adheres (inconsistently) to both this view and the earlier one. In later work, he explicitly endorses only the later view, stating quite specifically that validity claims are raised for the *content* of an utterance (OPC, 227). The development of this view coincides with his adoption of Dummett's "epistemic turn" in semantics, suggesting that he only later came to realize that the validity claim needs to be related to the compositional component the speech act in order to secure the desired relationship between meaning and justification.

61. TCA, 1:309 (format altered).

62. PMT, 73.

63. This is suggested at MCCA, 53, and TCA, 2:69.

64. This is the view that Joel Anderson refers to as "strong demarcationism," in *A Social Conception of Personal Autonomy* (Ph.D. dissertation, Northwestern University, 1996), §6.3.

65. See Brandom, *Making It Explicit*, 341.

328

Notes

66. In fact, in his latest work, Habermas explicitly drops the claim that all three validity claims are raised in every speech act. See OPC, 327.

67. When I make an assertion, there is a sense in which I "claim" to be sincere. Similarly, when I congratulate someone, I "claim" to be happy for them. This does not mean that I am raising a special "happiness claim" for my speech act, or that grasping the conditions under which this happiness claim could be redeemed is constitutive of my understanding of the utterance. It just means that there are certain normative expectations that go along with certain types of social actions. Lumping these sorts of "claims" together with the deontic commitments that establish the meaning of the utterance is needlessly confusing.

68. PMT, 80.

69. See Dummett, *The Logical Basis of Metaphysics*, 113.

70. Dummett, "What Is a Theory of Meaning? (II)," in *The Seas of Language* (Oxford: Clarendon Press, 1993): 34–93 at 39.

71. PMT, 73.

72. Michael Dummett, *Frege's Philosophy of Language*, 2nd ed. (Cambridge, MA: Harvard University Press, 1981), 305.

73. PMT, 77.

74. PMT, 83. It is also strongly suggested by Habermas's "Comments on John Searle: 'Meaning, Communication, and Representation,'" in E. LePore and R. Van Gulick (eds.), *Searle and His Critics*. (Cambridge: Blackwell, 1991): 17–29 at 24.

75. See Anderson, *A Social Conception of Personal Autonomy*. I assume that argumentation, inquiry, and even conversation take the form of different "discourses." I deny only that these discourses can be "isolated from one another," as Habermas suggests in MCCA, 105.

76. Ernst Tugendhat, "Habermas on Communicative Action," in *Social Action*, eds. G. Seebaß and R. Tuomela (Dordrecht: D. Reidel, 1985): 179–186 at 184.

77. PMT, 83.

Chapter 4

1. An exception to this rule is Jon Elster, *The Cement of Society* (Cambridge: Cambridge University Press, 1989).

2. See Talcott Parsons, Edward Shils, eds., *Toward a General Theory of Action* (New York: Harper & Row, 1951).

3. For discussion, see David M. Kreps, *Game Theory and Economic Modelling* (Oxford: Clarendon Press, 1990), 101.

4. Cristina Bicchieri, "Strategic Behavior and Counterfactuals," *Synthese* 76 (1988): 135–169, at 138.

5. Reinhard Selten, "Reexamination of the Perfectness Concept for Equilibrium Points in Extensive Games," *International Journal of Game Theory* 4 (1975): 25–55. Note that even these basic refinements are problematic, because they all use conditionalization to assign probabilities to counterfactuals. Since conditional and counterfactual probabilities are in fact not equivalent, these refinement strategies have given rise to some predictable difficulties. For an overview, see Bicchieri, "Strategic Behavior and Counterfactuals."

6. John Harsanyi and Reinhard Selten, *A General Theory of Equilibrium Selection in Games* (Cambridge, MA: MIT Press, 1988). Pareto-inferior (or suboptimal) equilibria are ones that produce an outcome in which one player does worse, and no one does better, than in some other available outcome.

7. Drew Fudenberg and Eric Maskin, "The Folk Theorem in Repeated Games with Discounting or with Incomplete Information," *Econometrica* 54 (1986): 533–554. See also Drew Fudenberg and Jean Tirole, *Game Theory* (Cambridge, MA: MIT Press, 1991), 150–160. Note that for such results to obtain players must not discount the future too heavily.

8. Joseph Farrell, "Meaning and Credibility in Cheap-Talk Games," *Games and Economic Behavior* 5 (1993): 514–531.

9. David Gauthier, *Morals by Agreement* (Oxford: Clarendon Press, 1986). For a more developed version of this criticism, see Joseph Heath, "A Multi-Stage Game Model of Morals by Agreement," *Dialogue* 35 (1996): 529–552.

10. See Roger B. Myerson, *Game Theory: Analysis of Conflict* (Cambridge, MA: Harvard University Press, 1991), 113–114.

11. Thomas Schelling, *The Strategy of Conflict* (New York: Oxford University Press, 1963).

12. Robert Sugden has argued that the way agents label their strategies can generate focal effects (Robert Sudgen, "A Theory of Focal Points," *The Economic Journal* 105 [1995]: 533–550), but he makes no attempt to explain how agents arrive at these labels. As a result, his analysis does not so much dispel the mystery as relocate it.

13. If the absence of a reason not to do something does not supply a reason to do it, then (RE) as it stands has the effect of eliminating mixed strategy and "weak dominance" equilibria. Those who favor mixed strategies might then want to weaken RE to say that player y need only have grounds to believe that player x has no good reason not to do S_x.

14. This is, in a sense, a persuasive definition, since there is no reason to think that these intentional states will represent moral constraints. They could just as easily express simple urges. However, use of the term "principle" is no more misleading that use of the term "desire" to refer to the agent's preferences over outcomes, since the term "desire" has strong noncognitivist implications that are in no way necessary to the model. The important point, however, is that the question of what type of *content* these intentional states have is entirely separate from any questions concerning the role that these states play in practical deliberation. Where the agent's beliefs, desires, and principles come from is, in Habermas's theory, to be determined by the theories of pragmatic, ethical, and moral discourse, respectively.

15. These are what result from following the standard procedure for representing preferences over outcomes as cardinal utilities associated with actions. For a clear exposition, see R. Duncan Luce and Howard Raiffa, *Games and Decisions* (New York: John Wiley & Sons 1957), 12–39.

16. John von Neumann and Oskar Morgenstern, *The Theory of Games and Economic Behavior*, 3rd ed. (New York: John Wiley & Sons, 1953), 27. For discussion, see Martin Hollis and Robert Sugden, "Rationality in Action," *Mind* 102 (1993): 1–35 at 28. The fact that the "revealed preference" account of decision theory is unable to distinguish between these structurally dissimilar features of the agent's motive is just one more reason for not subscribing to this doctrine. Other reasons include the fact that actions can be taken to reveal *different* patterns of preference, depending on how the agent's beliefs are construed. This means that the attribution of a system of belief and desire is always underdetermined by the evidence. See Donald Davidson, "A New Basis for Decision Theory," *Theory and Decision* 18 (1985): 87–98. There is also the fact that revealed preference theory has the consequence of denying that agents have introspective access to their own preference orderings. For other problems, see Amartya Sen, "Rational Fools: A Critique of the Behavioral Foundations of Economic Theory," *Philosophy and Public Affairs* 6 (1976–7): 317–344.

17. This is how I interpret some of the results in Judith Mehta, Chris Starmer, and Robert Sugden, "Focal Points in Pure Coordination Games: An Experimental Investigation," *Theory and Decision* 36 (1994): 658–673.

18. See Kenneth Binmore, *Game Theory and the Social Contract. Volume 1: Playing Fair* (Cambridge, MA: MIT Press, 1994), 140.

19. This could be made more sophisticated by introducing a system of deontic operators attached to the actions. See §5.2.

20. This is the same kind of conflict, discussed in §3.1, that can arise between commitment-based reasons, like "it's part of the plan" and instrumental reasons. In both cases it is because one type of reason attaches to actions directly, whereas another does so only indirectly via its outcome.

21. Here I follow Henry Allison, *Kant's Theory of Freedom* (Cambridge: Cambridge University Press, 1990), 126–127.

22. Immanuel Kant, *Religion within the Limits of Reasons Alone*, trans. T. M. Greene and H. H. Hudson (New York: Harper & Row, 1960), 32.

23. See John R. Silber, "The Ethical Significance of Kant's *Religion*," introduction to Kant, *Religion within the Limits of Reasons Alone*, for a gloss on this argument that emphasizes the appeal to authenticity, xc–xciv.

24. A claim made famous by H. A. Prichard's powerful essay, "Does Moral Philosophy Rest on a Mistake?" *Moral Obligation, and Duty and Interest* (London: Oxford University Press, 1968): 1–17.

25. Plato, *Republic*, trans. G. M. A. Grube (Indianapolis: Hackett, 1974), [351].

26. For a more detailed critique of the instrumental strategy, see Joseph Heath, "A Multi-Stage Game Model of Morals by Agreement."

27. This is, in my view, the plausible intuition at the heart of "externalist" conceptions of moral motivation, viz., that knowing what one should do does not automatically translate into a motivation to do it. What externalists ignore is the parallel phenomenon, viz., that knowing what is in one's best interests does not translate automatically into a motivation to do it either. Once an agent has decided to assign normative reasons priority in her deliberations, then knowing her obligations will translate automatically into the appropriate motivation, but simply knowing the normative reasons does not give her a reason to assign them priority over instrumental reasons, and

vice versa. The problem with externalism is that it conflates this higher-order choice problem with the simple problem of deciding what to do, and therefore mistakenly concludes that there is a problem explaining how moral reasons can motivate action.

28. See the general discussion in Jean Piaget, *The Moral Judgment of the Child*, trans. Marjorie Gabain (New York: The Free Press, 1965).

29. I generally use the term "norm-conformative" to refer to the former and "norm-governed" to refer to the latter, although the difference is merely a matter of degree. In this view, all action is "norm-governed" insofar as agents begin with a "deontic pruning" of their decision tree, then proceed to entertain instrumental reasons for and against the remaining actions. On pruning, see Georg Henrik von Wright, *An Essay in Deontic Logic and the General Theory of Action* (Amsterdam: North Holland Publishing Company, 1968), 68. This initial pruning may leave the entire tree intact, or reduce it to a single action.

30. Talcott Parsons, *The Social System* (New York: The Free Press, 1951), and Talcott Parsons and Edward Shils, eds. *Toward a General Theory of Action* (New York: Harper & Row, 1951).

31. Parsons, *The Social System*, 59–64. In contrast to Parsons, my own view does not distinguish sharply between affective and normative reasons, from the point of view of practical reason. The difference between them lies only in how the operative principle is derived, and whether it is shared among agents involved in the interaction.

32. Furthermore, norm-governed interaction generates something like a higher-order free-rider problem. In interactions where strategic reasoning produces highly indeterminate practical prescriptions, agents may begin shopping around for some type of norm to focus their expectations and regulate the interaction. However, as soon as they all adopt this norm as a reason for action, it has the effect of parameterizing the interaction problem. If all agents can be expected simply to follow the rule, then the strategic problem can immediately be reduced to a decision problem for all agents. This then eliminates the indeterminacy that made them incapable of resolving the problem from within an instrumental orientation. For any given agent, unilateral deviation from the normative orientation would allow her to reason instrumentally about the interaction problem. Naturally, if she anticipates that everyone else will deviate, this puts them all back where they started. However, the point is that the potential for reversion to an instrumental orientation is present in all norm-governed interactions, even when adoption of the latter is motivated by the indeterminacy of the original strategic problem.

33. See Michael Taylor, *The Possibility of Cooperation* (Cambridge: Cambridge University Press, 1987).

34. Gregory Kavka, *Hobbesian Moral and Political Theory* (Princeton: Princeton University Press, 1986).

35. Drew Fudenberg and Eric Maskin, "The Folk Theorem in Repeated Games." Also, as the title of this paper suggests, it is precisely a decentralized punishment mechanism of this type that permits proof of the folk theorem, which shows that equilibrium-selection in repeated games is massively indeterminate.

36. Emile Durkheim, *The Division of Labor in Society*, trans. George Simpson (New York: The Free Press, 1933), 426.

37. See discussion in Parsons, *The Social System*, 236–240.

38. Parsons, *Toward a General Theory*, 194.

39. Talcott Parsons, "An Outline of the Social System," in Talcott Parsons et al., eds., *Theories of Society* (New York: The Free Press, 1961), 76.

40. Parsons, *The Social System*, 96.

41. Parsons, *The Social System*, 275.

42. This is why organized crime does not arise spontaneously in all societies, but requires certain specific cultural prerequisites. Since higher levels of organization are impossible among instrumentally oriented agents, there must be some basis of normative control within the deviant group. This requires some source of particularlistic loyalty, e.g., the family, that allows for the formation of a deviant subculture. See Diego Gambetta, "Mafia: The Price of Distrust," in Diego Gambetta, ed., *Trust: Making and Breaking Cooperative Relations* (Oxford: Blackwell, 1988): 158–175.

43. This is the intuition underlying the common philosophical observation that morality counteracts the fact that human affairs are "liable to go very badly" when all agents adopt instrumental orientations. However, Parsons's analysis situates the phenomenon differently. Gauthier is a representative of a certain philosophical school of thought that takes the possibility of suboptimal strategic equilibria as providing a *direct* justification for particular moral constraints. Parsons, on the other hand, does not view morality as something that "steps in" when strategic interaction is suboptimal. The fact that strategic interaction is often suboptimal is what makes large-scale "opting out" of institutionalized interaction patterns extremely problematic. This means that deviance will usually be only episodic and can never be the basis of a stable social order. Thus suboptimality does not provide a reason (in the intentional sense) for agents to act morally; rather, it provides the reason (in the sociological sense) that agents usually find themselves assigning normative reasons priority in their deliberations.

44. Parsons, *The Social System*, 39.

45. Parsons, *The Social System*, 218.

46. Parsons, *The Social System*, 16.

47. Parsons, *The Social System*, 272. This may explain some of the empirical research on deviance, which suggests that sanctions must be perceived by the sanctionee as normatively motivated in order to have a socializing effect. If these sanctions are perceived as instrumental, this will often increase the tendency toward deviance.

48. Parsons, *The Social System*, 213.

49. This process of generalization can be traced out, through parents, authority figures, social roles, "society" in general, etc. until it becomes fully autonomous. See, e.g., Lawrence Kohlberg, *The Philosophy of Moral Development: Moral Stages and the Idea of Justice* (San Francisco: Harper & Row, 1981).

50. TCA, 2:20.

51. Incidentally, the burden of proof seems to fall on the sanctionee to show that the action was norm-governed, not on the sanctioner to show that it was instrumental. Harold Garfinkel, for instance, experimented with making strange chess moves that were not technically illegal—such as switching the position of two pawn tokens. Although his opponents complained about the "obscurity of his motives" they nevertheless sanctioned him by refusing to continue play until he

stopped. See Harold Garfinkel, "A Conception of, and Experiments with, 'Trust' as a Condition of Stable Concerted Actions," in *Motivation and Social Interaction*, ed. O. J. Harvey (New York: Ronald Press, 1963), 199.

52. Robert Brandom, *Making It Explicit* (Cambridge, MA: Harvard University Press, 1994), 141.

53. The Sellarsian narrative in question is otherwise known as the "myth of Jones." See Wilfrid Sellars, *Empiricism and the Philosophy of Mind* (Cambridge, MA: Harvard University Press, 1997), 102–107.

54. Brandom, *Making It Explicit*, 166.

55. Brandom, *Making It Explicit*, 167.

56. Brandom, *Making It Explicit*, 168.

57. Brandom, *Making It Explicit*, 195. Since the deontic score is interpersonally calibrated, one's own self-ascribed deontic status is always open to correction by the other participants in the game. For this reason, there is another way of speaking of beliefs, in which they are the commitments ascribed to the agent by others. This is the way of speaking that is used when we suppose that an agent's beliefs include all inferential consequences of the commitments that the agent explicitly acknowledges. The fact that the word "belief" is ambiguous between these two senses is what leads Brandom to favor the term "doxastic commitment."

58. TCA, 2:89.

59. See BFN, 158.

60. Harold Garfinkel, *Studies in Ethnomethodology* (Oxford: Polity Press, 1967).

61. BFN, 114.

Chapter 5

1. Karl-Otto Apel, "The a priori of the Communication Community and the Foundations of Ethics," in *Towards a Transformation of Philosophy*, trans. Glyn Ady and David Frisby (London: Routledge, 1972): 225–300.

2. I am interpolating a bit. What he says is: "If moral statements or utterances can be justified, then they have cognitive content," IO, 3. This formulation is a bit too nonspecific, so I have amplified it by adding the word "rational," and by explicitly invoking the comparison with belief that I take to be implicit in his view.

3. MCCA, 43–44.

4. There are, of course, well-known skeptical concerns about what it means to "apply" a rule. I am setting these worries aside because they do not raise any special difficulties for Habermas's position, since the problems that they raise are in entirely general in nature.

5. Habermas, *Justification and Application*, trans. C. Cronin (Cambridge, MA: MIT Press, 1993), 76 (Hereafter JA).

6. Habermas grants that the language in terms of which these needs and desires are interpreted can always be problematized, and so statements of this type do not provide an absolute stopping point for discussion (JA, 90). The point is simply that the desires themselves, although open to reinterpretation, do not themselves stand in need of justification.

7. See MCCA, 56.

8. He says as much at MCCA, 98.

9. MCCA, 56.

10. MCCA, 56.

11. For a helpful taxonomy, see Peter Railton, "Moral Realism: Prospects and Problems," in *Moral Knowledge?* ed. Walter Sinnott-Armstrong (Oxford: Oxford University Press, 1996): 49–81. As we shall see in the next chapter, Habermas's belief that he must defeat relativism in order to establish moral cognitivism is a source of further confusion.

12. Of course, many forms of noncognitivism trivially imply that agents are unlikely to reach agreement. The point is simply that, even if these types of noncognitivism are set aside, it does nothing to make the problem of relativism go away. Incidentally, relativism is to be understood here in a very loose sense, to include also what Habermas calls "subjectivism" and "decisionism."

13. This is, of course, to assume that "emotional states" are not propositional attitudes. Cf. Amélie Oskenberg Rorty (ed.), *Explaining Emotions* (Berkeley: University of California Press, 1980).

14. See Habermas, "Comments on John Searle 'Meaning, Communication, and Representation,'" in *Searle and His Critics*, ed. Ernest LePore and Robert Van Gulick (Cambridge: Blackwell, 1991): 17–29 at 25.

15. MCCA, 53.

16. P. F. Strawson, "Truth," *Proceedings of the Aristotelian Society*, supp. vol. 24 (1950): 129–156.

17. I take "deflationary" to include the redundancy, minimalist, and prosentential theories. For an overview, see Richard Kirkham, *Theories of Truth* (Cambridge, MA: MIT Press, 1992). Habermas officially distances himself from deflationism, but his reasons for doing so are, in my view, wholly mistaken (see note 82 below).

18. Alfred Tarski, "The Semantic Conception of Truth and the Foundation of Semantics," *Philosophy and Phenomenological Research*, 4 (1944): 341–375.

19. For the classic statement, see Frank Ramsey, "Facts and Propositions," *Proceedings of the Aristotelian Society*, supp. vol. 7 (1927): 153–170.

20. Dummett, "Truth," in *Truth and Other Enigmas* (Cambridge, MA: Harvard University Press, 1978): 1–24.

21. Habermas, "*Wahrheitstheorien*," in *Vorstudien und Ergänzungen zur Theorie des kommunikativen Handelns* (Frankfurt: Suhrkamp, 1984): 127–183 at 130. This view is one that Habermas has adhered to consistently. For a later statement see OPC, 362.

22. In this view, the difference between the Equivalence Schema and Schema T is determined simply by whether the propositional variable is slotted into the subject or object position.

23. See Dorothy Grover, *A Prosentential Theory of Truth* (Princeton: Princeton University Press, 1992).

24. Paul Horwich, *Truth* (Oxford: Basil Blackwell, 1990), 18.

25. For this analysis to be intuitively correct, it is important that the class of imperatives be restricted to those that are normatively authorized. Habermas argues, with some plausibility, that pragmatic or prudential imperatives are better analyzed as forms of assertion. PMT, 83–84.

26. Strictly speaking, he analyzes them as concealed threats, with the assumption that threats are forms of assertion. See TCA, 1: 301; also Jürgen Habermas, "Reply to Skjei," *Inquiry* 28 (1985): 105–113, and PMT, 57–87. See also Joseph Heath, "Threats, Promises, and Communicative Action," *European Journal of Philosophy* 3 (1995): 225–241.

27. MCCA, 53. Here I am simplifying Habermas's example by eliminating a contextualizing qualification. It should be noted that the grammatical structure of the second phrase is rearranged in the English translation in such a way as to significantly obscure Habermas's point. Cf. Jürgen Habermas, *Moralbewußtsein und kommunikatives Handeln* (Frankfurt: Suhrkamp, 1983), 63.

28. MCCA, 53.

29. Naturally, this means truth-conditions understood in the weak deflationary sense. See Michael Dummett, *The Logical Basis of Metaphysics* (Cambridge, MA: Harvard University Press, 1991), 157–164.

30. See Dagfinn Føllesdal and Risto Hilpinen, "Deontic Logic: An Introduction," in *Deontic Logic: Introductory and Systematic Readings*, ed. R. Hilpinen (Dordrecht: D. Reidel, 1970): 1–35 at 17.

31. The confusion shows up clearly in statements like the following: "Certainly we cannot simply assimilate moral insight to empirical knowledge without further ado, for the former tells us what we ought to do, whereas we only know something, strictly speaking, when we know how things stand in the world" JA, 20 (see also IO, 36). If "empirical knowledge" is construed this strictly, then we could not have "empirical knowledge" of past events. The above analysis is intended to show that just as modalities must be used to specify the sense in which claims about the past are true, modalities can also be used to specify the sense in which normative claims are true.

32. Cf. JA, 26.

33. For a more general discussion, see Sergio Tenenbaum, "Realists without a Cause: Deflationary Theories of Truth and Ethical Realism," *Canadian Journal of Philosophy* 26 (1996): 561–590.

34. J. L. Mackie, *Ethics: Inventing Right and Wrong* (London: Penguin, 1977), 6.

35. Mackie, *Ethics*, 30.

36. Mackie, *Ethics*, 39.

37. The relevant arguments are too complex to get into here. See Richard Rorty, *Philosophy and the Mirror of Nature* (Princeton: Princeton University Press, 1980).

38. Mackie, *Ethics*, 37.

39. Kant, *Critique of Pure Reason*, trans. Norman Kemp Smith (New York: St. Martin's Press, 1929), 386 [A409/B436]. If one opts to extend the regress to infinity, then the unconditioned in this context is the entire series. If one cuts it short, then the unconditioned is the first term in the sequence of syllogisms, first cause in the sequence of events, etc. Kant, *Critique of Pure Reason*, 391 [A417/B445]. Incidentally, Kant is using Aristotelian logical terminology here. One can think of the conditioned as simply the conclusion of an inference, and the conditions as the premises.

40. Kant, *Critique of Pure Reason*, 450 [A509/B537].

41. This is a denial of what Michael Williams calls "epistemological realism," which is not realism as a position taken within epistemology, but realism about the objects posited in epistemology. See Michael Williams, *Unnatural Doubts: Epistemological Realism and the Basis for Scepticism* (Cambridge: Blackwell, 1992).

42. Alvin Goldman, "What Is Justified Belief?" in *Naturalizing Epistemology*, ed. Hilary Kornblith (Cambridge, MA: MIT Press, 1994), 105.

43. Laurence Bonjour, *The Structure of Empirical Knowledge* (Cambridge, MA: Harvard University Press, 1985), 3.

44. Susan Haack, *Evidence and Inquiry* (Oxford: Blackwell, 1993), 20. She does not consider the possibility that contextualists might have principled reasons for changing the topic in this way.

45. This is taken from Hilary Putnam, *Reason, Truth, and History* (Cambridge: Cambridge University Press, 1981), 110–111. The key concept is that criterial conceptions attempt to *define* exhaustively what counts as rational.

46. Statement (2) provides a recursion clause, ensuring that the total belief set has a tree structure with only basic beliefs as terminal nodes.

47. This is intended to parallel Michael Dummett and Crispin Wright's use-constraint on the attribution of semantic knowledge. See Crispin Wright, *Realism, Meaning, and Truth*, 2nd ed. (Oxford: Blackwell, 1993), 13–23.

48. Michael Williams, *Unnatural Doubts*, 117–118. Wittgenstein citation from *On Certainty* (New York: Harper & Row, 1969), §250.

49. Chaïm Perelman and L. Olbrechts-Tyteca, *The New Rhetoric*, trans. John Wilkinson and Purcell Weaver (Notre Dame: University of Notre Dame Press, 1969), 68.

50. BFN, 226–227. Habermas makes this claim in the context of a critique of Ronald Dworkin's model of legal adjudication. It is noteworthy that Habermas does not object to the idealizations built in to Dworkin's conception of "Judge Hercules" as ideal adjudicator. Rather, he argues that because Dworkin's model of justification is *monological*, no amount of idealization will close the "rationality gap" opened up by the fact that any particular argumentation sequence will always be open-ended, or incomplete. See BFN, 228.

51. Richard Rorty, "Putnam and the Relativist Menace," *Journal of Philosophy* 90 (1993): 443–461 at 449. It has also been pointed out that Rorty's claim presupposes something of a God's-eye point of view. If some agreement must always be given, but this agreement is shared by both observer and participants, then it would not be thought in any way to impair the cognitive

status of any agreement that the participants subsequently achieve. To draw relativist conclusions, one must imagine an observer who interprets the interaction without sharing any of the background presuppositions of participants. Various theorists have pointed out that this is incoherent (e.g., Thomas McCarthy in David Couzens Hoy and Thomas McCarthy, *Critical Theory* [Oxford: Blackwell, 1994], 77), since one can only interpret speech as a virtual participant. In any case, such an observer perspective is precluded by Rorty's own Davidsonian commitments.

52. Rorty, "Putnam and the Relativist Menace," 450.

53. Jürgen Habermas, "A Repy to my Critics," in *Habermas: Critical Debates*, eds. John B. Thompson and David Held (Cambridge, MA: MIT Press, 1982), 273.

54. TCA, 1: 28.

55. Habermas, "*Wahrheitstheorien*," 161.

56. Jürgen Habermas, "On the Cognitive Content of Morality," *Proceedings of the Aristotelian Society*, vol. 96 (1996): 335–358 at 351 (reprinted with some changes in IO: 3–46 at 37).

57. TCA, 1: 26.

58. TCA, 1: 26.

59. MCCA, 87.

60. H. P. Grice, "Logic and Conversation," *Studies in the Ways of Words* (Cambridge, MA: Harvard University Press, 1989), 26 (my emphasis).

61. MCCA, 88.

62. MCCA, 89.

63. JA, p. 31.

64. E.g., BFN, 323.

65. OPC, 367.

66. Immanuel Kant, *Foundations of the Metaphysics of Morals*, 2nd ed., trans. Lewis White Beck (New York: MacMillan, 1990), 38 [421].

67. For instance, Kant admits that there is no contradiction in willing a state of affairs in which no man cultivates his natural talents, but suggests that as a rational being, man "necessarily wills that all his faculties should be developed." Kant, *Foundations of the Metaphysics of Morals*, 40 [423].

68. MCCA, 203.

69. Kant, *Foundations of the Metaphysics of Morals*, 54–56 [437–439].

70. This feature is emphasized by John Rawls, "Themes in Kant's Moral Philosophy," in *Kant's Transcendental Deductions*, ed. Eckart Förster (Stanford: Stanford University Press, 1989): 81–113.

71. MCCA, 93.

72. Kant says: "If I speak of an idea, then as regards its object, viewed as an object of pure understanding, I am saying a *great deal*, but as regards its relation to the subject, that is, in respect of its actuality under empirical conditions, I am for the same reason saying *very little*, in that, as being the concept of a maximum, it can never be correspondingly given *in concreto*." Kant, *Critique of Pure Reason*, 319 [A327/B384].

73. For a typical example, see David Estlund, "Beyond Fairness and Deliberation: The Epistemic Dimension of Democratic Authority," in *Deliberative Democracy*, eds. James Bohman and William Rehg (Cambridge, MA: MIT Press, 1997): 173–204 at 180.

74. BFN, 323.

75. See Raymond Geuss, *The Idea of a Critical Theory* (Cambridge: Cambridge University Press, 1981), 66, or Nicholas Rescher, *Pluralism* (Oxford: Clarendon Press, 1993).

76. Actually, even this argument is faulty. Most critics assume that counterfactuals with unrealizable antecedents are substantively false, whereas in fact they are trivially true.

77. On the latter, see Arthur Fine, "Truthmongering: Less Is True," *Canadian Journal of Philosophy* 19 (1989): 611–616.

78. Habermas, "A Repy to My Critics," 273.

79. William P. Alston, "Level Confusions in Epistemology," in his *Epistemic Justification* (Ithaca: Cornell University Press, 1989): 153–171.

80. Richard Rorty, "Pragmatism, Davidson, and Truth," in *Truth and Interpretation: Perspectives on the Philosophy of Donald Davidson*, ed. Ernest Lepore (Oxford: Blackwell, 1986): 333–355 at 334.

81. Rorty, "Putnam and the Relativist Menace," 460.

82. Habermas at one point describes the cautionary use as "the only nonredundant use of the truth predicate," OPC, 373. If this is indeed his view, then the analysis above should remove the final obstacle to his official endorsement of deflationism.

83. Habermas grants that he overstated similarities in early work. Thus in "A Reply" in *Communicative Action*, eds. Axel Honneth and Hans Joas (Cambridge, MA: MIT Press, 1991), he writes, "I do not understand the discourse theory of truth to mean that the consensus achieved discursively is a criterion of truth (as was the case in some of my earlier statements); rather, it should explain via the discursive redemption of validity claims the meaning of each element of unconditionality which we intuitively link with the concept of truth," 233.

84. JA, 32.

85. JA, 33.

86. MCCA, 85–86.

Chapter 6

1. MCCA, 105.

2. Habermas describes this principle as one that *"die Einverständnis grundsätzlich herbeizuführen erlaubt,"* in *Moralbewußtsein und kommunikatives Handeln* (Frankfurt: Suhrkamp, 1983), 66; or *"die Einverständnis ermöglicht,"* 76.

3. MCCA, 56. Recall that "moral noncognitivism" here refers to the view that moral statements are not susceptible to rational justification.

4. MCCA, 76.

5. Charles Taylor, "Explanation and Practical Reason," in *Philosophical Arguments* (Cambridge, MA: Harvard University Press, 1995): 34–60 at 55.

6. See Hilary Putnam, "Equivalence," in his *Realism and Reason: Philosophical Papers, Volume 3* (Cambridge: Cambridge University Press, 1983): 26–45.

7. MCCA, 66.

8. To use Peter Railton's term, "surface cognitivism" is all that is needed to establish moral cognitivism. See Peter Railton, "Moral Realism: Prospects and Problems," in *Moral Knowledge?* ed. Walter Sinnott-Armstrong (Oxford: Oxford University Press, 1996): 49–81 at 59–62.

9. For example, in his *Malaise of Modernity* (Concord: Anansi, 1991), Taylor presents a persuasive analysis of how various forms of radical individualism stem from the same underlying ideals of self-fulfillment that motivate a variety of communitarian projects.

10. Bernard Williams, *Ethics and the Limits of Philosophy* (Cambridge, MA: Harvard University Press, 1985), 136. This is merely a "best explanation" because it assumes the falsity of various skeptical hypotheses.

11. See Michael Dummett, "Realism," in *Truth and Other Enigmas* (Cambridge, MA: Harvard University Press, 1978): 145–165.

12. The same type of realist argument could be formulated using "rightness" instead of "truth." For it to be worthwhile arguing about a given moral issue, there must be some fact of the matter about what is right and wrong. That is, for any action p, it must be the case that either p is right or p is wrong. Suppose that we define wrongness on analogy with rightness, using the imperative game from §5.3:

(W) It is wrong that p iff $\neg p$.

Then if p is neither right nor wrong, by (R) and (W):

(n1) $\neg (p \text{ or } \neg p)$,

which is of course a denial of the law of the excluded middle, and in classical logic generates a contradiction. However, since every norm system contains "gaps," i.e., actions that are neither right nor wrong, moral reasoning will constantly be generating contradictions. Since the best explanation for the lack of convergence in moral argumentation is precisely the presence of such gaps, one might conclude that moral reasoning is not governed by principles of logical inference.

However, this argument can be avoided by rendering explicit the deontic operators that usually appear in normatively authorized imperatives, and then formulating the gaps in the norm system as cases where a particular action is neither obligatory nor forbidden. For example, if we say that:

(W′)   It is wrong that p iff Fp,

and define rightness in terms of what is "obligatory," then the claim that some action is neither right nor wrong states simply that:

(n2) $\neg \, (Op$ or $Fp)$.

In the standard system of deontic logic, this does not generate a contradiction, but rather the "principle of deontic contingency":

(n3) $(\neg Op$ and $\neg Fp)$ iff $(P\neg p$ and $Pp)$,

which does not generate any logical problems.

13. See Dummett, "The Philosophical Basis of Intuitionistic Logic," *Truth and Other Enigmas*: 215–247.

14. For evidence that Habermas retains this intuition, see "Reply to Symposium Participants," *Cardozo Law Review* 17 (1996): 1477–1557 at 1502.

15. Habermas, "Reply to Symposium Participants," 1502.

16. Paraphrasing MCCA, 65. It is not entirely clear that the "if and only if" is appropriate. However, I do not think that any important aspect of my argument turns on this question.

17. After writing the "Discourse Ethics" paper, Habermas introduces a distinction between three types of practical discourse: moral, ethical, and pragmatic, "On the Pragmatic, Moral, and Ethical Employments of Practical Reason," JA, 1–18. Since I regard this distinction as essentially action-theoretic (see §6.3 below), not discourse-theoretic, I will retain the earlier usage, in which practical discourse is assumed to be moral unless stated otherwise.

18. BFN, 107–111. Thus it is important that Habermas does not regard (U) itself as a rule of discourse, but rather as something that can be *derived* from the rules of discourse.

19. There is confusion on this point in Albrecht Wellmer's "Ethics and Dialogue," *The Persistence of Modernity*, trans. David Midgley (Cambridge, MA: MIT Press, 1991): 113–241 at 150–151.

20. For an example of confusion on this point, see Seyla Benhabib, "Afterword," *The Communicative Ethics Controversy* (Cambridge, MA: MIT Press, 1990): 330–369 at 345–346.

21. Jürgen Habermas, "Wahrheitstheorien," in *Vorstudien und Ergänzungen zur Theorie des kommunikativen Handelns* (Frankfurt: Suhrkamp, 1984), 165. See also Stephen Toulmin, *The Uses of Argument* (Cambridge: Cambridge University Press, 1964), 104.

22. See Robert Brandom, *Making It Explicit* (Cambridge, MA: Harvard University Press, 1994), 97–102.

23. Stephen Toulmin, Richard Rieke, and Allan Janik, *An Introduction to Reasoning* (New York: MacMillan, 1979), 46.

24. Brandom, *Making It Explicit*, 105–110.

25. MCCA, 89.

26. MCCA, 86.

27. TCA, 1:19.

28. This claim is defended at greater length in Joseph Heath, "The Problem of Foundationalism in Habermas's Discourse Ethics," *Philosophy and Social Criticism* 21 (1995): 77–100.

29. E.g., JA, 29.

30. Consider, e.g., the structure of Ronald Dworkin's argument against welfare egalitarianism. Dworkin, "What Is Equality? Part 1: Equality of Welfare," *Philosophy and Public Affairs* 10 (1981): 185–246.

31. MCCA, 66.

32. Talcott Parsons, *The Social System* (New York: The Free Press, 1951). This is also the main idea underlying Taylor's conception of strong evaluation. See Charles Taylor, "What Is Human Agency?" in *Human Agency and Language: Philosophical Papers 1* (Cambridge: Cambridge University Press, 1985):15–44.

33. Parsons, *The Social System*, 121.

34. Parsons, *The Social System*, 121.

35. JA, 90.

36. See Thomas Scanlon, "Preference and Urgency," *The Journal of Philosophy* 72 (1975): 655–669.

37. Thomas McCarthy, "Practical Discourse," *Ideals and Illusions* (Cambridge, MA: MIT Press, 1991): 181–199 at 191.

38. William Rehg, "Discourse and the Moral Point of View: Deriving a Dialogical Principle of Universalization," *Inquiry* 34 (1991): 27–48.

39. JA, 59.

40. He also notes at this point that the term "discourse ethics" is slight misnomer, since what he has formulated is really a "discourse theory of morality." JA, vii.

41. Georg Henrik von Wright, *Norm and Action* (London: Routledge, 1963); and *Varieties of Goodness* (London: Routledge, 1963).

42. BFN, 255–256.

43. BFN, 256. Translation modified slightly. See Jürgen Habermas, *Faktizität und Geltung* (Fankfurt am Main: Suhrkamp, 1992), 312.

44. MCCA, 108.

45. JA, 91.

46. JA, 91.

47. MCCA, 111 (n41).

48. BFN, 158.

49. This is something that Habermas loses sight of in BFN. Here he classifies morality as simply cultural knowledge, and only law as an action system. He thereby loses the Durkheimian insight at the core of his early analysis—that social norms are sanctioned expectations.

50. Habermas's use of "right" and "wrong" instead of the usual deontic modalities contributes to the confusion. Equating "right" with obligatory and "wrong" with forbidden suggests that any action that is neither is simply not subject to moral regulation. The problem is that one cannot handle negation with this system—"not right" is not the same as "wrong." This can only be corrected by introducing permission as a moral category.

51. George Henrik von Wright, *An Essay in Deontic Logic and the General Theory of Action* (Amsterdam: North Holland Publishing Company, 1968), 68.

52. See John Roemer, *Theories of Distributive Justice* (Cambridge, MA: Harvard University Press, 1996), 89–93; Joseph Heath, "Culture: Choice or Circumstance," *Constellations* 5 (1998): 183–200.

53. See Thomas Scanlon, "Contractualism and Utilitarianism," in *Utilitarianism and Beyond*, eds. Amartya K. Sen and Bernard Williams (Cambridge: Cambridge University Press, 1982): 103–128 at 119.

54. John Nash, "The Bargaining Problem," *Econometrica* 18 (1950): 155–162 at 155.

55. Nash also makes the assumption that the set of feasible outcomes is convex and compact, which follows naturally from the idea that all outcomes, and all randomizations over these outcomes, are to be considered possible outcomes for the purposes of solving the problem.

56. Expositions sometimes add a "scale invariance" axiom, which states that the numbers used to represent the agent's utility functions should not affect the outcome. This is implied, however, by the mere fact that the bargaining space is defined in terms of some set of utility functions.

57. See Nash, "The Bargaining Problem," 159. In a strange twist on the classic utilitarian formula, Nash's solution therefore suggests that instead of seeking the greatest sum of happiness, one should seek the greatest product of happiness.

58. Ehud Kalai and Meir Smorodinsky, "Other Solutions to Nash's Bargaining Problem," *Econometrica* 43 (1975): 513–518.

59. BFN, 165.

60. Ariel Rubenstein, "Perfect Equilibrium in a Bargaining Model," *Econometrica* 50 (1982): 97–109.

61. For instance, in *Morals by Agreement*, 143, Gauthier tries to suggest that a solution roughly equivalent to Kalai and Smorodinsky's follows directly from the instrumental model. He has since retracted this claim, in his "Uniting Separate Persons," in David Gauthier and Robert Sugden, eds., *Rationality, Justice, and the Social Contract* (Hemel Hempstead: Harvester Wheatsheaf, 1993): 176–192.

62. Eric Rasmusen, *Games and Information*, 2nd ed. (Oxford: Blackwell, 1990), 279.

63. This is what Gauthier's "Lockean proviso" is intended to achieve in his own system. Gauthier, *Morals by Agreement*, 205.

64. John Rawls, "The Idea of an Overlapping Consensus," *Oxford Journal of Legal Studies* 7 (1988): 251–276.

65. BFN, 166.

66. IO, 86.

67. Thanks to Cheryl Misak for pointing this out to me.

Chapter 7

1. BFN, 153. For analysis, see Joel Anderson, *A Social Conception of Personal Autonomy* (Ph.D. dissertation, Northwestern University, 1996), §6.3.

2. Some accommodation must be made for coarsening, which is considered permissible. Here I am treating input as "preprocessed," so that everything that comes in is intended to be preserved.

3. For instance, we may not be aware that we are projecting subjective responses onto the environment. See John L. Mackie, *Ethics: Inventing Right and Wrong* (London: Penguin, 1977), 42, where he calls this the "pathetic fallacy."

4. See Gilbert Harman, *The Nature of Morality: An Introduction to Ethics* (New York: Oxford University Press, 1977).

5. Crispin Wright, *Truth and Objectivity* (Cambridge MA: Harvard University Press, 1992), 92–93.

6. Melvin Pollner, *Mundane Reason* (Cambridge: Cambridge University Press, 1987). See also Thomas McCarthy's discussion, in David Couzens Hoy and Thomas McCarthy, *Critical Theory* (Oxford: Blackwell, 1994), 72–73.

7. Immanuel Kant, *Critique of Pure Reason*, trans. Norman Kemp Smith (New York: St. Martin's Press, 1929), 322–326 [A333–8/B390–6].

8. Eric Rasmusen, *Games and Information* (Cambridge, MA: Blackwell, 1989), 165.

Notes

9. Gary Becker, *Accounting for Tastes* (Cambridge, MA: Harvard University Press, 1996), 24.

10. Becker, *Accounting for Tastes*, 203–224.

11. Ludwig Wittgenstein, *Philosophical Investigations*, trans. G. E. M. Ancombe (Oxford: Blackwell, 1967), 117 [§381].

12. C. S. Peirce, *Collected Works of Charles Sanders Peirce*, vol. 5 (Cambridge, MA: Belknap, 1934), 359.

13. Donald Davidson, "A New Basis for Decision Theory," *Theory and Decision* 18 (1985): 87–98.

14. See Shaun P. Hargreaves Heap and Yanis Varoufakis, *Game Theory: A Critical Introduction* (London: Routledge, 1995), 52.

15. John Harsanyi, "Games with Incomplete Information Played by 'Bayesian' Players," 3 parts, *Management Science* 14 (1967–68): 159–182, 320–334, 486–502.

16. John Harsanyi, "Games with Incomplete Information Played by 'Bayesian' Players."

17. This is admittedly informal, but conveys the basic idea of Robert Aumann's argument in "Agreeing to Disagree," *The Annals of Statistics* 4 (1976): 1236–1239. For more general reflection on these issues, see Robert Aumann, "Correlated Equilibrium as an Expression of Bayesian Rationality," *Econometrica* 55 (1987): 1–18.

18. Aumann, "Correlated Equilibrium as an Expression of Bayesian Rationality," 12–15.

19. Consider, for instance, the examples assembled by C. S. Lewis, *The Abolition of Man* (London: Oxford University Press, 1944), 41–48.

20. Jürgen Habermas, "Reply to Symposium Participants," *Cardozo Law Review* 17 (1996): 1477–1557 at 1493.

21. This is captured by Kant's idea that moral reasoning is governed by the regulative idea of the kingdom of ends. The laws governing this realm have no substantive content, but are merely those that all could will in common. This is unlike the laws governing the physical realm, which are not only subject to the formal constraint that they be the same for all, but also have their substantive content fixed.

22. BFN, 162.

23. Will Kymlicka, *Multicultural Citizenship* (Oxford: Clarendon Press, 1995).

24. Emile Durkheim, *L'éducation morale* (Paris: Presses universitaires de France, 1963). *Moral Education*, p. 26 (my translation).

25. Durkheim, *The Rules of Sociological Method*, trans. W. D. Halls (New York: The Free Press, 1982), 67.

26. Although even here there are very high levels of agreement. See Pierre Bourdieu, *Distinction*, trans. Richard Nice (Cambridge, MA: Harvard University Press, 1984).

27. John Rawls, *Political Liberalism* (New York: Columbia University Press, 1993), xxiv–xxvii.

28. BFN, 229–233.

29. Ronald Dworkin, *Law's Empire* (Cambridge, MA: Belknap, 1986), 59.

Chapter 8

1. Jürgen Habermas, *Moralbewußtswin und kommunkatives Handeln* (Frankfurt am Main: Suhrkamp, 1983), 92.

2. Quoting, with slight modification, from Jerry Fodor and Ernest Lepore, *Holism* (Cambridge, MA: Blackwell, 1992), 261.

3. See Barry Stroud, "Transcendental Arguments," *The Journal of Philosophy* 65 (1968): 241–56 at 252–253.

4. Here I follow David Lewis, *Counterfactuals* (Oxford: Basil Blackwell, 1973), 5–6.

5. Stroud, "Transcendental Arguments," 254.

6. Richard Rorty, "The World Well Lost," *The Journal of Philosophy* 69 (1972): 649–665.

7. W. v. O. Quine, *Word and Object* (Cambridge, MA: MIT Press, 1960), 170.

8. See Robert Brandom, *Making It Explicit* (Cambridge, MA: Harvard University Press, 1994), 376–384.

9. Immanuel Kant, *Critique of Pure Reason*, trans. N. Kemp Smith (New York: St. Martin's Press, 1929), 267 [B306]. This explains, incidentally, why noumena are not the same as things-in-themselves.

10. Ludwig Wittgenstein, *Tractatus Logico-Philosophicus*, trans. D. F. Pears and B. F. McGuiness (London: Routledge, 1961), 56 [§5.6].

11. E.g., MCCA, 82.

12. Jürgen Habermas, *Knowledge and Human Interests*, trans. Jeremy J. Shapiro (Boston: Beacon Press, 1971), and Karl Mannheim, *Ideology and Utopia*, trans. Wirth, L. and Shils, E. (New York: Harcourt Brace Jovanovich, 1936).

13. Lewis Carroll, "What the Tortoise Said to Achilles," *Mind* 104 (1995): 691–693.

14. Michael Dummett, "The Justification of Deduction," *Truth and Other Enigmas* (Cambridge, MA: Harvard University Press, 1978): 290–318 at 304. Dummett goes on to reject this view, which he associates with semantic holism.

15. MCCA, 97.

16. MCCA, 81.

17. Jürgen Habermas, *The Philosophical Discourse of Modernity*, trans. Frederick Lawrence (Cambridge, MA: MIT Press, 1987), 284. See also Charles Taylor, *Sources of the Self* (Cambridge, MA: Harvard University Press, 1989).

18. Karl-Otto Apel, "The Problem of Philosophical Foundations in Light of a Transcendental Pragmatics of Language," in *After Philosophy*, eds. Kenneth Baynes, James Bohman, and Thomas McCarthy (Cambridge, MA: MIT Press, 1987), 280.

19. MCCA, 91.

20. MCCA, 95.

21. MCCA, 97.

22. Kant, *Critique of Pure Reason*, 68 [A24/B38].

23. Edmund Husserl *Cartesian Meditations*, trans. Dorion Cairns (The Hague: Martinus Nijhoff, 1977), 50–53.

24. MCCA, 89.

25. See Thomas McCarthy and David Couzens Hoy, *Critical Theory* (Oxford: Blackwell, 1994), 42.

26. MCCA, 98.

27. MCCA, 100.

28. MCCA, 97.

29. Hilary Putnam, "Philosophers and Human Understanding," in *Realism and Reason: Philosophical Papers, Volume 3* (Cambridge: Cambridge University Press, 1983): 184–204 at 193.

30. Lucien Lévy-Bruhl, *How Natives Think* (New York: Washington Square Press, 1966).

31. See E. E. Evans-Pritchard, *Nuer Religion* (Oxford: Clarendon Press, 1956).

32. Consider the moral overtones to Peter Winch's influential claim that in Evans-Pritchard's treatment of Zande witchcraft beliefs, "it is the European, obsessed with pressing Zande thought where it will not naturally go—to a contradiction—who is guilty of misunderstanding, not the Zande." "Understanding a Primitive Society," in Bryan R. Wilson, *Rationality* (Oxford: Basil Blackwell, 1970), 93. The assumption that one party is to be *blamed* for the misunderstanding is significant. The suggestion that the Zande are behaving "naturally" while Evans-Pritchard is "obsessed" then gives us a clear indication of where this blame should lie.

33. This should not be surprising, from a sociological perspective. Culture is reproduced through institutionalization, and institutions take the form of normative rules of action that separate proper from improper ways of acting. Thus a culture is never normatively neutral from the standpoint of its members. It takes a somewhat counterintuitive sociocognitive judgment to determine that these rules, while mandatory for members, may be optional or even forbidden for those who do not share the same cultural background, since this is precisely *not* the way the rules are taught to us over the course of primary socialization.

34. TCA, 2:145–148.

35. For more extensive discussion, see Joseph Heath, "Rational Choice as Critical Theory," *Philosophy and Social Criticism* 22 (1996): 43–62.

36. MCCA, 108 (translation modified). See Habermas, *Moralbewußtsein*, 117.

37. BFN (postscript), 460.

38. Habermas, "Remarks on Legitimation through Human Rights" (unpublished MS).

39. Cf. Joseph Heath, "Rational Choice as Critical Theory," *Philosophy and Social Criticism* 22 (1996): 43–62 at 51.

Bibliography

Alexander, J., ed. 1987. *The Micro-Macro Link*. Berkeley: University of California Press.

Allison, H. 1990. *Kant's Theory of Freedom*. Cambridge: Cambridge University Press.

Alston, W. P. 1989. *Epistemic Justification*. Ithaca: Cornell University Press.

Anderson, J. 1996. *A Social Conception of Personal Autonomy*. Ph.D. dissertation, Northwestern University.

Apel, K.-O. 1972. *Towards a Transformation of Philosophy*. Trans. G. Ady and D. Frisby. London: Routledge & Kegan Paul.

Apel, K.-O. 1987. "The Problem of Philosophical Foundations in Light of a Transcendental Pragmatics of Language." In K. Baynes, J. Bohman, and T. McCarthy (eds.), *After Philosophy*. Cambridge, MA: MIT Press.

Aumann. R. 1976. "Agreeing to Disagree." *The Annals of Statistics* 4: 1236–1239.

Aumann, R. 1987. "Correlated Equilibrium as an Expression of Bayesian Rationality." *Econometrica* 55: 1–18.

Austin, J. L. 1975. *How to do Things with Words*. 2nd edn. Eds. J. O. Urmson and M. Sbizà. Cambridge, MA: Harvard University Press.

Banks, J. S. and J. Sobel. 1988. "Equilibrium Selection in Signalling Games." *Econometrica* 55: 647–661.

Becker, G. 1996. *Accounting for Tastes*. Cambridge, MA: Harvard University Press.

Benhabib, S. 1990. "Afterword." In S. Benhabib and F. Dallmayr (eds.), *The Communicative Ethics Controversy*. Cambridge, MA: MIT Press, 330–369.

Bicchieri, C. 1988. "Strategic Behavior and Counterfactuals," *Synthese* 76: 135–169.

Binmore, K. 1993. "Bargaining and Justice." In D. Gauthier and R. Sugden (eds.), *Rationality, Justice, and the Social Contract*. Hemel Hempstead: Harvester Wheatsheaf, 131–156.

Binmore, K. 1994. *Game Theory and the Social Contract. Volume 1: Playing Fair.* Cambridge, MA: MIT Press.

Bonjour, L. 1985. *The Structure of Empirical Knowledge.* Cambridge, MA: Harvard University Press.

Bourdieu, P. 1984. *Distinction.* Trans. R. Nice. Cambridge, MA: Harvard University Press.

Brandenburger, A. 1992. "Knowledge and Equilibrium in Games." *Journal of Economic Perspectives* 6: 83–101.

Brandom, R. 1994. *Making It Explicit.* Cambridge, MA: Harvard University Press.

Braybrooke, D. 1985. "The Insoluble Problem of the Social Contract." In R. Campbell and L. Sowden (eds.), *Paradoxes of Rationality and Cooperation*. Vancouver: University of British Columbia Press, 277–305.

Carroll, L. 1995. "What the Tortoise Said to Achilles." *Mind* 104: 691–693.

Charon, J. M. 1989. *Symbolic Interactionism.* 3rd ed. New Jersey: Prentice Hall.

Cicourel, A. 1973. *Cognitive Sociology.* Harmondsworth: Penguin Education.

Cooke, M. 1994. *Language and Reason.* Cambridge, MA: MIT Press.

Crawford, V. P. and J. Sobel. 1982. "Strategic Information Transmission." *Econometrica* 50: 1431–1451.

Davidson, D. 1980. "Toward a Unified Theory of Meaning and Action." *Grazer Philosophiche Studien* 11: 1–12.

Davidson, D. 1984. *Inquiries into Truth and Interpretation.* Oxford: Clarendon.

Davidson, D. 1985. "A New Basis for Decision Theory." *Theory and Decision* 18: 87–98.

Davidson, D. 1996. "The Folly of Trying to Define Truth." *The Journal of Philosophy* 93: 263–278.

Deacon, T. W. 1997. *The Symbolic Species.* New York: W.W. Norton.

Dummett, M. 1978. *Truth and Other Enigmas.* Cambridge, MA: Harvard University Press.

Dummett, M. 1981. *Frege's Philosophy of Language.* 2nd ed. Cambridge, MA: Harvard University Press.

Dummett, M. 1991. *The Logical Basis of Metaphysics.* Cambridge, MA: Harvard University Press.

Dummett, M. 1993. *The Origins of Analytical Philosophy.* Cambridge, MA: Harvard University Press.

Dummett, M. 1993. "What Is a Theory of Meaning? (II)." In *The Seas of Language*. Oxford: Clarendon Press, 34–93.

Durkheim, E. 1933. *The Division of Labor in Society.* Trans. George Simpson. New York: The Free Press.

Durkheim, E. 1963. *L'éducation morale.* Paris: Presses universitaires de France.

Durkheim, E. 1982. *The Rules of Sociological Method.* Trans. W. D. Halls. New York: The Free Press.

Dworkin, R. 1981. "What Is Equality? Part 1: Equality of Welfare." *Philosophy and Public Affairs* 10: 185–246.

Dworkin R. 1986. *Law's Empire.* Cambridge, MA: Belknap.

Eatwell, J., et al., eds. 1989. *The New Palgrave: Game Theory.* New York: W. W. Norton.

Elster, J. 1986. "The Scope and Nature of Rational Choice Explanations." In B. McLoughlin and E. LePore (eds.), *Actions and Events.* New York: Blackwell, 60–72.

Elster, J. 1989. *The Cement of Society.* Cambridge: Cambridge University Press.

Estlund, D. 1997. "Beyond Fairness and Deliberation: The Epistemic Dimension of Democratic Authority." In J. Bohman and W. Rehg (eds.), *Deliberative Democracy.* Cambridge, MA: MIT Press, 173–204.

Evans-Pritchard, E. E. 1956. *Nuer Religion.* Oxford: Clarendon Press.

Farrell, J. 1993. "Meaning and Credibility in Cheap-Talk Games." *Games and Economic Behavior* 5: 514–531.

Fine, A. 1989. "Truthmongering: Less Is True." *Canadian Journal of Philosophy* 19: 611–616.

Fodor, J. and E. Lepore. 1992. *Holism.* Cambridge, MA: Blackwell.

Føllesdal D. and R. Hilpinen. 1970. "Deontic Logic: An Introduction." In R. Hilpinen (ed.), *Deontic Logic: Introductory and Systematic Readings.* Dordrecht: D. Reidel, 1–35.

Frege, G. 1968. *The Foundations of Arithmetic.* 2nd ed. Trans. J. L. Austin. Oxford: Blackwell.

Fudenberg, D. and E. Maskin. 1986. "The Folk Theorem in Repeated Games with Discounting or with Incomplete Information." *Econometrica* 54: 533–554.

Fudenberg, D. and J. Tirole. 1991. *Game Theory.* Cambridge, MA: MIT Press.

Gambetta, D. 1988. "Mafia: The Price of Distrust." In D. Gambetta (ed.), *Trust: Making and Breaking Cooperative Relations.* Oxford: Blackwell, 158–175.

Garfinkel, H. 1963. "A Conception of, and Experiments with, 'Trust' as a Condition of Stable Concerted Actions." In O. J. Harvey (ed.), *Motivation and Social Interaction.* New York: Ronald Press, 187–238.

Garfinkel, H. 1967. *Studies in Ethnomethodology.* Oxford: Polity Press.

Gauthier, D. 1986. *Morals by Agreement.* Oxford: Clarendon Press.

Gauthier, D. 1993. "Uniting Separate Persons." In D. Gauthier and R. Sugden (eds.), *Rationality, Justice, and the Social Contract*. Hemel Hempstead: Harvester Wheatsheaf, 176–192.

Gauthier, D. 1994. "Assure and Threaten." *Ethics* 104: 690–721.

Geuss, R. 1981. *The Idea of a Critical Theory*. Cambridge: Cambridge University Press.

Gilligan, C. 1982. *In A Different Voice:Psychological Theory and Women's Development*. Cambridge MA: Harvard University Press.

Goldman, A. 1994. "What Is Justified Belief?" In Hilary Kornblith (ed.), *Naturalizing Epistemology*. Cambridge, MA: MIT Press, 105–130.

Grice, H. P. 1989. *Studies in the Ways of Words*. Cambridge, MA: Harvard University Press.

Grover, D. 1992. *A Prosentential Theory of Truth*. Princeton: Princeton University Press.

Haack, S. 1993. *Evidence and Inquiry*. Oxford: Blackwell.

Habermas, J. 1971. *Knowledge and Human Interests*. Trans. J. J. Shapiro. Boston: Beacon Press.

Habermas, J. 1983. *Moralbewußtsein und kommunikatives Handeln*. Frankfurt am Main: Suhrkamp.

Habermas, J. 1979. *Communication and the Evolution of Society*. Trans. T. McCarthy Boston: Beacon Press.

Habermas, J. 1982. "A Reply to my Critics." In J. B. Thompson and D. Held (eds.), *Habermas: Critical Debates*. Cambridge, MA: MIT Press, 219–283.

Habermas, J. 1984a. *The Theory of Communicative Action*. Vol. 1. Trans. T. McCarthy Boston: Beacon Press.

Habermas, J. 1984b. "Wahrheitstheorien." In *Vorstudien und Ergänzungen zur Theorie des kommunikativen Handelns*. Frankfurt: Suhrkamp, 127–183.

Habermas, J. 1985. "Reply to Skjei." *Inquiry* 28: 105–112.

Habermas, J. 1987a. *The Philosophical Discourse of Modernity*. Trans. F. Lawrence. Cambridge, MA: MIT Press.

Habermas, J. 1987b. *The Theory of Communicative Action*. Vol. 2. Trans. T. McCarthy. Boston: Beacon Press.

Habermas, J. 1990. *Moral Consciousness and Communicative Action*. Trans. C. Lenhardt and S. Weber Nicholsen. Cambridge, MA: MIT Press.

Habermas, J. 1991a. "A Reply." In A. Honneth and H. Joas (eds.), *Communicative Action*. Cambridge, MA: MIT Press, 214–264.

Habermas, J. 1991b. "Comments on Searle: 'Meaning, Communication and Representation.'" In E. LePore and R. Van Gulick (eds.), *Searle and His Critics*. Cambridge: Blackwell, 17–29.

Habermas, J. 1992a. *Faktizität und Geltung*. Frankfurt am Main: Suhrkamp.

Habermas, J. 1992b. *Postmetaphysical Thinking.* Trans. W. M. Hohengarten. Cambridge, MA: MIT Press.

Habermas, J. 1993. *Justification and Application.* Trans. C. Cronin. Cambridge, MA: MIT Press.

Habermas, J. 1996a. *Between Facts and Norms.* Trans. W. Rehg. Cambridge, MA: MIT Press.

Habermas, J. 1996b. "On the Cognitive Content of Morality." *Proceedings of the Aristotelian Society* 96: 335–358.

Habermas, J. 1996c. "Reply to Symposium Participants." *Cardozo Law Review* 17: 1477–1557.

Habermas, J. 1998a. *On the Pragmatics of Communication.* Ed. Maeve Cooke. Cambridge, MA: MIT Press.

Habermas, J. 1998b. *The Inclusion of the Other.* Ed. C. Cronin and P. De Greiff. Cambridge, MA: MIT Press.

Habermas, J. 1998c. "Remarks on Legitimation through Human Rights." Unpublished MS.

Harsanyi, J. 1967–68. "Games with Incomplete Information Played by 'Bayesian' Players." 3 parts. *Management Science* 14: 159–182, 320–334, 486–502.

Heap, S. P. H. and Y. Varoufakis. 1995. *Game Theory: A Critical Introduction.* London: Routledge.

Heath, J. 1995a. "The Problem of Foundationalism in Habermas's Discourse Ethics." *Philosophy and Social Criticism* 21: 77–100.

Heath, J. 1995b. "Threats, Promises, and Communicative Action." *European Journal of Philosophy* 3: 225–241.

Heath, J. 1996a. "A Multi-Stage Game Model of Morals by Agreement." *Dialogue* 35: 529–552.

Heath, J. 1996b. "Rational Choice as Critical Theory." *Philosophy and Social Criticism* 22: 43–62.

Heath, J. 1997. "Foundationalism and Practical Reason." *Mind* 106: 451–474.

Heath, J. 1998. "Culture: Choice or Circumstance?" *Constellations* 5: 183–200.

Hobbes, T. 1991. *Leviathan.* Ed. R. Tuck. Cambridge: Cambridge University Press.

Hohengarten, W. M. 1991. *Language Games versus Communicative Action: Wittgenstein and Habermas on Language and Reason.* Ph.D. dissertation, Northwestern University.

Hollis, M. and R. Sugden. 1993. "Rationality in Action." *Mind* 102: 1–35.

Horwich, P. 1990. *Truth.* Oxford: Blackwell.

Hoy, D. C. and T. McCarthy. 1994. *Critical Theory.* Oxford: Blackwell.

Hume, D. 1978. *A Treatise of Human Nature.* 2nd edn. Ed. L. A. Selby-Bigge. Oxford: Clarendon Press.

Husserl, E. 1970. *Logical Investigations.* 2 vols. Trans. J. D. Findlay. London: Routledge.

Husserl, E. 1977. *Cartesian Meditations.* Trans. D. Cairns. The Hague: Martinus Nijhoff.

Johnson, J. 1993. "Is Talk Really Cheap? Prompting Conversation between Critical Theory and Rational Choice." *American Political Science Review* 87: 74–86.

Kalai, E. and M. Smorodinsky. 1975. "Other Solutions to Nash's Bargaining Problem." *Econometrica* 43: 513–518.

Kant, I. 1929. *Critique of Pure Reason.* Trans. N. Kemp Smith. New York: St. Martin's Press.

Kant, I. 1960. *Religion within the Limits of Reason Alone.* Trans. T. M. Greene and H. H. Hudson. New York: Harper & Row.

Kant, I. 1990. *Foundations of the Metaphysics of Morals.* 2nd edn. Trans. L. White Beck. New York: MacMillan.

Kavka, G. 1986. *Hobbesian Moral and Political Theory.* Princeton: Princeton University Press.

Kirkham, R. 1992. *Theories of Truth.* Cambridge, MA: MIT Press.

Kohlberg, L. 1981. *The Philosophy of Moral Development: Moral Stages and the Idea of Justice.* San Francisco: Harper & Row.

Kreps, D. M. 1990. *Game Theory and Economic Modelling.* Oxford: Clarendon Press.

Kreps, D. M. and R. Wilson. 1982. "Sequential Equilibria." *Econometrica* 50: 871–889.

Kymlicka, W. 1995. *Multicultural Citizenship.* Oxford: Clarendon Press.

Lafont, C. 1999. *The Linguistic Turn in Hermeneutic Philosophy.* Trans. José Medina. Cambridge. MA: MIT Press.

Lévy-Bruhl, L. 1966. *How Natives Think.* New York: Washington Square Press.

Lewis, C. S. 1944. *The Abolition of Man.* London: Oxford University Press.

Lewis, D. 1969. *Convention.* Cambridge, MA: Harvard University Press.

Lewis, D. 1973. *Counterfactuals.* Oxford: Blackwell.

Luce, R. D. and H. Raiffa. 1957. *Games and Decisions.* New York: John Wiley & Sons.

Mackie, J. L. 1977. *Ethics: Inventing Right and Wrong.* London: Penguin.

Mannheim, K. 1936. *Ideology and Utopia.* Trans. L. Wirth and E. Shils. New York: Harcourt Brace Jovanovich.

McCarthy, T. 1991. *Ideals and Illusions.* Cambridge, MA: MIT Press.

Mead, G. H. 1934. *Mind, Self, and Society.* Chicago: University of Chicago Press.

Mehta, J., C. Starmer, and R. Sugden. 1994. "Focal Points in Pure Coordination Games: An Experimental Investigation." *Theory and Decision* 36: 658–673.

Myerson, R. B. 1989. "Credible Negotiation Statements and Coherent Plans." *Journal of Economic Theory* 48: 264–303.

Myerson, R. B. 1991. *Game Theory: Analysis of Conflict*. Cambridge, MA: Harvard University Press.

Nash, J. 1951. "Noncooperative Games." *Annals of Mathematics* 54: 289–295.

Outhwaite, W. 1994. *Habermas: A Critical Introduction*. Cambridge: Polity Press.

Parsons, T. 1951. *The Social System*. New York: The Free Press.

Parsons, T. and E. Shils, eds. 1951. *Toward a General Theory of Action*. New York: Harper & Row.

Parsons, T. 1961. "An Outline of the Social System." In Talcott Parsons, et al. (eds.), *Theories of Society*. New York: The Free Press, 30–79.

Parsons, T. 1968. *The Structure of Social Action*. 2 vols. New York: Free Press.

Peirce, C. S. 1934. *Collected Works of Charles Sanders Peirce*. Vol. 5. Cambridge, MA: Belknap.

Perelman, C. and L. Olbrechts-Tyteca. 1969. *The New Rhetoric*. Trans. J. Wilkinson and P. Weaver. Notre Dame: University of Notre Dame Press.

Pettit, P. and M. Smith. 1996. "Freedom in Belief and Desire." *The Journal of Philosophy* 93: 429–449.

Piaget, J. 1965. *The Moral Judgment of the Child*. Trans. M. Gabain. New York: The Free Press.

Plato. 1974. *Republic*. Trans. G. M. A. Grube. Indianapolis: Hackett.

Pollner, M. 1987. *Mundane Reason*. Cambridge: Cambridge University Press.

Prichard, H. A. 1968. "Does Moral Philosophy Rest on a Mistake?" *Moral Obligation, and Duty and Interest*. London: Oxford University Press: 1–17.

Putnam, H. 1981. *Reason, Truth, and History*. Cambridge: Cambridge University Press.

Putnam, H. 1983. *Realism and Reason: Philosophical Papers, Volume 3*. Cambridge: Cambridge University Press.

Quine, W. v. O. 1963. "Two Dogmas of Empiricism." *From a Logical Point of View*. 2nd edn. New York: Harper & Row, 20–46.

Quine, W. v. O. 1960. *Word and Object*. Cambridge, MA: MIT Press.

Railton, P. 1996. "Moral Realism: Prospects and Problems." In Walter Sinnott-Armstrong (ed.), *Moral Knowledge? New Readings in Moral Epistemology*. Oxford: Oxford University Press, 49–81.

Ramsey, F. 1927. "Facts and Propositions." *Proceedings of the Aristotelian Society*, supp. vol. 7: 153–170.

Rasmusen, E. 1990. *Games and Information: An Introduction to Game Theory.* 2nd ed. Oxford: Blackwell.

Rawls, J. 1988. "The Idea of an Overlapping Consensus." *Oxford Journal of Legal Studies* 7: 251–276.

Rawls, J. 1989. "Themes in Kant's Moral Philosophy." In E. Förster (ed.), *Kant's Transcendental Deductions.* Stanford: Stanford University Press, 81–113.

Rawls, J. 1993. *Political Liberalism.* New York: Columbia University Press.

Rehg, W. 1991. "Discourse and the Moral Point of View: Deriving a Dialogical Principle of Universalization." *Inquiry* 34: 27–48.

Rescher, N. 1993. *Pluralism.* Oxford: Clarendon Press.

Roemer, J. 1996. *Theories of Distributive Justice.* Cambridge, MA: Harvard University Press.

Rorty, A. O., ed. 1980. *Explaining Emotions.* Berkeley: University of California Press.

Rorty, R. 1972. "The World Well Lost." *The Journal of Philosophy* 69: 649–665.

Rorty, R. 1980. *Philosophy and the Mirror of Nature.* Princeton: Princeton University Press.

Rorty, R. 1986. "Pragmatism, Davidson, and Truth." In E. Lepore (ed.), *Truth and Interpretation: Perspectives on the Philosophy of Donald Davidson.* Oxford: Blackwell, 333–355.

Rorty, R. 1991. "Postmodernist Bourgeois Liberalism." In *Objectivity, Relativism, and Truth.* Cambridge: Cambridge University Press, 197–202.

Rorty, R. 1993. "Putnam and the Relativist Menace." *The Journal of Philosophy* 90: 443–461.

Rowe, N. 1989. *Rules and Institutions.* Ann Arbor: University of Michigan Press.

Rubenstein, A. 1982. "Perfect Equilibrium in a Bargaining Model." *Econometrica* 50: 97–109.

Savage, J. 1954. *The Foundations of Statistics.* New York: John Wiley & Sons.

Scanlon, T. M. 1982. "Contractualism and Utilitarianism." In A. K. Sen and B. Williams (eds.), *Utilitarianism and Beyond.* London: Cambridge University Press, 103–128.

Scanlon, T. M. 1975. "Preference and Urgency." *The Journal of Philosophy* 72: 655–669.

Schelling, T. 1963. *The Strategy of Conflict.* 2nd ed. New York: Oxford University Press.

Searle, J. 1969. *Speech Acts.* Cambridge: Cambridge University Press.

Sellars, W. 1963. *Science, Perception, and Reality.* New York: Routledge & Kegan Paul.

Sellars, W. 1997. *Empiricism and the Philosophy of Mind.* Cambridge, MA: Harvard University Press.

Selten, R. 1975. "Reexamination of the Perfectness Concept for Equilibrium Points in Extensive Games." *International Journal of Game Theory* 4: 25–55.

Bibliography

Sen, A. 1976. "Rational Fools: A Critique of the Behavioural Foundations of Economic Theory." *Philosophy and Public Affairs* 6: 317–344.

Silber, J. R. 1960. "The Ethical Significance of Kant's *Religion*." Introduction to I. Kant, *Religion within the Limits of Reason Alone*. Trans. T. M. Greene and H. H. Hudson. New York: Harper & Row.

Smith, M. 1994. *The Moral Problem*. Oxford: Blackwell.

Skinner, Q., ed. 1985. *The Return of Grand Theory in the Human Sciences*. Cambridge: Cambridge University Press.

Strawson, P. F. 1950. "Truth." *Proceedings of the Aristotelian Society*, supp. vol. 24: 129–156.

Stroud, B. 1968. "Transcendental Arguments." *The Journal of Philosophy* 65: 241–256.

Sugden, R. 1995. "A Theory of Focal Points." *The Economic Journal* 105: 533–550.

Sugden, R. 1997. "Rationality and Experience: The Role of Inductive Reasoning in the Evolution of Conventions." Unpublished MS.

Tarski, A. 1944. "The Semantic Conception of Truth and the Foundation of Semantics." *Philosophy and Phenomenological Research* 4: 341–375.

Taylor, C. 1985. *Human Agency and Language: Philosophical Papers 1*. Cambridge: Cambridge University Press, 1985.

Taylor, C. 1989. *Sources of the Self*. Cambridge, MA: Harvard University Press.

Taylor, C. 1991. *The Malaise of Modernity*. Concord, ON: Anansi.

Taylor, C. 1995. *Philosophical Arguments*. Cambridge, MA: Harvard University Press.

Taylor, M. 1987. *The Possibility of Cooperation*. Cambridge: Cambridge University Press.

Tenenbaum, S. 1996. "Realists without a Cause: Deflationary Theories of Truth and Ethical Realism." *Canadian Journal of Philosophy* 26: 561–590.

Toulmin, S. 1964. *The Uses of Argument*. Cambridge: Cambridge University Press.

Toulmin, S., R. Rieke, and A. Janik. 1979. *An Introduction to Reasoning*. New York: MacMillan.

Tugendhat, E. 1985. "Habermas on Communicative Action." In G. Seebaß and R. Tuomela (eds.), *Social Action*. Dordrecht: D. Reidel, 179–186.

von Neumann, J. and O. Morgenstern. 1953. *The Theory of Games and Economic Behavior*. 3rd edn. New York: John Wiley & Sons.

von Wright, G. H. 1963. *Norm and Action*. London: Routledge.

von Wright, G. H. 1963. *Varieties of Goodness*. London: Routledge.

von Wright, G. H. 1968. *An Essay in Deontic Logic and the General Theory of Action*. Amsterdam: North Holland Publishing Company.

Weber, M. 1958. *The Protestant Ethic and the Spirit of Capitalism.* Trans. T. Parsons. New York: Charles Scribner's Sons.

Weber, M. 1978. *Economy and Society.* 2 vols. Eds. G. Roth and C. Wittich. Berkeley: University of California Press.

Wellmer, A. 1991. *The Persistence of Modernity.* Trans. D. Midgley. Cambridge, MA: MIT Press.

Winch, P. 1970. "Understanding a Primitive Society." In B. R. Wilson (ed.), *Rationality.* Oxford: Basil Blackwell, 78–111.

Williams, B. 1981. *Moral Luck.* Cambridge: Cambridge University Press.

Williams, B. 1985. *Ethics and the Limits of Philosophy.* Cambridge, MA: Harvard University Press.

Williams, B. and A. Sen, eds. 1982. *Utilitarianism and Beyond.* Cambridge: Cambridge University Press.

Williams, M. 1992. *Unnatural Doubts: Epistemological Realism and the Basis for Scepticism.* Cambridge: Blackwell.

Wittgenstein, L. 1961. *Tractatus Logico-Philosophicus.* Trans. D. F. Pears and B. F. McGuiness. London: Routledge.

Wittgenstein, L. 1967. *Philosophical Investigations.* Trans. G. E. M. Ancombe. Oxford: Blackwell.

Wittgenstein, L. 1969. *On Certainty.* Trans. D. Paul and G. E. M. Anscombe. New York: Harper & Row.

Wright, C. 1992. *Truth and Objectivity.* Cambridge MA: Harvard University Press.

Wright, C. 1993. *Realism, Meaning, and Truth.* 2nd ed. Oxford: Blackwell.

Index